# The Arts & Crafts in New England
# 1704-1775

Gleanings from Boston newspapers relating to painting, engraving, silversmiths, pewterers, clockmakers, furniture, pottery, old houses, costume, trades and occupations, &c

George Francis Dow

Alpha Editions

This edition published in 2020

ISBN : 9789354017100

Design and Setting By
**Alpha Editions**
email - alphaedis@gmail.com

As per information held with us this book is in Public Domain.
This book is a reproduction of an important historical work. Alpha Editions uses the best technology to reproduce historical work in the same manner it was first published to preserve its original nature. Any marks or number seen are left intentionally to preserve its true form.

# THE

## IN
## NEW ENGLAND
### 1704-1775

GLEANINGS
FROM BOSTON NEWSPAPERS
Relating to Painting
Engraving, Silversmiths, Pewterers
Clockmakers, Furniture, Pottery, Old Houses
Costume, Trades and Occupations
&c. &c. &c. &c. &c.

By
GEORGE FRANCIS DOW

TOPSFIELD, MASSACHUSETTS
THE WAYSIDE PRESS
1927

# PREFACE

IN THE present-day search for documentary information relating to the early arts and crafts in New England, an important source is the contemporary newspaper, too often neglected because thorough search requires a considerable expenditure of time. Here may be found valuable evidence concerning the work of painters, engravers, and early craftsmen not to be discovered elsewhere:—the work of the artist, the announcement of the recently completed engraving, the advertisement of the silversmith and the cabinetmaker, the shopkeeper's description of his stock of burnt-china and earthenware received in the last ships from England and Holland, the list of household goods and furniture to be sold at public vendue, the clockmaker's advertisement of his stock, the amazing list of fabrics offered for sale in the shops—all this and much more lies buried in the files of the early newspapers. Much of the value of this material will be found to exist in the exact knowledge it supplies of the productions of the arts and crafts at a known date and from these facts may be drawn deductions of real value to the antiquary and the artist.

The earliest newspapers printed in New England contained few advertisements and it was not until after 1720 that they increased in number and became more varied in character. Within the scope of the subject matter selected for this volume, the existing files of the following newspapers have been closely scanned, viz.:—

| | |
|---|---|
| Boston News-Letter, | 1704-1776 |
| Boston Gazette, | 1720-1765 |
| New England Courant, | 1721-1725 |
| New England Journal, | 1726-1740 |
| Boston Evening Post, | 1740-1764 |

The following "gleanings" have been made at various times, as opportunity permitted, in the libraries of the Massachusetts Historical Society and the American Antiquarian Society, and to the librarians of those societies grateful thanks are tendered for the many courtesies extended. Thanks are also extended to the Society for the Preservation of New England Antiquities and the Marine Research Society for the loan of engraved blocks and to the Essex Institute, the Robert C. Vose Galleries, Mr. Francis Hill Bigelow, Mrs. Harriette M. Forbes, Mr. John W. Farwell and Mr. Morgan B. Brainard for illustrative material. These "gleanings," of necessity, are disconnected and supply only a glimpse, now and then, of the matter-of-fact, every-day happenings and matters of general information which were well known at the time. As "gleanings" they are offered to the student and to the curious reader.

# TABLE OF CONTENTS

| | |
|---|---|
| Preface . . . . . . . . . . . *Page* | v |
| Table of Contents . . . . . . . . | vii |
| List of Illustrations . . . . . . . . | ix |
| Introduction . . . . . . . . . . | xi |
| **Painting and Engraving** | |
|     Painters . . . . . . . . . . . | 1 |
|     Paintings . . . . . . . . . . | 5 |
|     Engravers . . . . . . . . . . | 6 |
|     Engravings . . . . . . . . . . | 14 |
|     Maps and Charts . . . . . . . . | 26 |
|     Mezzotints . . . . . . . . . | 33 |
|     Wood Engravings . . . . . . . . | 37 |
| **Silver** | |
|     Silversmiths . . . . . . . . . | 41 |
|     Miscellaneous Silver . . . . . . . | 58 |
|     Jewellers . . . . . . . . . . | 66 |
| **Pewter** | |
|     Pewterers . . . . . . . . . . | 73 |
|     Miscellaneous Pewter . . . . . . . | 74 |
| **Pottery and Earthenware** | |
|     Potters . . . . . . . . . . . | 81 |
|     Earthen Wares . . . . . . . . . | 82 |
| **Glass** . . . . . . . . . . . | 97 |
|     Germantown (Braintree) Glass Works . . . | 103 |
| **Furniture** | |
|     Cabinetmakers . . . . . . . . . | 105 |
|     Furniture . . . . . . . . . . | 106 |
|     Looking Glasses . . . . . . . . | 127 |
|     Miscellaneous . . . . . . . . . | 129 |

## Table of Contents

Clocks and Watches
    Makers . . . . . . . . . *Page* 132
    Clocks and Watches . . . . . . . . 146

Wall Paper . . . . . . . . . . . 150

Fabrics . . . . . . . . . . . . 154

Costume . . . . . . . . . . . . 173
    Dress of Mechanics and Servants . . . . . 185

Architecture
    Houses and Buildings . . . . . . . . 204
    Architectural Books . . . . . . . . 221

Hardware and Cutlery . . . . . . . . 224

Paint . . . . . . . . . . . . . 237

Window Glass . . . . . . . . . . 244

Trades and Occupations . . . . . . . 252

Sweetmeats and Provisions . . . . . . . 292

Music and Musical Instruments . . . . . 297

Moving Pictures . . . . . . . . . 302

Seeds and Flowers . . . . . . . . . 305

Index . . . . . . . . . . . . 311

# LIST OF ILLUSTRATIONS

| | |
|---|---:|
| Nathaniel Hurd, Silversmith and Engraver *Frontispiece* | |
| Rev. Richard Mather — Woodcut by John Foster | xiv |
| The Boston Massacre — Engraving by Paul Revere | xvi |
| Rev. William Welsteed — Mezzotint by Copley | xviii |
| John Joy, Jr. — Portrait by Joseph Badger | xxii |
| The Day of Doom, by Rev. Michael Wigglesworth | xxvi |
| Gravestone of William Clark, 1742 | xxx |
| John Singleton Copley, painted by himself | 2 |
| Mrs. Theodore Atkinson — Portrait by Copley | 6 |
| Mrs. Timothy Fitch — Portrait by Blackburn | 10 |
| Seth Hudson's Speech from the Pillory | 12 |
| Prospect of Boston in 1723 — Drawing by Burgis | 16 |
| Prospect of the Colleges in Cambridge in 1726 | 20 |
| View of Harvard College — Engraving by Revere | 26 |
| Rev. Cotton Mather — Mezzotint by Pelham | 32 |
| Woodcut of a Ship in 1735 | 38 |
| Weights and Values of Coins — Engraving by Hurd | 38 |
| Silver Cream Jug made by Revere | 48 |
| Silver Teapot made by Edwards | 62 |
| Two-Drawer Connecticut Chest, about 1690 | 104 |
| One-Drawer Hadley Chest, about 1700 | 116 |
| Block-Front Secretary Desk, about 1760 | 128 |

LIST OF ILLUSTRATIONS

| | |
|---|---:|
| WALL-PAPER USED IN NEW ENGLAND | 150 |
| A QUILTING BEE IN THE OLDEN TIMES | 158 |
| COUNTERPANE OF QUILTED GALLOON | 168 |
| PARSON CAPEN HOUSE (1683), TOPSFIELD | 204 |
| PARLOR OF PARSON CAPEN HOUSE (1683) | 208 |
| PARLOR OF JOHN WARD HOUSE (1684), SALEM | 208 |
| WILLIAM CLARK MANSION (1715), BOSTON | 216 |
| PROSPECT OF YALE COLLEGE IN 1749 | 222 |
| HANDWROUGHT IRON-WORK FROM CONNECTICUT | 230 |
| DIAMOND-PANE, LEADED-GLASS SASH | 248 |
| CROWN GLASS WINDOW SASH | 248 |
| PRICE SHEET (1763), ENGRAVED BY HURD | 258 |
| QUILL WORK SCONCE MADE ABOUT 1720 | 266 |
| PETIT POINT PICTURE WORKED IN 1765 | 272 |
| GRAVESTONE OF MRS. SUSANNAH JAYNE, 1776 | 282 |
| WAX FIGURE MADE BEFORE 1748 | 286 |
| MODEL OF SHIP "AMERICA" BUILT IN 1749 | 290 |

# INTRODUCTION

IN ORDER to properly understand the disabilities under which the New England Puritans created, something should be said at the outset about the characteristics of the Puritans and especially something concerning their former environment and education; and as much has been written about their pilgrimage to a distant land in order to find new homes where they might worship God according to the dictates of their own consciences, in order to judge somewhat of their artistic temperament we should know something of their spirituality.

They were Englishmen, and when the first considerable emigration ceased about the year 1640, of the 25,000 settlers then living in the Colony, probably ninety-five per cent were small farmers or workmen engaged in the manual trades, together with many indentured servants who had come over under the terms of a contract whereby they were bonded to serve their masters for a term of years—usually five or seven. The remaining five per cent of the population was composed of those governing the Colony, the stockholders in the Company, so to speak; ministers enough to supply the spiritual needs of each town and settlement, however small; a few of social position and comparative wealth; one lawyer; and a sprinkling of shopkeepers and small merchants living in the seaport towns.

The founders of the colony in the Massachusetts Bay, and most of those who immediately followed them, were men who did not conform to the ritual and government of the Established Church in England. They were followers of John Calvin whose Geneva Bible was widely read in England and whose teachings had profoundly influenced English thought and manners. Calvin taught a great simplicity of life and a literal application of the teachings found in the Bible. In the Commonwealth that he set up in Geneva, the daily life and actions of its citizens were as closely guarded as if in a nursery for children. All frivolous amusements were forbidden, a curfew was established, and all were constrained to save souls and to labor for material development. There was a minute supervision of dress and personal conduct and a literal construction of Bible mandates was carried so far that children were actually put to death for striking their parents.

Calvin's theology was based on the belief that all men were born sinners and since Adam's fall, by the will of God, predestined from birth to hell and everlasting torment, unless, happily, one of the elect and so foreordained to be saved. In this belief the Puritans found life endurable because they considered themselves of the elect and in cases of doubt the individual found comfortable assurance in the belief that although certain of his neighbors were going to hell he was one of the elect. It naturally followed that the imagination of the Puritans was concentrated on questions of religion.

The teachings of Calvin spread rapidly in England and among his followers there came about an austerity of religious life and a great simplicity in dress and manners. Pomp and ceremony in church ritual was anathema and the usual adornments of the church edifice—the stained glass windows, the sculptured decorations, the pictures upon the walls, and even the monuments and brasses over the dead—became objects marked for destruction. During the reign of Queen Elizabeth there was much pulling down of shrines with their relics and of graven images in the churches that tended to adoration and superstition. Much painted glass having representations of Christ and the saints was also destroyed, leaving "religion naked, bare and unclad," to use the expression of a contemporary writer. But this was as nothing when compared with the violation of the churches by Puritan fanatics during the Commonwealth.

It is generally accepted that the Reformation was hostile or at least cold to the development of Art, and that sculpture, painting and architecture were but little regarded by the Protestant Church. This indifference blossomed into malignant destructiveness in the time of Cromwell and a Parliamentary Commission was appointed to go about England and destroy all "reliques of idolatry." At the University of Cambridge they complained that the Commission went about "like a Bedlam breaking glasse windowes, having battered and beaten downe all our painted glasse, not only in our Chapples, but (contrary to order) in our publique scholes, Colledge Halls, Librayes and Chambers, mistaking perhaps the liberall Arts for Saints (which they intend in time to pull down to)."

In the county of Suffolk, a fanatic named William Dowsing was appointed in charge of this fascinating work. He kept a journal in which he minutely recorded, day by day, the destruction that attended his progress about the shire. At St. Peter's, Sudbury, he destroyed about one hundred pictures and gave orders to take down a cross on the steeple. At Haverhill, he records "we broke down about an hundred superstitious Pictures; and seven Fryars hugging a Nunn." At Ipswich, the godly Dowsing smashed his way through twelve churches. Two days were profitably spent there. At St. Margaret's, a churchwarden, "a godly man," promised to take down and destroy the twenty or thirty pictures. The recital might be continued at great length without adding to the impression desired to be conveyed, viz., the antagonism of the Puritans in England to all forms of adornment in their church edifices; and one should also look behind the veil at the mentality that conceived such destructive work.

The same is true of the meeting houses of the Puritans in New England, for a long time after the settlement. Both in exterior and interior nothing could be plainer and more lacking in decorative features. And a century later when the steeples of the meeting houses in the larger towns began to take on the architectural forms of the Wren churches built in London after the fire, even then the introduction of simple paneling and mouldings about a cornice or a pediment was as far as the housewrights permitted themselves to go in building house or meeting house. Mural decorations and painted glass in the windows did not begin to appear until another century had passed and Unitarianism had set theological groups by the ears and caused many of the older churches to break away from the severe Calvinistic doctrines.

It is true that most of the settlers of New England were poor in purse and with many of them mere existence was a struggle for a long time. But the growth of wealth in the Colony, although it brought with it more luxury in living and better dwellings, did not add much to the refinement of the people. It was the influence and example of the royal governors and a more frequent commercial intercourse with England and the Continental peoples that brought about a desire for a richer dress and an introduction of some of the refinements of life. This by no means met the approval of the Puritan ministers who frequently inveighed against "Professors of Religion who fashion themselves according to the World." The Rev. Cotton Mather, the leading minister in Boston and the industrious author of over four hundred published sermons and similar works, again and again exhorted against stage plays and infamous games of cards and dice. "It is a matter of Lamentation that even such things as these should be heard of in New England," he exclaimed. "And others spend their time in reading vain Romances," he continued. "It is meer loss of time." The analysis of the Puritan opposition to bear baiting, will be recalled, which they did away with, not because of the pain to the bear, but for the pleasure it gave to the audience.

With such a background and burdened with such a far-reaching antagonism toward the finer things of life, that help to lighten the burden of existence and beautify the way, it is small wonder that the esthetics found little fertile soil in New England, and much of this prejudice and state of mind lingered until our day among the old families in the more remote and orthodox communities. Little more than a generation ago the comfortably situated New England family sparingly decorated its parlor walls with floral wreaths made of human hair snipped from the heads of relatives and friends. It was a form of domestic art. One or two engravings representing the deathbed of Daniel Webster, or Washington in a martial attitude, might be seen and probably a framed representation of flowers painted on velvet or worked in cross-stitch. In some room there would be a framed motto worked in cross-stitch — "Simply to Thy cross I cling," "God bless our

Rev. Richard Mather
From a wood engraving made in 1670 by John Foster

Home," or a similar sentiment. The parlor furniture would be black walnut covered with black haircloth and on a marble-topped table might be seen the artistic yearnings of the family in the shape of a Rogers' group or possibly wax flowers under a glass bell. Hooked or braided rugs on the floors exemplified the thrift and handicraft of the women of the household. These rugs, made from wornout clothing, didn't come into fashion until about a century ago and most of them were made during the Godey's Magazine Period.

The art of wood engraving began in New England with a portrait of Rev. Richard Mather, the minister at Dorchester, Mass., which was cut in 1669 by John Foster, a young man of his parish. The print is about five by six inches in size, and the engraving was made on the flat side of a board as the longitudinal grain of the wood can be detected in the engraving. The block was in two pieces or split in the cutting as the head and shoulders do not fit together with the body by nearly a quarter of an inch.

Six years later, in 1675, Foster set up the first printing press in Boston, "over against the Sign of the Dove," and in 1677 he printed "A Narrative of the Troubles with the Indians," written by Rev. William Hubbard, the minister at Ipswich, and for this book Foster engraved a map—"the first that ever was here cut," it is stated in the title. Unlike the usual way of showing the cardinal points, the top represents the West, and the bottom represents the East. It was cut on wood and the title was set up in type and morticed into the engraved block.

Foster made an engraving on wood of the Colony Seal, the well-known Indian with a bow and arrow, which appeared on the title-page of "The General Laws" and several other books of the period and he also made a drawing of the town of Boston taken from Noddles Island, now East Boston, which was sent to Amsterdam in 1680 to be engraved. There is evidence to show that the engraving was made and impressions struck off but not a single example is known to exist. Foster, "the cunning Artist," was only thirty-three years old when he died and in the inventory of his estate are listed "carveing tools," and "his cuts and coolors." Nine years later the printing office was burned and with it, probably, the tools of his handicraft and the blocks he had cut.

After the death of Foster the art of engraving seems to have languished in New England for a long time. Paper money, printed from rudely engraved copper plates done by John Coney, the Boston silversmith, was issued in 1690, and followed at different periods of stress by eight other issues, up to the time of the flood of paper money emitted at the time of the Revolution.

"A View of the Great Town of Boston" was proposed in 1722 by William Burgis who came from England to New York about 1718 and there published by subscription his "South East Prospect of the City of New York," an exceeding rare print. When he reached Boston he established himself at the Crown Coffee House, kept by Thomas Selby, and his first proposed "View of Boston" not receiving the support he hoped for, he drew a "Prospect" from the southeast and subscriptions were successfully solicited during the winter of 1723/4. The "Prospect" was engraved on three plates by John Harris, a London engraver, and measures 24½ by 52½ inches in size. It was advertised for sale by William Price, the Boston map and print seller, in Franklin's newspaper, the *New England Courant*, of Aug. 28, 1725. It shows twelve meeting houses and churches and fifteen shipyards and gives us the first American portrayal of a two-masted schooner, a form of vessel that originated in Gloucester in 1713. Boston, at that time, according to the legend under the "Prospect," had about 16,000 inhabitants.

Burgis produced several other views which were engraved and published including "A Prospect of the Colleges in Cambridge in New England"; a mezzotint view of Boston Light, showing an armed sloop; and a view of Castle William, with a fine representation of a ship of war in the foreground. All of these prints now exist in only a few examples.

Burgis married the widow of the tavern keeper where he lived and succeeded him as a "taverner," so he may be considered a Bostonian, but his training was wholly English and his plates were

THE BOSTON MASSACRE

From an engraving on copper made by Paul Revere in 1770, after a drawing by Henry Pelham

all engraved in London, so his work cannot be properly said to be the product of New England culture.

A more typical example is the "Boston Massacre" engraved by the many-sided Paul Revere. The original drawing was made by Henry Pelham, the half-brother of John Singleton Copley, who engraved a plate from which prints were sold.

Jonathan Mulliken, a Yankee clock-maker of Newburyport, also engraved a plate closely following the Revere plate.

Revere has many engravings to his credit that exhibit excellent work for his time. His perspective was extraordinary and his line at times uncertain, but his portraits, views, caricatures, bookplates, psalm-tunes and bill heads, show sincere work and met a demand not easily supplied at that time.

Before him came James Turner, also a silversmith and engraver, who soon removed to Philadelphia; and Nathaniel Hurd, born in Boston in 1730, who engraved bill heads, bookplates, loan certificates, a portrait or two, and a curious caricature of Dr. Seth Hudson, a native of Lexington, who was convicted of forgery and ordered to the pillory. In the crowd of spectators Hurd introduced the likenesses of well-known Boston characters of the time. The culprit was not only pilloried, with an exposure to ancient eggs, garbage, and a choice assortment of missiles, but he also was tied to the whipping post and soundly thrashed and then fined and imprisoned. Puritan punishments when inflicted were dealt with a generous hand.

Allusion has been made to William Price, the Boston shopkeeper who sold prints. Before his time pictures of various kinds were sold generally at public vendue. In 1712, pictures were sold that had been found in the cargo of the ship *St. Francisco*, a prize brought into Boston for adjudication. In 1720, the *Boston Gazette* published an advertisement of a "Collection of choice Pictures, fit for any Gentleman's Dining-room or Stair-case" to be sold at vendue at the Crown Coffee-House on the Long Wharf. Two years later a French gentleman came to town who advertised to do all sorts of engraving at reasonable rates.

In 1726 there arrived in Boston, Peter Pelham of London, portrait painter and mezzotint engraver. His son Henry, born in Boston, in 1749, was an engraver and painted beautiful miniatures. He also practiced engineering which probably was a more dependable means of support. He eventually was drowned in Ireland while superintending some construction work.

Peter Pelham, soon after his arrival in Boston, painted a portrait of Rev. Cotton Mather, and after that reverend gentleman died in February, 1728, he engraved this portrait in mezzotint, the first work of the kind done in New England. The prints were ready in June and sold at five shillings each. Thereafter he painted and engraved the portraits of a dozen or more ministers and public men, which found a market among the ministers of the Colony and the well-to-do of their congregations. When the Rev. John Whiting of Concord died, among the furnishings of his house were prospects and mezzotint prints; "also the Effigies of all the New-England Ministers ever done in Metzotints, among which is the Effigy of that worthy Gentleman, the late Rev. William Welsteed, deceased," the latter done by John Singleton Copley when thirteen years old.

But Pelham's portraits and mezzotints could not keep his family alive and so he kept a private school afternoons. A few years later he also taught painting on glass and all sorts of needlework. "Youth may be Boarded or half Boarded"—reads the advertisement. In 1748 his "Writing and Arithmetick School" was kept open "from Candle Light 'till Nine in the Evening, for the benefit of those employ'd in Business all the Day." He also sold "best Virginia Tobacco, cut, spun into the very best Pigtail, and all other sorts; also snuff, at the cheapest Rates." But this was after he had married the widow Copley, the mother of John Singleton Copley. The widow had inherited from her first husband a tobacco shop and she continued to keep it open after his death.

Worst of all, in order to support himself and family, Peter Pelham was driven to the makeshift of opening a dancing school and advertising monthly assembles. In a communication printed

REV. WILLIAM WELSTEED
From a mezzotint by John Singleton Copley

on the first page of the *Boston Gazette,* the next week after the announcement of the first assembly, a writer states that he has been startled and concerned at the birth of so formidable a monster in this part of the world, in a town famous for its decency and good order. He deplores the appearance of so licentious and expensive a diversion in which the great part of the pleasure consists in being gazed at and applauded. He invokes the interposition of public authority to prevent such expensive extravagance and closes with the following, "And if Madam and Miss are not suffered to shake their Heels Abroad, they will make the House and Family shake at Home."

The advertisements in the weekly Boston newspapers are an exact source for interesting information as to the artistic and decorative taste of the time.

In 1728, pictures painted with oil'd colours in carved frames, gilt, were advertised, together with a great variety of prints and maps, also picture varnishes, "which preserve them from the smoak and flies." There were metzotintoes to be had for painting on glass, in frames or without.

Maps were always in demand and were a favorite wall decoration. In 1756, Samuel Blodgett, near the sign of the Lamb, and opposite to Capt. Smith's, advertised Thomas Johnston's "Prospective Plan of the Battle fought near Lake George on the 8th of September 1755, between 2000 English with 250 Mohawks and 2500 French and Indians, in which the English were victorious." The print is in two sections and shows at the left a bird's-eye view of the march of the troops and at the right a view of the camp and the battle. The map shows the river and the forts.

Three years later Nathaniel Warner, at his shop near the Draw Bridge, had in stock a neat assortment of mezzotint pictures, such as, "the Hon. William Pitt. Esq., the King of Prussia, Mr. Gerrick, the actor; Mr. Beard, the singer; the twelve months, four seasons, four elements; the Rake's and Harlot's Progress; the idle and industrious apprentice; beautiful prospects, coloured and without; sea pieces, coloured; as also a neat assortment of Pictures painted on glass."

New England produced no portrait painter in oils, worthy of the name, until nearly a century had passed from the time of the settlement. Robert Feke came from abroad and appeared at Newport, R. I., about 1726. While in New England he painted a number of excellent portraits, several of which may be considered finer than any done by Smibert or Blackburn. He died in 1750 at the Barbadoes. John Smibert, a Scotchman, came to Rhode Island with Dean Berkeley, in 1728, and did most of his work in or about Boston. He married in Boston, in 1730, and like Pelham found it necessary to open a shop in order to increase a somewhat uncertain income from portrait painting. In 1734 he advertised "all Sorts of Colours, dry and ground, with Oils and Brushes, Frames of several sorts, the best Metzotints, Italian, French, Dutch and English Prints, in Frames and Glasses, or without, by Wholesale or Retail." The next spring he was forced to sell his private collection of prints which he had collected in Italy, France, Holland and England. "The Price of each single Print or Book to be mark'd upon 'em, and to be the same, which Mr. Smibert, who bought 'em at the best Hand, himself, gave for them," reads the advertisement in the *Boston News-Letter*. At the same time was sold a collection of pictures in oil colors.

Smibert's son Nathaniel, born in Boston, died in his 22d year. He followed in his father's steps, and his obituary states that "painting was his peculiar Profession." It also records that the young man "had no Relish for the Scenes of high Mirth and Gaiety, but chose those Pastimes which improved the Thought and left an agreeable Reflection," which, if true, makes it quite plain that he was foreordained for an early translation.

Another portrait painter from overseas was Joseph Blackburn, of whose origin and personality little is known. He seems to have reached New York in 1753, coming from Bermuda. In 1755 he was working in Boston and he remained there until 1763, when he strangely disappears. He could not have been well known in Boston a full year after he reached the town, as the postmaster then advertised in one of the local newspapers two letters that had been received addressed to him. Blackburn worked for a short time at Portsmouth, N. H., and may have painted portraits at Newport. His subjects came from the mercantile aristocracy of New England, their wives and daughters, with a sprinkling of governors and judges and their "ladies." His work frequently suggests that of Copley and it is supposed that the younger man may have studied with Blackburn. The mystery of his appearance in New England and his strange disappearance remains a problem yet to be solved.

Nathaniel Emmons, a native of Boston, died there in 1740, aged 36 years. He painted the well-known portrait of Judge Sewall, the diarist and condemner of witches, and also several other portraits that have been identified with his name. The obituary published at his death states that "He was universally own'd to be the greatest Master of various Sorts of Painting that ever was born in this Country. And his Excellent Works were the pure Effects of his own Genius, without receiving any instructions from others. Some of his Pieces are such admirable Imitations of Nature, both in faces, Rivers, Banks and Rural scenes, that the Pleased Eye cannot easily leave them; and some of his Imitations of the Works of Art are so exquisite, that tho' we know they are only Paints, yet they deceive the sharpest Sight while it is nearly looking on them and will preserve his Memory till Age or some unhappy Accident or other destroy them. He was sober and modest and minded accuracy more than Profit."

John Smibert died in Boston in 1751, and about the time when he was obliged to decline commissions, through failing health, Joseph Badger, a house painter and glazier of Boston, turned his hand to painting portraits. He was the son of a Charlestown tailor, of small means, and his own children became glaziers and tailors. Badger's humble origin and comparative poverty undoubtedly prevented him from obtaining social recognition. His portraiture shows no great artistic excellence and suffers in comparison with that of Feke, Smibert and Blackburn. His portraits also display marked mannerisms in the posing of his subjects. His men were usually represented standing with the right hand resting on the hip, the two first fingers outstretched and holding back the folds of the long-skirted coat of the period. His women were seated, one hand resting on the lap and sometimes holding a flower. Nearly thirty of his portraits represent children under fourteen years of age and while they express the primness of his time, they have a quaintness and naïve charm that is most appealing.

It is evident that Badger conscientiously aimed to produce a good likeness and allowance should be made for his evident lack of proper training and the non-existence in Boston of good paintings that he might study and hope to imitate for he lived in a Puritan town with an atmosphere not particularly congenial to art in any form. In 1757 he received £6 for painting the portrait of Timothy Orne, the Salem merchant, and five years later, when he was fifty-five years old, he painted five portraits for George Bray, a Boston baker, for which he received £12. To eke out a livelihood he painted signs and hatchments and, when nothing better turned up, he spread paint on the trim of houses. With the irony that Time inflicts, his work, until recently, has been attributed to other artists — Smibert, Blackburn or Copley — so that the man and his works have remained unknown.

John Singleton Copley, the first great American portrait painter, was born in Boston in 1737, from English parents who had arrived in the country only the year before so that it cannot be said that he very closely represents New England heredity or traditions. His father was in poor health and died in the West Indies about the time of his son's birth and the widow supported herself and son by the profits from a small tobacconist's shop. When the boy was about ten years old his mother married Peter Pelham, portrait painter, mizzotintest, school teacher and drawing master, and undoubtedly he received his first instruction in painting from his stepfather. When sixteen years old he was painting portraits and his skill and the number of his commissions increased with each succeeding year. He worked in pastel as well as oil and also painted miniatures. When thirty-two years old he made an advantageous marriage. At that time he was painting as many portraits as he could execute at prices ranging from five to

JOHN JOY, JR.
From a portrait by Joseph Badger, painted about 1758, now owned by Mrs. Charles H. Joy.

fourteen guineas each, and was in receipt of a comfortable income. The population of Boston at that time was about 18,000, which included a goodly number of well-to-do families of the merchant class, and also the members of the government, the justices of the courts and those engaged in the learned professions. It was the most important town in New England and represented its highest culture and social development.

Two years before Copley's marriage he had sent to Benjamin West, in London, a painting representing his half-brother, Henry Pelham, seated at a table, holding in his hand a chain to which a flying squirrel was attached. This picture is now known as the "Boy with the Squirrel." It was included in an exhibition of the predecessor of the Royal Academy, was warmly praised and his reputation in England was soon established. Copley was urged to remove to London; but such a step involved many risks and uncertainties. The three hundred guineas a year that he was earning in Boston must be increased to nine hundred in order to maintain an equal standard of living in London. But a desire to study the old masters and to improve his style persisted and the approach of the Revolution at last forced a decision. In 1774 he sailed for England where he received a cordial welcome and soon became the fashion. He never returned to America.

The building of houses was the first craft that was practiced by the Puritans after they landed in New England and for the larger number, at the outset, these were mere shelters. But the rude huts, tents, and wigwams were soon supplanted by wooden structures of the substantial character that the severe climate required. After the first imperative need for anything that furnished a shelter from the weather, the housewrights, who had been brought over to supply this anticipated want, proceeded to construct houses modelled along the lines of the structures with which they were familiar in their former homes in England. This was only natural. The apprentice system was in full swing in those days and a master taught his apprentices what he in turn had been taught by his master. The craft of building houses was passed along from one generation to another like the "mystery" of other crafts.

These housewrights, who landed at Plymouth, Salem, and Boston, as soon as they got their chests of tools ashore did not at once invent a new form of structure, framed and put together in a manner not known to them before. Oh, no! They proceeded to dig saw-pits and to saw up logs into timber and boards exactly as they had been taught to do in England through generations of apprenticeship.

The English housewrights, on reaching the Massachusetts Bay, found timber everywhere, to be had for the cutting, and wooden houses were commonly built, then as now. After the first need was met, larger and more substantial structures were erected with here and there a house of brick, usually in or near the seaport towns. A stone house north of Boston was almost unknown but in Rhode Island in parts of Connecticut, where a shaly rock was found, the stone house was the more usual thing.

As a typical example of the wooden house in the Massachusetts Bay and also elsewhere in New England during the last part of the seventeenth century, we may well take the Parson Capen house built in 1683, at Topsfield, Mass., which embodies several unusual decorative features, and the modern restoration of which was easily and accurately effected because comparatively few changes had been made in the original structure. The parson was a Harvard graduate and came to Topsfield from Dorchester. He married Priscilla Appleton of Ipswich, a town that adjoins Topsfield, and as the Appleton family were large land owners and rich, for the time, it is likely that young Priscilla was given a house as good as the countryside afforded.

It is a typical structure of its time with two large rooms on each floor and a huge central chimney. The second story overhangs the first, not for the purpose of permitting the parson to pour hot water on the heads of maurauding Indians, but because it was an architectural style and embellishment well known in England and naturally introduced on this side. This overhang disappears from New England houses soon after 1710 as the strength of the English structural tradition grew fainter. The pendants or "drops" under the overhang were further well-recognized embellishments as were the less common brackets under the projecting garret floor and on either side of the front door. The nail-studded door perpetuated a medieval tradition and the leaded-glass casement windows existed everywhere at that time. "New-fashion" sliding window sash, in the London mode, were introduced about 1710, in the houses of the well-to-do living in the large towns.

Beyond a molding of the sheathing used to cover the walls of the house and a simple chamfering of the summer beams, no effort was made to decorate the interior with one exception—the newel post and balusters of the stair rail. The rooms were severely plain and well suited to the theology of their occupants. The inventories made at death do not reveal any pictures on the walls but there was good furniture, a clock and silver plate. The parson's predecessor in the ministerial office owned a golden cup.

This house may be fairly characterized as typical of the New England house of its period, but in the large towns there were a few fine houses in which lived wealthy merchants and their number increased in the early 1700's. In the Price "View of Boston," engraved in 1725, eight three-story houses appear and attention is called to them in the table beneath the picture. One of them was built about 1715 by William Clark, a wealthy merchant and member of the governor's council. His death in 1742 was attributed by some to the loss of forty sail of vessels in the French War. In this house afterwards lived Sir Henry Frankland, Collector of the Port, who fell in love with Agnes Surriage, the beautiful sixteen year old maid-of-all-work at the *Fountain Inn* in Marblehead. Her romantic story is well known. This house differed but little from the dozen or so of its type to be found in Boston at the time, save in its rich and elaborate decoration of the north parlor, at the right of the entrance hall. Here, the walls were divided into panels by fluted pilasters supporting an elaborate cornice, the whole heavily gilded, and each of the panels was embellished with a landscape or other decoration painted in oils. Painted arabesques and heraldic devices covered all other flat surfaces and the floor was laid in a mosaic of various colored woods. Every inch of the surface of this parlor was the product of the imagination and skill of the painter, gilder or carver. But while this magnificence actually existed in New England, by no means was it typically representative of its culture or artistic development.

There was an important craft in New England that required much skill not only in construction but in wood carving, and that was ship building—a considerable industry practiced everywhere along the coast line from the early years following the settlement until the passing of the sailing ship in recent times. The oldest known ship model of a New England-built vessel is that of the "America," built at Portsmouth, N. H., in 1749, and in this model may be seen evidence of the elaboration of carved wood decoration required about the bows and sterns of all of the larger vessels. The bow had its figurehead and head rails, with an elaboration of brackets and trail boards covered with carving or painted decoration and the stern carried its succession of galleries and quarter galleries, with many cabin windows surrounded by much carved and gilded work and between each deck-level a carved frieze frequently embellished with representations of sea nymphs, mermaids and tritons. On the King's ships, a number of which were built on this side, the royal arms, with supporters, always appeared in the elaborate gingerbread-work about the stern. The woodwork in the ship's cabins also carried much modelling and carving and it was only natural that the architectural skill they attained should eventually be utilized in house construction as wealth and occasion permitted. One excellent example of a development of this skill may be noted at a later day in the case of Samuel McIntire of Salem, a man who began his career as a wood carver in ship work and after a time transferred his technical skill and training in wood carving to the designing and decorating of houses.

Printing, the art preservative of arts, was set up early in the Massachusetts Bay Colony as an adjunct to the newly founded college in Cambridge. After printing the "Freeman's Oath"—a small broadside—and an almanac for the year 1639, the "whole booke of Psalms" was turned into verse by "thirty pious and

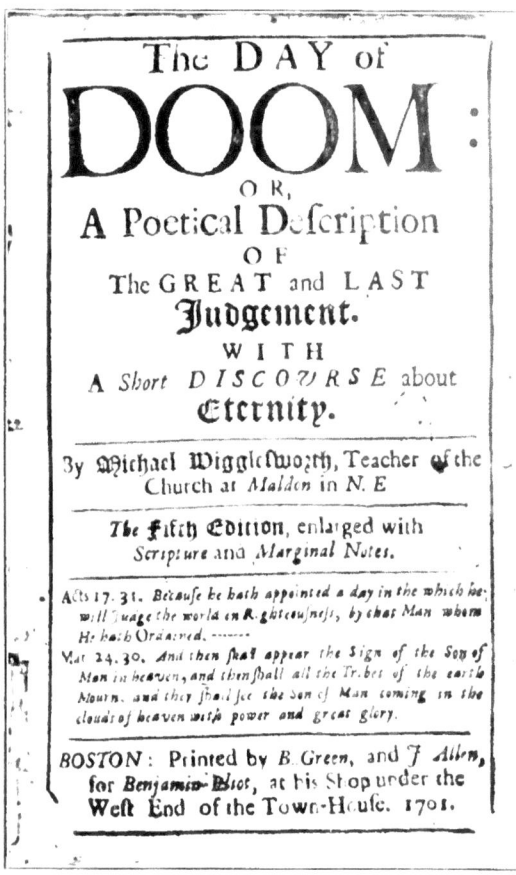

TITLE-PAGE OF "THE DAY OF DOOM"
From the original owned by John W. Farwell

learned Ministers," with the Rev. Richard Mather at their head—he of the woodcut portrait and this was put into type and was the first book printed in New England, the well-known "Bay Psalm Book." Previous to this the Puritans had used the version of the Psalms by Sternhold and Hopkins, which was not acceptable to the extremists who called it "Hopkins his Jigges."

How successful the thirty pious ministers were may be judged somewhat from the following lines:

> "O Blessed man, that in th' advice
>  Of wicked doeth not walk:
> Nor stand in sinners way, nor sit
>  in charyre of scornfull folk
>
> But in the law of Jehovah,
>  is his longing delight:
> And in his law doth meditate,
>  by day and eke by night."

During the late seventeenth century and well into the eighteenth, the books usually found in the average New England family were the Bible, the Psalm Book, an Almanac, the New England Primer, a sermon or two and perhaps a copy of Michael Wigglesworth's terrific poem—"The Day of Doom." The latter was first printed in 1662 in an edition of 1800 copies, not one of which has survived. Every copy was read and re-read until nothing remained but fragments of leaves. Seven editions of this poem were printed between 1662 and 1715 and few copies of any edition now exist. The book expressed the quintessence of Calvinism. Here is stanza 205, expressing the terror of those doomed to hell.

> "They wring their hands, their caitiff-hands,
>  and gnash their teeth for terrour,
> They cry, they roar, for anguish sore
>  and gnaw their tongues for horrour.
>
> But get away without delay,
>  Christ pities not your cry:
> Depart to Hell, there may you yell,
>  and roar Eternally."

During the Colonial period both type and printing press came from abroad and there was little or no originality in type composition. Type faces became worn and continued in use and, moreover, much of the ink was poor so that the printed page frequently was muddy and sometimes almost unreadable. The freedom of the press was restricted and it was not until 1704 that a newspaper was permitted. Benjamin Franklin is considered by many as the first American printer who produced really fine work, but he removed from New England while a young man and located in Philadelphia.

When it comes to a consideration of the production of objects having to do with everyday life and material comfort, the New England craftsmen were not far behind their fellow workers overseas. The cabinetmakers, silversmiths, pewterers and ironworkers successfully continued the traditionary forms introduced from England and some of them, before long, evolved an individual style truly American.

Oak chests, in which to store clothing, were brought from England and also were made everywhere on this side; but it was a cabinetmaker at Hartford, Conn., who introduced individualistic decorative forms on his chests that gave them distinction among others of their type and made them prize examples for the private collector and the museum of today.

Farther up the Connecticut valley, in the town of Hadley, Mass., another cabinetmaker struck out for himself and made chests of a different type covered with an incised decoration heightened with color in a manner that certainly may be considered distinctive. His product could not have had a very wide distribution and the "Hadley chest" therefore must be considered a highly localized production.

Most of the early oak chests, court cupboards, tables, chairs and other pieces of furniture made in New England in the seventeenth century, so closely followed English prototypes in their paneled and turned ornamentation, that frequently the pieces can only be differentuated by a close examination of the wood of which they are constructed. Two generations later, when the Chippendale and other styles were introduced, the principal differences between the New England product and the examples brought in from Old England lay in a greater degree of restraint in the carved ornamentation and perhaps a less heavy construction of the frame. The Windsor chair and the rocker may be considered developments of American craftsmanship but utilitarian rather than decorative in their form and construction.

One decorative form appearing in New England in the mid-eighteenth century, in the low chest of drawers, slant-top desk, secretary-desk and similar pieces of furniture, was the "block-front" cut from the solid wood. It seems to have originated in Newport, Rhode Island, passed into Connecticut and reached a high development in Philadelphia. By many it is considered one of the finest contributions to furniture design produced by the New England cabinetmakers and certainly it is not lacking in fine proportion nor in a dignified richness of design.

It would be fruitless to attempt here to elaborate upon the work of the New England cabinetmakers. The subject has been treated at length in numerous volumes containing a wealth of illustration.

The same is true of the work of the Colonial silversmiths. It has been carefully studied and beautifully illustrated and the student has at command much material upon which to base individual judgment. In general, the early silversmiths followed closely the London models and as a result the best examples of their workmanship compare most favorably with contemporary English work. There was much less wealth in the colonies, however, and therefore the additional cost of handwork, in an elaboration of decorative detail, usually resulted in a greater simplicity of design. The shapes, in general, followed the London fashion, and this was just as true in the time of Paul Revere as it was when John Coney impressed his mark with the symbol of a rabbit.

The craft of the pewterer does not seem to have been followed by many men in New England during the seventeenth century. The vessels were bringing shipments from London as demand required and, moreover, the bronze moulds used in making the ware were costly. Pewter was in use in nearly every household until well into the nineteenth century and as time passed a pewterer was located in every large town. But neither the material nor its utility were well adapted to highly decorative forms and the established English patterns were repeated in New England until well toward its disappearance from domestic use. And this, of course, may be largely attributed to the very general use of imported moulds.

In the olden time the domestic arts were not entirely confined to pattern weaving and fine needlework. According to numerous advertisements in the Boston newspapers private schools existed for instruction in featherwork, filigree and painting on glass. Turkey-work for handkerchiefs was taught and also flourishing and plain embroidery. Young misses were instructed in crewel-work on pocket books, in drawing and working of twilights, and in making lace and in working tent stitch. In 1738, Mrs. Susannah Condy, near the Old North Meeting House in Boston, advertised "all sorts of beautiful Figures on canvas, for Tent Stitch: the Patterns from London, but drawn by her much cheaper than English drawing." Twenty years later, Eleanor McIlvaine, who lived opposite the Governor of the Province, advertised that she taught "Dresden painting on Glass, Shell work, Tent Stitch, and other works proper for young ladies." It will be noted that she was quite Victorian in her limitations for instruction. There were many who taught drawing, painting on glass and japanning—which was invented in France "for the amusement and benefit of the Ladies and now practiced by most of the Quality and Gentry in Great Britain," reads one advertisement. David Mason also did coats of arms and framed pictures.

Another domestic art was working in wax. In the old days this usually resulted in floral effects or representations of the human figure. Mrs. Abigail Hiller was one of those who gave instruction in this art. She also taught "painting upon glass, quill-work, feather work, filligree and transparent." At sometime before 1751 she had made a series of wax figures representing kings, queens, etc., which she exhibited at her house upon payment of six pence, lawful money, for men and women, and four

GRAVESTONE OF WILLIAM CLARK, BOSTON MERCHANT
Made in 1742 by William Codner of Cambridge

pence for children. In this manner of displaying her art she followed one John Dyer who advertised in 1733, "a very curious waxwork, being a lively representation of Margaret, Countess of Heininburg, who had 365 children at one birth, occasioned by the rash wish of a poor Beggar woman, who is represented asking for her charity."

Sculpture in stone existed in New England but only upon gravestones. Here, the representation of Father Time, the Death's head, bats, the serpent, the hourglass, and symbolic fruits and flowers was a fitting climax for a life devoted to the contemplation of death and the horrors of hell.

There were three generations of Lamsons, the first, a son of a farmer living in Ipswich, who cut gravestones in and about Boston. Joseph, of the first generation, was a gifted child, for he combined with his skill as a stonecutter the occupations of builder, mariner, cordwainer and surveyor, as appears from various entries in the public records. He cut the stone which marks the grave of the Reverend Michael Wigglesworth, the minister who was "Maulden's physician for soul and body Two," and the author of that much-read poem—"The Day of Doom." Lamson was paid only £2.10 to £3 for cutting and setting up a stone so one can see why he turned his hand, for a part of the time, to shoemaking and surveying.

There is a beautifully carved stone in Copp's Hill Burying Ground, Boston, which marks the grave of William Clark, the wealthy merchant who built the three-story mansion, already described, in which afterwards lived Sir Harry Frankland and Agnes Surriage. Its eulogistic epitaph is characteristic of the time and the excellent carving of coat of arms and festoons of fruits on either side, that at once attract attention, were cut by William Codner, the son of a cooper living in Cambridge. Much of his work may be traced in the graveyards of Boston and vicinity.

Henry Christian Geyer, a stonecutter, of German ancestry, advertised "Stones fit for all sorts of Architect work," as early as 1762 and the next year he had in stock "a large assortment of Slate-Stones, fit for hearths or graves." In 1767 he had increased his business and could supply "some Frontice-Pieces work'd in with some of the compleatest mouldings of any in this Town." He sold "spout stones, gravestones, drean stones," and had fine marble slabs for tables.

"N. B. Said Geyer also makes Stone Coverts either of Marbel, Slate or Free Stones, which may be erected in any convenient place in a Gentleman's house, in order to preserve any Sort of Provision or Liquor from spoiling, and are very convenient for Gentlewomen to preserve their Milk, Cream and cold Victuals."

In 1768, Geyer began to make images of birds, cats, dogs, etc., in plaster of paris which were offered for sale in his shop opposite the South Fish Market, and two years later this branch of his business had increased so that he offered for sale busts of King George and Queen Charlotte, the King and Queen of Denmark and also Homer, Milton and Matthew Prior. He continued to cast birds and animals and advertised to supply in quantity to merchants, masters of vessels, country traders and shopkeepers.

This summary of the more outstanding creative work of the New England craftsmen is only intended to be suggestive. A study of original evidence and of the material that has been preserved until the present day will reveal much that is worthy of praise and also much that is merely curious. The line between the work of art and the antiquarian object is sometimes so obscurely drawn as to bewilder the ordinary observer. It is also very easy to arrive at pleasing conclusions when the will and the imagination have not been fortified by research.

THE
ARTS AND CRAFTS IN NEW ENGLAND
1704-1775

# THE
# Arts & Crafts in New England
## 1704-1775

### PAINTING AND ENGRAVING

#### PAINTERS

JOSEPH BADGER, of Boston, limner, was seized with an apoplectic fit about five o'clock in the afternoon and expired before eleven o'clock, the same night on Saturday last [May 11th].—*Boston Gazette*, May 13, 1765.

JOSEPH BADGER, late of Boston, painter, deceas'd, represented insolvent; advertisement of commissioners to receive claims.—*Boston Gazette*, Nov. 11, 1765.

JOSEPH BADGER, painter, late of Boston. His real estate lying in Temple Street, near the Rev'd Mr. Howard's meeting-house, was advertised to be sold a public vendue.—*Boston News-Letter*, Aug. 4, 1768.

JOSEPH BADGER, Mr., late of Boston, painter; his daughter Mrs. Campbell, wife of Mr. Campbell of Newport, R. I., printer, died there.—*Boston News-Letter*, Oct. 24, 1771.

JOSEPH BLACKBURN, Boston, and Mr. Blackburn, Boston, Letters for him were advertised in the *Boston Gazette*, Aug. 30, 1756.

JOHN SINGLETON COPLEY of Boston, was elected a Fellow of the Society of Artists of Great Britain on Sept. 2, 1767.—*Boston Gazette*, Oct. 19, 1767 (*sup.*).

JOHN SINGLETON COPLEY.—Last Evening Mr. John Singleton Copley was married to Miss Sukey Clarke, Daughter of Richard Clarke, Esq.—*Boston News-Letter*, Nov. 17, 1769 (*sup.*).

JOHN SINGLETON COPLEY.—Tomorrow Capt. Robson sails for London, in whom goes Passenger Mr. John Singleton Copley.—*Boston News-Letter*, June 9, 1774.

NATHANAEL EMMONS, of Boston, died May 19, 1740, aged

36 y. leaving a widow and 4 or 5 children. "He was universally own'd to be the greatest master of various Sorts of Painting that ever was born in this Country. And his excellent Works were the pure Effect of his own Genius, without receiving any Instructions from others. Some of his Pieces are such admirable Imitations of Nature, both in faces, Rivers, Banks and Rural Scenes, that the pleased Eye cannot easily leave them; and some of his Imitations of the Works of Art are so exquisite, that tho' we know they are only Paints, yet they deceive the sharpest Sight while it is nearly looking on them; and will preserve his memory till age or some unhappy accident or other destroy them. He was sober and modest; minded accuracy more than Profit."—*New England Journal*, May 27, 1740.

WILLIAM JOHNSTON, portrait painter, formerly of Boston, son of the late Mr. Thomas Johnston, Japanner, died suddenly at Bridge Town in Barbados.—*Boston News-Letter*, Oct. 1, 1772.

GEORGE MASON, Limner, begs leave to inform the Public, That (with a view of more constant Employ) he now draws Faces in Crayons for *Two Guineas* each, Glass and Frame included,—as the above-mentioned Terms are extremely moderate, he flatters himself with meeting some Encouragement, especially as he proposes to let no Picture go out of his Hands but what is a real Likeness:—Those who are pleased to employ him are desired to send or leave a Line at Mrs. *Coffin's* near *Green* and *Russell's* Printing-office, and they shall be immediately waited upon.—*Boston News-Letter*, Jan. 7, 1768.

MR. GEORGE MASON, Limner, died in Boston.—*Boston News-Letter*, July 1, 1773 (*sup.*).

CHRISTIAN REMICK, lately from *Spain*, Begs Leave to inform the Public, That he performs all sorts of Drawing in Water Colours, such as Sea Pieces, Perspective Views, Geographical Plans of Harbours, Sea-Coasts, &c.—Also, Colours Pictures to the Life, and Draws Coats of Arms at the most reasonable Rates.—Specimens of his Performances, particularly an accurate View of the Blockade of Boston, with the landing the British Troops on the first of October 1768, may be seen at the Golden-Ball and the

JOHN SINGLETON COPLEY
Painted by himself

Bunch of Grapes Taverns, or at Mr. Thomas Bradford's, North-End, Boston.—*Boston Gazette*, Oct. 16, 1769.

John Smibert, painter, sells all Sorts of Colours, dry or ground, with Oils and Brushes, Frames of several Sorts, the best Metzotinto, Italian, French, Dutch and English Prints, in Frames and Glasses, or without, by Wholesale or Retail, at Reasonable Rates; at his House in Queen-Street, between the Town-House and the Orange Tree, Boston.—*Boston News-Letter*, Oct. 10/17, 1734; also *Boston Gazette*, Oct. 14/21, 1734.

John Smibert.—To be Sold, at Mr. Smibert's, in Queen Street, on Monday, the 26th Instant, A Collection of valuable PRINTS, engrav'd by the best Hands, after the finest Pictures in Italy, France, Holland, and England, done by Raphael, Michael Angelo, Poussin, Rubens, and other the greatest Masters, containing a great Variety of Subjects, as History, etc, most of the Prints very rare, and not to be met with, except in private Collections: being what Mr. Smibert collected in the above-mentioned Countries, for his own private Use & Improvement: The Price of each single Print or Book to be mark'd upon 'em, and to be the same, which Mr. Smibert, who bought 'em at the best Hand, himself gave for them.

At the same Time, there will be Sold a Collection of Pictures in Oil Colours; the price of each Picture, to be mark'd upon it.

N. B. The Sale will last from Monday morning till the Saturday Evening following, and no longer: Those Prints, that shall remain then unsold, will be sent to England.—*Boston News-Letter*, May 15/22, 1735.

John Smibert.—At the Desire of several Gentlemen who were hindered the last Week from being present at Mr. Smibert's Sale, it will be continued till Saturday next; and those Prints that shall then remain unsold, will be sent to England.—*Boston News-Letter*, June 5/12, 1735.

John Smibert.—Ran-away on the 26th of this Instant September, from Mr. John Smibert of Boston, Painter, a Negro man Servant named Cuffee, who formerly belonged to Capt. Prince, and understands something of the business of a sailor, he is about 22 Years of Age, and speaks good English, a pretty tall well shap'd Negro with bushy Hair, has on a large dark colour'd Jacket, a pair of Leather Breeches stain'd with divers sorts of paints, and a pair of blue stockings. Whoever shall take up said Runaway and him safely convey to his abovesaid Master in Boston, shall have Three Pounds Reward and all necessary Charges paid. All Masters of Vessels are hereby warned against carrying off said Servant on penalty of the Law in that Case made and provided.—*Boston Gazette*, Oct. 3/10, 1737.

JOHN SMIBERT.—On Tuesday last died here, much lamented, Mr. John Smibert, well known for many fine Pictures he has done here, and celebrated in Italy, as well as Britain, for a good Painter, by the best Judges. As a Member of Society, he was a valuable Gentleman of a happy Temper, great Humanity and Friendship, a Kind Husband, tender Father, and steady Friend: But what is above all, an exemplary christian, eminently so in Patience and constant Resignation to the Will of God. We hear his Funeral will be Tomorrow Evening.—*Boston News-Letter*, Apr. 4, 1751.

NATHANIEL SMIBERT, 2d son of the late Mr. John Smibert, of this Town, died here after a short illness, last Wednesday afternoon [Nov. 3] aged 21 years. . . . "Painting was his peculiar Profession."—*Boston Gazette*, Nov. 8, 1756. 28 line obituary.

NATHANIEL SMIBERT.—On Wednesday last [No. 3d] departed This Life after a short Illness, and last Evening was decently inter'd, Mr. NATHANIEL SMIBERT, in the 22nd Year of his Age. He was the second Son of the late Mr. *John Smibert*, Painter, in which Business he succeeded his Father, and bad fair to equal him in his justly admired Skill. The amiable Qualifications of this lately esteemed, and now, much lamented Youth, are more than can conveniently or prudently be mentioned on this Occasion. . . . His natural Ingenuity was remarkably promising, and though he had not the Advantage of an Academical Education, yet he had made such Progress in the dead and living Languages, and in many of the Arts and Sciences, as would be esteemed to deserve the Honours: . . . He had no Relish for the Scenes of high Mirth and Gaiety, but chose those Pastimes which improve the Thought and left an agreeable Reflection.—*Boston News-Letter*, Nov. 11, 1756.

NATHANAEL SMIBERT.—The following wrote to a Friend of the Person so justly celebrated, would have been made Public sooner, had the author permitted it: yet 'tis hoped the Merit and Memory of the Deceased, will sufficiently atone for its Appearance now.

In obitum Magnae spei Juvenis,
NATHANAELIS SMIBERTI, &c.

[Then follows a latin poem of sixty-four lines signed Jo. Beveridge, Hartford, Conn., 1757].—*Boston Gazette*, May 2, 1757.

## PAINTINGS

THE QUEEN'S PORTRAIT was saved from the Town Hall at the time of the great fire.—*Boston News-Letter*, Mar. 1/8, 1711.

TWENTY SHILLINGS REWARD shall be given to any one who shall bring to Mr. Luke Vardy at the Royal Exchange near the Town Hall, a little painted Picture of a Young Lady, under a Crystal in a Shagreen Case lined with Green with Silver Clasps which hath been lost.—*Boston Gazette*, Sept. 5/12, 1726.

PICTURES AND PRINTS belonging to the estate of Governor Burnet, were sold at vendue in Boston.—*Boston News-Letter*, Oct. 7, 1729.

THE PICTURES of their Majesties King GEORGE II, and Queen CAROLINE, beautifully drawn at length, are put up in the Council Chamber in this Town, and according to the Inscription at the bottom of them, they are the Gift of His Majesty, to this His Province of the *Massachusetts* Bay.—*Boston News-Letter*, Oct. 8/15, 1730.

DUTCH PAINTINGS.—Household goods at auction, including a "curious collection of Dutch paintings, China punch bowls, glass decanters," etc.—*Boston Gazette*, Mar. 13/20, 1738.

THE PICTURES of their late Majesty's King WILLIAM and Queen MARY of blessed memory, at full length, which were done in London by the best Hands, at the charge of the Province, are come over in Capt. Jones. They are reckoned to be fine Pieces, and on Saturday last they were put up in the Council Chamber.—*Boston Gazette*, Dec. 1/8, 1740.

Lightning struck the house of Jacob Wendell, jr. of Boston, and among other damage it "scorch'd the Cieling and some Pictures that hung up near it."—*Boston News-Letter*, June 20, 1745.

"A Number of large Pictures painted on Canvas, with carv'd and gilt Frames," with household goods, etc., and part of the library of the Rev. Mr. John Checkley, deceased, were advertised at public vendue at the vendue room of Benjamin Church.—*Boston Gazette*, Oct. 24, 1757.

Game Pictures.—Lost at the late Fire, Two small Pictures of dead Game in their proper Colours, the one representing a Hare hanging by the hind Feet imboweled; the other a Lark falling, in plain gilt Frames and glaz'd. Whosoever has them it's desired they would inform the Printer, that the owner may send for them. —*Boston News-Letter*, May 15, 1760.

Col. Isaac Barre.—The Portrait of Col. Isaac Barre arrived from London last week and is to be placed in Faneuil Hall.—*Boston Gazette*, Jan. 26, 1767.

Hon. H. S. Conway.—The Portrait of Hon. H. S. Conway arrived from London, May 15, 1767 and is to be placed in Faneuil Hall.—*Boston Gazette*, May 20, 1767.

Negro Artist.—At Mr. McLean's, Watch-Maker, near the Town Hall, is a Negro man whose extraordinary Genius has been assisted by one of the best Masters in London; he takes Faces at the lowest Rates. Specimens of his Performance may be seen at said Place.—*Boston News-Letter*, Jan. 7, 1773.

## Engravers

MICHAEL DE BRULS.—Proposals for publishing by Subscription, two different Water Views, and two different Land Views, of the flourishing City of New York. The Editor and Engraver, has taken great Pains, and been very exact in laying down these four beautiful Prospects, with which the City presents itself to the Eye of every judicious Beholder. He hopes to meet with Encouragement from all Gentlemen and Ladies, &c, especially, as nothing of the Kind has been undertaken by any Body in this Part of the World.

MRS. THEODORE ATKINSON OF PORTSMOUTH, N. H.
From a portrait by John Singleton Copley, painted in 1765

*Conditions of Subscription.*

1. These above-mentioned four different Views, with the respective References, in English, High Dutch, and Low Dutch, will be curiously engraved on a Copper Plate of 21 by 12 Inches each, and printed on best large Paper.

2. A Plan of the Streets, &c., of this City, with their respective Names, will also be neatly engraved in another Copper Plate, and printed on best large Paper.

3. Each subscriber to sign his Name, and give his Quality and Place of abode.

4. These four Prints will be delivered on or before the first Day of February next to the several Subscribers at their Place of abode, at Twenty Shillings, *New York* Currency: One Half to be paid on subscribing, the other Half on the Delivery of the Five Prints.

5. The Subscription will be closed on the last Day of *January* next, after which none will be sold or disposed of.

6. A Separate Pamphlet will be published along with the Prints, giving an exact account of the wholesome Climate, pleasant Situation, Products, &c. of this Province, for the Benefit of the Subscribers, which they may chuse, either in English, High Dutch or Low Dutch.

The Editor and Publisher has settled a correspondence in the most noted Cities and Towns in *New York* Government, *New-England*, the *Jersies*, and *Pennsylvania*, for to deliver the Prints immediately after Publication, whereof Notice will be given in the publick News-Papers in *New York*, *Boston*, and *Philadelphia*, &c.

Subscriptions are taken in by *Edes & Gill*, and *T. & J. Fleet*, Printers, in *Boston*, and by *Michael De Bruls*, Publisher and Engraver of the above Plates, at the lower End of New-Street, next door to Col. Thodey, in *New York*.

P. S. Such Gentlemen, Ladies, and others, as shall be pleased to encourage this Undertaking, are desired to be expeditious in giving in their Names and Places of Abode, as they are intended to be printed and prefixed to the Pamphlet.

And in complying with this Request, they will greatly oblige their most obliged humble Servant.

*Michael De Bruls.*
—*Boston Evening Post*, Dec. 27, 1762.

Mr. Foster, copper plate printer, died in Boston.—*Boston News-Letter*, Mar. 30, 1775.

On the fatal First of November, 1765, was published, a caricatura Print, representing the deplorable State of America, and under what Influence her Ruin is attempted. - - - At the Top is a Figure representing France, holding in one Hand a Purse of Money to a Comet, marked with a Jack-Boot, and out of her Mouth a Label, by which we find she actuates the Star to shed its baneful Influence on Britannia; who presents a Box to America, telling her it is the St---p A--t: but on it is wrote *Pandora's Box* (which, according to the Poets, was fill'd with all Kinds of Calamities. America, who is in deep Distress, calls out to Minerva to secure her, *for she abhors it as Death!* Minerva (i. e. Wisdom) forbids her taking it, and points to Liberty, who is expiring at the Feet of America with a Label proper to his Extremity. Close by is a fair Tree, inscribed to Liberty; at whose Root grows a Thistle, from under it creeps a Viper and infixes its Sting in the Side of Liberty.--Mercury (who signifies Commerce) reluctantly leaves America, as is expressed by the Label.—Boreas, near the Comet, blows a violent Gust full upon the Tree of Liberty; against which Loyalty leans, and expresses her Fear of losing her Support.— Behind, a Number of Ships haul'd up and to be sold; a Croud of Sailors dismiss'd, with Labels proper to them. On the other Side a Gallows, with this Inscription, *Fit Entertainment for St---p M--n:* A Number of these Gentlemen, with Labels expressing various Sentiments on the Occasion. At the Bottom is a Coat of Arms, proper for the St---p M---n.

The above to be Sold by *Nathaniel Hurd*, near the Town House.—*Boston Gazette*, Nov. 11, 1765.

Thomas Johnson.—Mr. Thomas Johnson has just finish'd two of the Plates containing eight Bills, or manufactory Notes, to be forthwith emitted, by a number of Gentlemen in the County of

Essex, viz. of the Denominations of 1 *d.* 6 *d.* 9 *d.* 1 *s.* & 2 *s.* 3 *s.* and 5 *s.* The following is a Copy of a Bill of 9 *d* to pass four-fold.

THE BANK BILL

No.   NINE PENCE   (   )

*We jointly and severally, for ourselves and Partners, promise to take this Bill as* Nine Pence *lawfull Silver Money at 6s. 8d. per Oz. in all Payments, Trade and Business, and for Stock in our Treasury at any time, and to pay the same at that Estimation on Demand to Mr.* James Eveleth, *or Order, in the Produce or Manufactories enumerated in our Scheme, as recorded in the County of Essex Records, for Value receiv'd, dated at* Ipswich *the 1st day of* May, 1741. Motto, JUSTITIA REDIVIVA.—*Boston Gazette,* May 18/25, 1741.

THOMAS JOHNSTON.—Last Friday Morning died here Mr. Thomas Johnston, Japanner, Painter and Engraver, after a short illness, having been seized with an apoplectic fit a few Days before.—*Boston Evening Post,* May 11, 1767.

JAMES MARK, engraver, was convicted of counterfeiting the £4 bills of the Province of New York, and sentenced to be hanged. He had printed only thirteen bills when discovered. He afterwards was pardoned, on petition of "most of the Gentlewomen of the City."—*Boston News-Letter,* Sept. 7/14, 1713.

NATHANAEL MORSE, "an ingenious Engraver," died in Boston, June 17, 1748. He left a widow Sarah.—*Boston Gazette,* June 21, 1748.

THOMAS ODELL, who counterfeited a Twenty shilling Bill of Credit of the Province of Massachusetts Bay, was apprehended in Pennsylvania, and taken to Rhode Island, where he escaped, was recaptured and brought to Boston, where he was fined £300, and ordered imprisoned for one year.—*Boston News-Letter,* Nov. 5/12, 1705.

PETER PELHAM.—*The following Observations should have been inserted in last Monday's* Gazette, *but came too late for the Press; yet I hope not too late to prevent the Growth of an Evil too dangerous to be overlookt by any Person who has either a Value for Religion, or Love for his Country.*

Passing by the Town-House on Saturday the 11th of this Month, a piece of Paper was slipt into my Hand, giving notice of an Entertainment of Musick and Dancing, (call'd by the fashionable name of an Assembly) to be held at Mr. *Pelhams* Dancing School on the Thursday following, &c. which Entertainment, as I am inform'd is to be repeated Monthly, for the benefit of Gentlemen and Ladies.

I could not read this Advertisement without being startled and concern'd at the Birth of so formidable a Monster in this part of the World; and I began to consider what could give encouragement to so Licentious and Expensive a Divertion, in a Town famous for its Decency and Good Order, and at a Time when Poverty is coming upon us like an armed Man; when our Trade is Daily Decreasing, and our Debts and Poor Multiplying upon us; does the Tranquility of our Affairs at Home, or the unusual Success of our Commerce, invite us to new Pleasures and Expenses?

When we look back upon the Transactions of our Fore-Fathers, and read the Wonderful Story of their godly Zeal, their pious Resolution, and their Publick Virtues; how should we blush and lament our present Corruption of Manners, and Decay of Religious & Civil Discipline? They laid the Foundation of their Country in Piety, and a Sanctity of Life: This was Building upon a Rock; and by the Blessing of GOD they flourish'd exceedingly, and became the astonishment and envy of their Neighbours: Magistrates then discharg'd their Duty with Diligence and Fidelity, and Vice and Irregularities were carefully watch'd, and crop'd in the Bud. Then were their Sons a Virtuous and Industrious Race, and their Daughters rich in a modest, frugal, and religious Education. But this their Posterity are too delicate to follow their sober Rules, and wise Maxims, and crying out for Musick, Balls and Assemblies, like Children for their Bells and Rattles; as if our Riches flow'd in so fast upon us, that we wanted ways to dispose of them: Whereas it is too well known how our Extravigance in Apparel, and Luxury at our Tables, are hastening the ruin of our Country, and are evils which call loudly for a Remedy.

MRS. TIMOTHY FITCH OF BOSTON
From a portrait by Joseph Blackburn, painted about 1765, in the Essex Institute.
Contemporaneous frame.

In vain will our Legislature provide wholsome Laws to suppress this Epidemical profuseness. In vain will our Ministers preach Charity, Moderation and Humility, to an Audience, whose thoughts are ingaged in Scenes of Splendour and Magnificence, and whose Time and Money are consumed in Dress and Dancing. In vain will Masters secure their Treasure (the fruit of long toil and Industry) with Locks and Bolts, while their Wives and Daughters are invited to Balls & Assemblies, where a great part of the pleasure consists in being gaz'd at, and applauded, for the richness of their Cloaths, and the elegancy of this Fancy. This is laying a foundation for Pride, vain Emulation, Envy, & Prodigality.

Time was when our Maidens were the desire of all Countries that had any Dealings with; and tho' their Fortunes were small, yet their Minds were Humble: If we should now feed their Pride & Extravagance, without inlarging their Portions, we may perhaps dispose of them to some inconsiderate Lovers; but Woe be to the Men to whose Lot they fall! they will be a Moth in their Estates, and a Bane to their Happiness.

These & many more Mischiefs too tedious to mention, fatal to Modesty & Virtue, and Expensive to Families, will be the pernicious Consequence of Tollerating such Assemblies. And they are Mischiefs which demand a General Remedy, by the Interposition of Publick Authority: For what single Person tho' ever so Prudent or Stout-hearted, durst deny a beloved Wife, or favorite Daughter, the Liberty of a Pleasure indulged to all their Neighbours and Acquaintance? And if Madam & Miss are not suffered to shake their Heels Abroad, they will make the House & Family shake at Home.—*Boston Gazette*, Nov. 20, 1732.

PETER PELHAM.—At Mr. Pelham's House near the Town Dock is to be sold sundry sorts of Household Goods (for Cash) very Cheap, he having Intention to break up House-Keeping.

N. B. Attendance will be given from Eight till Twelve o'clock every morning, but not after that Hour on account of his preparing for his school in the Afternoon, which he continues to Keep as heretofore.—*Boston Gazette*, Apr. 5, 1734.

Mr. Peter Pelham, gives notice to all Gentlemen and Ladies in Town and Country, That at the House of Philip Dumerisque, Esq. in Summer Street (next his own Dwelling house) Young Gentlemen and Ladies, may be taught Dancing, Writing, Reading, Painting on Glass, and all sorts of Needle Work.—*Boston Gazette*, Jan. 16/23, 1738.

Mr. Peter Pelham gives notice to all Gentlemen and Ladies in Town and Country, That at the House of Philip Dumerisque Esq. in Summer street (next his own Dwelling house) Young Gentlemen and Ladies may be Taught Dancing, Writing, Reading, painting upon Glass, in all sorts of needle work.—*Boston Gazette*, Feb. 6, 1738.

Peter Pelham gives Notice to all Gentlemen and Ladies in Town and Country, that he has removed his School to the House of Mr. John Powel in Leveret Lane near the Town House, Boston, where he teaches Dancing, Writing, &c. N. B. Youth may be Boarded or half Boarded.—*Boston Gazette*, May 1/8, 1738.

Mr. Pelham's Writing and Arithmetick School, near the Town House (during the Winter Season) will be open from Candle Light 'till Nine in the Evening, as usual, for the benefit of those employ'd in Business all the Day: and at his Dwelling House near the Quaker's Meeting in *Lindell's Row:* All Persons may be supply'd with the best *Virginia* Tobacco, cut, spun into the very best Pigtail, and all other sorts: also Snuff, at the cheapest Rates.—*Boston Gazette*, Sept. 20, 1748.

Mr. Peter Pelham desires all Gentlemen and Ladies may be informed, that he has open'd a Dancing-School at *Mr. Maverick's* in King-street, Boston: Due attendance will be given on Mondays, Thursdays and Saturdays in the afternoon, under such private and regular Orders as formerly kept by him, for the benefit of his Scholars. N. B., He may be spoke with any other Time at his House in *Lindall's* Buildings, or at his Writing-School behind the Stone Cutter's Yard, near the Town House.—*Boston Gazette*, Mar. 21, 1749.

Peter Pelham, late of Boston, estate of, advertised as being

SETH HUDSON'S SPEECH FROM THE PILLORY
Caricature engraved in 1762 by Nathaniel Hurd

settled by Mary Pelham, widow and administratrix.—*Boston Gazette*, Aug. 4, 1752.

PAUL REVERE.—Just Published, and to be sold by Josiah Flagg, and Paul Revere, in Fish street, at the North End of Boston, A Collection of the best Psalm-Tunes, in two, three and four Parts, from the most celebrated authors: fitted to all measures, and approved by the best Masters in *Boston*, New England. To which are added, Some Hymns and Anthems: the greater Part of them never before Printed in America. Set in Score by JOSIAH FLAGG. Engraved by PAUL REVERE.—*Boston Gazette*, Nov. 5, 1764.

OWEN SULLIVAN.—We hear from Providence, in the Colony of Rhode Island, that [Owen] Sullivan, a well-known Engraver, has lately had both his Ears crop'd, and been branded in both his checks with the Letter C, for counterfeiting the Bills of Credit of that Colony.—*Boston Evening Post*, Oct. 9, 1752.

OWEN SULLIVAN.—New-York, May 17, Owen Sullavan, before he was turned off on Monday last, declared, That some Years ago he struck off near Twelve Thousand Pounds of the Rhode-Island money, and passed above Sixteen Hundred of it in one Day:—That of the New-Hampshire Currency he made Ten or Twelve Thousand Pounds:—Of Connecticut Cash he struck off above Three Thousand Pounds:—And of the New-York Currency he printed large sums of four different Emissions; the last of which was the Bills signed Oliver de Lancey, John Livingstone and Isaac De Peyster, and dated so late as March 25, 1755; to do which he had four Sets of Accomplices, who, he said, printed and passed other large Sums at Times unknown to him; and that he left the several different Plates and Stamps with his Confederates, all of whom he allow'd deserv'd the Gallows as well as himself; but he would not betray one of them, or be guilty (he term'd it) of shedding their Blood; soon after which he took a large Cud of Tobacco, and turning round to the People said, *I cannot help smiling, as 'tis the Nature of the Beast*, And being ask'd for the Benefit of the Publick of what Denomination the Bills were which he printed of the New-York Money, answered, *You must find out that by your Learning;* and so died obstinate.—*Boston Gazette,* May 24, 1756.

JAMES TURNER.—Just Published, a Treatise, proving (*a Posteriori*) that most of the Disorders incident to the *Fair Sex*, are owing to Flatulencies not seasonably vented. Wrote originally in Spanish, by Don Fart-inhando Puff-indost. Sold by J. Bushell, Printer in Newbury-street. Price Two Shillings, single. Also a Frontispiece to the same, from a Copper Plate, with the Author's Effigies, &c. Sold by J. Turner, Engraver, in Cornhill. N. B., The Book and Prints may be had together or a part of said Bushel or Turner, or of J. Buck, Print Seller in Cornhill.—*Boston Evening-Post,* Mar. 14, 1748.

JAMES TURNER.—We hear from Philadelphia, that Mr. James Turner, engraver, formerly of this Town, lately died there of the smallpox.—*Boston Evening-Post,* Dec. 10, 1759.

THOMAS WHITE, of Boston, engraver, had two young children burned to death in his house, Mar. 6, 1735-36.—*New England Journal,* Mar. 9, 1735/6.

## ENGRAVINGS

MAPS and pictures in gilt frames were advertised in the *Boston News-Letter*, Mar. 1/8, 1713/14.

PICTURES were sold at vendue, being a part of the cargo of Ship *St. Francisco,* captured by H.M. ship *Sapphire.*—*Boston News-Letter,* Apr. 28/May 5, 1712.

PICTURES.—On Wednesday the 20th Currant, will be sold at Publick Vendue at the Crown Coffee-House on the Long Wharff, a Collection of choice Pictures, fit for any Gentleman's Dining-room or Stair-case, to be seen at Mr. Shores in Queen Street, from Wednesday next to the time of Sale, between the hours of 9 and 12, and 3 to 6.—*Boston Gazette,* Apr. 4/11, 1720.

PSALM TUNES.—A Collection of 28 Psalm Tunes, with Instructions for Singing them, in the easiest Method which has yet been known. To be Sold by Samuel Gerrish Bookseller in Boston. Price 6 d. single, or 5 s. per Dozzen.—*Boston Gazette,* Apr. 27/May 1, 1721.

PSALM TUNES.—An Introduction to the Art of Singing by Note, fitted to the meanest Capacities, By the Reverend Thomas Walter, M.A. with a Collection of 24 Psalm Tunes in three parts, (6 of which are long Tunes) are very curiously & exactly ingraven on Copper Plates, to be Sold by Samuel Gerrish near the Brick Meeting-House in Cornhill, Boston.—Subscribers are desired to take Notice that the whole Number of Tunes intended, are now finished.—*Boston Gazette*, July 10/17, 1721.

PRINTS AND MAPS.—To be Sold, at the little Brick House near the East End of the Town-House in King-Street Boston, a Choice parcel of the best sort of Prints & Maps lately brought from London, all in Good Frames well black'd, at reasonable Rates, by Mr. William Price.—*Boston Gazette*, Aug. 14/21, 1721.

PROSPECT OF NEW YORK.—To be sold at the Picture-Shop over against the Town-House in Boston, an exact Prospect of the City of New York, with all Sorts of Prints and Maps, lately come from London, in Frames, or without, by *Will. Price*.—*New England Courant*, Aug. 13/20, 1722.

ENGRAVINGS.—At Mr. John Dorothy's in Windsor's-alley in Ann-Street lives a French Gentleman that does all sorts of Engraving Work at reasonable Rates, who lately came from England.—*Boston Gazette*, July 16/23, 1722.

VIEW OF BOSTON.—A View of the Great Town of Boston, taken from a Standing on Noddles-Island, and designed to be cut on Copper, will be carried on by Subscription, as such expensive Works generally are. Those Gentlemen that would encourage such a Design, may see the View at Mr. *Price's*, Print and Mapseller, over against the Town-House, where Proposals are to be had, and Subscriptions taken in.—*New England Courant*, Oct. 1/8, 1722.

VIEW OF BOSTON.—Whereas there has been an Advertisement lately publish'd, of a Design to print a View of this Town of Boston, taken from Noddles Island. This is to certify, that the Undertaker *William Burgis*, desires all Gentlemen to be speedy in their Subscription, in order to send the Drawing to England this Fall, that he may conform to the Proposal to that end lately published.

N. B. Sufficient Security is given to conform to the Conditions of the said Proposals, or to return the Advance Money.—*New England Courant*, Nov. 5/12, 1722.

PROSPECT OF BOSTON.—A Prospect of the Great Town of Boston, taken from Noddles Island—and designed to be curiously cut on Copper Plate, will be carried on by Subscription, as such expensive Works commonly are. Those Gentlemen that would encourage this Design may subscribe to the same at Mr Shelby's at the Crown Coffee House where proposals may be seen. The price is set lower than at first and those that do Subscribe to this Prospect now will have it cheaper than those who do not. Subscriptions are also taken in by William Price, Print and Map Seller, over against the Town House where the Prospect is to be seen: Where likewise you may have all sorts of Prints and Maps lately come from London, sold very cheap, framed or without. N. B. No money to be advanced by Subscribers but paid at the delivery of the printed copies. Those gentlemen who have subscribed to the former proposals will have their demands answered accordingly. The undertaker William Price desires all gentlemen to be speedy in their subscriptions in order to the speedy sending of the Drawing for England, for unless Subscriptions come in it will not be printed.—*New England Courant*, May 13/20, 1723; also *Boston Gazette*, May 6/13, 1723.

PROSPECT OF BOSTON.—Whereas a N-East Prospect of the Great Town of Boston in New England, has been taken, which is not so much to advantage as the S.-East Prospect: Now to be seen at Mr. Price's Print and Map Seller, over against the Town-House (also the Proposals) for all Persons that will be pleased to Subscribe to the Same, in order to be sent to London, to be Engraven, by the best hand.—*Boston Gazette*, Dec. 16/23, 1723.

PROSPECT OF BOSTON.—This Day is Published, A New and Correct Prospect of the Town of *Boston*, curiously Engraved on Copper, according to the Proposals some time ago printed in this Paper: they are newly arrived from London, and are to be Sold at Mr. *Wm. Price's*, Print & Map-seller over against the Town-House; where great variety of Prints and Maps are to be Sold,

PROSPECT OF THE HARBOR AND TOWN OF BOSTON IN 1723
From an engraving (central part only) after a drawing by William Burgis

and great variety of fine Looking-Glasses. Also Pictures are there Framed & curiously Painted, which will preserve their Beauty against the injuries of Smoak & Flies. Also an exact Plan of the Town, shewing the Streets, Lanes, and Publick Buildings.—*Boston Gazette,* Apr. 19/26, 1725.

PRINTS AND MAPS.—To be sold by Mr. William Price, Print and Map-Seller over against the Town-House, a new Chart of the British Empire in North America, with the distinct Colonies granted by Letters Patent, from Cape Canso to St. Matthia's River; Also a new and correct Prospect of the Town of Boston, curiously engrav'd, and an exact Plan of the Town, shewing its Streets, Lanes, and Public Buildings; likewise a great Variety of other Prints and Maps, in Frames or without, and great Variety of fine Looking-Glasses, Tea-Tables and Sconces, Toys and small Pictures for Children. At the same Place may be had all Sorts of Picture-Frames made, and the best Sort of London Crown Glass to put over Prints.—*New England Courant,* July 24/31, 1725.

PICTURES.—"A few very fine Pictures, some of which in Ebony Frames," with other items, were advertised for sale at Publick Vendue at the Inn Tavern.—*Boston Gazette,* Jan, 31/Feb. 7, 1725/6.

PRINTS AND MAPS.—To be Sold over against the West-End of the Town House in Boston, All Sorts of Looking-Glasses of the newest Fashion, & Jappan Work, viz. Chests of Drawers, corner Cubbords, Large & Small Tea Tables, &c. done after the best manner by one late from London; also Prints and Picture Varnishes, which preserves them from the Smoak & Flies, &c. At the same Place you may be supplied with a new Prospect & Plan of the Town of Boston, and another of the City of New-York, and all other sorts of fine Prints & Maps, &c. All sorts of Picture frames made, & children's Toys, Sold at reasonable rate by Mr. William Price.—*Boston Gazette,* Apr. 4/11, 1726.

PSALM TUNES.—In about Ten Days will be Printed from a Copper-Plate, a Collection of Psalm Tunes in Three Parts, Treble, Medius and Bass, with Letters instead of the Notes, fit to be bound up with Psalm books; or single, with an Introduction for the use of Learners, to be Sold by Samuel Gerrish, Bookseller in the lower end of Cornhill, Boston.—*Boston Gazette*, June 27/July 4, 1726.

HARVARD COLLEGE.—This Day is Published a Prospect of the Colleges in Cambridge in New England, curiously Engraven in Copper; and are to be sold at Mr. Price's Print-seller, over against the Town-House, Mr. Randal Jappaner in Ann Street, by Mr. Stedman in Cambridge, and the Booksellers of Boston.—*Boston News-Letter*, July 7/14, 1726.

REV. SAMUEL WILLARD.—Just Arrived from London, the Effigies of the Rev. & Learned, Mr. *Samuel Willard*, late Pastor of the South Church in Boston, and Vice-President of Harvard College in Cambridge, in New England, curiously Engraven: To be Sold by Benja. Eliot, at his Shop in King Street, and Daniel Henchman at his Shop in Cornhill, Boston.—*Boston News-Letter*, Jan. 5/12, 1726/7.

MEETING HOUSE.—This Day is Published, A Draught of the Meeting-House of the Old Church in Boston, with the New Spire & Gallery, & are to be Sold by Mr. *Price*, over-against the Town-House, and at the Booksellers in Boston.—*N. E. Journal*, June 5, 1727.

PRINTS AND MAPS.—To be Sold by William Price in King Street, near the East End of the Town-House in Boston, all Sorts of Looking Glasses & Pictures, Painted with Oil'd Colours in Carved Frames Gilt; and also a great variety of Prints & Mapps, and fine Metzotinto for Painting on Glass in Frames or without, likewise sundry Toys & Pictures, Sold by wholesale at reasonable rates to those that Sell them again, and also a fine Prospect of a Plan of the Town of Boston.—*Boston Gazette*, May 20/27, 1728.

REV. COLMAN.—Just Arrived from London, a Book Intitled, The Glories of our Lord Jesus Christ, Exhibited in Twenty Sacramental Sermons, By the Rev. Mr. Colman; with the Authors Effigies curiously Ingraven; Printed for T. Hancock at the Bible and Three Crowns near the Town Dock. To be Sold also at the abovesaid place the Pictures in Frames and Glaz'd.—*Boston News-Letter*, June 13/20, 1728.

CHARACTER BLANKS.— Boston, Feb. 17th, 1730.

Whereas a laudable Custom hath of long Standing prevailed in this Province of recommending, in the Publick Papers, the Virtuous actions, blameless Lives, and christian Deportment of Deceas'd Persons, to the worthy Imitation of the Sorrowful Living: and as the same, (we hope) has been attended with a wish'd for Success, to the Instruction, and Edification of the surviving Generation. NOW in Order to render the same more extensively Effectual; and to soften the Labours of those pious Gentlemen who have hitherto Employ'd their Pens & precious Moments to so Excellent a Purpose: It is humbly propos'd, That the Endeavours of a Person, lately Arrived from Great Britain may merit Encouragement, The said Person having with the utmost Care, and best Assistances prepar'd a Set of Characters, suited to both Sexes, Engraven on Copper Plates, by the most skilful Hands, with Void spaces for Name, Age, Distinction, and Profession, or such Particular and Eminent Qualities, as do not properly fall under the Notice of General Description.

P. S. Such as desire further Information may Receive the same by Lodging a Letter to Mr. C. H., at the Crown Coffee House.— *Boston News-Letter*, Feb. 18/25, 1730/1.

Boston, Mar. 1, 1730, 1.

To the Publisher of The Weekly Journal

Sir, Finding by an Advertisement in the *Weekly News-Letter*, that there hath lately arrived from the other side the Atlantick, a Famous Character-Drawer, who hath brought over a Fine Set there of curiously Engraven on Copper-Plates: and has therein Notified, That any one that stands in need of so useful a Creature, may receive the best of his assistance, by leaving a Line at the *Crown Coffee-House*, Directed to C. H. and least there should be any miscarriage, or failure in the Conveyance, I thought proper to put it in your paper, which will be the safest way, not only to gratify him with a sight of so reasonable Request, but may others, perhaps, with stirring them up to Emulation.

*To Mr. C. H. at the Crown Coffee-House.*

*Sir*, Reading the News-Paper some time since, and in Complyance to your Desire, and the general Report of your Ingenuity, make me presume, and I hope without offence, to send you the following Lines.

Truly *Sir*, It cannot but Rejoyce the Hearts of the Inhabitants of *New-England*, to hear of the Famous Mr. C. H., the Great Characterizer, lately arrived from *Great Britain;* being the first of that Profession that ever Inhabited this Continent: among the rest, allow me to Rejoyce, in the hopeful expectation of having a considerable Trouble taken off my Hands, by so useful a one as yours. You have doubtless heard of the Melancholly News, of the sudden and awful Death of the Noted Cryer of this Town, *Cornelius George* by Name; as for his Character (notwithstanding the many I have given) I am intirely at a loss, therefore crave the favour of you, to supply me with one, for the best Advantage and greatest Honour of the Deceas'd; out of the famous Set, which you have Industriously Procured; where he was Born signifies but little; *New-England* was the last place of his Abode; he Dyed Aged, I know not how many years, he was a Cryer by Occupation, and a Son of the *Church of England* by Profession.

I am, Sir, yours, etc,—*New England Journal*, Mar. 8, 1731.

PRINTS.—Albert Dennie, at his Warehouse on the late Gov. Belcher's wharf, advertised for sale as just imported from London, "the greatest variety of most curious Pictures, pick & chuse for 6 *d* & 12 *d* a Piece."—*Boston News-Letter*, Sept. 23/30, 1742.

PRINTS.—TO BE SOLD, *By* William Price, *at the* Looking-Glass & Picture-Shop *in* Cornhill, *near the* Town House, a New Prospect of BOSTON, neatly done, with the Addition of the Buildings, Churches, etc, to the present year; and also a Plan of the Town and Prospect of the Colledges in *Cambridge*, NEW-ENGLAND; and the greatest Variety of Maps and Prints of all sorts and sizes, in Frames and Glass, or without; Pictures painted in Oyl in gilt Frames, &c. also sells and frames all sizes of the best & newest fashion Looking-Glasses, Spectacles, Prospect-Glasses, brass and glass Arms, hard mettle Tea pots,* China Ware, Tea-

---

* Tinware was advertised for sale at public vendue at the *Royal Exchange*, Boston, in the next issue of the *News-Letter*. It was a part of the cargo of the ship *Success*.

PROSPECT OF THE COLLEGES IN CAMBRIDGE IN 1726
From an engraving after a drawing by William Burgis

tables, and Tea-chests, Flutes, Hautboys, Violins & Strings, Musick Books and Songs, English and Dutch Toys for Children, &c.

N. B. He has all the above Goods from London, at the very best hand.—*Boston News-Letter*, Sept. 22, 1743.

CHARACTER BLANKS.—If the Proprietor of the Copper-Plates for striking off CHARACTERS (who purely for the Benefit of the Public visited these Parts some years ago) is in any Part of North America, and will return again to this Town, he may depend upon it 'twill be very much for his Advantage: But if he does not incline to remove, he is desired to send a few Dozen of his *Blank Characters* (with the lowest Price) to the Publisher of this Paper, by the Post, and he may depend upon his Pay by the very first Conveyance, and may probably have an order for many more.—*Boston Evening-Post*, Sept. 1, 1746.

PRINTS AND MAPS.—TO BE SOLD, by Stephen Whiting at the *Rose and Crown* in Union Street, Boston,—Looking-Glasses, Double-Flint Decanters, single Flint Wine-Glasses by the Dozen, a choice Sortment of Maps, Prints and Metzotintoes. N. B. He also buys broken Glass.—*Boston News-Letter*, Sept. 29, 1748.

PLATE PRESS.—A Large Rolling-Press, for Printing off a Copper Plate to be Sold, Enquire of the Printer.—*Boston News-Letter*, May 11, 1749.

PROSPECT OF YALE COLLEGE.—Just published, and to be sold by James Buck, at the Spectacles in Queen-Street, a Prospect of YALE-COLLEGE in *New Haven*, neatly Engraved, where also may be had sundry Sorts of Maps, Prints, Metzotintos, &.c. in Frames and Glass, or without: small Looking-Glasses, Children's Toys, and sundry other small Articles.—*Boston Evening Post*, Dec. 11, 1749.

PRINTS AND MAPS.—Sold by William Price, at the Corner Shop next the old Brick Meeting-House, Boston:—China ware, all sorts of large and small Looking-Glasses, best Steel Temple and Nose Spectacles, &c., Reading-Glasses, Prospect Glasses, Hand Teaboards, Tea Chests, Hard-metal Tea-Pots, &c. a large Prospect, and Plan of BOSTON, the Colleges in *Cambridge*, A large Map of the British Empire in *North-America*, shewing the Boundaries of each Province, and the French Settlements behind us, &c. and all other Sorts of new Maps and Prints, fine large and small Metzotinto Prints in Frames, the best *London* Crown Glass, and good *London*-made Glew, Violins and Strings, English and German Flutes, Reeds for Hautboys, Musical Books, etc. *London* Babies, English and Dutch Toys, by Wholesale and Retail at reasonable Rates.—*Boston News-Letter,* May 10, 1750.

COURT HOUSE IN BOSTON.—To be Sold by James Buck opposite the Crown and Comb in Queen-Street. A South Prospect of the Court-House in *Boston,* also a Variety of Maps & Prints, small Looking Glasses, & sundry other Articles.—*Boston Gazette,* July 2, 1751.

PRINTS AND MAPS.—*To be sold* by STEPHEN WHITING in *Union Street,* A great Variety of Maps, Prospects and Metzotinto Prints, either in Frames or without; large Sconce & pier Glasses; small Looking-Glasses of different Sizes by the Dozen, suitable for the Country: where Traders may be supply'd at a reasonable Lay.—*Boston Gazette,* Aug. 27, 1751.

PROSPECT OF BOSTON.—To be Sold, By William Price, At the Old Glass and Picture Shop in Cornhill, near the Town House, A New Prospect and Plan of Boston: a Map of North America, Quarters of the World: and great Variety of fine Prints and Prospects, large and small: fine large and small Metzotinto Prints, Frames and Glasses, &c, all Sorts of large and small Looking-Glasses, Spectacles and Perspective Glasses, China Ware, fine Tea and Tea-Chests, Leaf Gold and Silver, Violins and Strings, &c., Flutes, Hautboys, and Musical Books, &c., London Babies, English and Dutch Toys, and best Glew.—*Boston Evening Post,* June 3, 1754.

PAPER MONEY.—The Government of *Piscataqua* having made an act for the Emission of *One Hundred and twenty Thousand Pounds,* old tenor, for carrying on the Present Expedition to C——n P——t, And last Week the Honourable *Joseph Newmarch,* and *Clement March,* Esqrs; two of their Committee, came to Town, and have agreed with an Engraver to strike off that Sum.—*Boston Gazette,* Apr. 28, 1755.

PROSPECT OF BATTLE AT LAKE GEORGE.—This Day Publish'd, and Sold by Samuel Blodget, at the South End of Boston, near the Sign of the Lamb, and opposite to Capt. Smith's.

A Prospective-Plan of two of the Engagements the English had with the French at Lake George, on the 8th of September, 1755; exhibiting to the Eye a very lively as well as Just Representation of them; together with Part of the Lake, the Camp, the Situation of each Regiment, with the Disadvantages attending them: the appearances of the Canadians, Indians and Regulars, as they made their approach to the Breast-work; the Form of the Land and the Enemy: together with the advantage they had in their Ambuscade against Col. Williams. As also a Plan of Hudson's River from New York to Albany: with such marks as will be of great Service to Navigation: Likewise the River and Waggon Road from Albany to Lake George; together with a Plan and Situation of each of the Forts that have been lately built, all which is carefully and neatly struck off from a large Copper Plate.

There will be Sold with each Plan a printed Pamphlet with Explanatory Notes, containing a full, tho' short History of that important affair from the Beginning to the End of it.—*Boston News-Letter*, Jan. 9, 1756.

PRINTS AND MAPS.—Stephen Whiting in Union Street, Boston, has to sell cheap for Cash, Large and Small Looking-Glasses, Glass and Brass Arms for Sconcers, Maps, Prospects, and Metzotinto Prints, fram'd and glaz'd; a compleat Set of Shop-Window Glass large London Crown with Compass Squares. At the same Place Looking-Glasses are Quick-silver'd, and Pictures and Maps framed and varnish'd.—*Boston News-Letter*, Feb. 24, 1757.

MEZZOTINTS.—Stephen Whiting of Boston, a Japanner, was declared a bankrupt, and his household furniture and shop goods were advertised to be sold at publick venue, including chairs with leather and harrateen bottoms, suit of red harrateen curtains, a great variety of very beautiful Metzotinto and other Pictures, wine glasses, beakers, Delph-ware, etc, etc.—*Boston News-Letter*, Apr. 7, 1758.

HUNTING PRINTS.—"Several hunting-pieces under Glass," to be sold at vendue.—*Boston Gazette*, Dec. 25, 1758.

GLAZED PICTURES.—"A handsome Set of glaz'd Pictures with a carv'd gilt Edge."—*Boston Gazette*, Apr. 9, 1759.

COPPER PLATE.—This Day Publish'd Adorn'd with a beautiful Copper Plate, representing a strong fortified Place, with the Method of a regular Approach, Attack, &c. Sold by Edes & Gill, and Green & Russell, at their Printing Offices in Queen Street. The Gentleman's Compleat Military Dictionary. . . . —*Boston Gazette*, May 7, 1759.

VIEW OF QUEBEC.—To be Sold by *Stephen Whiting*, at his Shop near the Mill-Bridge; a very neat View of the City of Quebeck, from the latest and most authentic French original, done at Paris. ☞ Some of the above Prospects to be Sold by the Printers hereof.—*Boston Gazette*, Aug. 13, 1759.

VIEW OF QUEBEC.—Just Printed from a Copper-Plate, (and to be Sold by Stephen Whiting, at his shop near the Mill Bridge, Boston.) A very neat View of the City of Quebeck, from the latest and most authentic French original, done at Paris. This Prospect may be framed and glas'd, with Glass of 10 by 8, and may be had of said Whiting very reasonably.—*Boston News-Letter*, Aug. 16, 1759.

PRINTS AND VIEWS.—Just Imported in the *Pitt* Pacquet, and to be sold by Rivington & Miller, at the London Book Store, Head of King Street, Boston. [Various books] also, a very great Collection of Pictures, containing all the celebrated and reigning Beauties in *Britain:* all the Statesmen, Generals, and Admirals, that have distinguished themselves this WAR: framed and gilded in the most elegant and neat Manner. Also, Large and splendid Views of some of the most remarkable Places in *North-America;* and of the most magnificent Palaces and Gardens in England.—*Boston News-Letter*, Apr. 23, 1762.

PICTURES AND PAPER HANGINGS.—Just imported from London and for sale by Thomas Lee, a great variety of articles including: "a large Collection of Pictures, framed and glazed, and in Sheets:

a fine Assortment of Gothic Paper Hangings."—*Boston News-Letter*, May 17, 1764.

PROSPECTS AND MEZZOTINTS.—To be sold by Stephen Whiting, opposite the Cornfields in Union Street; Sconce and Pier Looking Glasses, handsome Prospects, Setts of Metzatinto Prints, and the best London Crown Glass, to paint Pictures on,—At the above Place, Looking-Glasses are Silver'd, Needle-Work and Glasses framed and gilt.—Those that have left Frames to be filled with Glass, are informed they are done, and are desired to send for them.—*Boston Gazette*, June 3, 1765.

PRINTS.—Thomas Lee, "directly from London, with a large Assortment of English goods hath opened a shop opposite the Golden Ball" and advertised among other items "a most genteel collection of pictures, fram'd, glaz'd and gilt, and a vast quantity of those in sheets, among the latter are many humerous and saterical prints, more especially respecting the late war and the peace."—*Boston Gazette*, June 13, 1763 (*sup.*).

HOGARTH ENGRAVINGS.—"7 Cartoons and Harlots Progress under Glass," for sale at Public Vendue at Deshon's Newest Auction-Room.—*Boston Gazette*, July 8, 1765.

ENGRAVINGS.—A certain ——— has been lately rubbing up his Old Tools, and purchasing and making of new ones at S ——— and M ———, &c. in order to begin a Piece of Work in the engraving Way, which he thinks will be so acceptable on the other side of the Water as to atone for the late Injuries done the Revenue by the Instrumentality of a *Cockell*-Shell.—*Boston Gazette*, Oct. 14, 1765.

EUROPEAN PROSPECTS.—To be Sold at a shop on the north side of the *Exchange:* China and Glass ware, large curve and gilt Sconces, large Pier Glasses, curious Images, several fine Setts of Prospects of EUROPE, Several Pieces, &c. coloured in Ebony Frames curved and gilt under the best Crown Glass; also a Camera Obscura, with Pieces answerable: India and Cotton Counterpains; silver Equipages and Jewelry; Ladies gold and gilt watches; silver plated Tea Chests, Cases silver-handle Knives and

Forks: London made clocks, etc. etc.—*Boston News-Letter*, Apr. 23, 1767.

## Maps and Charts

SOUTHACK'S CHART.—There is now Published, and to be Sold at Mrs. *Joanna Perry*, Bookseller's Shop in King-Street near the Town House in Boston, Capt. *Cypran Southack's* large and Correct Chart or MAP of all the Sea Coast in the British America, on the Continent, *viz.* from Newfoundland, to Cape Florida: the like never yet Extant, of great Use to all, but especially Mariners.—*Boston News-Letter*, June 17/24, 1717.

SOUTHACK'S CHART.—To my Fellow Marriners, Gentlemen, I have now finished my general CHART of the *Sea-Coast* from *Cape-Cancer* to *Sandy Point* of *New York*, in *North America*, with the Harbours, Towns, Bays, Roads, Rocks, Sands, Fishing-Banks, Shoals and Shelves, Depths of Water, Latitudes, Bearings and Distances from Place to Place, the make of the Land, and the Variations. My Intent in putting out this Advertisement is for the Good of the Navigation, and that my *Chart* may be as Correct as possible before it is engraven: Therefore, lest my *Chart* should be imperfect if any Gentlemen will let me wait upon them at my House, and will assist me in any thing they shall find uncorrect, or will inform me of any Discoveries they may have made, which my *Chart* makes no mention of, they will very much oblige their humble Servant, *Cyprian Southack*.—*Boston News-Letter*, May 19/26, 1718.

CANSO HARBOR.—Engraven and Printed, the Map of Canso Harbour, with the Distance of the French shoar from Canso, and Islands Adjacent, and Rocks, Shoals, and Channel ways, etc. A very large Scale; to be Sold by Mr Samuel Phillips, near the Town House, Boston. Drawn by Capt. Cyprian Southack.—*Boston News-Letter*, Apr. 14/18, 1720.

MISSISSIPPI RIVER.—Engraven and Printed the General Chart from the Great River Messsippi to Cape Breton, the Map of Canso, and Map of Casco Bay, with the Harbour, Islands, Adjacents, Rocks, Shoals, Channel ways, &c. Very Large Scale; to be

VIEW OF HARVARD COLLEGE IN AUGUST, 1767

From an engraving by Paul Revere, after a drawing by Joseph Chadwick, in the Essex Institute

sold by Capt. Cyprian Southack at his House in Boston, living at the Head of Hanover Street, near the Sign of the Orange Tree: The Chart at Six Shillings for one, Casco Map at Eight Shillings for one, and Canso Map at Five Shillings for one.—*Boston News-Letter*, Apr. 10/13, 1721.

MAP OF BOSTON.—A Curious Ingraven Map of the Town of Boston, with all the Streets, Lanes, Alleys, Wharffs & Houses, the Like never done before, Drawn by Capt. John Bonner: and Sold by him at his House in Common Street, and also by Messieurs Bartholomew Green in Newbury Street, Samuel Gerrish & Daniel Henchman at their Shops in Cornhill, Boston.—*Boston News-Letter*, May 14/21, 1722.

CAPT. JOHN BONNER.—"On the Lords Day Morning last, Died here Capt. John Bonner, in the 84th. Year of his age, and was Decently Interred on Tuesday following. He was a Gentleman very Skillful and Ingenious in many Arts and Sciences; especially in Navigation, Drawing, Moulding of Ships, &c. One of the best acquainted with the coasts of North America, of any of his time; of great Knowledge and Judgment in Marine affairs; was very much consulted, improved and relyed upon by the Government as a Principal Pilate, in our Marine Expeditions." . . . —*Boston News-Letter*, Jan. 27/Feb 3, 1725/6.

MAP OF BOSTON.—Lately Published, A New Plan of the Town of Boston, and are to be Sold at the Crown Coffee-House, and by the Booksellers in Town and Country.—*Boston News-Letter*, June 26/July 3, 1729.

SEA CHARTS.—Came by Capt. Hammerden now from London, Fifty of my General Charts in Sheets, from Sandy Point of New York, unto Cape Canso in Nova Scotia, and part of Island Breton, with the Courses and Distances from Place to Place, set by the Meridian Compass, with the allowance of the Western Variation, and Towns on the Sea board, Harbours, Bays, Islands, Roads, Rocks, Sands, the Setting and Flowing of Tides, and Currents, with several other Directions of great Advantages to this part of Navigation in North America, a Large Scale almost half an Inch to one League: And to be Sold at my House near the Sign of the

Orange Tree. Cyprian Southack.—*Boston Gazette*, June 30/July 7, 1729.

PLAN OF BOSTON.—To be Sold by William Price at the King's Head and Looking-Glass, in Cornhill near the Town-House, Boston, a new Plan of the Great Town of Boston in New England, Shewing the many Additional Buildings and new Streets, Lanes and Allies with their Proper Names, to this Present Year, etc. and also a Large new South-East prospect of Boston, and great Variety of all Sorts and Sizes of the newest Maps and Prints by the best Masters, in Frames and Glass or without.—*Boston Gazette*, Jan. 1/8, 1733.

CHART OF CANADA RIVER.—New Engraven, Printed and Sold by Thomas Johnston, at his House in Brattle-Street, near Dr. Colman's Meeting-House. A Correct French Draft of the River of Canada, from the Island of Anticostie as far as Quebec, the Islands, Rocks, Shoals, and Soundings, as they appear at Low Water. The whole contains three sheets of Demi-Paper. Price 15/. Old Tenor.—*Boston News-Letter*, Aug. 8, 1746.

MAPS AND PROSPECTS.—A newly engraved draft of the River Canada; also a new map of the British Empire in North-America; also a new plan and prospect of the town of Boston, and a Prospect of the Colleges in Cambridge, with a great variety of maps and prints of all sorts in Frames or without, to be had of William Price, at the Picture Shop in Cornhill, Boston.—*Boston News-Letter*, Aug. 15, 1746.

PLAN OF LOUISBOURG.—This Day is Published, (Price Twenty Shillings, Old Tenor), A Plan of the City and Fortress of LOUISBOURG: with a small Plan of the Harbour. Done in Metzotinto on Royal-Paper by Mr Pelham, from the Original *Drawing* of Richard Gridley, Esq: Commander of the Train of Artillery at the Seige of Louisbourg. Sold by J. Smibert in Queen Street, Boston.—*Boston News-Letter*, Sept. 4, 1746.

MAP OF NOVA SCOTIA.—Imported in the last ship from London, and Sold by James Buck, at the Spectacles in Queen Street, Boston, (Price Fifteen Shillings Old Tenor.) A New and Correct Map of NOVA SCOTIA, with its Boundaries: Together with an exact Plan of the Harbour of Chebucto, and Town of HALLIFAX, as surveyed by Mr. Harris: As also a Perspective View of the Town of Hallifax, drawn from the Topmast Head.—*Boston News-Letter*, Aug. 23, 1750.

CHART OF NEW ENGLAND COAST.—London, England, July 4, 1751. This Day was published a new and correct Chart of the Sea-Coast of NEW-ENGLAND, from Cape Cod to Casco Bay, by Capt. Henry Barnsley.—*Boston News-Letter*, Sept. 19, 1751.

CHART OF NEW ENGLAND COAST.—Jarvis and Parker, at their Warehouse near the Insurance Office in King street, sold a great variety of fabrics, books, etc. also, A New Draught of the Coast of New-England, by Capt. Henry Barnsley, Marble, blue, Cartridge and brown Paper, Writing Parchment, Case Knives and Forks, Temple Spectacles, Fountain Pens, Pewter and Wood Ink-Chests, etc. etc.—*Boston Evening Post*, May 21, 1753.

CHARTS AND STATIONERY.—To be Sold by Michael Dennis, at the Corner of Scarlet's wharf, where may be had . . . a variety of single Plays and small Histories, Marriners Compasses and Callendars according to New-Stile, Coasting Pilots, a new Draught of the Coast of New England by Capt. Henry Blansley: likewise Accompt Books, large & small, all Sorts of Writing Paper, Marble, blue, Cartridge and brown Paper, Press Paper for Clothiers, Writing Parchment, Gunter Scales and brass Dividers, Case Knives and Forks, Jack Knives, Penknives, Ink-pots, Temple Spectacles, Letter Cases, Fountain Pens, Pewter & Wood Ink-Chests, Ivory and Horn Combs, Slates with Frames & without, Pencils, small Scales & Weights to weigh Money, and Silk Purses to carry it in.—*Boston Gazette*, June 5, 1753.

MAPS AND CHARTS.—Just Published, a Map of Kennebeck and Sagadahock rivers, and of part of the eastern coast of the Massachusetts, lying between Cape Elizabeth and Penobscot. Also a small MAP of part of North America, on the same sheet with the forgoing, exhibiting a general comprehensive view of the territories of the English and French, and the forts possessed by each in this part of America,—sold by Thomas Johnson, in Brattle-

Street, near the Rev. Mr. Cooper's Meeting-House, at half a Dollar.—*Boston Gazette*, June 16, 1755.

MAP OF MIDDLE COLONIES.—Just published, A General Map of the MIDDLE BRITISH COLONIES, in AMERICA: Viz. Virginia, Maryland, Delaware, Pennsylvania, New-Jersey, New-York, Connecticut, and Rhode-Island, and Country of the Confederate Indians, &c. By LEWIS EVANS. N. B. This Map includes all the Country depending on the English and French Passages to Ohio, Niagara, Oswego, and Crown Point.

☞ A Number of the said Maps colour'd, with the Pamphlets, are bro't hither from Philadelphia, and are ready to be delivered to the Subscribers, at the Post office in Cornhill.—*Boston News-Letter*, Oct. 23, 1755.

MAP OF NEW ENGLAND.—Just imported from LONDON, a Plan of the Four Governments of New-England, on four Sheets of Imperial Paper, showing the Townships in each Government, and the boundary Lines of each Jurisdiction are described by coloured Lines: Compos'd from actual Surveys, By the late Dr. William Douglass. Sold by Mr. Price, near the Town House; Mr. Stephen Whiting, in Union-Street; Mr. Thomas Robinson at the Green-Dragon; and by the Printers hereof.—*Boston Gazette*, Dec. 29, 1755.

MAP OF CROWN POINT.—This Day is Published (and Sold by Thomas Johnston in Brattle-Street, and Jacob Griggs, opposite the Town-House, Boston, & Timothy Clements, in Haverhill.),

A Plan of Hudson's River to Fort Edward, with the Waggon-Road to Lake George, and the Narrows: also, Part of Lake Champlain, Crown-Point, the South-Bay, and Wood-Creek, by the best accounts:—with an exact Plan of Fort Edward, and William-Henry:—and of the Land defended in the General Engagement on the 8th of September, 1755;—Likewise, our Army's Intrenchment after the Fight, with Sundry Particulars respecting the Engagement on said Day; with the Distance and Bearing of Crown-Point, and Wood-Creek from the Great-Falls on Connecticut-River a little below No. 4, as surveyed by Timothy Clements, Surveyor.—*Boston News-Letter*, May 13, 1756.

Mr. Lewis Evans, author of the map of the Middle British Colonies in America, died at New York, June 12, 1756, after a lingering Indisposition.—*Boston Gazette*, June 21, 1756.

Map of Canada River.—An exact CHART of Canada-River, (from the Island of Anticoste, as far up as Quebeck) the Islands, Rocks, Shoals and Soundings, as they appear at Low Water, (taken from the French) to be Sold by the Printers hereof, and by Thomas Johnston in Brattle-Street.—*Boston Gazette*, July 16, 1759.

Chart of Carolina Coast.—The Navigation on the Coast of *North* and *South Carolina* being very dangerous on account of the many Bars, Shoals, Sandbanks, Rocks, etc. The late Daniel Dunbibin, Esq: of *North Carolina*, has, at a very great Expence and Labour, draughted the Sea Coast of both the Provinces in a large whole Sheet Chart of 33 Inches by 23; together with all the Rivers, Bays, Inlets, Islands, Brooks, Bars, Shoals, Rocks, Soundings, Currents, &c. with necessary Directions to render the Navigation both easy and safe, and are much esteemed by the most expert Pilots:—A few of the Draughts may be had of the Subscriber if apply'd for directly. Edmund Quincy, jun, *Broker*.—*Boston Gazette*, Sept. 14, 1761.

Map of Crown Point.—This Day is Published, (Printed on a Sheet of Demy, from a Copper-Plate), Price Two Pistareens. A Plan of Part of Lake Champlain, and the large New Fort at Crown-Point, mounting 108 Cannon, built by General Amherst; Done from an actual Survey taken by Francis Miller. With References and Explainations of the different Plans.

On the same sheet are Perspective Views of Quebec and Montreal.

Sold in Boston by *John Draper* at his shop in Cornhill. *Thomas Johnston*, Engraver, in Brattle-Square. *Stephen Whiting*, Print seller, near the Mill Bridge. *Daniel Jones*, at the Hat & Helmit, South-End. And, by *Richard Draper*, in Newbury Street.—*Boston News-Letter*, May 20, 1762.

Chart of New England Coast.—The University of Aberdeen have conferred the Honour of Doctor of Divinity on the

Reverend Mr. *Samuel Langdon*, of Portsmouth, in New Hampshire in New England, he being a Gentleman eminent in Piety and Learning, and having lately obliged the Public with a Map of that Province, being the first that was ever published.—*Public Ledger, London, Aug.* 10. [In the above curious Map is laid down the Sea coast from Boston to Penobscot-Bay: also a General Map of the River St. Lawrence above Montreal to Lake Ontario, and the adjacent Country, dedicated to the Right Hon. *Charles Townsend*, His Majesty's Secretary at War.—A few of them may be had of *Edmund Quincy*, Junr.]—*Boston Gazette*, Nov. 1, 1762.

MAPS AND PRINTS.—Looking-Glasses and Pictures, That were imported in Capt. Bryant from London, to be Sold by STEPHEN WHITING, at his Shop opposite the Sign of the Cornfield in Union Street, and by STEPHEN WHITING, JUN'R, at his Shop a little below the Cornfield.

Large and handsome sconce and pier Looking-Glasses, small Glasses by the Dozen, suitable for Traders, Maps of the Four Quarters of the World, ditto of the four Provinces of Massachusetts, New Hampshire, Rhode Island, and Connecticut, a Variety of large and small Metzotinto Prints, plain and coloured, among which are the King and Queen, the late Lord Mayor Beckford, the Rev'd George Whitefield, the newest Impression, and others of Note, suitable for painting on Glass, with the best London Crown Glass for that use: The idle and industrious Apprentice, large and small coloured ordinary Pictures, single or by the dozen.

At the above Places Looking-Glasses are silvered, and Frames made for all sorts of Pictures, Looking-Glasses, Coats of Arms and Needle-Work, and gilt as best suits the Employer.

New Frames made for old Glasses or new Glasses put to old Frames. Also, Varnishing, Japanning and Gilding done to Frames of all Sorts, as well and reasonable as any are done in this Province.—*Boston News-Letter*, May 16, 1771.

MAPS AND PRINTS.—To be Sold. A Set of very handsome Prints, neatly framed and glazed, engraved from original Paintings by Claud Lorrain; also, a Set of the Elements framed and

REV. COTTON MATHER
From a mezzotint by Peter Pelham, made in 1728

glazed in the same Manner. Enquire of the Printer.—*Boston News-Letter*, July 8, 1773.

MAPS AND PRINTS.—Stephen Whiting, opposite the Corn-Fields in Union Street, and by Stephen Whiting, jun'r, at the Boston Store, near the Mill-Bridge; A variety of humorous Engravings and Mezzotinto Prints, plain and coloured, large and small, with and without Frames,—ordinary Pictures by the Dozen. N.B. Those that left Glasses to be silver'd or fram'd are desired to send for them as soon as possible.—*Boston News-Letter*, Sept. 23, 1773 (*sup.*).

## MEZZOTINTS

PORTRAIT OF REV. COTTON MATHER.—PROPOSALS for making a Print in *Metzotinto*, of the late Reverend Dr. Cotton Mather, by Peter Pelham. . . .

I. The Copper Plate to be 14 Inches by 10, which is the Common Size of most Plates in *Metzotinto*, by the said *Pelham*, and others.

II. It shall be done after the Original Painting after the Life by the said Pelham, and shall be Printed on the best Royal Paper.

III. Every Subscriber to pay *Three Shillings* down, and *Two Shillings* at the Delivery of the Print, which will be begun when a handsome Number of Subscriptions is procur'd: Therefore as the Author hopes to Compleat the work in *Two Months*, he desires all those who have a mind to Subscribe, to be speedy in sending their Names with the first Payment.

IV. For the Encouragement of Subscribers, those who take Twelve shall have a Thirteenth *Gratis*.

N. B. SUBSCRIBERS and others may see Some Prints in Metzotinto, of the Author's doing by way of Specimen, at his House in Summer St. . . . The Plate is now actually in hand. —*Boston Gazette*, Feb. 26/Mar. 4, 1727/8.

PORTRAIT OF REV. COTTON MATHER.—Notice is hereby given to Subscribers, &c. that the Prints of the late Rev. Dr. COTTON MATHER, will be deliver'd at the beginning of next Week: . . . —*Boston Gazette*, June 10/17, 1728.

MEZZOTINT PRINTS.—On Thursday the second of January next will be Sold by Vendue at the Sun-Tavern on Dock Square at five of the Clock in the afternoon, a parcel of Fine Missitinto Prints, the largest Cutts that has been seen in these parts, consisting of curious Battles, Riding, Hunting, Fowling, Fishing and History peices; also some Excellent Scripture peices.—*Boston Gazette*, Dec. 23/30, 1728.

PORTRAIT OF ANN ARNOLD.—*Mezetinto.* Just Published in Mezetinto, and to be Sold by J. Buck, at the Spectacles in Queen street, the Effigies of *Ann Arnold*, who generally goes by the name of *Jersey Nanny.*—*Boston Gazette*, Dec. 20, 1748.

PORTRAIT OF REV. WILLIAM COOPER.—Just Done, the Effigies of the Rev. Mr. William Cooper, in Metzo-Tinto, of the best Size and Sold by Stephen Whiting, at the Rose & Crown in Union Street, Boston.—*Boston News-Letter*, May 10, 1744.

PLAN OF LOUISBOURG.—This Day is Published, (*Price* Twenty Shillings, Old Tenor.) A Plan of the City and Fortress of LOUISBOURG: with a small plan of the Harbour. Done in Metzotinto on Royal Paper, by Mr. *Pelham*, from the original Drawing of *Richard* Gridley, Esq: Commander of the Train of Artillery at the Seige of *Louisbourg.* Sold by J. Smibert in Queen-Street, Boston.—*Boston Gazette*, Sept. 16, 1746; also *Boston News-Letter*, Sept. 4, 1746.

PORTRAIT OF WILLIAM SHIRLEY.—A curious Print of His Excellency, WILLIAM SHIRLEY, Esq. done in Mezzotinto, by Mr *Peter Pelham*, to be sold by him at his school, in Queen Street—at Mr. Stephen Whiting's, at the Rose & Crown, in Union Street,—and at Mr. James Buck's, near the Brazen Head, in Cornhill.—*Boston Evening Post*, July 27, 1747.

MEZZOTINT PRINTS.—Just imported, and to be sold by James Buck, at the Spectacles in Queen Street, a choice Assortment of Maps and Prints, plain and coloured, fine Mezzotintoes pick'd out for the Ladies to paint, with the very best of London Crown Glass, small Looking-Glasses, Spectacles, etc. He has also a very good Philadelphia Fire Stove to dispose of.—*Boston Evening Post*, Sept. 12, 1748.

PORTRAIT OF REV. THOMAS PRINCE.—To be Sold, by James Buck, at the Spectacles in Queen-Street, An accurate Print in Metzotinto of the Rev. Mr. Thomas Prince, A.M., Likewise all Sorts of Maps and Prints,—among which is a Set of Prints compleatly coloured, proper for viewing in *Camerae Obscura.*—*Boston News-Letter*, May 24, 1750.

MEZZOTINT PORTRAITS.—The Sett of Prints of the four Episcopal Ministers, grav'd in Metzotinto by *P. Pelham*, and Printed by him, are now ready to deliver to the Subscribers, and others, who may be supplied with Frames and Glass's of several Sorts, at his House near the *Quaker's* Meeting-House in Boston.—*Boston Gazette*, Mar. 12, 1751.

PORTRAIT OF REV. JOHN MOORHEAD.—This Day is Published and Sold by James Buck, at the Spectacles in Queen Street, an accurate Print in Metzotinto of the Rev. Mr. John Moorhead, where may be had the Rev. Thomas Prince's Picture, a Prospect of the Court-House in Boston; a Variety of Maps and Prints, small Looking-Glasses, &c. &c. N. B. The Subscribers for the Print of Mr. Moorhead, are desired to send for them.—*Boston News-Letter*, July 18, 1751.

PORTRAIT OF THOMAS HOLLIS.—TO BE SOLD, by P. Pelham, at his House near the Quaker's-Meeting-House, A Print in Metzotinto of THOMAS HOLLIS Late of *London*, Merchant, a most generous Benefactor to *Harvard College* in *New England*, having founded two Professorships and ten Scholarships in said *College*, given a fine Apparatus to Experimental Philosophy, and increased the Library with a large Number of valuable Books, &c. &c. done from a curious whole Length Picture by *Joseph Highmore* in *London*, and placed in the *College Hall* in *Cambridge*. Also sundry other Prints at said *Pelham's.*—*Boston Gazette*, Sept. 17, 1751.

PORTRAIT OF REV. JAMES HARVEY.—T. Bromfield, next the three Sugar-Loaves, in King Street, advertised for Sale "the Effigies of the Rev. Mr. James Harvey: together with several other valuable Prints: fram'd or without: also a Compleate sett of Tapestry Hangings."—*Boston Gazette*, Nov. 27, 1753.

MEZZOTINT PORTRAITS.—To be Sold. A Large Handsome Dwelling House, scituate near the Middle of the Town of Concord, which formerly belonged to the Rev. John Whiting, deceased, . . . enquire of Stephen Whiting, at his House in Union-Street, Boston; where he has to sell, large Sconce and Pier Looking-Glasses, small Glasses of almost all sizes, a Variety of Maps, Prospects and Metzotinto Prints: also the Effigies of all the New-England Ministers ever done in Metzotinto, among which is the Effigy of that worthy Gentleman the late Rev. William Welsteed, deceased.—*Boston Evening Post*, May 27, 1754.

PORTRAIT OF REV. JAMES HARVEY.—For sale by Thomas Bromfield, in King-Street, near the Three Sugar Loaves and Canister, the effigies of the Rev. Mr. James Harvey, with or without glass.—*Boston Gazette*, June 23, 1755.

MEZZOTINT PORTRAITS.—Just imported from LONDON, and to be sold by Nathaniel Warner, opposite to the Sign of the Schooner in Fish Street, near Mr. John Pigeon's at the North End, Boston,

A great Variety of new fashioned Looking Glasses, and Sconces, and also a Variety of Metzitento Pictures, painted on Glass, double Frames, neatly carved and gilt, viz. The Royal Family, the Judges of England, the months, the seasons, the four Parts of the Day, the senses, the Elements: very handsome Views of Sea Pieces; the Rakes & Harlots Progress, Maps, Gold Leaf, &c.

☞ Said *Warner* frames and quicksilvers Glasses in the neatest and best Manner, at a moderate Rate.—*Boston Gazette*, Jan. 17, 1757.

MEZZOTINT PORTRAITS.—Imported by Nathaniel Warner, in the last Ship from *London*, and to be Sold at his Shop next to the Draw-Bridge, at the lowest Rates for Cash, *viz*. Looking Glasses of all Sizes; a neat Assortment of Metzetinto Pictures, such as, The Hon. William Pitt, Esq; the King of Prussia; Prince Ferdinand; Marshal Keith; Admiral Boscawen; Mr. Gerrick, Actor; Mr Beard, Singer; The Twelve Months; Four Seasons; Four Parts of the Day; Five Senses; The Sciences; Four Elements; The City of Quebeck and the Draught of the River; The Rake's and Harlot's Progress; The idle and industrious apprentice; Beautiful

Prospects, coloured and without; Sea Pieces, coloured; Maps; The Six Dock Yards of England, done after the best Manner; Gold Leaf and Dutch Metal, as also a neat Assortment of Pictures painted in Glass. N. B. The said *Warner* makes all Sorts of Frames, and Quick Silvers Glasses after the neatest Manner.—*Boston Gazette*, Nov. 5, 1759.

PORTRAIT OF REV. JONATHAN MAYHEW.—Prints of the late Rev. Jonathan Mayhew, D.D. done in Metzotinto by Richard Jennys, jun. are sold by Nathaniel Hurd, Engraver, near the Exchange.—*Boston News-Letter*, July 17, 1766.

MEZZOTINT PORTRAITS.—To be sold by Stephen Whiting, *Glassman* and *Jappanner*, at his Shop in Union-Street, opposite the Cornfield, Boston, the following articles which were Imported in Capt. *Freeman*, one of the last Ships from London, viz: Sconce & Pier Looking-Glasses, with neat Walnut Frames plain and Gilt, Glass Plaits silver'd of different sizes for Book case Doors, small Glasses of almost all Dimensions, suitable for Traders in the Country; a Variety of Metzotinto Prints with or without Frames, among which are some of the most esteemed Patrons of America, compleat Setts of Metzotintoes for painting on Glass; also, best London Crown for that Use; Setts of Prospects, both Plain and Colour'd, ordinary Pictures by the large or smaller Quality: Cheap for Cash.—*Boston News-Letter*, Nov. 5, 1767.

## WOOD ENGRAVINGS, ETC.

THE first wood engraving to appear in the *Boston News-Letter* is a representation of the flag to be used by merchant vessels, thereafter, by proclamation dated at Windsor, 28th July 1707.—*Boston News-Letter*, Jan. 12/19, 1707/8.

The second wood engraving to appear in the *Boston News-Letter* is a mortice initial roughly representing two thistles with Prince's feathers [?] between and two roses beneath.—*Boston News-Letter*, Mar. 10/17, 1717/18.

New woodcut (ship & light house) and mortice initial letter (bird & rabbit) in *Boston Gazette*, Nov. 13/20, 1732; also, cut of ship in the advertisements and also advertisements broken up by rules.

Woodcut of flaming sun (with human head).—*Boston Gazette*, Apr. 16/23, 1733.

Wood cut of mortice initial (Britannia seated).—*Boston Gazette*, June 10/17, 1734.

Wood cut of new device of pine tree.—*Boston Gazette*, Oct. 14/21, 1734.

Wood cut of hanging sign of John Merritt, grocer, *The Three Sugar Loaves.—Boston Gazette*, Nov. 18/25, 1734.

Wood cut of devices at head of the newspaper.—*Boston Gazette*, June 16/23, 1735.

Wood cut of a ship and a run-away servant.—*Boston Gazette*, Aug. 11/18, 1735.

Wood cut:—a fine tail piece, used in some book [?].—*Boston Gazette*, Apr. 30, 1739 (*sup.*).

Wood cut:—a new mortice initial letter (good): St George slaying the Dragon.—*Boston Gazette*, June 29/July 6, 1741.

Wood cut:—a new mortice initial letter and new cuts in the heading, one showing the figure of a man in a street, with rows of houses and a church steeple.—*Boston Gazette*, Oct. 27, 1741.

Wood cut:—a mortice initial used,—a ship, house and man on horseback.—*Boston Gazette*, Dec. 13, 1744.

Wood cut representing an old man and two children; a new heading for the *Boston Gazette*,—Jan. 3, 1753; also another,—an Indian on the Massachusetts Seal (good),—Jan. 1, 1754.

Wood engraving of a snake severed in parts with the initials of the several Provinces in America, the words *"unite and conquer"* issuing from the mouth of the snake and the legend *"Join or Die"* beneath.—*Boston Gazette*, May 21, 1754.

Wood engraving of Britannia and a bird; she severing the confining cord; buildings in the distance.—*Boston Gazette*, Apr. 14, 1755.

Wood cut:—new heading of *Boston Gazette* (good); Indian Seal of Massachusetts freely treated.—Jan. 28, 1755.

WOODCUT OF A SHIP

From the Aug. 11/18, 1735, issue of the *Boston Gazette*

THE WEIGHTS AND VALUES OF COINS

From an engraving made about 1765 by Nathaniel Hurd

Wood cut of a brig, in a ad. of the privateer snow *Boston*, desiring gentlemen seamen.—*Boston Gazette*, Oct. 11, 1756.

Rude wood cut of a man carrying a pack crossing a stone bridge of three arches, to head an advertisement of the Newbury bridge lottery (1st part); the Parker river bridge.—*Boston Gazette*, Feb. 6, 1758.

Device at the head of *Boston Gazette*, newly re-engraved.— Aug. 14, 1758.

Wood cut of a brig, one inch square.—*Boston Gazette*, Jan. 22, 1758.

Wood cut of a sloop, in an advertisement.—*Boston Gazette*, July 2, 1764.

ALABASTER EFFIGIES, prints and maps, to be sold at auction.— *Boston Gazette*, Apr. 24/May 1, 1738.

PORTRAIT MEDALS.—To be Sold, by Peter M'Taggart at New Boston [West End], Sundry Medals of his present most Sacred Majesty GEORGE III. struck on a fine white Metal. One Side contains an exact Portrait of His Majesty: The other Side a Heart encircled with Oak and Laurel Branches; the Motto ENTIRELY BRITISH. Also sundry other Articles.—*Boston Gazette*, June 22, 1761.

PORTRAIT MEDALS.—Left at Green & Russell's Printing-Office for Sale. A Parcel of Curious Medals of the KING and QUEEN, neatly done in yellow and white Mettal, [*Price 6 Coppers single.*]

☞ Good allowance will be made to those who buy by the Dozen. —*Boston News-Letter*, Feb. 11, 1762.

PORTRAIT BUSTS.—"Handsome images of Shakespear, Milton and others in marble" were listed among household goods to be sold "at the new brick Store" formerly occupied by Mr. John Gould, by the Septre and Crown, Back Street, Boston.—*Boston News-Letter*, Apr. 28, 1768.

BOSTON MASSACRE.—"In the Evening [of Mar. 5, 1772] was exhibited on the Balcony at Mrs. Clapham's in King Street, a Lanthorn of transparent Paintings, well drawn by an ingenious Young Gentleman, representing in Front the Melancholly Scene which was transacted near that Spot. Over which was inscribed, 'The fatal Effects of a Standing Army, posted in a free City.'—At the East End, was a Representation of a Monument inscribed to the Memory of those who were Killed, with their Names, &c.—At the West End was the Figure of America sitting in a Mourning Posture, and looking down on the Spectators."—*Boston News-Letter*, Mar. 12, 1772.

# SILVER

## SILVERSMITHS

ISAAC ANTHONY, goldsmith, at Newport, R. I. His daughter Mary died suddenly aged 20 years.—*Boston Gazette*, Mar. 21/28, 1737.

——— AUSTIN.—Taken out of a House in Cambridge, a silver Can, which holds a full Ale pint, mark'd at the Bottom E S L and the maker's Name Austin. . . .—*Boston Gazette*, Aug. 14, 1750.

I. B.—Advertisement of stolen silver (various pieces) having the following maker's marks, viz. I B; I C; E W; R S; R N.—*Boston News-Letter*, Feb. 10/17, 1706/7.

I. B.—Taken out of a Gentleman's House in this Town, on the 28th ult. a Silver Pepper Caster fashioned eight square, mark'd at the bottom I H A, the Maker's Mark on the side I B. If the Person suspected or any other Person will bring it to the Publisher hereof, shall have 20 s. Reward, and no questions asked.—*Boston Gazette*, Sept. 25/Oct. 2, 1738.

JOHN BALL, goldsmith, in Concord, advertised for Sale in Concord, a small dwelling house, brick Shop, and 14 acres of land. —*Boston News-Letter*, Mar. 17, 1763.

JOHN BALL of Concord, goldsmith, advertised his land and buildings for sale.—*Boston Gazette*, May 4, 1767 (*sup.*).

I. BLOWERS.—Lost last Thursday night, a Gold Thimble mark'd M. H. I. Blowers. Whoever will bring it to the Publisher of this Paper, shall be satisfied without any Questions ask't, if offered to be pawn'd or sold, 'tis desired it may be stopt.—*Boston Gazette*, Mar. 13/20, 1738.

I. BLOWERS.—Lost or stolen out of a House in Boston, a large new fashion'd Silver Spoon mark'd R R L the makers Name *I. Blowers*. Twenty shillings reward.—*Boston Gazette*, Dec. 23, 1746.

ZECHARIAH BRIGDEN.—His wife Sarah, died in Boston, Mar. 30, 1768, aged 44 years. She was a daughter of the late Thomas Edwards.—*Boston News-Letter*, Mar. 31, 1768 (*sup.*).

ZECHARIAH BRIGDEN.—Just Imported from London, and to be Sold by Zechariah Brigden, Goldsmith; at his Shop opposite the West Door of the Town House, Coral Beeds, and Stick Coral for Children's Whistles; Money Scales and Weights; neat Watch Plyers; Sliding Tongs; Shears and Hand Vices; coarse and fine Iron Binding Wire; Brass Hollow Stamps and Blow Pipes; an Assortment of Files for the Goldsmith's Use; Gravers; Scorpers; Dividers; Sand Paper; Sandever; Black Lead Pot; large and small Crucibles; Wood and Bone Polishing Brushes; Borax; Salt Petre; Rotton and Pumice Stone; Moulding Sand by Cask or Retail.

ALSO, Shoe, Knee and Stock Stone Buckles; Buttons; Christal and Cornelian Seals; Neat Stone Bosom Broaches; Garnet; Hoop Rings. ☞ A few Pair of neat Stone Earings sett in Clusters, in Shagreen Cases, Cheap for Cash.—*Boston Gazette*, Nov. 19, 1764.

JOHN BRULEMAN, silversmith, was executed for murder, in Philadelphia, Pa., [see extended account].—*Boston News-Letter*, Sept. 8, 1760.

S. BURRILL was the maker of a pint silver porringer that was advertised as lost or stolen.—*Boston Evening Post*, Dec. 20, 1742.

S. BURRILL, *see also* R. Greene.

JOHN BUTLER, goldsmith, at the corner of Clark's ship yard, Boston, advertised the loss by robbery of stone rings, grape gold rings, Heart and Hand rings, stone Buttons, Stone Ear-Rings set in Gold, silver buckles, neck clasps, etc.—*Boston News-Letter*, Nov. 30, 1758.

R. C.—Advertisement of the loss of a tankard, maker's mark R C.—*Boston News-Letter*, Oct. 21/28, 1706.

E. C.—Advertisement of the loss of a pair of Gold Buttons marked R. G., the maker's mark E C.—*Boston Evening Post*, Dec. 22, 1746.

SAMUEL CASEY.—His house at South Kensington, R. I., was destroyed by fire, including "Drugs, Medicines, etc." . . . "occasioned by a large Fire being kept the Day preceding in his Goldsmith's Forge."—*Boston News-Letter*, Oct. 1, 1764.

THOMAS CLARKE, goldsmith, of Boston, lost a son, aged about 6 years, by drowning on July 18, 1766.—*Boston News-Letter*, July 25, 1766.

JOHN COBURN, goldsmith, at the head of the Town Dock, advertised that he had stopped a silver spoon supposed to have been stolen.—*Boston News-Letter*, Nov. 2, 1750.

JOHN CONEY.—This Evening the remaining part of the Tools of the late Mr. Coney are to be Sold. About 5 a Clock.—*Boston Gazette*, Nov. 5/12, 1722.

JOHN CONEY.—Advertisement of the loss of "a Fashionable Silver Spoon of Mr. Coney's make, Crest with a Talbotts (or Dog's) head erased."—*New England Journal*, Nov. 10, 1729.

JOHN COVERLY, goldsmith, late of Boston, an insolvent debtor, —a meeting of his creditors was advertised.—*Boston News-Letter*, Dec. 11, 1766.

JOHN COWELL, goldsmith, at the South End, Boston, advertised for sale "choice good Coffee."—*Boston News-Letter*, July 11/18, 1728.

WILLIAM COWELL, goldsmith, died in Boston, Aug. 3, 1736, aged 53 years.—*Boston News-Letter*, July 29/Aug. 5, 1736.

WILLIAM COWELL, goldsmith, at the South End of Boston, advertised several pieces of silver stopped by him on suspicion of having been stolen.—*Boston News-Letter*, Apr. 24/30, 1741.

WILLIAM COWELL, late of Boston, goldsmith, deceased, advertisement of settlement of his estate by *Hannah Simpson* and *Rebecca Cowell*, of said Boston, administratrixes. "To be sold . . . a very good Assortment of Goldsmith's Tools: a good Silver Watch: a Quantity of Lead, Bullets and Shot: Old Iron, Brass, and Bell-Metal. ☞ Those Persons who have left any Work to be done are desired to call for it."—*Boston Gazette*, Sept. 14, 1761.

WILLIAM COWELL, late of Boston, goldsmith, deceased, settlement of estate advertised by Hannah Simpson and Rebecca Cowell, administratrixes.—*Boston News-Letter*, June 10, 1762.

NATHANIEL CROSWELL, goldsmith, married Polly Whitman, in Boston.—*New England Chronicle*, Nov., 1776.

I. D.—Advertisement of a stolen silver tankard, maker's mark I D.—*Boston News-Letter*, Feb. 3/10, 1706/7.

JOHN DIXWELL.—Advertisement of stolen silver made by John Dixwell and Mr Dummer.—*Boston News-Letter*, Apr. 13/20, 1713.

JOHN DIXWELL.—Advertisement of the loss of a quart tankard made by Mr John Dixwell, marked T S E and stolen from the *Crown Coffee House*. Reward of five pounds offered.—*New England Courant*, Oct. 1/8, 1722.

JOHN DOANE, goldsmith, formerly of Boston, died at the Island of Barbadoes, where for some years he had been resident.—*Boston News-Letter*, Aug. 13, 1767.

T. E.—Stolen out of a certain House, a Silver Spoon with a Crest Three Pikes on the Handle, with the Goldsmith's Mark T E. Twenty Shillings Reward for the Discovery.—*Boston Gazette*, Nov. 14/21, 1737.

JOHN EDWARDS, goldsmith, "a Gentleman of a very fair Character and well respected by all that knew him," died April 8, 1746, aged 75 years.—*Boston Evening Post*, Apr. 14, 1746 (*sup.*).

THOMAS EDWARDS.—Advertisement of the settlement of the estate of Mr John Edwards, goldsmith, "NB. The Goldsmith's Business is carried on at the Shop of the deceased, as usual, by his Son, Thomas Edwards."—*Boston News-Letter*, May 8, 1746.

JOSEPH EDWARDS, JR.—Whereas the Shop of the Subscriber was last Night broke open, and the following Articles stolen, viz:

34 pair of wrought Silver Shoe Buckles,—20 pair of ditto, Knee ditto,—6 pair plain Shoe ditto,—2 Silver Snuff-Boxes,—1 ditto Tortoise Shell Top,—2 Silver Pepper Castors, stamp'd I. E.—12 Tea spoons, same stamp,—2 large ditto, Name at length; 9 stock Buckles; 3 gold Necklaces; 5 gold Rings; 1 Cream pot, stamp'd I. E.; 1 Punch-ladle, same stamp; several pair Stone Buttons; 3 pair brilliant Stone Earings, set in Gold; 5 pair Cypher ditto; several ditto set in Silver; several stone Rings; a Box of gold Beads; 3 pair Tea Tongs; gold Earings; 2 pair small Buckles, R.; 1 pair old Tea-Tongs, I. M.; 1 old spoon; 3 child's Whistles; 1 pair small Scales and Weights; 1 pair gold Buttons; 1 silver Pipe.

Whoever will make Discovery of the Thief or Thieves, so that they may be brought to Justice, and that I may recover my Goods again, shall receive TWENTY DOLLARS Reward, and all necessary Charges paid by JOSEPH EDWARDS, JUN'R.—*Boston News-Letter,* March 21, 1765.

JOSEPH EDWARDS, JUN.—Friday last Joseph Pomroy received 40 stripes at the publick Whipping Post, for stealing a Quantity of Plate, &c. from Mr Joseph Edwards, jun, &c. of this Town.—*Boston Gazette,* Nov. 25, 1765.

SAMUEL EDWARDS, goldsmith in Boston, advertised that he had stopped a large silver spoon supposed to have been stolen.—*New England Journal,* Nov. 6, 1739.

SAMUEL EDWARDS.—Last Wednesday Night [Apr. 14] died here after a few Days Illness of a violent Fever, in the 57th Year of his Age, Mr. *Samuel Edwards,* Goldsmith: who, for several Years has been one of the Assessors of the Town; and esteemed as a Man of Integrity: exact and faithful in all his Transactions; His Death is lamented as a publick Loss.—*Boston Gazette,* Apr. 19, 1762.

SAMUEL EDWARDS, of Boston, goldsmith, deceased; his household furniture was advertised for sale at public vendue, including "some wrought Plate, viz. Tankards, Porringers, Spoons, &c"; also a negro man "who has had the Small Pox and is Honest."—*Boston Gazette,* Oct. 31, 1763.

SAMUEL EDWARDS, late of Boston, goldsmith, deceased. His executors "once more" desire payments of indebtedness, and advertise for sale "a Variety of Articles at the Apprizement, viz. Silver Snuff Boxes, Ditto Salts, Porringers, Cans, Tankards, Cream Pots, Sugar Dishes, two Tea Pots, Salvers, Punch Strainers, Punch Ladles, Table and Tea spoons large and small, Shoe, Knee and Neck Buckles, Thimbles, Gold Beads, a pair Gold Buckles, Gold Buttons, with many other Articles of Gold and Silver, too many to be enumerated. Any Person that will buy the whole, and either pay the Cash or give good Security, may have them to great advantage.—Enquire of *Joseph Edwards* in Cornhill.—*Boston Gazette,* June 17, 1765.

THOMAS EDWARDS.—A Large Silver Spoon, sundry Tea Spoons, and a Silver Spur, lately offer'd to Sale, suspected to be Stolen, have been Stop'd. The owner or owners thereof, may have them again upon telling the Marks, and paying the Charge; Inquire of Mr Thomas Edwards, Goldsmith in Cornhill.—*Boston News-Letter*, Nov. 19, 1747.

THOMAS EDWARDS.—Advertisement of Sarah Edwards, Executrix of the estate of Capt. Thomas Edwards, late of Boston, Goldsmith, desiring speedy payment of indebtedness.—*Boston Gazette*, Mar. 1, 1756.

——— FENTER, goldsmith, at New York City, had his house partly destroyed by fire on Aug. 21, 1761.—*Boston News-Letter.*

EDWARD FOSTER, late of Boston, goldsmith, administrator's notice in the *Boston News-Letter*, Jan. 25, 1753.

JOSEPH GOLDTHWAIT, goldsmith, is removed from Mr Burril's shop, to the House adjoining to the Sign of the Red Lyon, where any Gentleman or Woman may be supplied with any sort of Pocket Instrument Cases at a very reasonable Rate.—*Boston News-Letter*, Apr. 15/22, 1731.

JOHN GRAY, goldsmith, was in possession of a house near the Old South Meeting House, Boston, advertised to be sold or let.—*Boston News-Letter*, July 15/22, 1717.

R. GREENE.—Lost or stolen two Silver Spoons, on one is Engrav'd the Crest of a Tyger's head with the Maker's name, R. Greene, at length, the other is mark'd T. B. with the maker's name, S. Burril. at length, etc.— *Boston News-Letter*, July 26/Aug. 2, 1733.

DAVID GRIFFITH.—Four Pair of old Silver Shoe Buckles, and a Lump of Silver weighing 1 oz. 14 dwt. supposed to be Stollen, were stop'd last Week by Mr. David Griffith, Goldsmith, at Portsmouth [N. H.].—*Boston News-Letter*, Nov. 5, 1768.

B. H.—Advertisement of three silver spoons lost or stolen, maker's name B. H.—*New England Journal*, July 6, 1730.

G. H.—Stolen out of a House in Boston, a Silver Can that will hold a Wine quart, mark'd R P M made by G H. Whoever can stop the said Cann, and will bring it to the Publisher of this Paper, shall have Forty Shillings Reward, and no Questions asked.—*Boston Gazette*, Sept. 1/8, 1740.

GEORGE HANNAH, goldsmith, at his House at the Dock-Head, Boston, advertised a pocket book with some paper Bills in it that he had "stopt."—*Boston News-Letter*, July 11/18, 1720.

GEORGE HANNERS.—By a Vessel last week from Louisbourg, we have Advice of the Death of Capt. George Hanners, of a Provincial Company, belonging to this Town.—*Boston Gazette*, Jan. 28, 1760.

JOHN HASTIER, goldsmith, of New York City, was approached by Samuel Flood and Joseph Steel and asked "if he could engrave a Copper plate" like a five shilling New Hampshire bill, which was shown. Hastier replied that he could and was requested to do so and be expeditious about it. He reported the circumstances to a Magistrate and the intended counterfeiters were arrested.—*Boston Gazette*, Mar. 12/19, 1739.

MR. ——— HEALEY, goldsmith, died in Boston about Nov. 15, 1773.—*Boston News-Letter*, Nov. 18, 1773.

WILLIAM HOMES, of Boston, goldsmith, was attorney for John Franklin, executor of the estate of Josiah Franklin, late of Boston, tallow chandler.—*Boston Gazette*, July 21, 1752.

WILLIAM HOLMES.—A Spoon stopt about Ten Days ago, suspected to be Stole; inquire of *William* Holmes, Goldsmith, near the Draw-Bridge.—*Boston Gazette*, May 21, 1759 (*sup.*).

JACOB HURD.—Lost, a New Silver Spoon, mark'd I. L. the maker John (*sic*) Hurd. Ten Shillings reward and no Questions ask'd.—*Boston Gazette*, Aug. 2/9, 1731.

JACOB HURD, goldsmith, at the south side of the Town House, Boston advertised a reward of forty shillings for the return of a string of gold beads of small size with a heart stone locket.—*Boston News-Letter*, Sept. 21/28, 1732.

JACOB HURD, silversmith, his large and new house in Atkinson's Street was struck by Lightning, and considerably damag'd, but the Lives of all in the Family were mercifully preserved.—*Boston Gazette*, May 15/22, 1738.

JACOB HURD.—Lost or Stolen out of a House in this Town on

Tuesday last a Silver Spoon, the Crest a Pelican upon a Nest feeding her Young, the maker's Name, I. Hurd. Whoever brings said Spoon to the Publisher, shall be well rewarded and no Questions ask'd.—*Boston Gazette*, Oct. 16/23, 1738.

JACOB HURD, Capt., goldsmith, formerly of Boston and late of Roxbury, "being in Town at a Relation's House, was seiz'd with an Apoplexy, in which he continued speechless till Friday Evening, when he departed this Life," Feb. 17, 1758.—*Boston News-Letter*, Feb. 23, 1758 (*sup.*).

JACOB HURD, Capt.—Boston, Feb. 20. Last Wednesday in the Afternoon Capt. Jacob Hurd, (formerly of this Town,) a noted Goldsmith, was seized with a Lethargy, in which he continued till Friday Evening, and then expired, much lamented.—*Boston Gazette*, Feb. 20, 1758.

JACOB JENNINGS.—Whereas the Shop of the Subscriber, living in Norwalk, in the Colony of Connecticut, was broke open on the Sixth Day of April Instant at Night, and robb'd of the following Things, viz. a Silver Cream Pot, 6 large Spoons, 2 or 3 Dozen Tea Spoons, a great many pair of Stone Buttons, Gold Buttons, Gold Studs, Jewels and Silver Buttons; several Pair of Silver Buckles, some with Fluke & Tongs and some without, and sundry other Articles, to the Value of above £100. Lawful Money.—This is to give Notice to any Person or Persons that will apprehend said Thief and commit him to any of His Majesty's Goals, so that he may be convicted and send word to Levi Jennings, of Boston, or to the Subscriber, Goldsmith, living at Norwalk, in Connecticut, shall have TWENTY DOLLARS Reward, paid by JACOB JENNINGS. —*Boston Gazette*, Apr. 18, 1763.

DAVID JESS, goldsmith, died in Boston, Jan. 13, 1705/6.— *Boston News-Letter*.

———— JOHNSON, silversmith, lived near the Oswego Market in New York City. His house was broken into in July, 1765.— *Boston News-Letter*, July 25, 1765.

JEFFERY LANG, goldsmith, of Salem, advertised a run away servant.—*Boston Evening Post*, June 10, 1745.

KNIGHT LEVERETT.—A new silver porringer marked with the

SILVER CREAM JUG
Made by Paul Revere and owned by George Francis Dow

maker's name *K. Leverett*, advertised as supposed to have been stolen.—*Boston News-Letter*, Oct. 26/Nov. 2, 1738.

SAMUEL MINOTT, at his Shop opposite William's Court, Cornhill, advertised tea, spices, and groceries; also cream colored, Delph, brown and flint ware; also silver mounted Swords, Coral beads, Plate and Jewellery.

☞ He carries on the Goldsmiths Business in all its Branches as usual, at his other Shop, Northward of the Draw-Bridge, near the Drum-Maker's.—*Boston News-Letter*, Oct. 1, 1772.

OBADIAH MORS, goldsmith, in King Street, Boston, advertised the theft of twenty-three large silver coat Buttons, and eleven ditto for a Jacket, marked Mors on the back side of each, etc.— *Boston News-Letter*, Dec. 13/20, 1733.

JOSEPH MOULTON.—Newbury, October 24, 1754. A large Silver Spoon was offered to Sale at my Shop, and suspecting it was stolen, I went to a Justice of the Peace, who stop'd it till the Person could give better Satisfaction how he came by it; and I have not seen him since; Therefore any Person who can lay just claim to it may have it, only paying Reasonable Costs and Trouble, Joseph Moulton.—*Boston Gazette*, Mar. 4, 1755.

I. N.—Advertisement of the theft of a silver tankard, with a coat of arms, "with three water pouches or buckets," and the workman's mark I. N. etc.—*Boston News-Letter*, Mar. 8/15, 1707/8.

DANIEL PARKER, Goldsmith, Hereby informs his Customers and others in Town and Country, that he has removed from his Shop near the BLUE BALL, to a Shop in Merchants Row, between the *Golden Ball* and the *Sign of Admiral Vernon*, where may be had good Moulding Sand, black Lead Pots, and Crucibles.—*Boston Evening Post*, Dec. 11, 1752.

DANIEL PARKER.—To be Sold cheap for CASH, A few Pieces of fine Bagg Hollands: Also an Assortment of Jeweller's and Goldsmith's Ware, viz: Cypher and Brilliant Button and Earing Stones of all Sorts, with a Variety of small Tools, Files, &c. By Daniel Parker, Goldsmith, at his Shop near the Golden-Ball, or at his House next Door to Deacon Grant's in Union Street.—*Boston Gazette*, Nov. 6, 1758.

DANIEL PARKER.—This is to inform the Publick, that the Subscriber has still missing a Variety of Articles that were stole from him the 8th Instant, at Night, viz. Three large Silver Spoons stamp'd *D. Parker*, 12 Tea spoons, most of them stamp'd *D. P.* 3 pair Silver Tea Tongs, not stamp'd, one large Gold Locket, 4 pair Stone Earings set in Silver, with Gold Wires, 3 pair round Stone Buttons in Silver, 14 pair large open-work'd Silver Shoe Buckles with Steel Chapes, several odd Shoe Buckles, sundry pair Silver Knee Buckles, and some odd dittos: . . . Ten Dollars Reward, paid by me, DANIEL PARKER.—*Boston Gazette*, June 4, 1759.

DANIEL PARKER.—Tuesday Night last the Shop of Mr. Daniel Parker of this Town, Goldsmith, was broke open, and robbed of Silver Shoe and Knee Buckles, large and small Spoons, Gold Necklaces and Earings, Stone Buttons set in Silver, &c. to the value of several Hundred Pounds: and last Saturday two regular Soldiers, in a Sailor's dress (who had deserted) which were concerned in sharing the Plunder, were bro't to Town from Marlboro', and carried to their respective Companies, which were embark'd, and 'tis not doubted but they will meet with their deserved Reward.—*Boston Gazette*, May 14, 1761.

DANIEL PARKER.—Imported in the Neptune, Capt. *Binney*, and to be Sold by *Daniel Parker*, Goldsmith, at his Shop near the Golden-Ball, Boston, an assortment of articles in the Goldsmith's and Jeweller's Way, viz. brilliant and cypher'd Button and Earing Stones of all Sorts, Locket Stones, cypher'd Ring Stones, brilliant Ring Sparks, Buckle Stones, Garnetts, Emethyss, Topaz and Saphire Ring Stones, neat Stone Rings sett in Gold, with some Diamond Sparks, Stone Buttons in Silver, by the Card, black ditto in Silver, best Sword Blades, Shoe and Knee Chapes of all Sizes, Files of all Sorts, freezing Punches, Turkey Oyl Stones, red and white Foyl, moulding Sand, Borax, Saltpetre, Crucibles and black Led Potts, Money Scales, large ditto to weigh Silver, Piles of Ounce Weights, Penny Weights & Grains, Coral Beeds, Stick ditto for Whistles, Forgeing Anvils, Spoon Teats, plain ditto, small raizing Anvils for Cream Potts, fine Lanceshire

Watch Plyers, Shears and Nippers, Birmingham ditto, with sundry other Articles cheap for Cash.—*Boston Gazette*, Feb. 12, 1761.

DANIEL PARKER, Goldsmith, near the Golden Ball, Boston, Hereby informs his Customers that he has just imported from London, in the *Boscawen*, Captain Jacobson, a general Assortment of articles in the Goldsmith's and Jeweller's Way: where they may be supply'd in reasonable Terms for Cash or short Credit. —*Boston Gazette*, Oct. 5, 1761.

EBENEZER PITT, jun., of Taunton, goldsmith and watchmaker, was married April 8, 1762, to Miss Lydia Cudworth, "a shapely young Lady, graceful in her Carriage, agreeable in her Conversation, and endowed with every necessary Qualification to render the Marriage State agreeable, being crowned with a considerable Fortune. This Mr Pitt is thought to be a Relation of the Right Hon. *W—m P—tt*, Esq., he being a Man of great Ingenuity."—*Boston Evening Post*, Apr. 26, 1762.

DANIEL PARKER.—Imported in the last Ships from London, a general assortment of Articles and Tools in the Goldsmith's, Jeweller's and Watchmaker's Way, and to be sold by *Daniel Parker*, at his Shop next Door to Samuel Grant's, Esq. in Union Street, Boston.—*Boston Gazette*, Nov. 28, 1763.

DANIEL PARKER.—Imported from London, in the ship *Devonshire*, Capt. Hunter, and to be Sold by *Daniel Parker*, next door to Deacon Grant's in Union Street; a general Assortment of Stones, Chapes and Tongs, Melting Pots, and all other Necessaries for the Goldsmiths and Jeweller's Use, with Some Watch Articles, cheap for Cash.—*Boston Gazette*, May 21, 1764.

DANIEL PARKER.—Imported from *London* and to be Sold by DANIEL PARKER, goldsmith, at his Shop next Door to Samuel Grant, Esq. in Union-Street, Boston, a variety of Goldsmith's, Jewellers & Watch Makers Tools and Wares, *viz.* Cypher'd Earing and button christials, with cyphers for ditto; Brilliant earing top and drop Christials; round and square brilliant button stones; Buckle & locket stones; Cypher'd ring stones; Brilliant ditto; Garnet, amethysts, and topaz ring Stones; Diamond ring sparks; Christial ditto; Red & white foyl, amethyst & topaz ditto; Silver thimbles steel ends; Coral beeds & stick coral for children's whistles; Best buckle & ring brush; Watch christials, main-springs, silver pendants, hour hands, fuzze chains & enamel'd dial plates; Scales and weights; Money ditto; a few neat small pocket ditto with box end beams in shagreen cases; Neat glazier's diamonds; Fine & Coarse emery; Flour of putta, rotten stone, pummice stone, Thimble Stamps; Sand over sand & emery paper; Borax & salt petre; assortment of Files; Penny wts. and grains; a Variety of round and square best fine quality steel shoe & knee chapes and tongues; Forging & raising anvils for tankards, cans and cream pots; Spoon teasts plain ditto; Sparhawks or beek irons; Death head and heart in hand ring swages; Plane ditto; Forging and plannishing hammers; Hand vises, shears, clock and watch plyers; Polished spring ditto; Polish'd draw plates; Common ditto; Fine screw dividers; Steel & stone burnishers; Brass borax boxes; Brass hollowing stamps; Brass & iron rivet wire; Fine iron binding wire; Steel gravers; Freezing punches; Brass blow pipes; Upright drill stocks with bitts; moulding sand; Sword blades; Turkey oil stones; German ditto; Bohemia polishing stones; Crucibles, black lead pots. ☞ Also may be had at the above *Shop*, a variety of ready made Plate, Jewellry, &c. cheap for Cash.—*Boston Gazette*, Sept. 10, 1764.

DANIEL PARKER, Goldsmith, in Union Street, Boston, Hereby informs his Customers and others. That he has just imported in Capt. *Jarvis* from LONDON, a General Assortment of Articles in the Goldsmith, Jeweller's & Watchmaker's Way, which he will sell cheap for Cash.—*Boston Gazette*, May 20, 1765.

DANIEL PARKER, Goldsmith, in Union Street, Boston, Hereby informs his Customers and others, That he has just imported in Capt Jarvis from London, a general Assortment of Articles in the Goldsmiths, Jewellers and Watchmaker's Way; which he will sell cheap for cash.

N. B. He desires those that are indebted to him either by Note or Book to make immediate Payment.—*Boston News-Letter*, June 20, 1765.

DANIEL PARKER, Goldsmith, Imported from London, and to be sold by, at his Shop next Door to Samuel Grant, Esqr. in Union-Street, Boston, a variety of Goldsmiths, Jewellers & Watchmakers Tools and Wares, viz. Cypher'd Earing & Button Christials with cyphers for ditto, Brilliant earing top & drop christials, Round & square brilliant button stones, Buckle and locket stones, Cypher'd ring stones, Brilliant ditto, Garnet, amethysts, and topaz ring stones, Neat Diamond Rings, Diamond ring sparks, Christial ditto, Neat stone, stone, Knee & stock buckles, with bosom broaches, Red & white foyl, amethyst & topaz ditto, Silver thimbles steel ends, Coral beeds & stick coral for children's whistles, Best buckle & ring brushes, Watch christials, main springs, silver pendants, hour hands, fuzze chains & enamel'd dial plates, Scales and weights, Money ditto, A few neat small pocket ditto with box end beams in shagreen cases, Neat glaziers diamonds, Fine & coarse emery, Thimble stamps, Sand over sand & emery cloth, Borax & salt petre, Assortments of Files, Penny wts. and grains, A variety of round and square best fine quality steel shoe & knee chapes and tongues, Forging & raising anvils for tankards, cans and cream pots, Spoon teasts, plain ditto, Sparhawks or beek irons, Death head and heart in hand ring swages, Plain ditto, Forging and plannishing hammers, Hand vices, shears, clock and watch plyers, Polish'd spring ditto, Polish'd draw plates, Common ditto, Fine screw dividers, Steel & stone burnishers, Brass borax boxes, Brass hollowing stamps, Brass & iron rivet wire, Fine Iron binding wire, Steel gravers, Freezing punches, Brass blow pipes, Upright drill stocks with bitts, Moulding sand, Sword blades, Turkey oil stones, German ditto, Bohemia polishing stones, Flour of putta, rotton stone, pummice stone, Crucibles, black lead pots. ☞ Also may be had at the above SHOP a variety of ready made Plate, Jewellry, &c cheap for Cash.—*Boston Gazette*, Oct. 28, 1765.

DANIEL PARKER, goldsmith, Union St., Boston, advertised in the June 8, 1767, *Boston Gazette*.

DANIEL PARKER, goldsmith, of Boston, a child of, fell through the scuttle at Christ's Church, July 20.—*Boston Gazette*, July 20, 1771.

BENJAMIN PIERPONT.—Lost four silver Table Spoons, two London made, marked crest, a Spread Eagle; two no mark, Maker's Name, *B. Pierpont;* If offered for sale, it is desired they may be stopped.—*Boston News-Letter*, Oct. 31, 1771 (*sup.*).

EBENEZER PITT, JUN'R. of Taunton, Goldsmith and Watchmaker, was married April 8, 1762, to Miss Lydia Cudworth, "a shapely young Lady, graceful in her Carriage, agreeable in her Conversation, and endowed with every necessary Qualification to render the Marriage State agreeable, being crowned with considerable Fortune. This Mr. Pitt is thought to be a relation of the Right Hon. W———m P———tt, Esq., he being a Man of great Ingenuity."—*Boston Evening Post*, April 26, 1762.

PAUL REVERE, goldsmith, is Removed from Capt. Pitts, at the Town Dock, to the North End over against Col. Hutchinson's.—*Boston News-Letter*, May 14/21, 1730.

PAUL REVERE.—We hear that the Week before last was finished, by Order and for the Use of the Gentleman belonging to the Insurance Office kept by Mr. *Nathaniel Barber*, at the North-End, an elegant Silver BOWL, weighing *forty-five* Ounces, and holding *forty-five* Jills. On one Side is engraved within a handsome Border—*To the Memory of the glorious* NINETY-TWO *Members of the Honourable House of* REPRESENTATIVES *of the* MASSACHUSETTS-BAY, *who undaunted by the insolent Menaces of Villians in Power, and out of a strict Regard to Conscience, and the* LIBERTIES *of their Constituents, on the* 30*th of June* 1768, VOTED NOT TO RESCIND.—*Over which is the Cap of Liberty in an Oaken Crown. On the other Side, is a Circle adorned with Flowers, &c. is No.* 45. WILKES AND LIBERTY, *under which is General Warrants torn to Pieces. On the Top of the Cap of Liberty, and out of each Side, is a Standard, on one is* MAGNA CHARTA, *the other* BILL OF RIGHTS.—On Monday Evening last, the Gentlemen belonging to the Office made a genteel Entertainment, and invited a Number of Gentlemen of Distinction in the Town, when 45 Loyal Toasts were drank, and the whole concluded with a new Song, the Chorus of which is, *In Freedom we're born, and in Freedem we'll live*, &c.—*Boston Gazette*, Aug. 8, 1768.

PAUL REVERE.—Whereas many Persons are so unfortunate as to lose their fore Teeth by accident, and otherwise, to their great Detriment, not only in looks, but speaking both in Public and Private:

☞ This is to inform all such, that they may have them replaced with false ones, that looks as well as the Natural, and answers the End of Speaking to all intents by PAUL REVERE, Goldsmith, near the head of Dr. Clark's Wharf, Boston,—

All Persons who have had false Teeth fixt by Mr. *John Baker*, Surgeon-Dentist, and they have got loose (as they will in Time) may have them fastened by the above, who learnt the Method of fixing them from Mr. *Baker*.—*Boston News-Letter*, Aug. 25, 1768.

WILLIAM ROWSE, goldsmith, died in Boston, Jan. 20, 1704/5.—*Boston News-Letter*.

B. S.—Stolen out of the House of Mr Gilbert Warner, Distiller in Boston, last Week a Silver Spoon, mark'd with the Letters G. W. S. Goldsmith's mark B. S. If offered to be Sold its desired it may be stopt and the Person in Possession thereof.—*Boston Gazette*, May 24/31, 1736.

WILLIAM SIMPKINS, goldsmith, near the Draw Bridge, Boston, advertised for sale the library of the late Rev. Robert Stanton of Salem.—*Boston News-Letter*, June 20/27, 1728.

WILLIAM SIMPKINS, goldsmith, of Boston, advertised the loss of a piece of silver three inches broad, ¼ inch thick and weighing about fourteen ounces.—*Boston Evening Post*, Jan. 27, 1746.

WILLIAM SWAN.—Last Night the Dwelling-House of William Swan, of Worcester, was broke open, and the following Articles stolen, viz.

      5 Pair Stone Earings,
      ½ Doz. Tea spoons partly finished,
      5 Pair Stone Sleeve Buttons,
      1 Gold Necklace

Sundry Pair Silver Shoe Buckles; one Pair partly finished; together with about Twelve Pounds in Cash, viz. 1 Johanna, 1 Guinea, 6 Crowns, the Remainder in Dollars.

Also well disposed Persons are desired to apprehend the Thief, for which a Reward of Six Dollars will be given. If the Articles are offered for Sale, its desired they may be Stopped.

Worcester, 25th May, 1773.      WM. SWAN.
      —*Boston News-Letter*, May 27, 1773.

WILLIAM SWAN, goldsmith, formerly of Boston, died at Worcester, a few days after Apr. 14, 1774.—*Boston News-Letter*, May 5, 1774.

JOHN SYMMES, Goldsmith, near the Golden Ball, Boston, advertised Best Shoe and Knee Buckles, Fluke and Tongs, ruff and Smooth Files, Bone Buckle Brushes, Freezing Punches, Binding Wire, Steel Top Thimbles, Cypher and Brilliant Button Stones, Ring Sparks, Motto Ring Stones, Amethysts, Garnetts, Brilliant and Cypher Earing Stones, Amethysts Foyle, red & white do, Stone Bosom Buckles, Crusables, and black Lead Melting Pots, &c. all cheap for Cash.—*Boston Gazette*, May 4, 1767.

——— SYMPSON.—Taken out of a House in Boston, a Silver Pepper Box, mark'd W. M. C. The maker's name *Sympson*. Whoever will stop or take up said Box, so that the Owner may have it again, shall be well rewarded.—*Boston Gazette*, Nov. 7, 1752.

JOHN TOWZEL.—The Subscriber's Shop in Salem was BROKE Open the first of this Instant, in the Night, and the following Articles were Stolen from him, viz:

One pair square Stone-Buckles, 4 pair Stone Earings set in gold, 6 or 7 Gold Rings, 5 or 6 pair or Cypher Stone Buttons set in silver, 50 or 60 pair Silver shoe and Knee Buckles, 6 strings of Coral Beeds, Part of a Gold Necklace, 1½ Dozen Tea-Spoons marked *I : T*, one large Spoon, Maker's Name *J. Towzel*, 7 pair silver Sleeve Buttons, together with Neck-Buckles, etc. etc. etc.

Any Person that will discover the Thief or the Goods, that the Owner may recover them again, shall have TEN DOLLARS Reward and all necessary Charges paid by me. *John Towzel*, Goldsmith. —*Boston News-Letter*, Nov. 5, 1767.

ANDREW TYLER, goldsmith, died in Boston, Aug. 12, 1741.— *Boston Gazette*.

JAMES TYLER, goldsmith, was injured at Hartford, Conn., when the school house was blown up on May 20, 1766.—*Boston Gazette.*

PETER VAN DYKE, silversmith, in New York City, the sudden death of his wife mentioned.—*New England Journal*, Feb. 4, 1733/4.

BARNABAS WEBB.—Taken up in Cambridge some Time Since, a Gold Ring: The owner by describing the same, may have it again, paying the Charge; inquire of Barnabas Webb, Goldsmith, near the Market.—*Boston Gazette*, Nov. 15, 1756.

BARNABAS WEBB, Goldsmith, Informes his Customers, that since he was burnt out near the Market, he has opened a Shop in Back-Street opposite Mr. *Brown's* Meeting-House, formerly occupied by Mr. *Edward Whittemore.*—*Boston Gazette*, Jan. 19, 1761.

BARNABAS WEBB, goldsmith, "Takes this Opportunity to acquaint his Town and Country Customers, That he hath removed his Shop to *Ann-Street*, near the Market, Where they will be well used."—*Boston News-Letter*, Apr. 1, 1762.

BARNABAS WEBB, stopped part of a large Silver spoon on suspicion that it had been stolen.—*Boston Gazette*, July 29, 1765.

E. W.—Silver stolen from the house of Rev. Joseph Moss of Derby, Conn., had the following maker's marks, viz. a tankard, E. W.; one handle cup in the fashion of a mug, I. D.; spoons, E. W., I. D.; and I. N.—*Boston Gazette*, Aug. 22/29, 1726.

E. W.—Stolen "a silver Panakin with the Handle broke almost off in the Socket, marked at the Bottom either with E. W. or R. G." Twenty shillings reward.—*New England Journal*, Mar. 24, 1740/1.

E. W.—Dropt from a Person's Sleeve yesterday a Gold Button, the Maker's Name *E. W.* Any Person that hath found it is desired to bring the same to the Printer and they shall be rewarded to their satisfaction. If offer'd to be sold, it's desir'd it may be stop'd.—*Boston Gazette*, Mar. 2, 1742.

EDWARD WEBB, goldsmith, of Boston, died Oct. 21, 1718, and "having no poor friends in England that wanted, and getting his money here, he bequeathed Two Hundred Pounds . . . for the use of the poor of Boston."—*Boston News-Letter*, Nov. 17/24, 1718.

——— WEBB.—Silver spoons with maker's marks WEBB and COWELL were advertised as stolen.—*Boston News-Letter*, Aug. 30/Sept. 6, 1739.

EDWARD WINSLOW, goldsmith, Advertisement of.—*Boston News-Letter*, Oct. 1/8, 1711.

W. WRIGHT.—Stolen a Silver Mugg, the Goldsmith's Name W. Wright. Reward £3. old Tenor and no Questions ask'd.—*Boston Gazette*, Sept. 20, 1743.

S. Y.—A silver spoon with "a Lyon with a Flower D'luce in his paw" engraved on the shank, and near the bowl stamped two letters S. Y. was advertised as lost or stolen.—*Boston Gazette*, Feb. 21/28, 1725/6.

## MISCELLANEOUS SILVER

DEER'S FOOT.—Lost on Tuesday last the 12 Instant at *Boston*, a small Guinea Dear's foot Tipt with Gold; whosoever shall find the same and bring it in unto *John Campbell* Post-Master shall be sufficiently rewarded.—*Boston News-Letter*, Sept. 11/18, 1704.

TANKARD.—Stollen on Saturday the 4th Currant, from *Mrs Susanna Campbell* Widow in Boston, A Silver Tankard, that holds about two Wine Quarts, has Sir Robert Robinson's Coat of Arms engraven on the fore-part of it, wherein are three ships, and the Motto in Latin. Whoever can give any true Intelligence of the same, so as that the Owner may have it again, shall be sufficiently rewarded.—*Boston News-Letter*, Nov. 6/13, 1704.

SNUFF BOX.—Dropt in *Boston* on Wednesday the last 12th Currant, A Snufh Box almost Square, the bottom and sides are of Silver, and the top steel, the Inside wash'd with Gold; Whoever finds the same, or can give any Intelligence of it to the Post-Office at *Boston*, so that the true Owner may have it again, shall have Twelve Shillings Reward.—*Boston News-Letter*, Dec. 10/17, 1711.

SNUFF BOX.—A Gentleman has lost a Tortoiseshell Snuff Box (with Scaramouch on the Top of it.) Whoever brings it to the Post office in Boston, shall have Twenty Shillings Reward, with Many Thanks.—*Boston News-Letter*, June 16/23, 1718.

SILVER TOOTHPICK CASE.—Lost some time since a Silver Toothpick Case: Whoever will bring the same to Mr Brooker in Boston, shall have the value paid 'em in Silver.—*Boston Gazette*, May 16/23, 1720.

HORSE RACE.—On the 2d of June next at 4 in the afternoon, A Silver Punch Bowl Value Ten Pounds will be run for on Cambridge Heath, Three Miles by any Horse, Mare or Gelding 13 hands 3 inches High, none to exceed 14, carrying Nine Stone Weight, if any Horse is 14 hands high to carry Ten stone weight; The Horses that put in for the Plate are to Enter at the Post-Office in Boston on the 1st of June between the Hours of 8 & 12 in the morning, and pay down Twenty Shillings. The winning Horse to pay the charge of this Advertisement.—*Boston News-Letter*, May 15/22, 1721.

SILVER SNUFF BOX.—Lost on Tuesday the 4th ultimo, an oval Silver Snuff Box, the Cover Gilt inside and out, and the Rivell of the heathen gods in raised work on the Cover. Whoever will bring it to Mr. Musgrave Postmaster of Boston, shall have Twenty Shillings Reward.—*Boston Gazette*, Sept. 3/10, 1722.

TOBACCO STOPPER.—Lost: a double Tobacco Stopper, tipt with silver in a crooked piece of Wood.—*Boston News-Letter*, June 3/10, 1725.

CORRALL.—The Person who borrowed a Silver Corrall Engraved about Three Years ago, is desired to return it from where it was borrowed.—*Boston Gazette*, Sept. 18/25, 1727.

MOURNING RING.—Lost last Friday, a Mourning Ring with this Posie, (Acceptance is Requital) if found and brought to the Post Office, the Person shall be well Rewarded.—*Boston Gazette*, Jan. 27/Feb. 3, 1728/9.

SILVER STOLEN.—*Whereas last Week on Tuesday Night the House of Dr.* Lawrence Dolhonde, *in Pond-Street, was broke open by some evil-minded Person or Persons, who stole and carried off the following Plate, viz.* F.

*A Silver Quart Tankard, mark'd* C. M. *almost New, with a Rim round the middle.*

*Six large Silver Porringers, some holding a Pint and some more.*
*Twelve Silver Spoons.*
*And Two Silver Pint Cans.* D.
*Each of which were mark'd* L. E.

*This is therefore to give Notice, That whoever shall discover the Person or Persons who has stolen the abovesaid Plate, so as they may be brought to Justice, and the Things restored, shall have* Twenty Pounds *Reward.*

*These are also to desire every Goldsmith or any other Person, to stop the said Plate, or any Part of it, if offered to be Sold or Pawn'd, and give Notice to the Owner.*

*And if the Person who took the same, will restore it, it shall be received and no Questions ask'd.* — Boston News-Letter, Apr. 28/May 5, 1737.

HOARD OF SILVER MONEY.—We hear from Salem that on Friday last a Servant of William Brown, Esq. the youngest surviving Son of the Hon. Col. Brown, deceased, in freeing a Cellar of his from Water and Rubbish, struck his spade against an Earthen Jarr of Silver buried in a Hole wherein was five Jarrs more, containing together one thousand ninety three Ounces of Silver of several species, among which was about six thousand New England shillings scarcely discolour'd.—*Boston Gazette,* July 11/18, 1737.

PUNCH BOWL.—Newport, May 5, 1738. On Wednesday Night last was taken out of the House of Mr Joseph Wanton, a large Silver Punch Bowl, being a present from the Boston Gentlemen to William Wanton, Esq., deceased, whoever will bring said Punch Bowl to me the Subscriber or give any Intelligence of it, so that the owner may have it again, shall have Twenty Pounds Reward, and no Questions asked, and if said Bowl be offered to Sale, it is desired it may be stopt. GEORGE WANTON.—*Boston Gazette,* May 18, 1738.

PORRINGER.—Lost, "an oldfashioned Silver Porringer that holds a Pint," Reward: 20 shillings.—*Boston News-Letter*, Sept. 21/28, 1738.

CHURCH FLAGGONS.—On Thursday Night last was lost from off a Horse at Mrs Brown's Door, two Flaggons, one mark'd, *The Gift of the Rev. Mr.* Perley Howe *to the Church of Christ in* Dudley, 1740. The other, *The Gift of* William Carter *to the Church of Christ in* Dudley. Whoever shall take them up and bring them to the Printers hereof, shall be well rewarded.—*Boston Gazette*, Feb. 2, 1742.

BEZIL, or rim of the lid of a tankard stopped.—*Boston News-Letter*, Jan. 19, 1744.

PRESENTATION SILVER.—On Friday last several of the Merchants of this Town made an Entertainment for Capt. *Richard Spry*, Commander of his Majesty's Sloop the Comet-Bomb, and presented him with a handsome Piece of Plate, in Gratitude for his gallant Behaviour and good Conduct in taking a French Privateer Ship, commanded by Capt. *Le Grotz*, from Cape Breton, which had for some Time infested our Coast.—*Boston News-Letter*, Dec. 27, 1744.

SILVER-HANDLE knives and forks, wormed wine-glasses, etc. just imported to be sold at Capt. Philip Viscount's in Cross Street, Boston.—*Boston News-Letter*, Mar. 14, 1746.

SNUFF BOX.—Lost in removing Goods in the late Fire at the Court House, a Silver Snuff Box marked *Sa. Butler*, a Lyon engrav'd thereon, any Person who will bring it to the Owner, or to the Printer, shall have 20 s. old Tenor Reward; and if offer'd to sell, its desir'd it may be stop'd.—*Boston Gazette*, Dec. 29, 1747.

BURYING RING.—A Burying-Ring marked *N. Hubbard*, Esq; Ob. 10, Jan. 1747-8. Æt. 69, lost in Boston. The person who has found the same, and brings or sends it to the Printer, shall be well rewarded.—*Boston Gazette*, Nov. 15, 1748.

GOLD SLEEVE BUTTON.—Taken up last Tuesday, a large Gold Sleeve-Button; the Owner may have it again, telling the Marks and paying the Charge of this Advertisement. Enquire of the Printer.—*Boston News-Letter*, Mar. 7, 1746.

STAY HOOK.—Taken up near *Gersham Flagg's*, Glazier, in Boston, a Silver Stay Hook, with 5 Stones, the owner may have it, paying Charges. Inquire at said Flagg's.—*Boston Gazette*, Oct. 3, 1749.

POPE'S NIGHT DISASTER.—Last Monday, the 6th Instant, at Night, some of the Pope's Attendance had some Supper as well as Money given 'em at a House in Town, one of the Company happen'd to swallow a Silver Spoon with his Victuals, marked I H S. Whoever it was is desired to return it when it comes to Hand, or if offer'd to any Body for Sale 'tis desired it may be stop'd, and Notice given to the Printer.—*Boston Gazette*, Nov. 14, 1749.

SILVER PLATE.—To be sold at Publick Vendue, at the Vendue House on Dock Square, by William Nickols, the following Goods taken by Execution, viz.

Sundry pieces of Plate, viz. a Can, Tankard, Porrenger, Salts, Spurs, Salvers, Soupe Spoon, Sword, Punch Strainer, Pepper Box, Silver Watch, &c. &c. also Diamond Rings; two handsom Clocks, one without a Case, the other with a handsom japan'd Case, etc. etc.—*Boston Evening Post*, Mar. 30, 1752.

SILVER PLATE.—To be Sold at Public Vendue at the House of the late *Mr. Benjamin Edwards* in Back street. Sundry Pieces of Plate, viz. a Tankard, a Salver, four Porringers, three Casters, Pewter Dishes and Plates, a fine Silk Bed, and Bedsted, . . . a fine Clock, a Shays, a Negro Man and a Negro Woman. . . . —*Boston Gazette*, Nov. 14, 1752.

JOURNEYMAN GOLDSMITH.—If any Journeyman-Goldsmith (Master of his Business) wants Employ, he may meet with Encouragement by inquiring of the Printers hereof.—*Boston Gazette*, Aug. 23, 1756.

FLOWERED SILVER BUCKLE.—Lost yesterday between the Rev. Mr. *Cooper's* Meeting-House, and Quaker-Lane, a flower'd Silver Buckle: Whoever will bring it to the Printers hereof shall be satisfied for their Trouble.—*Boston Gazette*, Jan. 31, 1757.

BROKEN SILVER.—Found by a Search Warrant, a large Quantity of broken Silver, as Tea Spoons, Part of a Silver Tea Pot,

SILVER TEA POT

Made by Samuel Edwards of Boston in 1759. From the Francis Hill Bigelow Collection

Pieces of a Strainer and Sweet-meat Fork, and a number of other Pieces, some whole large Silver Spoons,—also a Walking Cane, with a large Ivory Head, with a Silver Ferrel under-neath marked; Any Person who has lost any of the above Articles, may know where to see them by inquiring of the Printers.—*Boston Gazette*, June 13, 1757.

SILVER BUCKLES.—The following affair happened at Salem some time since, viz. An Irish Fellow named James Clark, one of the listed Soldiers in the present Expedition, not being content with the Bounty, had marked a Goldsmith's shop, and when he came to try it, could not break it open, but got upon the roof and threw off an arch which was built over the Top of the Chimney, and got down that way, and carried off about £100, O. T. in Silver Buckles, &c. and there being no-body with him but a Dog, they could not prove it against him, but committed him to Goal on Suspicion; and when he came on Trial, the Dog was call'd into Court, (for they were both seen together that same Night) and the poor Fellow fearing the Dog should turn King's Evidence, and he be convicted, confess'd the Fact, pled Guilty, and received twenty Stripes at the publick Post; The poor Dog that was with him has since been guilty of Murder, in Killing a Lamb; for which Crime (his Master being Chief Judge) he is condemned to Transportation.—*Boston Gazette*, Aug. 1, 1757.

SILVER PLATE.—Sold at public vendue by Benjamin Church, at his usual place of Sale, a variety of Household Furniture with a large Quantity of wrought Plate, viz. Tankard, Porringers, Chaffin-Dishes, Spoons large and small, knives and forks, etc. . . . — *Boston Gazette*, Aug. 15, 1757.

EPERGNE.—To be Sold, A neat polish'd Epergne, with gadrooned and peirced Bason Saucers, and 4 Saucers, and 4 Nozzels and Pans, wt. 191 oz. 13 dwt. . . . Apply to Mr. Stephen Deblois at the Concert Hall; as the Owner in all Probability will soon embark for Europe.—*Boston Gazette*, Oct. 10, 1757.

SNUFF BOX.—Taken up in the Street last Thursday, a Silver Snuff Box, with a Mourning Ring in it. The owner may have them again by telling the Marks and paying for this advertisement.—*Boston Gazette*, Dec. 19, 1757.

SILVER CLASPS.—Taken out of the Rev. Mr. Cooper's Meeting-House on the 5th Instant, a small Gilt Bible, with Silver Clasps mark'd M. H. if offer'd for Sale, it is desired that it may be stopt, and bro't to the Printers hereof, who will satisfy the Person for his Trouble.—*Boston Gazette*, Feb. 13, 1758.

SILVER PLATE.—John Welch of Hanover Street, Boston, "purposing to go for England in a short time," advertised his household effects to be sold at public vendue. The silver was listed as follows:—"A Beautiful large Tea-Kettle, a wrought Bowl which will hold 5 pints, with Handles, a large Sugar Box and Salver, a Quart Tankard, Cans, Porringers, Salts, Pepper and Mustard Boxes, a Case of Silver Haft Knives and Forks for Sweet-Meats, &c."—*Boston Gazette*, Apr. 24, 1758.

SILVER PLATE.—The Cargo of a prize, the French ship *Fripponne*, was sold at public vendue in Boston. Among the items listed in the advertisement were: "a Quantity of Silver Plate, consisting of Soup and other Spoons, Spoon Forks, and Cups, and a Number of Jewels."—*Boston Gazette*, Sept. 11, 1758.

SILVERSMITH.—Wanted, to go to Halifax, a Journeyman Silver-Smith, or Watchmaker, that can be recommended; Inquire of the Printer.—*Boston News-Letter*, Oct. 12, 1758.

SPECTACLES.—Lost on the 3d Instant, on the Road from Boston to Roxbury, a Pair of spectacles set in Silver, and Temple Springs, the maker's Name, *Ribright*, engrav'd on them, the Case polish'd, and tipt with Silver. Whoever hath taken them up, and will bring them to the Printers hereof, shall be well rewarded.—*Boston Gazette*, Nov. 6, 1758.

APPRENTICE.—Wanted, as an Apprentice to a *large* and *small* Work, Goldsmith, for the Term of seven Years, a faithful Honest Lad that can be well recommended. Enquire of the Printers hereof.—*Boston Gazette*, Dec. 31, 1759.

SILVER PLATE.—Dr. John Cutler, physician, of Boston, having died, his household effects were advertised to be sold at public auction at his late dwelling-house in Long Lane, including "A

Quantity of wrought Plate, among which are Tankards, Porringers, Spoons, Sugar chest, Candlesticks, Snuffers and Stand, Chafindishes, Tea-Pot, Saucepans, Spout Cup, Bowl, large Cup with a Cover, Waiters, and sundry other Articles in Silver; also half a Dozen Gold Tea-Spoons."—*Boston Gazette*, Oct. 12, 1761.

GOLD WHISTLE.—To be sold at public vendue at the New Auction-Room over Mr Thomas Walley's Grocery-Store, . . . a very handsome Gold Whistle, with Bells and Coral . . . N. B. Secondhand Plate is much enquired for. . . . —*Boston Gazette*, Aug. 23, 1762.

SILVER PLATE.—Dr. Hugh Kennedy, physician of Boston, having died his household effects were advertised at public vendue including "Silver Tankards, Silver Tea Pot, Cans, Porringers, Salts, Spoons, Cups, and other Articles of wrought Plate—a good Clock, . . . sundry Desks,—a Commode—5 or 6 Looking Glasses, &c.—a very neat Jack compleat: . . . —*Boston Gazette*, Aug. 23, 1762.

SPOONS.—Two dollars Reward. Lost or stollen, two oldfashioned Silver Spoons, marked N G—E G. If returned there will be no Questions asked. N. B. The Handles are likewise mark'd downwards IS. IS. N. &c. Notice should be given to the Printers. —*Boston Evening Post*, Nov. 22, 1763.

CAN.—Stolen from the house of Capt. David Baldwin of Sudbury, "a Silver Can, which will hold near a Wine-Quart; also a new-fashioned Silver Pepper Box, both mark'd B." Reward $6. —*Boston Gazette*, Dec. 19, 1763.

NUTMEG GRATER.—"Silver Snuff Boxes, a Silver Nutmeg Grater, and Silver Watches, to be disposed of at Private Sale" at Moses Deshon's Newest Auction Room, opposite the West End of Faneuil Hall.—*Boston Gazette*, Sept. 3, 1764.

MOURNING RING.—Taken up in Boston, a few Days since, a Mourning Ring. The owner may have it again telling the Marks and paying Charges; inquire of Edes and Gill.—*Boston Gazette*, Nov. 19, 1764.

PENCIL CASE.—*Lost*, a Silver fluted Pencil Case, about 5 Inches long, with a Cypher (L. D.) at one End, Also a small wrought Silver Shoe Buckle, mark'd S. D. If found, send to the Printers hereof and reasonable satisfaction shall be made.—*Boston Gazette*, June 10, 1765.

## Jewellers

DANIEL BOYER.—Imported from London, & to be Sold by Daniel Boyer, Jeweller, at his Shop opposite the Governor's in Boston:

Stone Shoe, Knee & Neck Buckles, Stone Broaches, Pair Cluster Earings with three Drops, Steel top Thimbles, best Brilliant & Cypher Ear-ring & Button Stones, Brilliant and Cypher Ring Stones, Garnets, Armethistes and Topazes, Ring & Buckle Sparks, Diamond Sparks, Locket Stones & Cyphers, Ruby, white & amethiste foyle Coral Beeds, Corals for Whistles, best Shoe and Knee Chapes, rough and smooth Files binding Wire, Brass ditto, Brass Stamps, friezing Punches and Gravers, blow Pipes, Brass Borax Boxes, Money Scales and Weights, Buckle & Ring Brushes, Polishing Ditto, small Shears & Plyers, Screw Dividers, fine Drawing-Irons, large Ditto, Hand Vices, small & Large Ditto, Anvills, Spoon Teasts, planishing Ditto, Thimble stamps, Ingots and Skillets, Forging and Drawing Tongs, upright Drills with Bitts, Turkey Oyl Stones, Borax & Salt Petre, large Pomice Stone, Rotton Stone, Crucibles and black Pots, Moulding Sand, &c.

At said Shop may also be had most sorts of Jewellers and Goldsmiths Work, cheap for Cash.—*Boston News-Letter*, Oct. 22, 1767.

Daniel Boyer.—Just Imported from London, and to be Sold by Daniel Boyer, jeweller, at his Shop opposite the Province House in Boston, An Assortment of Articles for the Jewellers and Goldsmith's use; which will be sold cheap for the Cash.—Also at said Shop may be had most Sorts of Jewellers and Goldsmiths Work.—*Boston News-Letter*, Mar. 14, 1771.

Daniel Boyer.—Imported from London, and to be Sold by Daniel Boyer, jeweller, at his shop opposite the Province-House, in Boston; Best brilliant and cypher Ear-ring Stones, round, oval, square, brilliant and cypher Button Stones, brilliant and cypher

Ring Stones, Coffin Stones, Garnets, Amethists, Topazes, Ring and Buckle Sparks, Locket Stones with cyphers, Ruby, white and amethiste foyle Coral Beeds, Corals for whistles, best shoe and Knee Chapes, rough and smooth files, binding wires, Brass ditto, Brass Stamps, Borax, Boxes blow Pipes, Freizing Punches, Gravers, Money Scales and Weights, Buckle and Ring Brushes, small Shears and Plyers, Screw dividers, Draw-plates, Hand Vices, small and large Bench Vices, forging and planishing Hammers, Anvils, Spoon Teasts, palnishing ditto, Thimble-stamps, Ingots and Skillets, forging and drawing Tongs, upright Drills, Oil-Stones, Borax, Salt Petre, Pommice and Rotton Stone, Crucibles and Blackpots, moulding Sand, Plated-buckles, also, stone shoe, knee, and neck Buckles, Stone Broaches, Hair Pins and Sprigs, garnet and paste Ear rings, with most sorts Jewellers and Goldsmiths Work, which he will sell cheap for Cash.—*Boston News-Letter*, Aug. 29, 1771.

Cox & Berry, at their Store near the British Coffee-House in King Street, have Imported in the last Ships from London, a great Variety of Articles, including Plate, as Tankards, Coffee-Pots, Cans, Waiters, Frames and Castors, Sugar Baskets, Punch Strainers, Cream Pails, Pepper Castors, Cream Ewers and Urns, Salts, Wine Funnels, Sauce Boats & Ladles, Tureen Ladles, Table and Tea Spoons, Salt Ladles and Shovels, Punch Ladles, silver, gilt, plain and chas'd Corrals, Spring Tea Tongs, Decanter Labels, Decanter Corks with Silver Tops, Silver Thimbles, Nutmeg Graters; a great Variety of Silver Buckles, Silver-mounted Swords and Hangers, Etwee and Pencil Cases, Silver, Snake and Jack Watch Chains, Scissar Chains, Silver-mounted Snuff Boxes, Gold Stock Buckles, plated Tea Urns, Coffee Pots, Tankards, Cans, Candlesticks, Frames & Castors, Waiters, Bottle Stands, Sugar Baskets, Sauce Boats, Ink Stands, Spur, Buckles, India Plate Coffee Pots, Frames and Castors, Decanter Stands, Salts, Candlesticks, Snuffers and Stands, Japan'd Tea Urns, Plate Warmers, Tea Trays, Waiters of all sizes, Tea chests, Ink Stands, Comb Trays, Quadrille Pools, Bread Baskets, Tea Tongs, Bottle Tickets, etc. . . . — *Boston News-Letter*, Jan. 9, 1772.

FIFTY DOLLARS REWARD. Last Night the Dwelling-House of the Subscriber was broke open, and from thence were taken the following articles, viz. one Pair of Silver Chaffing-Dishes; one Pair of Butter Cups; on Silver Can; two large Soup Spoons; one Pepper Box; six large Table Spoons; six Tea ditto & a Strainer, mark'd E. D. Maker's Name D. Henchman, all except the Spoons which have a Hand for a Crest; a Silver Tea Pot; one ditto Sugar Dish; a Boat for Tea Spoons; one Pair Tea Tongs; five Tea Spoons and a Cream Cup; two Porringers and two Salt-Cellars, all mark'd E. S., one Silver Tankard without a Lid, mark'd I. S. S. one Silver Can mark'd I. D. E. an old fashioned Pepper Box, marked A. D. E. six large Table Spoons, mark'd E. S. one Silver Salver, no mark on it, the Foot resembling the Mouth of a Tunnel; a Silver Tankard marked A. B. one Silver Porringer without any Mark; three Table Spoons marked A. B. one old Spoon mark'd I. S. S. four Tea Spoons no mark; one Pair Tea Tongs; Maker's Name of these not D. Henchman; I. Hurd, some of them, and some B. W., with other small articles.

Whoever will take up the Thief or Thieves, so as he or they may be brought to Justice, and the Plate recovered, shall be paid the above Reward, and a reasonable Reward for any Part of the Plate, in proportion to its Value, per me,

*Fairfield, Conn.* THADDEUS BURR

*March* 15, 1774.   —*Boston News-Letter*, Mar. 24, 1774.

COX AND BERRY, intending to embark for England in a short Time, desire all Persons who are indebted to them to make immediate Payments, to prevent further Trouble. They have for Sale at their Store near the British Coffee-House, in King-street, a great Variety of Articles, among which are the following, viz. A large and valuable Assortment of Jewellry . . . a great Variety of Plates, as Tankards, Coffee-Pots, Cans, Waiters, Frames and Castors, Sugar Baskets, Punch Strainers, Cream Pails, Pepper Castors, Cream Ewers and Urns, Salts, Wine Funnels, Sauce Boats and Ladles, Tureen Ladles, Table and Tea Spoons, Salt Ladles and Shovels, Punch Ladles, silver, gilt, plain and chased Corrals, Spring Tea-Tongs, Decanter Labels, Decanter Corks with

Silver Tops, Silver Thimbles, Nutmeg Graters; a great variety of Silver Buckles, Silver-mounted Swords and Hangers, Etwee and Pencil Cases, Silver, Snake and Jack Watch Chains, Scissor Chains, Silver-mounted Snuff Boxes, plated Coffee Pots, Tankards, Cans, Candlesticks, Frames and Castors, Waiters, Bottle Stands, Sugar Baskets, Sauce Boats, Ink-Stands, Spurs, Buckles; japanned Tea Urns, Plate Warmers, Tea Trays, Waiters of all sizes, Candlesticks, Coffee Potts, Tea Chests, Ink Stands, Quadrille Baskets, Tea Tongs, Bottle Tickets; Silver and Ivory Handle Knives and Forks, in mahogany and Shagreen Cases; Horn snakes, Paper Snuff Boxes; etc. etc. Gold Horizontal Watches, Silver and Pinchbeck of most sorts, etc. etc.—*Boston News-Letter*, Aug. 25, 1774.

JAMES BOYER.—This is to inform the Publick, That Mr. *James Boyer*, Jeweller, from London, living at Mr. Eustone's, a Dancing Master in King Street, Boston, setts all manner of Stones in Rings, &c. and performes every thing belonging to that Trade. N.B. Said Mr. Boyer is lately recovered of a Fit of Sickness.—*New England Courant*, Dec. 31/Jan. 7, 1722/3.

JAMES BOYER, jeweller of Boston, died intestate and insolvent. Advertisement of the appointment of Commissioners.—*Boston Gazette*, July 13/20, 1741.

WILLIAM CARIO.—By applying to Mr Cario, Jeweller, may be seen a Silver Spoon that was taken up in the Street about three weeks ago and has not been advertised.—*Boston Gazette*, Mar. 7/14, 1737.

WILLIAM CARIO.—Notice is hereby given, that William Cario is removed from his late Dwelling near the Rev. Dr. Colman's Meeting House, to the South End of the Town over against the White Swan, where all sorts of Jeweller's work is made & sold after the best and newest Manner, likewise fine Sword Blades, and Canes Sold and mounted there.—*Boston Gazette*, Oct. 23/30, 1738.

JOSEPH COOLIDGE, jun'r, has just Imported from London, and has to sell at his Shop opposite Mr. William Greenleaf's, Foot of Cornhill, A Variety of Jewellry, among which are; Paste shoe-buckles, knee and stock ditto, paste, rose and star earings, garnet ditto, paste, marqueset and garnet sprigs and pins, paste combs, plain tortoise-shell ditto, stay-hooks, broaches, watch-seals, cornelian and moco buttons; also, plated buckles and spurs, watch-chains, keys and hooks, steel-top thimbles, coral beeds, teeth brushes, money-scales, sets of penny weights and grains, pinchbeck buckles and buttons, and many other articles, with all kinds of Goldsmiths and Jewellers Work.

Goldsmiths and Jewellers may be supplied with all sorts of christal, garnet, white and red foyle, shoe and knee chapes, large black lead pots, crucibles, moulding sand, buckle brushes, sand-paper, iron and brass bar wire, binding wire, borax, pumace stones, gravers, knife tools, scorpers, frezing punches, sandover, files, flour of emery, &c.—*Boston News-Letter*, May 9, 1771.

JOHN DEXTER, Jeweller, has opened a Shop in Fish Street, a little to the Northward of Cross Street, near Mr. Pigeon's; where he makes and sells, and likewise mends, all Sorts of *plain* and *Stone* Rings, Earings, Buttons, and every other kind of Stone-Work, at the Cheapest Rates—Has also to sell Stones, Foil, &c. &c. and expects soon a larger Assortment.

☞ Goldsmiths in Town or Country may be supplied with the above-mentioned Articles.—N.B. Choice Kipper's Snuff, Indigo, and several Sorts of Cutlery Goods.—*Boston Gazette*, Nov. 7, 1757.

JOSEPH HILLER, advertised Electrical Experiments exhibited near the Old North Meeting House, Boston, in two parts, price one pistarene each part. "N. B. Said Hiller also does all sorts of Jeweller's Work in a neat Manner."—*Boston Gazette*, Mar. 5, 1754.

JOSEPH HILLER, Jeweller, at his House near Concert Hall, advertised that Electrical Experiments, with Methodical Lectures, are again exhibited by him, beginning at six o'clock in the evening, one Pistereen each Lecture.—*Boston Gazette*, Jan. 9, 1758.

THOMAS READ.—Fifteen Pistoles Reward. Ran-away from the Subscriber, (living at Annapolis, in Maryland) in June last, a Convict Servant Man, named *Thomas Read*, alias *Cuthbert*, about 25 or 30 Years of Age, 5 Feet, 4 Inches high, well set, grey Eyes, large Nose, and had short brown curl'd Hair. He is supposed to be in *Boston,* or some of the Northern Governments; is a Jeweller, and Motto-Ring Engraver, and is a very artful talkative pert Fellow:—can write pretty well, and has doubtless help'd himself to a Discharge, Pass, or any other Writing to deceive, and suit his Purpose: His apparel is probably genteel, as he had Money with him, a Watch in his Pocket, and a large Stock of Pride; by what Name he now goes is uncertain, as he has Impudence eno to pick & chuse any he should think proper. . . . JOHN INCH.

Annapolis, Sept. 15, 1759.—*Boston Gazette,* Nov. 12, 1759.

ASABEL MASON, late of London, Jeweller, deceased, his estate represented as insolvent. Rev. Mr. McClenacon of Chelsea and Deacon Henry Prentiss of Cambridge, were appointed administrators.—*Boston Gazette,* Dec. 19, 1752.

ROBERTS AND LEE, Jewellers, Opposite the Old Brick Meetinghouse, Cornhill, Boston, has received by the last ships from London, a large and valuable Assortment of Jewellry, with a great Variety of Watches, and other articles, consisting of plated pillar'd candlesticks of the Gothic and Corinthian order, ditto snuffer stands with snuffers, plated tankards, pints, ditto spurs very neat, ditto shoe & knee buckles very cheap, plated swords and hangers, mehogany cases with silver-handled knives, forks & spoons the newest fashion, stain'd ivory knives and forks both chap'd & plain, patent razors warranted good, ditto penknives & strops, with all sorts of cutlary, compleat setts of fish, &c. with pools for quadril, patent ass-skin memorandum books, an elegant assortment of japan ware, patent night lamps which tells the time of night, and may be used in the nicest bed-chamber, without the least offence, and with the greatest safety, hair powder scented & plain, powder knives, dressing and tail combs, tortoise shell pole combs, black hair pins, tooth powder which may be depended on to be no quackery, tortoise-shell and bone tooth brushes.

Town and Country Goldsmiths may be supplied with every article usually imported in that way, on very advantageous terms. —They make and repair every article in the Jewellery way, as neat and reasonable as in London. Mourning Rings made with Expedition. N. B. Ready Money for old Gold, Silver and Lace. —*Boston News-Letter*, Nov. 19, 1772.

JONATHAN TROTT, jeweller, his shop next door to the White-Horse tavern in the Southerly part of Boston, was broken open, and various articles were stolen including "one large Gold Necklace, one pair of Stone Earings set in Gold, two pair of wrought open Silver Shoe Buckles, and four odd ditto." All goldsmiths and others were desired to "stop" the same if offered for sale. Reward $8.00.—*Boston Gazette*, Nov. 6, 1758.

JOHN WELSH, Jeweller, in Fish Street, near Doctor Clark's, Hereby informs his Customers and others, That he has removed his Shop the opposite side of the Way; where may be had all Sorts of Jeweller's Works, and all kinds of loose Stones, at the lowest Rate. ALSO, Red and White Tois, Coral Beads, Borax, Salt-Petre, Pommace-Stone, Rotton-Stone, Steel Shoe and Knee Chapes and Tongs, Files, Bending Wire, and sundry other Articles, very cheap.—*Boston Gazette*, Oct. 16, 1758.

JOHN WELSH, Jeweller, in Fish Street, hereby informs his Customers and others, That he hath removed his Shop a little further to the Northward, next to Mr *John Pigeon*'s Insurance Office.—Where he carries on the Jeweller's Business, and where also may be had, all Sorts of loose Stones, Steel Shoe and Knee Chapes, Crucibles, and a variety of Articles in the Goldsmith's and Jeweller's Way, very reasonable.—*Boston Gazette*, Dec. 17, 1764.

STEPHEN WINTER, Jeweller, at the South End, Boston, advertised silver spoons supposed to have been stolen.—*New England Journal*, Jan. 27, 1740/1.

## PEWTER

### Pewterers

NATHANIEL AUSTIN, Pewterer; next Door to Mr. Boylston's in Charlestown, makes and sells (as cheap for Cash or Old Pewter, as any Person in Boston) the following Articles, *viz.* Quart and Pint Pots, Quart and Pint Basons, Plates and Porringers of all Sizes, &c.

He has also to dispose of at a reasonable Rate, a small Assortment of Brazier's Ware, viz.—Brass Kettles, Warming Pans, Skillets, Frying Pans, Tea Kettles, Iron Pots and Kettles, Shovel and Tongs, Candlesticks, best *London* Glue, Bellows, Hand-Saws, Files, Rasps, Aul Blades, Tax, Brads, best shoe Knives, Penknives, Knives & Forks, London Pewter, &c.—*Boston Gazette*, Oct. 3, 1763.

JOHN CARNES, pewterer, of Boston, advertised loss of paper money.—*Boston Gazette*, Oct. 28/Nov. 4, 1723.

JOHN COMBER, of Boston, pewterer, estate settled.—*Boston News-Letter*, Nov. 27/Dec. 4, 1721.

DAVID CUTLER.—To be Sold by DAVID CUTLER, Pewterer, at the Sign of the Great Dish, (with his Name on said Dish) in *Union-Street*, near the Town Dock; all sorts of Pewter, Viz. Dishes, Plates, Basons, Porringers, Quart Pots, Pint Pots, Cans, Tankards, closestools, Pans, &c. by Wholesale or Retail, at the cheapest Rates for Money or old Pewter, and the Ware made thick and substantial.—*Boston Gazette*, Mar. 14, 1757.

EDWARD KNEELAND, Pewterer, in Union Street, near the Conduit, Boston, Makes and sells the best *New-England* Pewter, in large or small Quantities, at the very lowest Prices for Cash, or old Pewter, Brass or Copper. N. B. Cash for old Pewter.—*Boston News-Letter*, Nov. 3, 1768.

DAVID LYELL.—This is to give notice, that a Journeyman Pewterer, who is a good workman in Hollow-ware, may have constant work, and good Wages, if they will go to New York, and apply themselves to Mr. *David Lyell*, or they may write to him and know further.—*Boston News-Letter*, Aug. 23/30, 1714.

John Skinner, advertised the removal of his Shop to Union Street, "where he continues to make and sell all sorts of the best *New-England* Pewter, in small or large Quantities, extraordinary cheap for Cash or old Pewter."—*Boston News-Letter*, Oct. 1, 1761.

John Skinner, Pewterer, adjoining on the North-side of the Mill Bridge, next to Deacon Barrett's in Boston, Makes and Sells by Wholesale or Retail, very cheap for Cash or old Pewter,

Plates of different sizes, hammer'd the same as London, very neat Canns, Quart and Pint Pots, Quart and Pint Basons, Porringers of five different sizes,—pewter Beakers, &c. all warranted the best of fine Pewter; also Rum-Measures, from Quart to Jill Pots; —also sells Tea-Kettles, the best London Pewter; etc.

☞ Gentlemen Traders may be supplied at the above Place at the very lowest Rate.—*Boston News-Letter*, July 7, 1763.

John Skinner, Pewterer, Hereby informs his Customers and others, That he has removed from the front of the House adjoining the Mill-Bridge, to his work-shop at the back end of said House, in the Lane leading to the Mills; Where he continues to make hammer'd Plates the same as London, of different Sizes; also Wine Measures from Quarts to Jills, with all other sorts of Pewter Ware usually made in New England, where Gentlemen and Ladies that trade in Pewter may be supply'd with large or small Quantities, at the very lowest Rate for Cash or old Pewter.

N. B. The highest Price is given by said *Skinner* for Old Pewter.—*Boston Gazette*, July 1, 1765.

## Pewter

Braziers and Pewterers.—A Good Set of Sundry Sorts of Braziers and Pewterers' Moulds, and other Tools, as good as New, belonging to the Estate of Mr. Thomas Thacher, deceased, To be sold by Oxenbridge Thacher at his Shop near the Town Pump, Boston. And also almost all sorts of Brass, Pewter and Iron Ware, viz. Nails, Locks, Hinges, Pots, Kittles, &c. . . . — *Boston News-Letter*, Sept. 17/24, 1724.

PEWTER WORM.—*To be SOLD, A Very good Copper Still about Seventy Gallons, with a pewter Worm suitable for the same, as also a good Copper of about Ten Barrels, to be seen at Mr. Ellis Wilson's Shop at the lower End of School Street.*—*Boston News-Letter*, Dec. 7/14, 1732.

WATER PLATES.—The best of Hard mettal Plates, Dishes, Dish covers, Cullenders, Water-Plates & Water-Dishes. To be sold seasonably by Thomas Hubbard, at the Head of the Town Dock.—*New England Journal*, Mar. 12, 1732/3.

PEWTER BUTTONS.—TAKEN from off a Saddle at the House of *Mr.* John Rachell *at* Winnisimet, *the 11th Inst. a blew Great Coat, with a Cross stampt Pewter Buttons. Any Person that will give Information of the said Coat to said* Rachell *so as he may have it again, shall have* Twenty Shillings *Reward and no Questions ask'd, by said* Rachell.—*Boston Gazette*, June 23/30, 1735.

PEWTERER'S MOULDS.—A good set of Pewterer's Moulds to be sold either in whole or part, very cheap, by Mr. Oxenbridge Thacher.—*Boston Gazette*, Mar. 28/Apr. 4, 1737.

DIAL MOULD.—"Spoon and dial moulds & other Tinker's tools" found in possession of a runaway negro servant.—*Boston News-Letter*, Apr. 8/15, 1742.

BLOCK TIN CANN.—If a Pint Block-Tin Cann, marked on the Handle with E D M is offered for Sale, it is desired it may be stop'd, and Notice given the Printer hereof: and the Person shall be well rewarded.—*Boston Gazette*, June 16, 1747.

COMMUNION FLAGONS.—"Neat hard-mettle two Quart Communion Flaggons, made after the newest manner."—*Boston News-Letter*, Apr. 29, 1748.

LONDON PEWTER.—Imported by Edmund Crowley in the Sloop *Mary*, late Capt. Hussey's from London, and to be Sold at the upper Part of Capt. Cheever's Store, opposite the Insurance-Office, King-Street; A Quantity of Pewter of Sorts, with Water-Dishes and Plates; Tea-Chests of Sorts, Tea-Boards, silver-fashioned Waiters, and Bottle-Stands with green cloth Bottoms, English brown China Tea-Pots of Sorts, with a rais'd Flower, Women's Russel Shoes of all Colours, and Children's of all sizes, with black Leather Clogs and Goloshoes, and a few black shammy Shoes: Also, Threads, Tapes, Quality-Binding, cotton-Laces, Pins, Needles, Men's and Women's common Thimbles, shirt Buttons, twist and deaths-head Buttons, with a small Assortment of Ribbons, Men's worsted Stockings, Caps, Gloves, and Muffatees; Clocks and Watches; Slop-Clothes for Sailors of all Sorts, and Osnabrigs;—Clover, Rye and Saint field Grass Seed.—Very good twice-laid Rope and Hawsers, from two Inches to six, at Eleven Pounds old Tenor per Hundred:—As also the best T. B. Wool-Cards.—All the above Goods to be Sold very low for ready Money, by Wholesale or Retail.—*Boston News-Letter*, Oct. 18, 1750.

PEWTER AND BRASS WARE.—To be sold by Gilbert and Lewis Deblois, at the sign of the Crown and Comb, in Queen Street, A large assortment of Brass Kettles, Skillets, Tea Kettles, Warming Pans, &c. best London Pewter Dishes, Plates, Basons, Porringers, Tankards & Tea Pots, etc.—*Boston Gazette*, Sept. 17, 1751.

PEWTER CRANE.—"A large Pewter Crane" advertised for sale at vendue, together with tinman's tools, etc. in Boston.—*Boston Gazette*, May 3, 1756.

LONDON PEWTER.—Jacob Richardson, at his shop and storehouse in Brenton's-Row, Newport, R. I. advertised "London pewter dishes, plates, basons, porringers, &c."—*Boston Gazette*, June 7, 1756.

LONDON PEWTER.—Just Imported from London and to be Sold by wholesale or retail by Gilbert Deblois, at the sign of the *Crown and Comb* near the Prison in Queen Street, Boston: . . . London pewter dishes, plates, basons, porringers, breakfast bowls, table spoons, pint and quart pots, cans, tankards, butter cups, newest fashion tea pots, table salts, sucking bottles, plate & dish covers, cullenders, soop kettles, new fashion roased (*sic*) plates, communion beakers and flaggons, pewter measures, chamber pots, bed and close stools. . . . —*Boston Gazette*, July 26, 1756.

OLD PEWTER.—Any Person that has old Pewter to sell, may have Seven Shillings O. T. a Pound, at the Sign of the great Dish, in Union-Street, near the Town Dock.—*Boston Gazette*, Nov. 8, 1756.

OLD PEWTER.—Any Person that has old Pewter to sell, may have *Seven Shillings*, O. T. a Pound, not only at the Great-Dish, but at any of the Braziers Shops in Union Street.—*Boston Gazette*, Nov. 22, 1756.

LONDON PEWTER.—William Molineaux, at his warehouse opposite the East End of Faneuil-Hall, sells very cheap for Cash, or short Credit, best London Pewter, at one Shilling and five Pence per Pound.—*Boston Gazette*, Sept. 26, 1757.

PEWTER, BRASS AND STEEL.—Wickham & Deblois, at the sign of the *Golden Eagle*, opposite to Dr. Tweedy's; and at their store opposite to Col. Malbone's Brick House [in Newport, R. I.] advertised "a Beautiful and large Assortment of hard ware Goods, Consisting of (almost) every Article that is made in Brass, Pewter, Steel and Iron," imported in the last ship from London.—*Boston Gazette*, Sept. 26, 1757.

LONDON PEWTER.—Mary & William Jackson, at the Brazen Head in Cornhill, Boston, advertised by Wholesale and Retail a great variety of hardware and utensils imported from London and Bristol, including the following pewter:—London dishes, plates and basons, tankards, quart and pint cans, quart and pint pots, tea pots of all sizes, cream pots, spoons, pewter measures, porringers, bed and closestool pans, turrenes, tea kettles and copper coffee pots, kettle pots, brass and copper saucepans, copper drinking pots. . . . —*Boston Gazette*, Oct. 3, 1757.

HARD-METAL DISHES.—Ebenezer Coffin, at the *Crown and Bee-hive*, opposite Deacon Phillips in Cornhill, Boston, advertised as imported in the last ships from London, a great variety of hardware and utensils including:—"Best London hard-metal and common Pewter Dishes, Plates, Basons, Porringers, Quart-Pots, Tankards, Soup-Kettles, Communion Flaggons and Cups, Tea-pots and Spoons, Bed and Close-stool Pans, Measures, etc."—*Boston Gazette*, Oct. 10, 1757.

CANDLE MOULDS.—"Pewter Candle Moulds" were advertised to be sold with other goods at public vendue.—*Boston Gazette*, Apr. 10, 1758.

OLD PEWTER.—Lewis Deblois, dealer in hardware, etc. at the

Sign of the Golden-Eagle in Dock Square, Boston, advertised that "Old Pewter will be receiv'd as Cash for Goods."—*Boston Gazette*, Apr. 24, 1758.

DISH COVERS.—John Welch of Hanover Street, Boston, "purposing to go for England in a short time," advertised his household effects to be sold at public vendue. Among which were listed— "Water-Plates, Hard Metal Covers for Dishes, Oval Dishes, Plates and other Pewter."—*Boston Gazette*, Apr. 24, 1758.

BLOCK TIN Cream Potts, were advertised.—*Boston Gazette*, Aug. 14, 1758.

LONDON PEWTER.—Ebenezer Coffin, Imported in the last Ships from London, and to be Sold at the Crown and Bee-Hive, opposite Deacon Phillip's in Cornhill, Boston, very Cheap for ready Cash, or on short Credit, A Large assortment of best London, hard-metal and common pewter dishes, plates, basons, porringers, quart-pots, tankards, soup-kettles, communion flaggons and cups, christening basons, tea-pots and spoons, bed and close stool pans, measures, &c.—*Boston Gazette*.—Aug. 13, 1759.

PEWTERER'S TOOLS.—A Sett of Pewterer's Tools to be Sold. Enquire of the Printers hereof.—*Boston Gazette*, Apr. 7, 1760.

LONDON PEWTER.—James Green, in a new Shop, at the Sign of the Elephant, at Providence, R. I. advertised a great assortment of goods including "London pewter dishes, plates, basons, porringers, tea potts, spoons, &c."—*Boston Gazette*, Sept. 15, 1760.

CANDLE MOULDS.—"Lewis Deblois, lately returned from London, has open a Store at the Bottom of King Street," and advertised a great variety of goods including:—"pewter dishes, plates, basins, porringers, tea-pots, hard metal candle moulds, spoons, &c."—*Boston Gazette*, Jan. 5, 1761.

LONDON PEWTER.—Imported in the last ships from London, and to be Sold by John Cutler at the Golden Cock, Marlborough-Street, over against *Doctor Ashton's*, Boston, . . . best London pewter Dishes, Plates, Basons, Tankards, Quart pots, Porringers, Spoons, and Bed-pans, best large Hard mettle Plates, Dishes, Canns, Teapots and Spoons . . . —*Boston Gazette*, Jan. 19, 1761.

BREAKFAST BOWLS.—"London hard-metal and common pewter dishes and plates, basons, quart and pint pots, quart and pint cans, tankards, teapots, tea and table spoons, hard metal breakfast bowls, best large bed pans, pewter wine measures," just imported in the last Ships from *London* and *Bristol*, By *Edward Blanchard*, and to be sold at his Shop in Union-Street, near the Conduit.—*Boston Gazette*, July 27, 1761.

BATH METAL.—Best London and hard metal Pewter Dishes, Plates, Basons, Tankards, Cans, Spoons; a great Assortment Bath metal, Tortoise Shell and Horn Coat and Waistcoat Buttons. . . . imported in the last Ships from London and Bristol, and to be sold by *Timothy Newell* at his shop on Dock Square.—*Boston Gazette*, Nov. 16, 1761.

TEA POTS.—William Bowes informed his customers and others that he had removed his shop to Dock Square, where he had to sell by wholesale and retail, viz. "The best *London* Pewter and Hard Metal Dishes & Plates, Hard Metal and common Table Spoons, Tea Spoons, best Hard Metal Tea Pots of all Sizes, Quart and Pint Cans, &c. &c." . . . —*Boston Gazette*, Jan. 10, 1762.

LIGHTNING struck the house of Giles Hall at Wallingford, Conn. and among other damage done "it melted some Pewter that hung upon the Post, run through a Shelf of Pewter, and melted each Thing at the Places were it entered, and went from it;"—*Boston Gazette*, June 14, 1762.

SPOONS.—Pewter and alcumy spoons, for sale.—*Boston Gazette*, Nov. 29, 1762.

SOUP KETTLES.—*Richard Billings*, at his Shop in Cornhill, near the Post-office, (at the Sign of the Crown and Comb) advertised as just imported in the last ships from London and Bristol, a great variety of hardware, including "best London hard mettle pewter dishes, plates, basons, porringers, soupe kettles, dish covers, communion flaggons, christening basons, mugs, cans, bed and close stool pans, &c. pewter ink stands. . . . —*Boston Gazette*, July 4, 1763.

LONDON PEWTER.—Joshua Gardner & Co. at their store in King Street, Boston, advertised as just imported from London, a great variety of hardware, etc., also, pewter and hard metal dishes, plates, basons, porringers, tea pots, cream pots, pepper castors, table and tea spoons, sugar tongs, pewter measures from half jill to a quart, stool and bed pans, pewter ink standishes and stands, painted snuff boxes, very neat paper ditto, etc. etc.—*Boston Gazette*, May 14, 1764.

BOTTLE CRANES.—Jeremiah Allen informs his Friends and the Publick, that he has received per the *Dolphin*, Capt. Scott, from London, a new supply of Goods in the Hardware Branch, among which are, . . . London Pewter Dishes, Plates & Basons, Cans, Tankards, Tea-Pots and Bottle-Cranes, Wine Measures, Table and Tea Spoons, Bed and Close-Stool Pans, Brass Knockers, Bed Caps, Cloak Pins, Kitchen Jacks, Silver, Ivory and Bone Handle Knives and Forks, Temple & Dutch Spectacles, 6 by 8, 7 by 9, 8 by 10 London Crown Window-Glass, Bambo, Dogwood, Solid Joint, and Hazel Angling Rods, a large Assortment of Looking Glasses, also a few pair in the Palmyra taste, with Jerendoles, etc. etc. etc.—*Boston News-Letter*, Nov. 4, 1773.

## POTTERY AND EARTHENWARE
### Potters

SAMUEL HALE, potter, of Philadelphia, advertised a runaway servant.—*Boston Gazette*, July 8/15, 1734.

JONATHAN HALL, JR, of Medford, potter, settlement of estate advertised.—*Boston Gazette*, May 28, 1754.

JONATHAN HALL, potter, of Roxbury, an incendiary attempted to set fire to his "Work-House," near his dwelling house. A reward of £100. was offered for information leading to conviction of the "Inventor of said Villainy."—*Boston Gazette*, Jan. 31, 1763.

JONATHAN HALL, potter, of Roxbury, lost his Shop by fire together with its contents "of a considerable value."—*Boston Gazette*, Oct. 24, 1763.

POTTER'S HOUSE, with the Works and Cooper's Shop, Warehouse, Mansion House, Barn, and Lands adjoining, just by Concord Meeting House (a good seat for Trade) will be sold by Public Vendue, March 6th next, it being the estate of Seth Rose, Innholder, late of Concord, deceased.—*Boston Gazette*, Feb. 11, 1765.

DAVID SIMONS.—*Earthen Ware* made, and sold by Wholesale or Retail, by *David Simons* at *New Boston*, Potter, on the North side of Doctor *Mayhew's* Meeting-House.—*Boston Gazette*, June 18, 1751.

THOMAS SYMMES.—Made and Sold reasonably by *Thomas Symmes* and Company at *Carlestown*, near the Swing Bridge, blue and white stone Ware of forty different sorts; also red and yellow Ware of divers Sorts, either by Wholesale or Retail.—*Boston Gazette*, Apr. 16, 1745.

JOHN WEBBER.—John Webber, a potter, at Charlestown, was injured by the explosion of a cannon while celebrating the marriage of the Princess Royal.—*Boston News-Letter*, May 16/23, 1734.

CHARLESTOWN EARTHENWARE.—To be sold on reasonable Terms, A Dwelling-House & Land in Charlestown, near the Swing-Bridge, with a House & Kiln for the making of Earthen Ware; as also a Warehouse and other Conveniences necessary for that Business, Inquire of the Printer.—*Boston News-Letter*, Nov. 1, 1744.

CHARLESTOWN EARTHENWARE.—To be sold by publick Vendue on Tuesday the 16th Currant, two o'Clock Afternoon, at the Three Crane Tavern at Charlestown, a Dwelling House, Potter's Kiln House and Kiln in Wapping Street in Charlestown aforesaid, any Person minding to purchase the same before said Time may inquire of Michael Brigden or Grace Parker.—*Boston Gazette*, Dec. 9, 1746.

### EARTHENWARES

EARTHENWARE, part of a ships loading, listed in a sale at auction.—*Boston News-Letter*, Sept. 3/10, 1711.

EARTHENWARE.—"Six Hogsheads of Earthen Ware, as Tea Pots," were to be sold at public vendue.—*Boston News-Letter*, Feb. 9/16, 1712/13.

EARTHENWARE.—To be sold by Capt. Arthur Savage at the White House near Mr. Colmans Church, Boston, Earthern Ware and Glasses per the Hogshead, fine Holland Tiles, Earthern and Stone Ware in Parcels, likewise the long London Tobacco Pipes, all very Reasonable.—*Boston News-Letter*, Apr. 23/30, 1716.

CHINA TEA CUP and brass lamp stolen.—*Boston News-Letter*, Oct. 13/20, 1718.

DUTCH TILES for Chimneys, advertised.—*Boston News-Letter*, Aug. 3/10, 1719.

CHINAWARE, lately imported, for sale.—*Boston Gazette*, Sept. 18/25, 1721.

EARTHENWARE.—Just imported, and to be sold by William Randall, in the middle of Cross-Street, at Capt. Philip Viscount's, Hogsheads of Earthen Ware, white stone Tea-Cups and Saucers, Bowls, Plates, Salts, Milk Pots, handsome cut Salts, cotton, silk and Barcelona Handkerchiefs, Ribbons, Women's silk, russel, callimanco and shammey Shoes, Cloggs & Pattoons, Gloves & Mittens, Women's & Children's Fans of all Sorts, Necklaces, Chints, Calicoes, striped Cottons, demy Chince Borders, best London Pipes, Hunters, pewter Plates, Gentlemen's hunting Bottles and walking Canes, Books, Wax, Wafers, Knives, Buckles, Scizars, Needles, Pins, and sundry other Goods.—*Boston News-Letter*, Jan. 17, 1724.

DUTCH TILES.—"Square Dutch Tiles to be set in Chimnies," for sale.—*Boston News-Letter*, Apr. 29/May 6, 1725.

DUTCH TILES.—Several Sorts of Neat Dutch Tiles, to be set in Chimnies. To be sold by Mr. Richard Draper, at the lower end of Cornhill, Boston.—*Boston News-Letter*, May 6/13, 1725.

LIVERPOOL WARE.—Just imported from Liverpool, Several sorts of Earthen Ware, Pipes and Woolens. To be sold by Benjamin Foster at his Ware House No. 7 on the Long-Wharfe.—*Boston Gazette*, Oct. 11/18, 1725.

BURNT CHINA.—A Parcel of super fine Burnt China Plates, Cups & other Furniture for a Tea Table; as also a very handsome Japann'd Tea Table lately imported from London; To be Sold, Inquire of the Publisher hereof.—*Boston Gazette*, Jan 24/31, 1725/6.

CHINAWARE.—"Very good China, Blue & White Plates, and burnt Bowls, Cups & Sawcers," for sale.—*Boston Gazette*, May 2/9, 1726.

BLUE AND WHITE PLATES.—To be Sold by Mr. Nicholas Davis, living over against the Custom-House near the Orange Tree, A parcel of very good China, Blue & White Plates, and Burnt Bowls, Cups & Sawcers, just arrived from London.—*Boston Gazette*, May 9/16, 1726.

BURNT CHINA.—"Blew, White and burnt China all in Setts," for sale.—*Boston Gazette*, Nov. 11/18, 1728.

STONEWARE in hampers, just arrived from Holland.—*Boston Gazette*, Feb. 10/17, 1728/9.

FIGURED TILES.—Very good Figured Dutch Tyle for Chimneys, to be Sold by the Dozen, at Mr. Jacob Royalls, in Union St.—*Boston Gazette*, Sept. 1/8, 1729.

DUTCH TILES.—Good Dutch Tiles of Various Figures for Chimneys, also Stampt Paper in Rolls for to Paper Rooms. To be Sold by John Phillips, Bookseller.—*New England Journal*, Oct. 26, 1730.

DELFT WARE.—Dutch Stone and Delft ware from Holland.—*Boston News-Letter*, Dec. 16/23, 1731.

YELLOW WARE.—James King, next Door to the King's Arms joining to the Mill-Bridge, Sells, Double and Single Flint Glass; white Flint Cups and Saucers, Tea, Saffron and Milk Pots, Sugar Boxes, Slop and Breakfast Bowls, Punch Strainers & Sauce Porringers, fine Delft and course Earthern Ware, of the above sortments yellow ware Hollow and Flat by the Crate, and Bohea Tea, at 28 *s.* a pound.—*Boston Gazette*, Apr. 16/23, 1733.

FLINT WARE.—"White Earthern, Delph & Flint Ware" lately imported from Liverpool; also Maple & Horn case knives and forks.—*Boston News-Letter*, May 17/24, 1733.

POTTERY AND GLASS.—Just Imported and to be Sold Reasonably, By Mehetabel Kneeland, At the King's Arms adjoining the Mill Bridge in Boston, A choice Sortment of Delph, Stone, and Glass Ware, *Viz.* Bowls of divers Sizes, Plates of all Sorts, and Dishes, Cups and Sawcers, Breakfast Bowls, Strayners, Mugs of divers Sorts, &c. Wine Glasses double and single Flint, Jellys, Whip Sullibubs, Baskets, Punch Ladles, Cream Pots pearl'd and plain, Bird Fountains, Tankards and Salvers, &c. By Wholesale or Retail. Where may also be had Choice Tea and Coffee, and other Sorts of Grocery.—*Boston Gazette*, Apr. 25/May 2, 1737.

ENAMELLED CHINA.—To be Sold Cheap, by Adam Brown, At the Eliphant in King-Street, up one pair of Stairs, some compleat Setts of Blue China, Blue and Gold ditto, Enamuel'd ditto, Tea Setts, and Coffee Bowls & Basons sorted, Patty pans, Cups blue handled, China plates Soop & shallow, Enamuel'd ditto, & Dishes sorted.—*Boston Gazette*, Apr. 25/May 2, 1737.

DELPH AND STONEWARE.—Just Imported, and to be Sold Reasonably, By Mehetabel Kneeland, at the King's Arms adjoining the Mill Bridge, Boston, A choice Sortment of Delph, Stone & Glass ware, viz. Bowls of divers Sizes & Colours, Plates of all Sorts & Dishes, Tea Pots, Cups and Sawcers, Strayners, Mugs of divers Sorts and Colours, &c. Wine Glasses double and single Flint, Jellys and Whip Sullibubs, Baskets, Punch Ladles, Cream Pots, pearl'd and plain, Bird Fountains, Tankards and Salvers, &c. By Wholesale or Retail. Where may also be had Choice Tea and Coffee, with other Sorts of Grocery.—*Boston News-Letter*, Apr. 28/May 5, 1737.

YELLOW EARTHENWARE.—Yellow and Brown Earthen Ware, for sale.—*Boston Gazette*, Oct. 24/31, 1737.

DUTCH TILES.—To be sold, at Capt. Stephen Richard's in Queen Street, Boston, All sorts of Dutch Tyles viz, Scripture (round and square), Landskips of divers sorts, Sea Monsters, Horsemen, Soldiers, Diamonds, &c. And Setts of Brushes: London Quart Bottles: And a Chest of Delph Ware.—*Boston Gazette*, Feb. 6/13, 1738.

LIGHTNING struck the house of Thomas Fisher at Wrentham, "the Casements in the lower Room were all beat off; The Earthern Vessels and Glasses on the Mantletree Shelf were thrown with such Force that they made deep Impressions in the Ceiling at the other End of the Room."—*New England Journal*, Mar. 20, 1738/9.

DELPH WARE.—A parcel of Delph Ware, Tea Cups and Saucers, Coffee Cups, Sugar Dishes, Tea Pots, Boats for Spoons, were advertised, among other things "Just Imported."—*Boston News-Letter*, Nov. 18, 1742.

CHINAWARE, and most other India Goods, Hogsheads of blew & white Earthen, and Glass Ware, Boxes of long London Pipes, &c. &c. were advertised by Robert Jenkins, opposite to the North Side of the Exchange, Boston.—*Boston News-Letter*, Dec. 23, 1742.

BRISTOL YELLOW WARE.—William Bell advertised a variety of Goods lately imported from Bristol, including "Crates of Yellow Earthen Ware, Tea Table Bells, Stands of Crewits, Ladies Bobs, Ear-Rings, Temple Spectacles, etc. etc.—*Boston Evening Post*, May 7, 1744.

FIGURED TILES.—Blue and white Dutch Tile for Chimneys,

handsomely figur'd to be Sold by John Phillips at the Stationer's Arms in Cornhill, Boston.—*Boston News-Letter*, June 14, 1744.

WHITE STONEWARE.—*Earthen Ware*. Just imported, and to be Sold by William Randall, in the middle of Cross-Street, at Capt. Philip Viscount's, Hogsheads of earthen Ware, white stone Tea-Cups and Saucers, Bowls, Plates, Salts, Milk Pots, handsome cut Salts, cotton, silk and Barcelona Handkerchiefs, Ribbons, Women's silk, russel, callimanco and shammey Shoes, Cloggs & Pattoons, Gloves & Mittens, Women's & Children's Fans of all Sorts, Necklaces, Chints, Calicoese, striped Cottons, demy Chince Borders, best London Pipes, Hunters, pewter Plates, Gentlemen's hunting Bottles and walking Canes, Books, Wax, Wafers, Knives, Buckles, Scizars, Needles, Pins, and sundry other Goods.—*Boston News-Letter*, Jan. 17, 1745.

WHITE STONE CUPS.—To be Sold by William Randall, in the middle of Cross-Street, at Captain Philip Viscount's,—White Stone Tea Cups, and Saucers, Salts, Milk-Pots, handsome cut Salts, silk Hankerchiefs, cotton ditto, Women's and Children's Fans of all Sorts, Necklaces, best London Pipes, Hunter's, pewter plates, Gentleman's hunting Bottles, and walking Canes, Knives, Buckles, Silver Knives and Forks in shaggreen Cases, scenting Bottles, silver Sleeve Buttons, Wine Glasses, and sundry other Goods.—*Boston Gazette*, May 28, 1745.

EARTHENWARE.—Just Imported, and to be Sold by William Randall, at Capt Philip Viscount's in Cross Street, Hogsheads of Earthen Ware, wormed Wine Glasses, Silver handle Knives and Forks in Shaggreen Cases, etc. etc.—*Boston Evening Post*, Dec. 1, 1746.

BURNT CHINA.—Burnt and enamelled China bowls, handsome sets of blue and white cups and saucers, double Flint Wine-Glasses and Decanters, English Earthern Ware, etc. were advertised in the *Boston News-Letter*, Sept. 22, 1748.

QUILTED PLATES.—To be Sold at the Blue Boar, South End; Fine blue and white quilted China Plates, at Eleven Pounds per Dozen, or Six Pounds the Half Dozen.—*Boston Evening Post*, Jan. 30, 1749.

CHINA PLATES.—*China* plates at £11. per dozen, advertised.—*Boston News-Letter*, Mar. 9, 1749.

DELPH WARE.—Imported and Sold by William Randall, in Back-Street, opposite to the Sign of the Chest of Drawers:—Hogsheads of Earthen Ware, and Glass, variety of all Sorts of Wine Glasses, Decanters, Cruets, Tumblers and Salts, and many other Articles of Glass. Also Window-Glass, a handsom Sortment of Blue and White Delph Bowls and Plates, also White and Brown Stone Ware, etc. etc.—*Boston Evening Post*, May 8, 1749.

LIVERPOOL PLATES.—"Liverpool Earthern Plates, very neat," for sale.—*Boston Gazette*, Nov. 28, 1749.

CHINA TEA CUPS.—Very handsome Setts of blue and white China Tea-Cups and Saucers, to be Sold by William Ballantine near the Mill-Bridge.—*Boston News-Letter*, Oct. 4, 1750.

EARTHENWARE.—"Water Dishes and Plates, Fish Dishes and Strainers, White Stone Plates and Dishes, ditto Tea Cups & Saucers," for sale.—*Boston Gazette*, Nov. 27, 1750.

YELLOW EARTHENWARE.—Painter's Colors, Chalk by the Ton or Hundred, yellow Earthen ware, ink horns, etc. etc. were advertised by Nathaniel Loring.—*Boston Evening Post*, Mar. 11, 1751.

WHITE STONEWARE.—Imported in the last Ships, and to be Sold by HENRY BARNS, at his Store the lower End of King-Street, next Door above Mr. *Dowse's* Insurance-Office.

*A Great Variety of Glass and Earthen Ware, consisting of single and double Flint Wine Glasses, Crewits, Decanters, Salt-sellers, Beakers, Cyder Ditto, half pint, pint and quart Cans, Ditto Salvers, Jelly Glasses, Mustard Pots, 3 Feet Salts and Cream Pots, Bird Fountains, &c. &c. fine Delph Ware, as Plates, Dishes, Bowles, Tea Dishes, Flower Bottles, Wash Basons, Mint Stands, &c. &c. white Stone Dishes, scolloped Plates, quart pint and half pint Mugs and Tea Dishes, &c. blue and white spriged Stone scolloped Dishes, Plates, quart pint, and half pint Muggs, Ditto Dutch & white Chamber Pots, blue & white Stone Mugs sorted, with a great Variety of other Ware, opened for the conveniency of Shops, where they may be supplyed as cheap as by the Hogshead, and Country Customers may have these Sortments packed in such a manner as they may be transported any Distance by Land without Breakage; likewise choice Starch, Rice, Pepper, Allspice, Ginger, split & round Pease, Oatmeal, Mustard & Flour of Mustard, long and short Pipes, with sundry other Grocerys, at the lowest Rates.*—*Boston Gazette*, Oct. 15, 1751.

LIVERPOOL DELFT WARE.—"Liverpool Delft ware in Hogsheads," for sale.—*Boston Gazette*, Oct. 22, 1751.

EARTHENWARE & cider were a part of the Cargo of a New England sloop wrecked near Capt Hatteras.—*Boston Gazette*, Jan. 23, 1753.

TORTOISE-SHELL WARE.—"New fashion'd Turtle-shell Tereens," for sale.—*Boston Gazette*, Apr. 9, 1754.

EXCISE ON WARE.—Saturday last was published an Act passed by the General Court in their present Session, intitled, *An Act for granting unto his Majesty an Excise upon Sundry Articles hereafter enumerated, for and towards the Support of his Majesty's Government of this Province.*

N. B. The articles are, viz. Tea, Coffee, and East-India Ware, called China-Ware.—The Act takes Place the first Day of July next.—*Boston Evening Post*, June 17, 1754.

Bow CHINA.—A Variety of Bow China, Cups and Saucers, Bowls, &c. Women's silk and worsted Shoes and clogs, Children's shoes of all Sorts, just imported by Philip Breadnig, and to be sold at his House in Fish Street.—*Boston Evening Post*, Nov. 11, 1754.

BROKEN CHINA.—This is to give Notice, to all those that have any broken CHINA, that at the *Lion* and *Bell*, in *Marlborough-Street, Boston*, they may have it mended by riveting it together with Silver or Brass Rivets: it is first put together with a Cement that will stand boiling Water, and then Riveted.—*Boston Gazette*, Oct. 20, 1755.

BLACK STONE COFFEE POTS.—White and black Stone Coffee Pots; glass tumblers, beakers and Jacks; Delph Soop and plain Dishes and Plates, painted dust pans, block Tin Cream Pots, table knives and forks, etc. for Sale.—*Boston Gazette*, June 5, 1758.

PRUSSIAN PLATES.—To be sold cheap, in Cold Lane, next Door to Capt. Hall's: White Stone, Prussian & Basket work'd Plates and Dishes, brown Stone Dishes and Patter pans.—*Boston Gazette*, Nov. 13, 1758.

TORTOISE-SHELL Stone Ware by the Crate.—*Boston Gazette*, Sept. 15, 1760.

DELPH WARE.—To be Sold by *Rebecca Walker*, at the corner Shop in Union-Street, opposite the *Blue Ball*, A Variety of Delph and Stone Ware, viz.

Setts of Fish Dishes, Baking Dishes of several sizes, Patter-pans of all Sizes, plain and flower'd Plates, Coffee Pots, large and small Toys, and sundry other Articles, by Wholesale or Retail.—*Boston Gazette*, Oct. 27, 1760.

CHINAWARE.—"A variety of blue & white china plates; blue and white China cups and saucers; china sauce boats; china handle coffee cups and butter plates; a fine assortment of glass, delph & stone ware," just imported, and to be Sold by *Samuel Fletcher* near the Draw-Bridge, Boston.—*Boston Gazette*, Jan. 5, 1761.

TORTOISE-SHELL STONEWARE.—"White, blue and white and Tortoise-shell Stone Ware," just imported from London and for sale by James Jackson at his shop in Union Street.—*Boston Gazette*, Feb. 2, 1761.

ENGLISH CHIMNEY TILES.—"A few Hogsheads of handsome Delph Ware, Crates of white Stone Tea Cups and Saucers, English Chimney Tiles, Boxes of short Pipes," imported from London, and for sale by William Greenleaf, fronting Cornhill, Boston.—*Boston Gazette*, June 1, 1761.

DELFT WARE.—William Greenleaf, fronting Cornhill, advertised:—a few Hogsheads of handsome Delft Ware, crates of white Stone Tea-Cups and Saucers, English Chimney Tiles, Boxes of short Pipes, Bar Lead, Bohea, Green and Hyson Tea, window glass, 9 by 7, and 8 by 6, Guinea Pepper, etc.—*Boston News-Letter*, June 11, 1761.

ENAMELLED CHINAWARE.—Just Imported, and to be Sold for Cash, a great Variety of new-fashioned China and Glass, viz. Blue and White China Plates of all Sorts, blue and white Dishes;

pint, quart, and two quart blue and white best burnt China Bowls, Coffee Cups and Saucers, handle Coffee Cups; a great Variety best blue and white and enamel'd China Tea Cups and Saucers; Sauce Boats, Butter Plates, Pudding and Salad Dishes of all Sizes, oval Dishes, flower'd Decanters, flower'd wine, cyder, and beer Glasses, neat japann'd Salvers, Glass Salvers, neat japann'd Bread Baskets, &c. together with a fine Assortment of Groceries, Boxes of Window Glass, 7 x 9—By *S. Fletcher*, near the Draw-Bridge.—*Boston Gazette*, July 13, 1761.

LIVERPOOL WARE.—Crates of Liverpool Earthern Ware, Hogsheads of Delph Ware, Nails, Glass, etc. were advertised by Nathaniel and Benjamin Greene.—*Boston News-Letter*, Aug. 6, 1761.

WHITE STONEWARE.—"White and Tortoise shell Stone Ware," imported in the last ships from London, to be sold by *James Jackson*, at his Shop in Union Street.—*Boston Gazette*, Aug. 17, 1761.

CHINAWARE.—Just imported and sold by *Samuel Fletcher*, Blue and white China Dishes and Plates, Quart and two Quart best blue and white, and burnt China Bowls, Coffee Cups and Saucers, a great Variety of blue and white and burnt China Tea Cups and Saucers, Handle Coffee Cups, Sauce Boats, Butter Plates, blue and white China Pudding Dishes of all sizes, oval Fish Dishes, flower'd Wine Glasses, Bread Baskets, Waiters and Salvers, the finest Hyson Tea, with a fine Assortment of Groceries. —*Boston Gazette*, Oct. 5, 1761.

ENGLISH CHIMNEY TILES.—William Greenleaf, fronting Cornhill, Boston, Has imported from London and Bristol . . . Looking Glasses, China Ware, a few Hogsheads of Delph Ware, Crates of white Stone Ware sorted, Crates of white Stone Tea Cups and Saucers, red & white, and blue & white English Chimney Tiles, Apothecary's Phials, long and short Pipes. . . . —*Boston Gazette*, Feb. 22, 1762.

CHINA IN STATUARY.—A variety of curious fine China in Statuary: also some of the best enamel'd China, sold at public auction at the House next to the Orange Tree in Hanover Street. —*Boston Gazette*, May 17, 1762.

ENAMELLED WARE.—Imported and to be Sold by Green & Walker, at the North Corner of Queen Street. . . . "a fine assortment of China Ware, viz. blue & white and burnt China Dishes, soupe ditto, blue & white baking ditto, blue & white and burnt plates, soupe ditto, blue & white quart and two quart Bowls, blue & white and burnt pint and half-pint ditto, enamelled quart, pint and half-pint Mugs, blue & white baking Cups, blue & white and burnt Tea-Cups and Saucers, Coffee ditto, beautiful compleat Tea-Setts, Also, Glass Candlesticks, quart, pint and half-pint Mugs, quart & pint Decanters, Crewets, Wine-Glasses, Wine & Water & Beer ditto, Jelly & Syllabub ditto, Beakers, Salts, etc. etc.—*Boston News-Letter*, June 24, 1762.

CHINAWARE.—To be Sold by *Samuel Fletcher*, near the Draw Bridge, Boston, . . . Best blue and white, and burnt China Plates and Dishes, China Mugs, Butter Boats and China Bowls of all Sorts, Soup and Pudding Dishes, blue and white and burnt China Cups and Saucers, Butter Plates and Coffee Cups, Glass Salvers, japan'd Salvers and Tea Chests, Wine Glasses, Compleat Sets of best China Candlesticks, Cans, plain and flower'd Decanters, Salts, Cream-Pots, Beer and Cyder Glasses, Glass Pitchers, Tumblers of all Sorts, Glass Lamps, and Sugar Dishes; Boxes of Single Flint Glass; Boxes of Pipes of all Sorts, . . . Chimney Tiles, . . . Coffee Pots, Tea-Pots, Bowls and Cream Pots, Earthern and Stone Ware of all Sorts, . . . beautiful Setts of best China Ware, Fruit Baskets, . . . —*Boston Gazette*, June 28, 1762.

STONE STATUES.—*Joshua Blanchard*, at his shop in Dock Square, advertised for sale "stone statues, Indian screens, paper for rooms, neat chimney pieces," etc.—*Boston Gazette*, Nov. 15, 1762.

ENAMELLED WARE.—Green and Walker, at their Store at the North Corner of Queen St. advertised among other goods:—

*China Ware*, viz. Blue and white enamell'd Plates and Dishes; soop ditto; long Dishes, octagon Dishes and Plates; blue and white Bowls of all Sizes; burnt Ditto; Mugs, Sauce-boats, Butter Saucers, Pastry Pans, Custard-Cups, Tea-Cups and Saucers, and Coffee Ditto with and without Handles; Tea-Pots, Cream-Pots, compleat Tea-Setts, &c. &c.

*Glass Ware,* viz. plain and flower'd Champaign and round Decanters; Crewits, Wine-Glasses, wine and water-colour'd Ale ditto; Jelly and Syllabub-Glasses; Beakers, Mugs, Salvers, Fruit-Baskets, Mustard Pots, Salts, Glass Stands, &c. &c.—*Boston News-Letter,* Apr. 28, 1763.

YELLOW LIVERPOOL WARE.—Crates of yellow *Liverpool* Ware, Hogsheads of Stone and Delph, Boxes of Glass Ware, and Window Glass, 6 by 8, 7 by 9, and 10 by 8, in half and quarter Boxes, just imported from London and Bristol, were advertised by Robert Gould.—*Boston Gazette,* June 6, 1763.

ENGLISH DELPH WARE.—"Delph Ware, Stone Ware, Chimney Tiles, Apothecary's Phials, etc. just brought from England, were advertised by William Greenleaf at his Store fronting Cornhill, Boston.—*Boston Gazette,* Oct. 31, 1763.

CHIMNEY TILES.—"Red and white and blue and white Chimney Tiles, Delph and Stone Ware, long and midling Pipes, half Pint flat bottles, Apothecary's Phials, Looking Glasses, Window Glass, 10 by 8, 9 by 7, and 8 by 6; a few very handsome Persia Carpets 4 yards and 3 yards square, &c." for sale by *William Greenleaf,* at his Store Fronting Cornhill, Boston.—*Boston Gazette,* Dec. 12, 1763.

BASKET PLATES.—To be sold very cheap, Two or three Crates of white Stone Ware, consisting chiefly of the new-fashioned basket Plates and oblong Dishes. Enquire of the Printers.—*Boston News-Letter,* Mar. 29, 1764.

LONDON PIPES.—"Square Quart Pickle Bottles, a new Assortment of China Bowls from a Pint to 3 Quarts, glaz'd 18 inch London Pipes per Box, neat Mehogany Tea Chests," etc. for sale by *Samuel Fletcher,* near the Draw Bridge, *Boston.*—*Boston Gazette,* May 28, 1764 (*sup.*).

PAINTED STONEWARE.—"A Variety of white and painted Stone Ware, such as Plates; Dishes round and oval; Bowls of all Sorts, Cups & Saucers; Mugs of all Sorts, Tea Pots, Fruit Baskets, . . . also Glass Ware, such as Decanters of all Sorts, Mugs, Tumblers, Wine Glasses, Salts, &c., with many other Articles, which will be Sold in Small Quantities, or by the Hogshead," at Public Auction, at the East End of Faneuil-Market.—*Boston Gazette*, May 28, 1764 (*sup.*).

LIVERPOOL WARE.—"Crates of flat and hollow Liverpool Ware, hogsheads of Delph Ware, Crates of blue and white Cups and Saucers," etc. just imported from England, for sale by Thomas Russell at the warehouse on Green's Wharf.—*Boston Gazette*, July 16, 1764.

FLINT WARE.—Just imported from England and for sale at the House of Mrs Parrot in Kelby St.: Six crates of flint Ware of several Colours, assorted.—*Boston News-Letter*, Aug. 9, 1764.

STONE JUGS.—Chimney Tile of different Figures and Colours: and Two and Three Gallon Stone Juggs, advertised by Thomas Walley at his Store in Dock Square, Boston.—*Boston Gazette*, Sept. 17, 1764.

LIVERPOOL STONEWARE.—A general assortment for Sale by Lewis Gray, at Store No. 1, Butler's Row.—*Boston Gazette*, Sept. 16, 1765 (*sup.*).

NOTTINGHAM MUGS.—John Hazro at his Shop opposite the Town House, advertised among other items: Nottingham Mugs, delph bowls, black tea pots, ditto sugar bowls, ditto cups or saucers, tortoishell tea pots, cream-colour'd coffee and tea pots, white stone ware.—*Boston News-Letter*, Nov. 8, 1770.

STAFFORDSHIRE WARE.—Now opening at the *Staffordshire* and *Liverpool* Warehouse, in King Street, a fresh Assortment of China, Glass, Delph & Stone Ware, which are to sell as low as they were ever sold in America, viz.

CHINA. Blue & white, red & gold, pencil'd & guilted Coffee-Pots, Tea-Pots, Bowls, Sugars, Ewers, Cannisters, Spoon Trays, Sauce Boats, Tea, Coffee & Chocolate Cups and Saucers, &c.

GLASS. Double & single Flint, plain enamel'd, Engrav'd & Cut Wines, Crewits, Salts, Beakers, Decanters, Cans, Pattys, Plates, &c.

DELPH. Bowls of all sizes, Plates, Dishes, Bottles & Basons, &c.

STONE. Printed, Printed & guilt & plain Cream colour, enameled, double & single Rose, Agate, Tortorise, Mellon, Colly flower, Pine-apple, Fruit Pattern, black, white, blue & white & Crown Ware of every sort, a good assortment of Chimney Tiles.

N. B. Great allowance to those who buy to sell again.—*Boston News-Letter*, Apr. 4, 1771.

ENGLISH WARE.—A Large Assortment of Cream-coloured, Fruit Pattern, enameled ditto, Colly flower, Pine-apple, Melon, Tortoise-shell, Agate-coloured, and divers other sorts of Earthern, Delph and Glass Ware, consisting of almost every Article of the kind usually wanted, great Part of which arrived in one of the last Vessels from England,

To be Sold at the Three Sugar-Loaves in Cornhill, a few doors Northward of the Heart and Crown, where those who incline to purchase by the Crate, may have an agreeable assortment packed up at very moderate Prices, as low as they are generally sold elsewhere. Among others are the following Articles; A Fine Assortment of Tea-pots, Coffee-pots, Sugar-pots, Milk-pots, Cups and Sawcers, Cannisters, &c. A great Variety of Mugs, Pitchers, Bowls and Basons, Tureens of various sizes, long and square Dishes, round and oval ditto, round & eight-square Plates, Breakfast Plates, plain, fruit pattern & enameled, Sauce-boats, Buttertubs, Desert Dishes, Nappies, Pudding Dishes & Patties, fine white stone Plates, very fine Delph Plates little inferior to China, Coarser ditto, several compleat Tea-table Sets of Children's cream-coloured Toys, Glass Salvers, with Jelly, Syllibub, and top Glasses, Decanters, Tumblers, and Wine Glasses, plain and engraved, Wine & Water, Cyder, and Beer Glasses, round and oval Pillar Cut Salts, and bonnet ditto, Cans, Mustards, etc. etc. —*Boston News-Letter*, Nov. 28, 1771.

PRINTED WARE.—E. Bridgham, at the STAFFORDSHIRE and LIVERPOOL Ware House in King street, advertised for Sale the largest Assortment of China, Glass, Delph, and Flint Ware, to be met with in any Part of America, including elegant Table Service compleat of printed, and printed and gilt Ware, Tea Setts of ditto, cream colour Pyramids, candlesticks, Ink stands, Chamber Lamps and a great Variety of other Articles never before imported; Glass Pyramids with Jelly Glasses, &c. Sconces, Globe and Barrel Lamps, etc. etc.—*Boston News-Letter*, Dec. 5, 1771.

DUTCH CHIMNEY TILE.—Thomas Walley, at his Store on

Dock Square, advertised Dutch Chimney Tile, from 3 s. to 9 s. per Dozen, Dutch Looking Glasses, Field Glasses, Bolting Cloths from "5 to 9 Dollars" each, Sheathing and White Brown Paper made at Milton, by the Ream, etc. etc. N. B. A Quantity of Mohogany Plank, to be sold very cheap.—*Boston News-Letter*, May 7, 1772.

INDIA CHINA WARE.—China Ware, Cheap for Cash. To be Sold by Samuel Gray, at the Three Sugar Loaves in Cornhill, near the Heart and Crown.

A neat assortment of India China Ware, viz: A Variety of pudding, sallad, and soop Dishes, round, eight-square, scolloped, and oval. Also, octagon, and mackrel Dishes, of different sizes,— and others, of various Forms and sizes. Likewise, a Variety of Table Plates and Butter Dishes, Patty pans, Sauce Boats, Bowls, Tea Cups and Saucers, Coffee ditto, and other articles—exceeding low for Cash, much cheaper than they are usually sold, (Cups and Saucers only excepted) and many of the Articles will be retailed at the first Sterling Cost.—*Boston News-Letter*, May 14, 1772.

WHITE AND BROWN LIVERPOOL WARE.—John Crosby, at the Sign of the Basket of Lemmons, South End, Boston, advertised, "a good assortment of white and brown Liverpool Bakeing Pudding Pans of the large and middling Size. Also, Meat Pyes, to be ready between 7 & 8 in the Evenings."—*Boston News-Letter*, Oct. 22, 1772.

CROCKERY WARE extreme cheap. *Ebenezer Bridgham* has now for Sale at his Staffordshire and Liverpool Warehouse in King Street, a Very Large Assortment of China, Glass, Delph & Flint Ware, viz. A beautiful Variety of printed and gilt and plain Cream-coloured Plates, Dishes, Candlesticks, Salvers, Pyramids, Egg Stands, Fruit Baskets and Drainers, Pickle Stands, Steak Dishes & Covers, Flummery Moulds, and Many other Articles *never before imported into this Place*. All Sorts of Agate, Tortoise, Pineapple, Colly flower, Fruit pattern, enamel'd, black, brown, white, blue & white and red Ware. Very neat cut, engrav'd and labell'd Gallon, two quart, quart and pint Glass Decanters, Tumblers, Beer, Wine and Cyder Glasses, Salts, Candlesticks, Salvers, and every kind of Glass Ware, Boxes of Glass Ware, neatly sorted for Shop Keepers, China coffee pots, tea pots, sugars, bowls, cups & saucers, &c. &c. a few compleat sets of Tea China.—*Boston News-Letter*, Dec. 31, 1772.

CREAM COLORED DELPH WARE.—Elizabeth Perkins has for Sale at her shop, two doors below the British Coffee House in King-Street, Boston,

A very fine and Genteel Assortment of Cream colour'd Delph, Flint & Glass Ware, wholesale or retail, among which are cut, label'd, enamel'd, engrav'd and plain Quart, Pint and ½ Pint Decanters, Cruits, Salts, Wine and Water Glasses, Tumblers, Jellies, Syllabub Glasses, Orange Glasses, Salvers, Sugar Dishes, Pattie, Sweetmeat and Pickle Saucers, Royal Arch Mason Glasses, Salt Linings, Water Glasses, Candle Sticks, etc.—*Boston Evening Post*, July 2, 1773.

# GLASS

BRISTOL WARE such "as Pipes, Glasses, Bottles," &c. were advertised by Messieurs Banisters.—*Boston News-Letter*, June 9/16, 1712.

BRISTOL GLASS.—"Drinking Glasses, Decanters," imported from Bristol.—*Boston News-Letter*, Apr. 26/May 4, 1719.

GLASS LAMPS.—Lately imported from London, a fresh Parcel of choice Looking-Glasses of divers Sorts and Sizes; as also fine Glass Lamps and Lanthorns well gilt and painted, both convex and plain; being suitable for Halls, Stair-cases, or other Passageways. To be sold at the Glass-Shop in Queen Street, Boston. There is likewise Japan-work of all Sorts done and Sold, and Old Looking-Glasses are new Quick-silver'd at the Place above said by William Randle.—*Boston News-Letter*, Aug. 17/24, 1719.

ENGLISH GLASS.—Lately Imported from England, and to be Sold by Mrs. Rebecca Abbot in Cornhill near the Town Dock, Fine Glass Ware, viz. Decanters, Salvers, Punch Bowls, Sugar Pots, Candlesticks, Barrel Canns, Whip Syllabub, Jelly & double Flint Wine Glasses; with sundry other sorts. Likewise fine white Glass Japann'd; Also all sorts of Common Glasses, with divers sorts of fine Earthern & Stone Ware. All which may be had in larger or smaller quantities.—*New England Journal*, Jan. 24, 1731/2.

She also advertised in the July 31, 1732, issue of the *New England Journal*; Glass Montelks, Baskets, Bird Fountains, Pistols; Tea Setts of White, Blew and Jappan'd Glass; Also all sorts of White, Brown & Blew Stone and fine Earthern Ware.

WORMED WINE GLASSES and silver-handled knives and forks, for sale.—*Boston News-Letter*, Mar. 13, 1746.

BROKEN GLASS.—To be sold, by Stephen Whiting, at the Rose and Crown in Union Street, opposite Capt. Storer's, Looking-Glasses, Double-Flint Decanters, single Flint Wine Glasses by the Dozen, a choice Sortment of Maps, Prints and Metzotintoes.

N. B. He also buys broken Glass.—*Boston News-Letter*, Sept. 29, 1748.

FLINT GLASS.—Imported in the last Ships, and to be Sold by Henry Barnes at his Shop at the lower End of King street, a variety of single flint and double flint Glass Ware, consisting of Wine Glasses, Beakers, Salt sellers, Cruits, Decanters, Pitchers, green and white Pocket Bottles, Mugs, Cans, washing Cups and Saucers, Candlesticks, incorperating Cruets, Urinals, Jellys, Sillabubs, Bird Boxes, Fountains, likewise a large Assortment of Earthern Ware, as Plates, Dishes, Bowles, Chamber Pots, Cups and Saucers, stand Basons, white stone quart and pint Mugs, Tea Cups and Saucers, Bowles, Punch Strainers, Dutch Ware, as gallon Jugs, two quart Jugs, quart and pint Mugs, Chamber Pots, etc. etc.—*Boston Evening Post*, Apr. 30, 1750.

FLINT GLASS.—Henry Barnes, at his Shop at the lower end of King Street, advertised among other items:—Double and Single Flint Glasses, Saltsellers, Crewits, Beakers, Milk Pots, 3 Feet Salts ditto, Salvers in sets, Candlesticks, Bird Fountains, Mustard Pots, &c. white and blue and white Stone Tea Cups and Saucers, Tea Pots, Bowles, quart Mugs, Milk Jugs, handled Cups, white and brown, Cream coloured and Tortoiseshell Tea Pots, Sugar Dishes, black Tea Pots and Milk Pots, Chamber Pots, Delph Bowles, etc., There also is a very large Looking Glass, with a gilt Frame, six Feet long, and two Feet two Inches wide, very cheap for the Cash.—*Boston Evening Post*, Mar. 11, 1751.

TWIST STEMED WINE GLASSES.—Just Imported and to be Sold by Henry Barnes, at his Shop at the lower end of King street:—Double Flint new fashion twist stemed Wine Glasses, Quart, Pint and half Pint Glass Cans, Jelly and Syllabub Glasses, Salvers, Cyder Glasses, Patty Pans Ditto, Decanters, with ground Tops, incorporating Crewits, etc. etc. blue and white Dutch Stone Ware of all sorts, Delph and Stone Ware, consisting of Plates, Bowles, Dishes, Mugs, flower pots, Coffee and Tea Dishes, Butter Plates, brown Stone Mugs, Dishes and Patty Pans, Pickle Pots, 3 gallon Jugs, etc., long and short Pipes, etc.—*Boston Evening Post*, May 27, 1751.

CIDER BEAKERS.—Henry Barnes advertised a variety of articles including:—Cyder Beakers; Delph Flower Bottles, Wash Basons, Mint Stands, &c. White Stone scolloped Plates; blue and white sprigged Stone scolloped Dishes, Ditto Dutch and White Chamber Pots, etc. etc.—*Boston Evening Post*, Oct. 14, 1751.

GLASS FOR CHARIOT.—Any Gentleman that has got a spare Front Glass for a Chariot, either in one or two Parts, of the following Dimensions, viz.
Without a Frame, 3 Feet, 1 Inch long and 2 Feet & half wide.
With the Frame, 3 Feet, 3 & ¼th Inch long and 2 Feet & 2 & ¾th Inches wide.
As also a Garden Rolling Stone, Eighteen Inches long, to dispose of at a Reasonable Rate, may hear of a Chapman for both or either of the above Particulars (with his Cash ready) by enquiring of the Printer hereof.—*Boston Evening Post*, Nov. 19, 1753.

GLASS BOTTLES.—To be Sold by Jonathan Williams, at his Warehouse, on the South Side of the Town-Dock, near the Stamp-Office: Sundry sorts of glass bottles, viz. square, case and round bottles, from one pint to a gallon, Philadelphia Flour, Wheat and good Bohea Tea.—*Boston Gazette*, Jan. 12, 1756.

GLASS BOTTLES.—To be sold by *Jonathan Williams*, on the south-side of the Town Dock, near the Stamp Office; all sorts of Glass Bottles, by large or small quantities, Case and Pickle Bottles from one quart to a gallon; quart and pint Black Bottles by the Gross, Glasses for Chymists, and Window Glasses of different sizes.—*Boston Gazette*, Aug. 23, 1756.

LAMP.—"A large Lamp," sold with other household goods. —*Boston Gazette*, Sept. 27, 1756; also in Mar. 7, 1757.

WORMED GLASS.—"New fashioned Worm'd and cutt Wine Glasses, the best gilded and painted servers," for sale.—*Boston Gazette*, Dec. 12, 1757; also "a large Glass Lanthorn for an Entry Way."

FLINT GLASS.—To be sold by John Dobel, in King street, at the Sign of the Two Sugar-Loaves, A good Assortment of double and single Flint Wine-Glasses, Decanters, Beakers, Salts, Crewits, large Wine and Water Glasses; a good Assortment of blue and white Stone Ware, consisting of Plates, Dishes, Mugs, Tea-Pots, black Stone and Tortoise-shell Ware.—*Boston News-Letter*, Mar. 21, 1760.

CASE BOTTLES.—"Quart, half Gallon and Gallon square Case Bottles, half Gallon and Gallon wide-mouth'd Pickle Bottles," by Jonathan Williams near the Swing Bridge.—*Boston Gazette*, July 28, 1760.

ENGRAVED GLASS.—"Hogsheads best engrav'd flower'd wine glasses and decanters; crates of white stone cups and saucers, (boxes of China tea cups and saucers, plates and bowls), London pipes; 7 by 5, 8 by 6 and 9 by 7 window glass; crate glass," just imported from London and Bristol and for sale by Lewis Deblois. —*Boston Gazette*, June 8, 1761.

WINE GLASSES.—"Wine-Glasses of the newest engrav'd and cutt-fashion, of different Patterns; decanters, flowered & lettered jappan'd Roman Waiters, jappan'd Bread and Fruit Baskets, large jappan'd Trays, and Earthern Ware," to be Sold by *William Maxwell*, in King Street.—*Boston Gazette*, July 6, 1761.

TABLE GLASS.—To be Sold by Mary Gallop, in Hanover-Street, near the Blue-Ball, Boston; a Variety of newfashion, plain and engrav'd Wine Glasses, Crewets and Decanters; compleat Setts of Salvers with Top Glasses; cut Shells for Sweet-Meats; Glass Baskets; Jelly Glasses; Sillibub Glasses; engrav'd Free-Mason Glasses, with a Number of other Articles of Glass Ware; blue and white and burnt China Tea Cups and Saucers; together with a large Assortment of Stone, Delph and Tortoishell Ware. . . . —*Boston Gazette*, Nov. 23, 1761.

NEW FASHION GLASS.—Samuel Fletcher advertised to sell for Cash:—capers, oil, anchovies, raisins, currants, Turkey figgs, etc., Castile soap, Redwood, chimney tiles, best blue and white China cups and saucers, dishes, butter boats, and plates, China plates of all sorts; coffee cups, handle ditto, quart and two quart bowls. A variety of new fashioned Glass, as Wine Glasses, Beer Glasses, and Cyder Glasses, Vinegar and Oil Crewits, Mustard Pots, Sugar ditto, Beakers, Decanters of all Sorts, Freemason Glasses, Glass Inks, Glass Cans, Salts and Cream Pots, Glass Lamps and

Pitchers, Glass Candlesticks; japanned Salvers; a great variety of Earthern, Stone and Delph Ware; etc. etc.—*Boston News-Letter*, Jan. 7, 1762.

NEWCASTLE BOTTLES.—Best New-Castle Bottles, (full Quart) either in Hampers, or loose, to be sold by *Arthur Savage* and Comp. at their Store on the Town Dock.—*Boston Gazette*, Apr. 12, 1762.

BRISTOL GLASS.—"Boxes of Glass Ware, and Hogsheads of Earthen Ware, neatly sorted, Wine and Beer Glasses and Decanters curiously engrav'd with the Mason's Arms," imported in the last Ships from London and Bristol, were advertised by Joseph Barrell, at his store on King Street.—*Boston Gazette*, July 11, 1763.

NEWCASTLE QUART BOTTLES, at £15. per groce.—*Boston Gazette*, July 25, 1763.

FLOWERED DECANTERS.—Mary Gallop, in Hanover-Street, has for Sale Flower'd Decanters, Wine Glasses, Cruets, Glass Salvers of all sizes, brown Stone Baking Dishes, Muggs, Bowls, with a variety of other Stone Ware.—*Boston Gazette*, Nov. 26, 1764.

GLASS BOTTLES in Hampers, to be Sold by Nathaniel Coffin.—*Boston News-Letter*, Feb. 14, 1765.

GLASSWARE.—Samuel Gray, at the Shop of Captain Pattin, deceased, in Cornhill, has for sale, a large and elegant Assortment of GLASS WARE, Consisting of Salvers of different sizes, & top Glasses, cut shank Wine Glasses & Bumpers, cut shank ditto, engraved, Orange Water Glasses ditto, cut Quart Decanters ditto, and other Decanters of different sizes, Tall Wine Glasses, engrav'd, cut round & oval Pillar Salts, cut Bonnet Salts, Pint and Half-pint Cans, Nest Tumblers, engraved Tumblers, & tall ditto, cut Crewits, tall Crewits, plain Wine Glasses, Bumpers, ribb'd Jellies, ribb'd Syllibubs, Mustard Pots, &c. &c.

Also, a great variety of Cream-coloured Ware, Delph, and Stone Ware and a general Assortment of Groceries.—*Boston News-Letter*, May 16, 1771

STIEGEL GLASS.—Philadelphia, June 27. At the last Meeting

of the *American Philosophical Society* held in this city, were exhibited several specemins of Flint-Glass, viz. decanters, wine glass, beer glasses, &c. manufactured by Mr. William Henry Stiegel, of Lancaster county, which was judged equal in beauty and quality to the generality of Flint Glass imported from England.—*Boston News-Letter*, July 11, 1771 (*sup.*).

DIAMOND CUT GLASS.—William Lambert, at the three Sugar Loaves, a little above the Draw Bridge, advertised an Assortment of Glass and China Ware, viz: Diamond Cut Cruits, plain ditto with Cut Tops, Mason Glasses, engraved with the different Jewels with the hand and hand Flower, enamel'd Ale Glasses, ribb'd ditto, double flint Pint and half Pint Mugs, a Variety of the newest Fashion enamel'd and cut Decanters, Jelly Glasses, Mustard Pots, ribb'd Top Glasses, etc.—*Boston News-Letter*, Oct. 10, 1771.

FLINT GLASS.—A great Variety of double and single Flint Glass, cream-coloured, Delph and Stone Ware, (Part of it being fresh Assortments of the newest Fashion) to be Sold Wholesale and Retail by *Samuel Gray*, at his Shop in Cornhill (near the Heart and Crown) and Crockery Store in Pudding-Lane (a little Southward of the Lower End of the Town House). Among the other Articles are the following, Glass Salvers or Waiters, chiefly from 9 to 13 inches, to be sold either in Pyramids or singly, Orange or Top Glasses, & Wine Glasses, of various sorts, Common Jellies and Syllabubs (some very neat) from 5 s. to 8 s. a dozen, a Quantity of Decanters of almost every Kind, plain and engraved, a few dozen best Diamond Cut Jellies and Syllabubs, a beautiful Assortment of Wine and Water, Cyder and Beer Glasses, Quart, pint, and half-pint Glass Mugs and Canns, Tumblers or Beakers of many sorts and sizes, Crewits, plain, cut and engraved, Salts of the best and common sort, Glass Sugar Bowls, Cream Jugs, and Mustard Pots, Water Guglets, Bird Fountains, sinking Proofs, &c. A large Assortment of cream-coloured and other sorts of Tea-Pots, Middling & small Coffee Pots, large do elegantly printed, Cups and Saucers and Cream Jugs of many sorts, Sugar Tubs and Canisters, Cream coloured Oval Dishes, royal Pattern, in Nests, or singly, Cream coloured Plates from 4 s. 8 d. to 6 s. 8 d. a dozen, White Stone Plates, Various Sizes of cream coloured baking Dishes from 1 s. to 1 s. 8 d. a piece. Delph, cream coloured, brown, Tortoishell & enameled Bowls of many sizes, Cream col'd Wash Basons, best Delph Guglets & Basons, Cream coloured, brown, blue & white, Tortoishell, & other Mugs and Pitchers, Turrenes, Butter Tubs, Sauce Boats, Mustard Pots, also a very good Assortment of China Pudding Dishes and other China Ware.—*Boston News-Letter*, Dec. 31, 1772.

WHITE FLINT GLASS.—To be sold for cash, White Flint Glass Ware per Box, viz. Common sorted Crewets & Salts, ditto. Tumblers, ditto. Wine Glasses, all 25 to the Doz. at 4/6 d. Ster. per Dozen, Ditto Mustard Pots, 25 to the Doz. at 6/6 d. per doz. Per the Crate, Apothecaries green Glass Vials sorted at 10 s. Sterling per Groce. Per the Crate, Green Half-Point [*sic*] Dram Bottles, 144 to the Groce, at 10/6 d. Sterl. per Groce. Brass Kettles, at 16½ Sterling per lb. Enquire of the Printers. —*Boston News-Letter*, Nov. 17, 1774.

### GERMANTOWN (BRAINTREE) GLASS WORKS

TUESDAY last [Sept. 19] a ship arrived here from Holland, with about 300 Germans, Men, Women and Children, some of whom are going to settle at Germantown (a part of Braintree), and the others in the Eastern Parts of this Province. . . . among the artificers come over in this Ship, there are a number of Men skilled in making of Glass, of various Sorts, and a House proper for carrying on that useful Manufacture, will be erected at Germantown as soon as possible.—*Boston Evening Post*, Sept. 25, 1752.

Notice is hereby given, That for the future none will be admitted to see the new manufactory at Germantown [Braintree], unless they pay at least one shilling lawfull money; and they are desired not to ask above three or four Questions, and not to be offended if they have not a satisfactory answer to all or any of them.

*Note.*—The manufactory has received considerable Damage, and been very much retarded by the great Number of People which are constantly resorting to the House.—*Boston Gazette*, Sept. 4, 1753.

We hear from German Town, that the Glass-House erected there was struck by Lightning on Thursday Night last, which set Fire to the same, and in a short Time it was entirely consumed. —*Boston Gazette*, May 26, 1755.

About Three o'Clock last Thursday Morning, the Glass-House in *Braintree* was set on Fire by Lightning, and entirely consumed in Ashes, with Six other Buildings contiguous to it, together with all the Utinsels and Stock therein.—*Boston Evening Post*, June 2, 1755.

These are to Advertize the Publick, That Jonathan Williams has undertaken to carry on the Glass-Works at Germantown, during one Fire at least, and expects to make Glass in about a month or five weeks at farthest: And such Persons as may want Bottles, Case-Bottles, Retorts, or other Kinds of Glass, may be supply'd in Reasonable Terms, by applying (by Letter or otherwise) to said Williams, on the Mill-Bridge, in Boston, or to Joseph Palmer, in Germantown.—*Boston Evening Post*, July 14, 1755.

Lottery for the encouragement of Germantown in Braintree and for carrying on the Cyder manufactory there, advertised, according to act of the General Court passed Apr., 1757. [One column in length.]—*Boston Gazette*, Oct. 3, 1757.

Joseph Palmer of Germantown in Braintree, makes (equal to any imported) Snuff-Bottles, Pint, Quart, two Quart and Gallon Bottles, &c. Also Pots for Pickles, Conserves, &c., of all sizes; Likewise most sorts of Chymical Vessels, &c. N. B. He gives a Pistareen per Hundred Weight for broken green and black Glass; and two Coppers per Pound for White Glass.—*Boston News-Letter*, Apr. 4, 1760.

Manufactured at *Germantown*, by Joseph Palmer, and to be Sold by William Belcher, opposite the Old Brick Meeting House; Round and square Bottles, from one to four Quarts; also Cases of Bottles of all Sizes and Chymical Vessels, &c. Also to be Sold by said Belcher, a few Chests of Glass Ware, and an Anchor about 1100 wt.—*Boston Gazette*, July 28, 1760.

Front and End View of a Two-Drawer Connecticut Chest

# FURNITURE

## CABINETMAKERS

BENJAMIN ALLEN, of Braintree, cabinet maker, sold land.—*Boston Gazette*, May 23, 1757.

PIERPONT BACON, of Colchester, Conn., cabinet maker, lost his shop, tools and stock of furniture by fire; Loss £100. L. M.—*Boston Gazette*, Jan. 14. 1760.

JOHN BROCAS was a cabinet maker with a shop in Union St. Boston, in Feb. 1736-7.—*New England Journal*, Mar. 8, 1736/7.

MR. BROCAS, cabinet maker, of Boston, lost his shop and tools by fire.—*Boston Gazette*, Feb. 28/Mar. 7, 1737.

WILLIAM COFFIN, cabinet maker, of Boston, advertised that his wife had run away from him.—*Boston Gazette*, Dec. 25, 1758.

DANIEL COLLINS, cabinet maker, of Boston, settlement of estate. —*Boston Gazette*, Sept. 25, 1758.

JOB COIT, deceased, of Boston, settlement of estate.—*Boston News-Letter*, Dec. 16, 1742.

JOB COIT, cabinet maker, of Boston, settlement of estate.—*Boston Gazette*, Oct. 22, 1751.

MR. JOHN DAVIS, Cabinet-Maker in Summer-Street, has for sale extraordinary good English Glew, by Wholesale or Retail, at the cheapest Rates, for ready Cash.—*Boston News-Letter*, Apr. 8/15, 1736.

WILLIAM FULLERTON, chairmaker, of Boston, mentioned.— *Boston News-Letter*, Mar. 11/18, 1742.

WILLIAM FULLERTON, of Boston, chairmaker, settlement of estate.—*Boston Gazette*, Mar. 20, 1750.

THOMAS GIBBONS and LENIER KENN, cabinet-makers in Boston, advertised dissolution of partnership.—*Boston News-Letter*, Aug. 23/30, 1739.

FRANCIS HUNT, joiner, of Boston, settlement of estate.—*Boston Gazette*, Mar. 13, 1753.

JOHN JENKINS, joiner, of Boston, settlement of estate.—*Boston Gazette*, Apr. 21, 1747.

SARAH LANE, widow of John Lane, carries on the Business of Caining Chairs.—*New England Journal*, June 14, 1737.

SAMUEL MATTOCKS, chairmaker, of Boston, mentioned.—*Boston News-Letter*, Mar. 6/13, 1728/9.

THOMAS SHERBURNE, cabinet maker, of Boston, settled the estate of Captain Sherburne.—*Boston Gazette*, May 22, 1753.

THOMAS SHERBURNE.—Made and sold by Thomas Sherburne, at his Shop in Back-Street, Boston; all sorts of Cabinet-Ware, in the neatest Manner; such as Desks and Bookcases, Cases of Drawers, Buroe Tables, Chamber Tables, Dining Tables, Tea-Tables, Screens, &c.—*Boston Gazette*, Apr. 22, 1765.

DAVID SNODEN, chairmaker, of Boston, settlement of estate.—*Boston Gazette*, Jan. 27, 1747.

SAMUEL WHEELER, chair maker, of Boston, estate settled.—*Boston News-Letter*, Mar. 17, 1748.

## FURNITURE

CANNOPIE BEDS.—A Couple of very good Cannopie Beds lately come from England to be Sold on reasonable terms, by Rupert Lord Upholsterer, and to be seen at Mr. Ramies House in Corn-Hill the next door to the Post Office, Boston.—*Boston News-Letter*, Jan. 4/11, 1713/14.

CANE CHAIRS, lately arrived from England.—*Boston News-Letter*, Apr. 19/26, 1714.

NEW FASHIONED BED.—To be Sold a Fine new Fashioned Bed that came over in the last ship, new Fashioned Chests of Drawers, Walnut-Tree, and Wainscot Desks, Tables, Glasses, Book Cases, &c. All of the best workmanship. To be seen at Mr. Bannister's Warehouse near the Swing Bridge, Boston.—*Boston News-Letter*, May 10/17, 1714.

LOOKING-GLASSES of all sorts, Glass Sconces, Cabbinetts, Escrutoires, Chests of Drawers, Tables, Beaufetts, Writing Desks, Bookcases with Desk, old Glasses new Silvered, and all sorts of Japan-work. Done and Sold by *William Randle* at the Sign of the Cabbinett, a Looking-Glass Shop in Queen-Street near the Town-House, Boston.—*Boston News-Letter*, Apr. 25/May 2, 1715.

CANE FURNITURE.—Lately arrived from England, Cain chairs and Couches, with a Silk Bed and Cushions, new Fashion Looking-Glasses and Chimney-Glasses, to be sold by Messeurs *Hedman* and *Lewis*, at the Lower end of King-Street, Boston.—*Boston News-Letter*, May 9/16, 1715.

BED-SCREWS.—Mr. *John Barnard* of Boston, having some time since Lent a Pair of large Bed-screws, These are desiring the Borrower to return them again to the owner, as he desires to Borrow again, & avoid the Curse due to the Wicked, that Borrow but never Pay.—*Boston News-Letter*, Oct. 22/29, 1716.

SCONCES.—Lately come from England, a parcel of Large Looking-Glasses, Sconces, Cabinets, Desks and Book Cases with Glass Doors; To be sold at Reasonable Rates, and to be seen at *William Hutchinson*, Esq: his Warehouse in Merchants Row at the Town Dock in Boston, up one pair of Stairs.—*Boston News-Letter*, June 2/9, 1718.

SLATE TABLES and slate mentioned (no other furniture).—*Boston News-Letter*, Sept. 29/Oct. 6, 1718.

DUTCH TEA TABLES.—Lately Arrived from London, & are to be Sold by Giles Dulake Tidmarsh at his Warehouse No. 4 on the Long Wharffe, Fine Dutch Tea Tables, as Hand Boards and Looking Glasses, new Fashion.—*Boston Gazette*, Nov. 19/26, 1722.

LOOKING GLASSES.—William Price, against the West-End of the Town-House in Boston, advertised "All Sorts of Looking-Glasses of the newest Fashion, & Jappan Work, viz. Chest of Drawers, Corner Cupboards, Large & Small Tea Tables, &c. done after the best manner by one late from London."—*Boston Gazette*, Apr. 4/11, 1726.

HOUSEHOLD FURNISHINGS.—*At Vendue*, by Mr Daniel Goffe, at the *Sun Tavern* in Dock Square, three Feather Beds, two Bedsteads and Curtains, three or four large Looking-Glasses, Cane Chairs, Couches, Sconces, Tea-Tables, Pewter, New and Second-

Handed, one Clock, Ruggs, Quilts, some Pictures, together with Sundry other things.—*New England Journal*, Mar. 20, 1727.

EMBROIDERED BED.—"A fine Imbroidered Bed and Curtains," at auction.—*Boston Gazette*, Apr. 8/15, 1728.

CEDAR DESK.—A fine Red New Cedar Desk, to be Sold a Pennyworth for ready money. Inquire of the Printer hereof. —*Boston News-Letter*, Nov. 28/Dec. 5, 1728.

BEDSTEAD.—A Handsome Bedstead with Calaminco Curtains, Vallens, Tester & Window Curtains, & also a Walnut Tea Table to be sold enquire of Mr. John Boydell.—*Boston Gazette*, Mar. 31/Apr. 7, 1729.

GOV. BURNET'S FURNITURE.— Boston, October the 2d. 1729. *To be exposed to Sale by Publick Vendue on Tuesday next at Two in the afternoon, at the House wherein his late Excellency Governour* Burnet *dwelt in* Boston, *sundry sorts of Household Goods & Furniture viz. Clocks, Glass-sconces, Tables, China-ware, Glass-ware, Pewter, Kitchen Utensils of Copper, Tin, Brass & Iron, a Japan'd Cabinet, Tea Tables, a Scriptore with Glass doors, Bedsteads, Beds and Bedding of sundry sorts, Gilt Leather Screens, Table Linnen, Sadles, Bridles, and other Horse Furniture, Horses for a Coach and Saddle, a Coach, a Chariot, and a Chaise with their Carriages and Harness, Fuzees & Pistols: Two Negro Women; about* 12 *Years Service of a Malatto Boy: sundry Pictures & Prints, two Water Engines, Glass Bottles, sundry sorts of Liquor in Bottles, a Pipe of old Madera Wine, Sweet-meats & Pickles, and sundry other things.*

*The Sale to be continu'd from day to day 'till all Sold.*—*Boston News-Letter*, Sept. 25/Oct. 2, 1729.

GOV. BURNET'S FURNITURE.—On Monday next at 2 o'Clock in the Afternoon, will be exposed to Sale by Publick Vendue, at the House wherein his late Excellency Governour Burnet have dwelt, sundry sorts of Household Goods, viz.: a Japan'd Cabinet, a fine Scriptoire, Gilt Leather Skreens, Clocks, Tables, Chairs, Bedsteds, a fine Chints Bed, with other Beds and Bedding, an Easy Chair, Pewter, a large Jack, and other Kitchen Utensils of Copper, Brass, and Iron. Saddles and Bridles, 3 Coach-Horses, a Negro Woman, about 12 Years service of a Mollatto boy, sundry curious Prints and Pictures, 2 Water Engines, Empty Glass Bottles, some gilt and Plain Paper, some Sugar, Rice, Pease, Candles, Pickles and Sweetmeats, and sundry other Things.

*N.B.* The Goods may be viewed 2 or 3 Days before the Sale, and there is also to be view'd and sold (but not for Publick Vendue) a Coach, a Chariot, a Chaise and a Sley with their Carriages, &c. as also a Harpsicord and other Musical Instruments, and sundry Mathematical Instruments.—*Boston Gazette,* Oct. 6/13, 1729.

Gov. Burnet's Furniture.—*This present Thursday at 2 o'th'Clock in the Afternoon will be exposed to Sale at Publick Vendue, at the House wherein his Excellency Governour* Burnet *here dwelt in; sundry sorts of Household Goods, &c. viz a Japann'd Cabinet, a fine Scruitore, Gilt Leather Screens, a handsome Clock, an easy Chair, a fine Chints Bed, with other Beds & Bedding, Tables, Chairs, Bed-steads, Pewter, a large Jack, and other Kitchen Utensils of Copper, Brass and Iron, Saddles, a Coach horse, Water Engines, Empty Glass Bottles, A Negro Woman, About 12 Years Service of a Mollatto Boy, Curious Prints & Pictures, some Gilt & Plain Writing Paper, Sugar, Rice, Pease, Candles, Pickles & Sweet-Meats, and sundry other things.*—*Boston News-Letter,* Oct. 16/23, 1729.

Publick Vendue.—At 5 o'Clock in the Afternoon will be sold by T. Fleet, at the Heart and Crown, in Cornhill.—Bedding, Several Suits of Curtains and Bedsteads, a fine new Silk Damask Quilt and Quilted Cushions of the same, Black Walnut Chest of Drawers and Desk, Brass Candlesticks, Iron Dogs, sundry Suits of wearing apparel for men, new Castor Hats, China Ware, Rummolds, Druggets, . . . —*Boston News-Letter,* May 18/25, 1732.

Publick Vendue.—This Day at Five o'Clock in the Afternoon, will be Sold by Publick Vendue, at the Sign of the Heart and Crown in Cornhill, Boston, sundry sorts of valuable Household Goods, viz.: Feather Beds, Chest of Drawers, Cane and Leather Chairs, a Tea Table, . . . a Dressing Glass, . . . a fine

Chamber Grate, Wiggs and Boxes, . . . *N.B.* The Buyers may depend upon having fair Play, good Liquor, and if they are Wise, good Bargains.—*Boston News-Letter*, Mar. 23/30, 1732.

HOUSEHOLD FURNISHINGS.—This Afternoon at 3 o'Clock will be Sold by PUBLICK VENDUE, by Daniel Goffe, at the Dwelling House of Mr. Jonathan Barnard, over against the Town-House in Cornhill, sundry sorts of Household Goods, consisting of Beds, Bedding, a Couch, Chairs, handsome Japan'd Tea Tables, Walnut and Mahogany Tables, Chest of Drawers, Peer Glasses, Sconces, Glass Arms, China Ware, Metzotinto and other Prints, several valuable large Pieces of Paintings, one handsome large Carpet 9 Foot 6 Inches by 6 Foot 6 Inches, a fashionable yellow Camblet Bed lin'd with Satten, a great easy Chair and Window Curtains, suitable for a Room, a Field Bedstead and Bed, the covering a Blew Harrateen, Kitchen Furniture, as Pewter of the best sort, Copper, Brass and Iron, a parcel of Books and some Shop Goods. —*Boston News-Letter*, May 8/15, 1735.

BEDSTEAD—A Coach-head Bed and Bedstead with its Curtains and Vallents, &c. as it stands, being a blew China. To be disposed off. Inquire of the Printer.—*Boston Gazette*, June 16/23, 1735.

BED HANGINGS.—To be sold by Mrs. Susanna Condy, near the Old North Meeting House, a fine Fustian Suit of Curtains, with a Cornish and Base Mouldings of a beautiful Figure, drawn in London, on Frame full already worked; as also enough of the same for half a dozen Chairs. *N. B.* The Bed may be had by itself.—*Boston Gazette*, May 24/31, 1736.

PRESS BED.—A Very good Press-Case for a Bed, to be Sold. Enquire of the Printer.—*Boston News-Letter*, Oct. 28/Nov. 4, 1736.

MOHAIR BED.—To be Sold reasonably for ready money, or on good Security, a yellow Mohair Bed lined with a Persian of the same Colour, and six Chairs of the same Mohair, little the worse for wear. Inquire of J. Boydell.—*Boston Gazette*, Oct. 17/24, 1737.

FURNITURE AT AUCTION.—To be sold by Auction, Household Furniture of the late Mr. Pyam Blowers, including: Fine Sconce

Glasses, large Looking Glasses, Leather-Bottom Chairs, sundry Mehogany and other Tables, a good Couch Squab and Pillow, a very handsome Yellow Damask Bed, an Easy Chair, a neat case of Drawers, . . . two Silver Watches, sundry sorts of good China Ware, etc.—*Boston News-Letter*, May 17/24, 1739.

"FINE WICKER CRADLE lined with Silk handsomely quilted," with quilt, to be sold at vendue.—*Boston Gazette*, Dec. 25, 1744.

PHANCERED DRAWS.—"A beautiful phancer'd Case of Draws" and "a very large Black Walnut Table fit for an Ordinary," to be sold at vendue.—*Boston Gazette*, May 21, 1745.

FURNITURE AT AUCTION.—To be Sold by Publick Vendue on Monday next at 3 o'Clock, Afternoon, at the House of Charles Paxton, Esq., the following Goods, viz.: A fashionable crimson Damask Furniture with Counterpain and two Sets of Window Curtains, and Vallans of the same Damask. Eight Walnut Tree Chairs, stuft Back and Seats covered with the same Damask, Eight crimson China Cases for ditto, one easy Chair and Cushion, same Damask, and Case for ditto. Twelve Walnut Tree chairs, India Backs, finest Cane, and sundry other valuable Household Furniture.—*Boston News-Letter*, Jan. 9, 1746.

DAMASK FURNITURE.—Thursday next at four o'Clock in the Afternoon, at the Royal Exchange Tavern in King street, Boston, will certainly be Sold by publick Vendue, the following Goods, viz.: A fashionable crimson Damask Furniture [*sic*], with Counterpain & two Setts of Window Curtains, and Vallans of the same Damask. Eight Walnut Tree Chairs, Stuff Back and Seats, cover'd with the same Damask, Eight crimson China Cases for ditto. One easy Chair and Cushion same Damask, and Case for ditto. Twelve Walnut Tree Chairs, India Back, finest Cane, with Sundry other valuable Household Goods.—*Boston Gazette*, Jan. 21, 1746.

COACH BED.—To be Sold, A crimson Harrateen Coach, Bed, Bedstead, and Feather-bed, six small chairs, and one two-arm Chair, with crimson Harrateen Seats, a Table, and two small Pictures. Enquire of the Printer.—*Boston News-Letter*, June 25, 1747.

HOUSEHOLD FURNITURE.—To Morrow being the 21st Instant will be Sold by Benjamin Church. A Variety of Choice Household Furniture, viz. One work'd Cloth Bed, lin'd with Silk, and Bedstead, one Quilt, one Easy Chair yellow China with a green Damask Cover, six black Walnut Chairs, with work'd Cloth bottoms; one India Cabinet, with a carv'd Gilt Frame; one Green Camblet Bed and bedstead, one large Looking Glass; about a Dozen Cane Chairs, one ditto Couch; one India Tea Table; a brass Hearth Shovel and Tongs; two fine large Matts for Floors. Said Articles to be seen before the Sale: and the Sale to begin at 3 o'Clock.—*Boston Gazette*, Dec. 20, 1748.

LOOKING GLASS.—At a public vendue of the household goods of the late Mr. Samuel Haly, "Painter stainer," at his Mansion house near Charlestown Ferry, were sold, among other items: a large handsome Looking Glass, blew, white and yellow Earthen Wares, 2 large Jarrs for salting down Pork, a large Stone Jarr for Pickles, a Bedstead in a Painted Press, Pictures in Gilt and Black Frames, etc.—*Boston Gazette*, Jan. 30, 1750.

BUREAU.—"New-fashion buro, oval tables," etc., for sale.—*Boston Gazette*, May 1, 1750.

LOOKING GLASS.—To be Sold an Extraordinary handsome and fashionable Looking Glass, with one of the best of Stones; A handsome pair of Large Brass Andirons; A large China Bowle, and a Mahogany Table, one Dozen of the largest Size of Massatento gilt Pictures. Inquire of the Printer.—*Boston Gazette*, April 30, 1751.

STONE TABLES.—To be Sold by Publick Vendue, at the late Dwelling House of Mr Thomas Hawding at New-Boston [West End of Boston]: a variety of fashionable Furniture, consisting of Mahogany, India and Stone Tables, Buroes, Chairs, Chest Drawers, several Harrateen Beds, Pear and Sconce Glasses, with a beautiful eight Day Clock, etc.—*Boston Evening Post*, July 29, 1751.

BUREAU.—To be Sold a handsome well finish'd Mehogany Desk, also a very neat made Beurau; inquire of the Printers.—*Boston Gazette*, Sept. 3, 1751.

MARBLE TABLE.—To be sold a publick Vendue, European goods of various sorts, including a large Marble Table, a handsome Black Walnut Desk, a Pair of beautiful Guilt Sconces, etc.—*Boston Gazette,* Oct. 22, 1751.

CARPETS.—Taken off a Shop Window at Noon, 2 small English Carpets for Bed sides, etc. etc.—*Boston Evening Post*, Feb. 24, 1752.

BLACK WALNUT CHAIRS.—To be sold at Publick Vendue, at the House of Mr. Woodle's at the lower end of Cold Lane, Boston,—Black Walnut Chairs, Mehogany Tables, a beautiful Clock, a marble Side-Table, Desk and Bookcase, Bedsteds of black Walnut, Curtains, etc.—*Boston Gazette,* Oct. 10, 1752.

HARRITEEN CURTAINS.—"Chairs with Hariteen, Leather and Straw Bottoms" and "a compleat Suit of green Harriteen Curtains," were advertised at public vendue by Benjamin Church.—*Boston Gazette*, Jan. 23, 1753.

MAHOGANY CHAIRS.—To be sold by Benjamin Church, at Publick Vendue, "a Variety of Choice Household Furniture, viz. A large Mehogany Case of Draws, made after the best Fashion, with a Chamber Table, a Buroe Table, and sundry other Tables, all Mehogany; half Doz. Carv'd Frame Mehogany Chairs; half Doz. black walnut Ditto; all new Work; and to be seen the Day before the Sale."—*Boston Gazette,* Nov. 20, 1753.

LEATHER BOTTOM CHAIRS.—To be Sold, half a Dozen Chairs with Leather Bottoms, a large black Walnut Table, and a Number of Metzitento Pictures. Inquire of the Printer.—*Boston Gazette*, Mar. 26, 1754.

TURKEY CARPET.—To be sold at Publick Vendue on THURSDAY NEXT, the 28th Instant, at 3 o'Clock afternoon, at the Dwelling House of the late Mr. *Ebenezer Holmes*, in King Street, Boston, a Parcel of valuable Household Stuff, among which are a very large *Turkey* Carpet, measuring Eleven and an half by Eighteen and an half Feet, an Iron Chest, a very handsom Sedan, sundry pieces of Plate, Books, Pictures, Beds, China Wares, &c. &c.—*Boston Gazette*, Mar. 26, 1754.

MARBLE CHIMNEY PIECE.—To be Sold, the owner intending soon for Europe, a Universal single and double Microscope, with a solar Apparatus, Frog Frame, &c.

A Farenheit's Thermometer, graduated to boiling Water.

A large Concave Mirror.

A Barometer.

Two Botanick Thermometers on Box.

A four Foot Reflecting-Telescope, the largest Size, six Inches Diameter.

A new-invented Organ in a Mohogony Case and Frame on Castors, the Pipes gilt; with two additional Barrels.

A beautiful Statuary Marble carved Chimney-Piece and Picture; two fine China Chandeliers, fitted with Flowers and Branches; with three Plaister Figures of *Shakespear, Milton and Pope.*

An Electrical Machine and two spare Globes.

A Magick Lanthorn, with three Dozen Pictures.

Two large Salmon double-walled shew Nets, never used; one 40 Yards by 10 Feet; the other 21 Yards by 6 Feet.

Four Dozen Glass Lanthorns and Burners, proper to illuminate a House on publick Nights.

A large Marquie and Walls, A Ticking Tent, with an Alcove at each End and lined with a printed Cotton, with Poles, Pinns, &c. compleat; quite new.

A small Sperma-Cæti Press, with an Iron Screw, &c. compleat.

A pair of double Girandoles with Pans and Nossels.

An Air-Gun, which discharges ten Times without Powder in half a Minute.

With sundry other Articles for the Sterling Cost, without any Charge of Commissions, Freight or Insurance:

They are all Compleat and very little used.

Enquire at Mess'rs *Gilbert* and *Lewis Deblois's* Shop in Queen Street.—*Boston Gazette,* May 21, 1754.

TURKEY CARPET.—Stolen out of a House in Boston, "a Turkey Carpet of various Colours, about a yard and half in length, and a Yard wide, fring'd on each End." Three dollars reward.—*Boston News-Letter,* Feb. 20, 1755.

MARBLE TABLES.—To be Sold, Marble Tables of different Colours and sizes.—*Boston Gazette*, Sept. 15, 1755.

MAHOGANY CHAIRS.—To be Sold, at public Vendue, "an exceeding good Sett of Mehogany carv'd Chairs, new Fashion, and a Sett of black ditto, Leather Bottoms, a beautiful Mehogany Desk and Book Case," etc.—*Boston Gazette*, Nov. 17, 1755.

LOOKING GLASSES.—To be Sold at Publick Vendue by Savage & Winter at their Vendue-Room in Wing's Lane; Large and small Looking Glasses, Sconces, Wine Glasses, Hoop-Pettycoats, Rolls of Paper, several new Jacks, a Brass Grate and Copper Coal Scuttle, two Tobacco Presses and a snuff Mill, some Lignum Vitae, etc.—*Boston Gazette*, June 28, 1756.

COMPASS SEAT CHAIRS.—To be sold at publick vendue by Benjamin Church, at his usual place of Sale; a variety of European Goods; Among the rest—Half a dozen Compass Seat Black Walnut Leather Bottom Chairs new, Mehogany Tables, Feather Beds, etc.—*Boston Gazette*, Aug. 16, 1756.

CASE OF DRAWS.—To be sold at public vendue by Benjamin Church, at his usual place of sale; a variety of European Goods; among the rest—a beautiful Mehogany Case of Draws, with an Oger Top, and brass'd off in the best Manner; half a Dozen of Black Walnut Chairs, open Backs and Leather Bottoms, a second hand Chaise, &c.—*Boston Gazette*, Sept. 27, 1756.

PILLARED TABLES.—Mahogany pillared Tables, large and small Looking-Glasses, and three silver Watches, to be sold at public vendue.—*Boston Gazette*, Jan. 10, 1757.

DESK.—"A choice new Mahogany Desk, made after the best Manner" was advertised for sale at the Vendue-Room of Samuel Smith on Colman's Wharf.—*Boston Gazette*, May 16, 1757.

COACH BED.—To be sold by *Samuel Smith*, at his Vendue-Room on Colman's Wharff. . . . a Coach Bed with all the Furniture, viz. a beautiful Suit of red Harriteen Curtains, double Valians, a Tester and Head Cloth, a sacking Bottom Bebstead; a beautiful Body of a Riding Chair new, a Silver Watch, a Chimney Piece imitating Adam and Eve in Paradise, wro't with a Needle after the best Manner. . . . —*Boston Gazette*, May 23, 1757.

OVAL TABLE.—"A Mahogany oval Table new Fashion," at auction.—*Boston Gazette*, July 4, 1757.

BUREAU TABLE.—A Mahogany Case of Draws, a Bureau Table, half a dozen Mehogany Chairs Leather Bottoms with Brass Nails, etc. sold at auction.—*Boston Gazette*, July 18, 1757.

TABLE DECORATIONS.—To be Sold, a handsome Post-chariot, a neat polished silver Epergne, a curious neat Chamber Organ, and "A compleat Set of Desert Frames, with Arbours, Alcoves, Hedging, China Flower Pots, &c. with spare Grass and Gravel for ditto." . . . Apply to Mr. Stephen Deblois, at the Concert Hall; as the Owner in all Probability will soon embark for Europe.—*Boston Gazette*, Oct. 17, 1757.

CASE OF DRAWS.—"A beautiful Mahogany Case of Draws, with a Compass Top" and other furniture, sold at public vendue.—*Boston Gazette*, Oct. 31, 1757.

SETTEE.—"Mehogany and Black-Walnut Tables and Stands, a Settee, a Suit of Cloth Curtains, Feather-Beds, a good large Jack, a large Glass Lanthorn for an Entry Way," at auction.—*Boston Gazette*, Dec. 12, 1757.

DUMB-BETTY, "A new Dumb-betty" for sale at vendue.—*Boston Gazette*, Jan. 9, 1758.

TABLES.—"Marble and other Tables, . . . Desks, a beautiful Desk and Book Case, with Glass Doors, Pictures. . . . Also a handsome 8 Day Clock, and an Iron Chest," were to be sold at public vendue.—*Boston Gazette*, Feb. 13, 1758.

IRON BEDSTEAD.—To be sold at public Vendue, the household furniture of Mr. Henry Quincy of Braintree, "consisting of Feather Beds, Bedsteads and Curtains, Mehogany and Black Walnut Tables, Mehogany and black Walnut framed Chairs, a handsome Chimney Glass, a handsome Marble Slab with a Mehogany Frame, a fine Assortment of China, a beautiful 8 Day Clock with Mehogany Case, an Iron Bedsted with screws, a Parcel of Pictures, a Turkey Carpet, a fine large Harpsicord, a case of Silver haft Knives and Forks, a handsome pair of Silver Chaffin Dishes, 3 Silver Cans, . . . also one Negro Man, one

ONE-DRAWER HADLEY CHEST
Made at Hadley, Massachusetts, about 1700

Negro Woman, and three Negro Girls." . . . —*Boston Gazette*, Apr. 17, 1758.

MARBLE TABLE.—John Welch, purposing to go for England, advertised to be sold at Publick Vendue, at his house opposite to Jacob Royall, Esq, in Hanover Street, among other items, the following:—Large and small Sconces, Looking-Glasses, Chimney and Dressing-Glasses, a very handsome japan'd Chest of Drawers and Buroe, a marble Table supported by Carved Eagles, Delph Flower Pots, with Handles, suits of green and red Harrateen Curtains. Several Pieces of Plate, viz: a beautiful large Tea-Kettle, a wrought Bowl which will hold 5 Pints, with Handles, a large Sugar Box and Salver, a Quart Tankard, Cans, Porringers, Salts, Pepper and Mustard Boxes, a Case of Silver Haft Knives and Forks for Sweetmeats, &c. A Number of Metzitinto Prints, large and small Pictures suitable for a Stair-Case; a handsome Brass Hearth, etc. etc. etc.—*Boston News-Letter*, Apr. 20, 1758.

BRASS HEARTH.—John Welch of Hanover Street, Boston, "purposing to go for England in a short time" advertised the sale of his household furniture at public vendue, including "Large and small Sconces, Looking Glasses, Chimney and Dressing Glasses, a very handsome Japan'd Chest of Draws and Buroe, one fine ditto and Table; a Marble Table supported by carv'd Eagles; a good eight Day Clock; burnt China Dishes, Plates and Bowls; Delph Flower Pots, with Handles; a Suit of green Harateen Curtains, a suit of Red ditto; . . . A number of Metzitinto Prints, large and small Pictures suitable for a Stair-Case; a handsome Brass Hearth, brass Andirons, Kettles and Candlesticks; Water-Plates; Hardmetal Covers for Dishes; oval Dishes, Plates and other Pewter; two Dozen of Candle-Moulds, some large and rib'd," etc.—*Boston Gazette*, Apr. 24, 1758.

PRESS BEDSTEAD with sacking Bottom, advertised.—*Boston Gazette*, May 15, 1758.

MAHOGANY TEA-BOARDS and Bottle-Stands, advertised.—*Boston Gazette*, July 3, 1758.

LOOKING GLASSES.—Thomas James Gruchy, intending shortly for Europe, advertises for sale, at Publick Vendue, etc . . . part of his Household Furniture; as, an 8 day Clock, of extraordinary Materials, and admirable Workmanship; a Looking-Glass of 8 feet by 5, with carved and gilt Frame; and sundry other Looking-Glasses; two Settees, with chairs suitable to them; an Escrutoire with Glass Doors; Sundry Pieces of Plate, amongst which is a Pair of beautiful Chaffing-Dishes; a parcel of China Ware; Bureau and other Tables, also a Card-Table; jappan'd Chest of Draws and Table; black Walnut ditto; . . . —*Boston News-Letter*, Nov. 2, 1758.

GREAT CHAIR.—"A marble slab for a table, a japan'd chamber table, a good great chair," for sale at the Vendue Room of Samuel Smith, on Chardon's Wharf.—*Boston Gazette*, Nov. 13, 1758.

JACK CHAIRS.—To be Sold at the Vendue Room of Arthur Savage, Boston, "a couch frame, mehogany, black birch and jack chairs, some with blue leather bottoms, a lolling chair frame, a field bedsted and furniture, a desk bedstead, a swinging cott, an iron grate, . . . with sundry other articles belonging to the estate of Joseph Grant, jun.—also Six new Mehogany Chairs neatly carv'd.—*Boston Gazette*, Nov. 13, 1758.

MAPLE CHAIRS.—"Handsome set Maple frame Chairs."—*Boston Gazette*, Jan. 8, 1759.

CARPETS.—Just imported from London, in the last ships and to be sold at Mr. Blanchard's in New Boston [West End]; a large assortment of fine Carpets for Rooms, very cheap for ready Cash. —*Boston Gazette*, Jan. 22, 1759.

FIELD BEDSTEAD, Maple fram'd chairs with straw Bottoms, "a beautiful Instrumentum Proferendi Lucim," a handsome set of glaz'd Pictures with a carv'd gilt edge, to be sold at auction.— *Boston Gazette*, Jan. 29, 1759.

STRAW BOTTOM CHAIRS.—"Maple fram'd Chairs Straw Bottoms," at auction.—*Boston Gazette*, Mar. 26, 1759.

IRON BEDSTEAD, a pallat bedstead, a brass plate warmer, to be sold at auction.—*Boston Gazette*, June 18, 1759.

PIER GLASSES.—To be Sold at Public Vendue . . . at the House of the late Honourable Paul Mascarene, Esq. in School Street, Boston, A Variety of best Household-Furniture, consisting of Beds, Bedding and Bedsteads, (amongst which is a very rich and handsome crimson mohair Bed and Chairs,) Pier and Sconce-Glasses, Chests of Drawers, glaz'd and other Pictures, Tables and Chairs, a good eight Day Clock, a neat Desk and Book-Case, . . . a new imported and neatly polish'd Coal-Grate, . . . Likewise, Sundry Mathematical Instruments, a good Thermometer, and a genteel made new invented Microscope, with its proper Apparatus. . . .—*Boston Gazette*, June 9, 1760.

EASY CHAIR.—To be sold by Public Vendue, this day, the 7th of August, at the House adjoining Messi'rs Green and Walker's store, in Dassett's Lane, near the Rev. Mr. Cooper's Meeting House.

Very good Household Furniture; amongst which is, A large handsome Mahogony Case of Drawers and Table; a neat Beauro; sundry Mahogony Tables—handsome Chairs; Beds, Bedsteds, a suit of green Curtains, &c.—an easy chair; Looking Glasses; China Ware, etc., An exceedingly good Jack compleat; also, Pewter, Brass, Iron, etc., As likewise, Sundry Turkey Carpets, sundry pieces of Plate, Two Silver Watches, &c. The Sale to begin at 11 o'Clock.—*Boston News-Letter*, August 7, 1760.

HANGINGS FOR ROOMS.—Jane Savell acquaints her Customers, that since the Fire she is Removed to a Chamber at the Upper End of Milk-Street, near the South Meeting-House, where she has got several pieces of beautiful painted Canvas Hangings for Rooms, some stone pickled Pots and Jugs; a Quantity of pickled Cucumbers & Mangoes, pickled Oysters done after the best manner. —*Boston Gazette*, Sept. 15, 1760.

PERSIAN CARPETS.—William Greenleaf imported from London and Bristol and had on sale at his store in Cornhill: Rich Persian carpets, 3, 4, and 4 by 5 yards square, list carpeting for stairs, earthern ware, large and small stone ware, chimney tiles, etc. etc. —*Boston News-Letter*, Jan. 29, 1761.

LEATHER SCREEN.—An elegant gilt Leather Screen, imported last spring from London for sale at the Dwelling-House of Thomas Walker in Bacon-Street.—*Boston Gazette*, Aug. 3, 1761.

CARPETS.—Very large and handsome Carpets; roles [*sic*] of

carpeting, etc. Consigned from Quebec, were advertised for sale at public Vendue at Wheelwrights Wharf.—*Boston News-Letter*, Jan. 13, 1762.

CHARIOT MOONS.—To be Sold at Public Auction, at the house next the Orange Tree in Hanover Street: Two large Mahogany Bedsteads, sacking Bottom.—Two Maple ditto with Furniture.—A Pair of Charriot Moons.—One large Mohogany Cloaths-Press, with three Draws.—A Mahogany Bureau, with a Writing-Table.—A Variety of curious fine China in Statuary; also Some of the best enamel'd China; a Parcel of double Flint Glass; a handsome Set of desert Knives and Forks and 12 Silver Spoons.—Yellow and crimson Silk Damask Window Curtains, compleat. . . . A large Garden Rolling-Stone.           M. DESHON.
—*Boston News-Letter*, May 13, 1762.

CHAIRS.—To be Sold at the Vendue Room of Benjamin Church, "half a Dozen Leather Bottom Chairs Mehogany Frames."—*Boston Gazette*, May 31, 1762.

CHAMBER TABLE.—To be sold at the Vendue Room of Benjamin Church, "A beautiful Mehogany Case of Draws and Chamber Table, new Fashion."—*Boston Gazette*, June 21, 1762.

GREAT CHAIRS.—To be Sold at Public Vendue, at the Dwelling-House late in the Occupation of *James Otis*, Esq, near the King's Chapel in School-street,—Household Furniture belonging to a Gentleman about leaving the Province,—consisting of second-hand Pewter; Copper Fish Kettle; a good, large Jack complete; . . . A Copper Brewing or Soap boiling Kettle, and Trevit. Also, a Set of great Chairs with *Crimson Damask* Backs and Bottoms; and a Set of great Chairs with strong Cane Bottoms and Backs, contrived for easy Transportation, as they may be speedily onfram'd and fram'd again without Damage; a large *Settee*, covered with crimson Damask; Tapestry Settee; Tappestry Hangings; 5 or 6 Looking Glasses; some plate; Feather Beds, &c. &c.

N. B. Amongst said Household Goods, are 4 or 5 handsome *square* Tables—a large Scritore; a *Parlor's* Case of Drawers, valuable second-hand Articles. GERRISH [the auctioneer].—*Boston Gazette*, June 28, 1762.

CARPETING.—"A quantity of stout Carpeting both for Floors and Stairs," at auction.—*Boston Gazette*, Dec. 6, 1762.

PAINTED SCREEN.—To be sold at Public Vendue. . . . "a large Mahogany Table, a handsome Looking Glass, a handsome Screen, beautifully painted in colours representing many perspective views of London." . . . —*Boston Gazette*, Feb. 21, 1763.

OIL CLOTHS.—"Handsome Oyl-Cloths for Tables," for sale. —*Boston Gazette*, Mar. 21, 1763.

CHINA STOVE.—To be sold at public auction tomorrow (if fair weather) at 11 o'clock, A. M., at Mr Hancock's warehouse— Sundry things belonging to the late Major General Whitmore, among which, are two Setts of Chairs with Velvet Cushions, a Settee, Tables of Several Sorts, an Alarm Clock, a China Stove, a hand Organ, a double Shey, a Sedan Chair Lin'd with Velvet, with many other Articles.—*Boston Gazette*, May 16, 1763.

TURKEY CARPETS.—At the Mansion House of William Fletcher, Boston, were to be sold at public Vendue various articles of household furniture including: Sundry neat Pieces of imboss'd Plate, of the newest Fashion; two handsome Shagreen Cases of Solid Silver; handsome Piece Sconce; and Chimney-Glasses; a red Harateen-Bed; one green ditto; Turkey and English carpets, etc. etc.—*Boston News-Letter*, June 16, 1763.

CHERRY-TREE CHAIRS.—To be sold at public Vendue at the Mansion house of William Fletcher, Esq, in New Boston [West End] . . . Sundry neat Pieces of imboss'd Plate, of the newest Fashion; two handsome Shagareen Cases of solid Silver handle Knives and Forks; handsome Piece Sconce, and Chimney-Glasses; a good Eight-day Clock; a handsome Set of Mahogany leather-bottom'd Chairs; Cherry-tree Ditto; Mahogany Tables, Desks, and Book-Cases, and Cases of Drawers; a handsome red Harateen-Bed; one green Ditto; *Turkey* and *English* Carpets; . . . —*Boston Gazette*, June 20, 1763.

COUCH AND SQUAB.—"Cain Couch and Squab, Harrateen Bed, Sacking Bottom Bedsteed, Mehogany Desk and Book Case, Mehogany Square and Round Tables" and other household furniture to be sold at Auction.—*Boston Gazette*, Aug. 29, 1763.

BLACK WALNUT CHAIRS.—"Half a Dozen Leather Bottom Chairs, of the newest Fashion, Black walnut Frames," advertised for sale at Benjamin Church's auction room.—*Boston Gazette*, Oct. 31, 1763.

DRESSING GLASSES.—To be sold by publick auction on Friday next, At the Royal Exchange Tavern in King Street, Boston, The following articles of Household Furniture (almost new) taken by Execution, viz: Mehogany Leather Bottom Chairs, Black Walnut ditto, Sconce Glasses and Dressing ditto, China Curtains and Window ditto and Squabs, Feather Beds & Bedsteads, Tongs and Shovels, Chest of Drawers, Bureau Tables, Tea ditto, China Ware, Screens & Carpets, Pictures, Brass & Iron Andirons, Brass & Copper Kettles, Kitchen Chairs & Jack, &c. &c.—*Boston Gazette*, Nov. 26, 1764.

BLACK WALNUT CHAIRS.—A handsome set of Black-walnut Frame Chairs, scarlet cloth, offered at private sale by *Moses Deshon* at the Newest Auction-Room, opposite the West End of Faneuil Hall.—*Boston Gazette*, Jan. 14, 1765.

FURNITURE.—Made and Sold by Thomas Sherburne, at his shop in Back Street, Boston; all sorts of Cabinet-Ware, in the neatest manner; such as Desks and Bookcases; Cases of Drawers, Buroe Tables, Chamber Tables, Dining Tables, Tea-Tables, Screens, &c.—*Boston Gazette*, Apr. 22, 1765.

"HANDSOME SCONCE LOOKING GLASS, Mahogany Tables, Mahogany Bedsted, a Sett quilted China, Black Walnut Chairs, Green China Bed, Sacking Bottom Bedsteads, Pewter, Brass, Copper, and other Kitchen Furniture," at public auction on June 11th "at X o'Clock Forenoon" at the House of Mr *Gordon* at the Lower end of Cold Lane.—*Boston Gazette*, June 3, 1765.

CASES FOR WAX WORK, Two Cases of Drawers, curious Pictures, Silver Sugar Box, &c. at public Vendue.—*Boston Gazette*, June 17, 1765.

HARPSICORD.—"Peer, Sconce and Chimney Looking Glasses, a Large proved Harpsicord, with two Rows of Keys, a genteel Sett of Mohogony Chairs with Horse hair Bottoms, Mohogony Tables of different Sizes, Mohogony Tea Table, Two handsome Chests of Drawers with Tables, a genteel Sett of China Dishes and Plates and Soup Plates, a Crimson Harrateen Bed and Chairs, several Setts of Chairs, a variety of Metzotinto Prints, a large Kitchen Jack with other Kitchen Furniture. ☞ Also, a small Chair Chaise for a single Person." To be sold at Public Vendue at Three o'Clock Afternoon, at the House opposite to Mr Joseph Gale in Sudbury Street.—*Boston Gazette*, June 17, 1765.

Gov. Hutchinson's Furnishings.—The following Articles, taken among the rest from the Lieutenant-Governor's House, the 26th Instant, if offered for Sale, in this or any other Government, it is desired they may be stopped, or if seen in any Persons Possession, that Notice may be given to either of the Lieutenant-Governor's Sons, at their Warehouses on the Dock:

A Silver Hilt of a Sword which had been wash'd with Gold, the Blade is found; two mourning Swords; a chased Gold Head of a Cane, with the Lieut. Governor's Crest; a Lady's chased Gold Watch, Hook & Chain; a new fashion'd Gold Chain and Hook for a Lady's Watch; a Set of large Silver Plate Buttons for Coat and Breeches; 2 sets ditto covered with Silver Wire, and very uncommon; several Funeral Rings, particularly one, the late *Tho. Lechmere*, Esq; another the late *Tho. Hancock*, Esq; several ancient coins; a Pair of Ruby Earings set in Gold, and Necklace; Garnet Earings and Necklaces in Gold; Paist Earings and Necklaces; Stone Girdle Buckles; 2 Pair Stone Shoe Buckles; 2 Pair Stone sleeve Buttons set in Gold; rich embroidered christening Blankets, Sleeves, Cradle Quilt and Curtain, and a set of Childbed Linen; Gauze Handkerchief & Sattin Apron, both flowered with Gold; silk Shoes; brocaded Silk, Padusoy, Damask Lutstring Gowns & Petticoats; laced Petticoats; Head-Cloaths & other Linen; Bundles of old Gold and Silver Lace; Bundles of Bone Lace; Silver Spoons; Silver Handle Knives and Forks; Sweetmeat Knives, Forks & Spoons, gilt, and other Articles of Plate; a large Octavo Bible richly Bound and in an outside Turkey

Leather Case, a Direction in one of the defensive Leaves signed by *Thomas Coram*, Esq.,

AND Whereas a Manuscript History of the *Massachusetts Province*, from the Year 1692 to the Year 1730, was among the Spoil, and Part thereof has been found; if any of the remaining Sheets should be discovered, it is desired they may be sent, as also any other of the Lieutenant-Governor's Papers or Books, to the Reverend Mr. *Eliot.*—*Boston News-Letter*, Sept. 5, 1765.

SCREENS.—At a sale of household goods at the new brick Store formerly occupied by Mr. John Gould, by the Septre and Crown, Back Street, Boston, the following items, among others, were enumerated:—Silver equipages; with sundry of jewelry ware; handsome images of Shakespear, Milton and others in marble; a pair of handsome painted window blinds or skreens; a handsome painted chamber skreen; tea boards; mehogany and copper waiters; two sets of surgeon's second-hand instruments; a set of fine large crown glass sashes with weights, bolts, lines, pullies, shutters, and furniture suitable for the front of a large commodious shop, with fine scroll irons; night lamp & irons for the street, etc. also, a worsted carpet, and painted floor-cloth.—*Boston News-Letter*, Apr. 28, 1768.

Gov. BERNARD'S FURNITURE.—On Tuesday 11th Day of September, at Ten o'Clock in the Morning, will be sold by PUBLIC VENDUE, at the PROVINCE HOUSE, all the genteel House Furniture of Sir. FRANCIS BERNARD, Bart. Among which are:

8 Mohogo dining Tables
2 genteel Card Tables
3 Tables forming a Horse Shoe for the Benefit of the Fire in the Winter
1 Excellent 8 day Clock
6 setts of Leather bottom Chairs
2 Screens Moho. frames
Turkey and other Carpets
3 Cases of China handled Knives and Forks with Silver Spoons to each
1 Case Silver handled do

1 Case of Desert ditto
1 Walnut Desk and Paper Case
2 Iron Grates with Shovel, Tongs, Fender, Poker.
1 Neat Chimney Glass.
A Variety of genteel Sconts and Pier Glasses
12 Mohogo carv'd frame Chairs with crimson damask bottoms
2 Crimson damask Window Curtains and window Cushions
1 Pair Prince metal Handirons & Shovel, Tongs and Chimney Hooks.
1 suit of Nett Curtains for a Bed with Chair Coverings
1 Mohogony four Post Bedsted, with Crimson Moreen Furniture, and 2 Window Curtains
8 Choice Feather Beds
1 Mohogony four Post Bedsted with Red and white Furniture Check and 3 Window Curtains
1 Suit of blue and white Chints Curtains
1 Walnut Case of Draws
1 Mohogony four Post Bedsted with yellow Moreen Furniture, and 2 Window Curtains.
1 sett of yellow bottom Chairs
4 Toilet Tables
1 fine Mattrass
8 pair Blankets
5 pair tow Sheets
2 Bed Quilts
1 Rich Chints Counterpane very neat
6 Red bottom Chairs
1 Walnut Case of Draws with Shelves for Books
1 Mohogony Ward Robe
1 Mohogony Tea Tray
2 four Post Bedsteds with coarse Blue Woolen Curtains
A great variety of Rich China and Glass Ware
1 genteel Coach with Harness
Sundry Mathematical Instruments
Some fine Garden Glasses and Garden Tools
2 large Ships Stoves

All Kinds of Kitchen Furniture in Brass, Copper, Iron and Tin
Madeira, white Port and other Wines in Casks and Bottles
100 Orange, Lemon, Fig and Cork Trees
Also, a Library of Books, a Catalogue of which may be had at the
    Time and place of Sale.

The Furniture may be viewed on Saturday the 8th, and Monday the 10th. of September, where a catalogue of the whole may be seen.           J. Russell, auctioneer.
          —*Boston News-Letter*, Aug. 30, 1770.

FLOOR CARPETS.—William Jackson at the Brazen Head, Cornhill, advertised as just imported from London—a few very handsome Wilton Floor Carpets; Stair ditto; a fine Assortment Paper Hangings for Rooms; japan'd Waiters, all sizes; japan'd Breadbaskets; pinching Irons and curling Tongs; very neat Hawks bill and Key-draught Teeth-pullers; 15 & 18 Inch London T. D. Pipes, &c. &c. &c.—*Boston News-Letter*, May 23, 1771.

CARPET.—William Gale in Corn-Hill, advertised for Sale "a Carpet 14 Feet by 12, more Elegant than any which have been imported into this Province."—*Boston News-Letter*, July 11, 1771.

HOUSEHOLD FURNISHINGS.—The furniture of the late John Apthorp, Esq. "which is far more elegant than any ever offered to Public Sale in this Town," was advertised to be sold at auction in the Concert Hall, on May 18, 1773. Among the items described were the following:—

Seven Cases of the very best Silver handled Knives and Forks, most of them lately imported, and of the newest Fashion.

A very rich Silk Damask Bed, with Window Curtains, Chairs, and an easy Chair, all in the newest Taste.

A large Sopha and ten Chairs covered with the best crimson Silk-Damask, and four large Window Curtains of the same.

A small Sopha and five Chairs of the same Damask, in the Chinese Taste.

A neat blue and white Copper-Plate Bed, with Window Curtains and Chairs for ditto.

Four very handsome Window Curtains of red and white Copper-Plate, almost new. A very fine India Cabinet. Two very handsome Spring Clocks. Turkey and Wilton Carpets, etc.—*Boston News-Letter*, May 13, 1773.

CANVAS FLOOR CLOTHS.—The household furnishings of the late Charles Hamock, wine merchant, of Boston were sold at public vendue. Among the items advertised were the following: Chest on Chest Draws, Dining Tables, Tea Tables, Leather-Bottom and Hair-Bottom Chairs, Chamber clocks, a Red and White Copper-Plate Bed and Window-Curtains, a neat Settee Bed with Curtains, Mohogany frame, a Scotch carpet, and Painted Canvass Floor-Cloths, etc. etc.—*Boston News-Letter*, Nov. 11, 1773.

## LOOKING GLASSES

LOOKING GLASSES, Several sorts, lately arrived from England, from 23 to 43 inches long. At wholesale or retail by Capt James Pitts at his house in Clark Square, Boston.—*Boston News-Letter*, June 30/July 7, 1718.

LAMPS AND LANTHORNS.—Lately imported from London, a fresh Parcel of choice Looking-Glasses of divers Sorts and Sizes; as also fine Glass Lamps and Lanthorns, well gilt and painted, both convex and plain: being suitable for Halls, Stair-cases, and other Passageways, To be Sold at the Glass-Shop in Queen Street, Boston.—*Boston News-Letter*, Aug. 31/Sept. 7, 1719.

LOOKING GLASSES.—New-fashioned looking glasses for Sale. —*Boston Gazette*, May 18/25, 1724.

LOOKING GLASSES.—"Glass Sconces and chimney-glass, of the newest fashion in gilded Frames," for sale.—*Boston Gazette*, Nov. 20/27, 1732.

SWINGING GLASSES with drawers and without, advertised.—*Boston News-Letter*, Sept. 22/29, 1737.

LOOKING GLASSES.—"A parcel of sizable new fashioned Looking Glasses, a large black walnut table suitable for an Ordinary, a new yellow Cheney rais'd Bed, compleat and Masqueraded Stuffs, Suitable for Gowns and Banyans," for sale.—*Boston News-Letter*, Mar. 4/11, 1742.

PIER AND SCONCE Looking-Glasses, Chimney and Pocket Ditto,

Mezzo Tinto Prints, painted on Glass in gilt Frames, ditto in both Pair-Tree and Pine Frames, Mahogany and Japan'd Tea Chests, best Prospectives, Barometers and Thermometer, sold by Stephen Whiting in Union Street.—*Boston Evening Post*, Jan. 23, 1743/4.

LOOKING GLASSES.—"New fashion plain'd and carv'd Edge Looking Glasses," for sale.—*Boston News-Letter*, Mar. 8, 1744.

LOOKING GLASSES.—To be sold by *Stephen Whiting*, at the Rose and Crown in Union Street; A Variety of large Sconce and Pier Looking Glasses, also small Looking Glasses by the Dozen, &c. suitable for Traders and others.—*Boston Gazette*, May 23, 1749.

PIER GLASS.—Note. Whereas it has been reported, that Peter Burn was going to quit his shop in Fish-street, near Doctor Clark's, which is entirely groundless, and still continues to occupy the same, in selling great Variety of Irish linens, etc. etc. Also, a large Pier Glass, with a gilt Frame with Branches, and a Gold chased Watch, and Silver ditto, two white grey Hair Wigs, with Feather Tops, made in the newest Taste at London, to be disposed of.—*Boston Evening Post*, Dec. 31, 1753.

CHIMNEY GLASS.—"A Chimney-Glass, a Turkey Carpet, India Counterpanes," etc. to be sold at an auction sale of furniture.—*Boston Gazette*, Jan. 8, 1754.

LOOKING GLASSES.—"Looking-glasses of several sizes in Mahogany Frames," for sale.—*Boston Gazette*, Apr. 9, 1754.

LOOKING GLASSES.—To be Sold by Moses Belcher Bass, In Ann Street, near the Conduit, A Variety of Looking-Glasses, some with neat carved gilt frames, just imported.—*Boston News-Letter*, August 7, 1760.

DUTCH LOOKING GLASSES were advertised for Sale by John, Robert and John Gould at Boston, also Chimney Tiles and Hampers of blue and white Stone Ware.—*Boston Gazette*, Sept. 15, 1760.

SCONCES.—Imported from London by *Samuel Whitney*, and to be Sold at his Shop at the Sign of the Looking Glass in Union Street, a fine Assortment of gilt and plain Sconces; a few hand-

BLOCK-FRONT SECRETARY-DESK
Made by John Goddard of Newport, R. I., and now owned by
Messrs. Brown & Ives of Providence

some large gilt Piedmont Glasses: . . . N. B. Curtains ready made, may be had at the said Place, as cheap as can be bought in Town.—*Boston Gazette*, Feb. 1, 1762.

LOOKING GLASSES.—To be sold at Public Vendue at the Mansion House of the late Madam *Sarah Wendall*, in School Street, near the King's Chappel: . . . two very handsome Large Looking Glasses, about Eight Feet in Height, several pair of Large Sconces, a very handsome Jappan'd Eight Day Clock. . . . — *Boston Gazette*, Sept. 6, 1762.

PIEDMONT LOOKING GLASSES.—William Bowes, has imported in the ship *Mary*, Captain Deverson, from London, A fine Assortment of Pedmont Sconce Looking Glasses of all Sizes, which he will sell at the lowest Rates for Cash at his Shop on Dock Square.—*Boston Gazette*, June 27, 1763.

LOOKING GLASSES.—Piedmont, Sconce, and Pier Looking Glasses, for sale.—*Boston Gazette*, Mar. 5, 1764.

GLASSMAN AND JAPANNER.—To be Sold by Stephen Whiting, *Glassman* and *Jappanner*, at his Shop in Union-Street, opposite the Cornfield, Boston; Large and Small Sconce and pier Looking-Glasses, made of the best Stone, and in any sort of Frames that will suit the Buyer: . . .

☞ *Said Whiting does more at present towards manufacturing Looking-Glasses than any one in the Province, or perhaps on the Continent, and would be glad of Encouragement enough to think it worth while to live.*—*Boston News-Letter*, Nov. 12, 1767.

## MISCELLANEOUS

MAHOGANY AND OTHER WOODS.—To be Sold behind Numb. 4, on the Long Wharffe, Lignumvitee, Box wood, Ebony, Mohogany Plank, Sweet Wood Bark, and wild Cinnamon Bark.—*Boston Gazette*, Aug. 22/29, 1737.

MAHOGANY.—To be sold at publick Vendue at the Exchange Tavern, on Thursday, the first of December next, at three o'clock Afternoon; 50 Pieces of fine Mahogany in 10 Lots, No. 1 to 10, being 5 Pieces in a Lot, to be seen at the Long Wharffe before the Sale begins.—*Boston Gazette*, Nov. 21/28, 1737.

MAPLE TREE KNOTS.—Whoever has got any curious Maple-Tree Knotts, to Sell, may hear of a Purchaser from the Publisher. —*Boston Gazette*, Apr. 30/May 6, 1739.

MAHOGONY WOOD, was part of the cargo of a Spanish prize ship brought into Newport, R. I.—*Boston News-Letter*, June 24/July 1, 1742.

MAHOGANY.—Just arrived—a parcel of Lignam vitae and 3½ in. Mahogany.—*Boston Gazette*, Dec. 25, 1744.

MAHOGANY PLANK, lignum-vitae, part of the cargo of a prize ship retaken from the French, sold at auction in Boston.—*Boston News-Letter*, Dec. 26, 1745.

GRATE FOR COAL.—*A Large Grate for Coal, fit for a Kitchin, To be Sold Reasonably by* Arthur Savage, *at his Store No. 7 on the Long Wharffe in* Boston.—*Boston News-Letter*, Dec. 7/14, 1732.

DUTCH STOVE.—A Large Dutch Stove well compleated, to be sold. Inquire of the Printer.—*Boston Gazette*, Dec. 8, 1741.

STOVES.—New-fashion Fireplaces or Stoves from Philadelphia, to be sold by Thomas Wade. Also in same issue, "Just Published an account of the new-invented Pennsylvanian Fire-places."— *Boston News-Letter*, Feb. 7, 1745.

IRON HEARTH.—On the 11th Instant, early in the Morning, a Fire broke out at *Mr. Pierpont's* House near the Fortification, occasioned by the Heat of the Iron Hearth of one of the newly invented Fireplaces, whereby the Floor was set on Fire; the People being in Bed, perceived a great Smoke, got up, and happily discover'd and timely distinguished [*sic*] the Fire.—*Boston Gazette*, Dec. 22, 1747.

DUTCH STOVE.—Any Person who has a large Dutch Stove to dispose of may hear of a Purchaser by enquiring of the Printer. —*Boston Evening Post*, Nov. 26, 1753.

CANNON STOVES.—Benjamin Andrews, jun. at his Store opposite the swing-bridge, Boston, has for sale, Cast iron cannon stoves, of different sizes, and new constructions, the larger very suitable for a vessel's cabin, or the room of one or more Persons who are inclined to be *upon the saving order*, as besides the advantage of their heat, with very small expense of fuel, they are fitted for the various methods of cookery, the smaller are of a less size and price, and better suited for shops, &c. than any heretofore made in this Country. He has also an assortment of iron hollow ware, Philadelphia pig iron, Deer's leather breeches, small anchors, etc.—*Boston News-Letter*, Feb. 1, 1770 (*sup.*).

QUEBEC STOVE.—To be Sold, a handsome Quebec Stove, with twelve feet cast Funnel, very convenient for a School-House or any Room where a Number of Persons are employed. Enquire of the Printer.—*Boston News-Letter*, Nov. 8, 1770.

# CLOCKS AND WATCHES

## Makers

JAMES ASBY, Watch-maker & Finisher from London, opposite Mess. Cox & Berry's Store in King Street, Boston, Having Imported in the last Ships from London, a large Quantity of Clocks, with curious Paintings and Motions in the Arches. Likewise a compleat Assortment of Gold, Silver, Pinchbeck and Metal Watches, of different Prices; particularly one Gold Watch, calculated to keep Longitude at Sea, it having every advantageous Improvement from Watches of a common Construction, not only having a Steel Horizontal Wheel and a ruby Cyllender, tho' being very advantageous against Friction, the main Spring also Keeps the same elastic Force while the Watch is winding up, which is a particular Improvement that no Common Watch has, and therefore must lose time when winding up; it has an Expansion slide, which must be allowed by all Judges of Mechanism, is the greatest Improvement ever made on Watch Work, which Use is to make the Watch keep regular Time in both extreme Heat and Cold, which occasioned the great Mr. Harrison a long Study before compleated. Likewise a compleat assortment of Watch Chains, Sword Swivels, Seals, &c.

The Subscriber cleans and repairs repeating, horizontal and plain Watches, at the most reasonable Rates.   JAMES ASBY.
—*Boston News-Letter*, May 16, 1771.

JAMES ASBY.—Just Imported in Capt. Callahan from London, and to be sold by James Asby, watch-maker, nearly opposite the British Coffee-House in King-Street, Boston, a Compleat Assortment of Watches. N. B. All Sorts of Clocks, as well as Watches, are Repaired in the most compleat Manner.—*Boston News-Letter*, Sept. 24, 1772.

JAMES ASBY.—A compleat Assortment of Clocks and Watches, etc. Imported and to be Sold by James Asby, Watch-Maker and Finisher from London, nearly opposite the British Coffee-House, in King-Street, Boston. N. B. All Sorts of Clocks and Watches Repaired in the compleatest Manner.—*Boston News-Letter*, Nov. 26, 1773.

JAMES ATKINSON, Watch-Maker, in Cornhill, near the Market in *Boston*, from the North-Side of *Royal Exchange* in London, Makes and Sells all Sorts of Watches and Clocks made in a compleat Manner of his own Name warranted, a variety of both he has now by him: Also repairs all Sorts of Watches in a careful and expeditious Manner; finishes the Dial Plate, &c. and fits them up in all Respects compleat and as reasonable as in London; sells Ladies Chains for Watches, and all sorts of Men's Chains, Seals, Gold and Silver and plain Watch Strings, Ear-Rings, Diamond Rings, &c. N. B. Buys Second Hand Plate, and all Sorts of Gold and Silver.—*Boston Gazette*, Jan. 8, 1745.

JAMES ATKINSON, Watch-Maker from *London*, is removed from Cornhill into King Street, near the Exchange, Boston.—*Boston Gazette*, Aug. 6, 1745.

JAMES ATKINSON, Watch-maker, upon the Exchange in Boston, All Sorts of repeating and plain Clocks, with or without Cases at reasonable Rates.—*Boston News-Letter*, June 30, 1748.

JAMES ATKINSON, watchmaker, deceased, late of Halifax, his estate was administered by Philip Freeman of Boston.—*Boston Gazette*, Nov. 15, 1756.

THOMAS BADELY, late of Boston, watchmaker, his estate was declared insolvent.—*Boston Gazette*, Mar. 6/13, 1720/1.

BENJAMIN BAGNALL.—Died, Benjamin Bagnall, watch maker, one of the people called Quackers; he came from England early in Life and has long resided in this place, died July 11, 1773, aged 84 years.—*Boston News-Letter*, July 15, 1773.

BENJAMIN BAGNALL, watch-maker, deceased, of Boston. His insolvent estate was advertised.—*Boston News-Letter*, July 28, 1774.

COLBORN BARRELL at his Store on the Dock near Mr John Head's advertised "A Fine Eight Day Spring Clock with Alarum, good Silver Watches with Chains and Seals. A Fine Watch for a Physician, with Second Hand."—*Boston News-Letter*, May 28, 1772.

JAMES BATTERSON.—This is to give Notice to all Gentlemen and others, that there is lately arrived in Boston from London, by the way of Pennsylvania, a Clock Maker: If any person or persons hath any occasion for New Clocks, or to have Old Ones turn'd into Pendelums; or any other thing either in making or mending; Let them repair to the Sign of the Clock Dial of the South Side of the Town-House in Boston, where they may have them done at reasonable Rates. Per James Batterson.—*Boston News-Letter*, Oct. 6/13, 1707.

JAMES BICHAUT, lately Arrived from London, Makes and Mends all sorts of Clocks and Watches.—*Boston Gazette*, July 21/28, 1729.

JOHN BRAND, Watch-Maker, from London, Maketh and Mendeth all Sorts of Clocks and Watches, at very easie Rates, and is to be found at the Sign of the Spring Clock & Watches, near the Draw-Bridge in Anne-Street, Boston.—*Boston News-Letter*, Jan. 21/28, 1711/12.

JOHN BRAND, watch-maker on the north side of the Town-House, Boston, advertised that his German Servant Man, John Copler, aged about 26 years, had run away.—*Boston News-Letter*, Aug. 24/31, 1713. He also advertised "several Compleat New Pocket Watches London Made."—*Boston News-Letter*, Oct. 18/25, 1714.

JOHN BRAND, watch-maker, in King Street, Boston, "designs for a Time to go for England" and requests all having dealings "without delay to come and make up accounts with him."—*Boston News-Letter*, Oct. 25/Nov. 1, 1714.

GAWEN BROWNE.—Imported from LONDON, and Sold by GAWEN BROWNE, Clock and Watch maker, below the Exchange in *King Street, Boston*. A Variety of new Silver Watches, and some double gilt Pinchback Watches, Stone Seals set in Silver, curious Pinchback Seals, with a great Assortment of common Seals, Watch Keys, &c. Likewise all sorts of new Clocks either repeating or plain at the lowest Prices.—*Boston Gazette*, June 16, 1752.

GOWEN BROWNE.—"Made and sold by Gowen Browne, In King-Street, *Boston*, All sorts of Clocks, cheaper than can be imported from *London;* also a Variety of best Stone Seals, *viz.* onyx and Cornelian Stones, curiously set in Silver, and double gilt Pinchbeck.—*Boston Evening Post,* Dec. 11, 1752.

GAWEN BROWN, Clock and Watch Maker, has removed from his Shop in King-Street to Union-Street next Door to Mr. John Salter, Brazier, opposite the Conduit, at the Head of the Town Dock, Boston.—*Boston Gazette,* Feb. 26, 1754.

GAWEN BROWN.—Imported in the *Jupiter,* Capt. Bull, from London, and to be sold by Gawen Brown, in King-Street, Boston, cheap for Cash or Province Notes;—A Number of Gold, Silver and Pinch-Beck Watches, fine wro't Chains for Ladies Watches, Steel ditto, Eight Day Clocks, &c.—*Boston Gazette,* Dec. 29, 1760.

GAWEN BROWN.—Imported in Capt *Farr,* and sold by *Gawen Brown,* sundry new Silver Watches of exquisite Workmanship, one Gold ditto, Eight Day Clocks, Clock Bells, best Watch Strings, Silver Pendants, Main Springs, London White Varnish, &c. &c. curious Chains for Ladies Watches.

N. B. Some of the Watches goes on Diamonds, and some shews the Day of the Month.—*Boston Gazette,* June 22, 1761.

GAWEN BROWN.—This is to acquaint the Public, that *Gawen Brown,* Watchmaker, in King Street, has remov'd his Shop 3 Doors below, the same side of the Way, next Door to *Richard Dana,* Esq, where he will be glad to wait on his former Customers. He has to sell sundry 8 Day Clocks, a genteel Gold Chas'd Watch, suitable for a Lady, 1 plain ditto for a Gentleman, 2 Silver ditto, go on Diamonds, plain Silver Watches, &c. &c.—*Boston Gazette,* Oct. 12, 1761.

GAWEN BROWN.—Imported in Capt. Hulme, and to be Sold by *Gawen Brown,* Watch-maker in King-Street, Boston; A number of new silver Watches, silver Chains, Seals, Strings, &c. eight day Clocks, a spring Clock, a gold Watch second hand, &c. &c.—*Boston Gazette,* Feb. 8, 1762.

GAWEN BROWN.—Imported in Capt. Hunter, and Sold by *Gawen Brown* in King-street, A variety of good Silver & Pinchbeck Watches, Silver Chains; Seals, Keys, Main-Springs, Glasses, etc. etc.—*Boston Gazette,* June 21, 1762.

GAWEN BROWN.—Imported in the Captains *Adams* and *Loring*, a Number of Clocks and Watches, to be sold cheap for the cash, by *Gawen Brown*, in King Street, Boston. Also a Gold Chas'd Watch.—*Boston Gazette*, Nov. 1, 1762.

GAWEN BROWN.—Just imported from London, and to be Sold by *Gawen Brown*, at his shop in King-Street; a number of fine Silver Watches, some Pinch beck ditto, one genteel Gold Chais'd Watch, Silver and steel Chains, best silk Strings, &c. at the most reasonable Prices.—*Boston Gazette*, July 4, 1763.

GAWEN BROWN.—Imported in Capt. *Hunter*, and sold by *Gawen Brown*, sundry good Eight Day Clocks, China Dial Plates, Clock Bells, Strings for 30 Hour Clocks, &c. and sundry new Watches, warrented to perform well,—Also a second hand small Gold Watch.—*Boston Gazette*, Nov. 21, 1763.

GAWEN BROWN.—Good Eight Day Clocks, with Mehogany Cases, new Silver Watches, Strings for 24 Hour Clocks, and two second-hand Clocks in Cases, to be sold at the lowest Prices by *Gawen Brown*, Watchmaker, in King-Street, Boston.—*Boston Gazette*, Apr. 16, 1764.

GAWEN BROWN.—Just Imported in Capt. *Coffin*, and to be sold by Gawen Brown, *in King-Street*, Sundry new Silver and Pinchbeck Watches; a variety of Paste and Stone Seals set in Silver and Pinchbeck; Eight Day Clocks, Clock Bells, Strings for 30 Hour Clocks, &c.—*Boston Gazette*, Oct. 22, 1764.

GAWEN BROWN.—Imported in Captain *Marshall*, from London, Sundry good Silver Watches, Pinchbeck ditto, Eight Day Clocks, with Mahogany Cases; silver Chains for Watches; best silk Strings, Seals, &c, to be sold very Cheap by GAWEN BROWN in King Street.—*Boston Gazette*, Dec. 9, 1765.

GAWEN BROWNE.—At the Town Meeting [held in Boston, Mar. 14, 1768] were exhibited the Frames and principal Movements of a superb stately Town-Clock, made by Mr Gawen Browne, of this Town: The two great Wheels took near 90 lb. weight of cast Brass: It is calculated for eight Days to shew the Hours and Minutes: will have three grand Dials, and a mechanic Lever to preserve the Motion during the winding up. The Pendulum Wheel and Pallets to perform the dead Beat. The Works are nicely executed: The Steel Pinions and Teeth of the Wheels are finely polished, which must greatly abate the Friction, add to its Regularity and Duration. It will have a curious mathematical Pendulum that may be altered the 3500 Part of an Inch while the Clock is going.—From the exquisite finishing of the Parts already done good Judges are of opinion it will be a Master piece of the Kind, and an Honor to America.—*Boston News-Letter*, Mar. 17, 1768.

GAWEN BROWN.—To be Sold cheap for Cash, New Eight-Day Clocks, with Mahogany Cases, New Silver Watches with Bar Movements, warranted good.—Silver Chains, Steel ditto, Silk Strings, &c. Enquire of Gawen Brown, in King-Street.—*Boston News-Letter*, Nov. 28, 1771.

GAWEN BROWN.—"An excellent eight Day Clock, made by *Gawen Brown*, (handsome Mahogany Case, Brass Balls, &c)," was offered for sale with other furniture by George Erving, Esq.—*Boston News-Letter*, Apr. 29, 1773.

WILLIAM CLAGGET.—"To be Sold a new Fashion'd Monethly Clock & Case lately arrived from London, also a new Fashion'd Camblet Bed lin'd with Satten, to be seen at Mr. *William Clagget*, jun. Clock-Maker, near the Town-House.—*Boston News-Letter*, Dec. 26/Jan. 2, 1715/16.

THOMAS CLARK, Clock and Watch-Maker from London, Takes this Method to inform all Gentlemen and Ladies in Town and Country, that he has to sell at his Shop the South Side of the Court-House; A Fine Assortment of the neatest made CLOCKS and WATCHES, of all Prices; he will also warrant the same, as they are of his own Make, and will be sold cheaper than any ever imported in the Country; the Clocks he will sell with or without the Case as it shall suit the Purchaster. He also mends and cleans either in the best Manner.—*Boston Gazette*, Nov. 5, 1764.

ELIJAH COLLINS, watchmaker, over against the dwelling house of the late Samuel Lynde, Esq., Boston, advertised for sale "a quantity of good Pickled Fish call'd Menhaden, choicely procured in Barrels suitable to send to the West Indies."—*Boston Gazette*, Aug. 21/28, 1727.

RICHARD CRANCH.—WATCH-TOOLS. To be Sold by Richard Cranch, near the Mill-Bridge, in Boston, a Great Variety of Watchmaker's Tools; with Stock of too many Sorts to enumerate in an Advertisement. Also, various Tools for Clock-Makers, among which are all Sorts of Clock-Files. He has also to sell a Pair of 12 Inch Globes, and a neat Compound Microscope.—*Boston News-Letter*, Dec. 20, 1770.

RICHARD CRANCH informs such of his Friends as may want to have CLOCKS clean'd or mended, that they may have them done at his Shop, by a Clock-maker, lately from LONDON, who will do them carefully, and at a reasonable Rate.—*Boston News-Letter*, Apr. 1, 1773.

RICHARD CRANCH, Near the Mill-Bridge, Boston, Informs his Customers and others, That he has receiv'd directly from the Makers, a good Assortment of Watches, some of which are of the best Quality. Also good Eight-day Clocks, and a Variety of Articles for Clock & Watch Makers; among which are Clock-Bells and Hands, Clock and Watch Files, Watch Springs and Glasses, a Variety of Watch-Maker's Tools and sundry other Articles; which he will sell at a reasonable Rate.—*Boston News-Letter*, Apr. 29, 1773.

RICHARD CRANCH, near the Mill-Bridge, Boston, informs his Customers, That he has just received by Capt. Scott, a good assortment of WATCHES, some of them very elegant, shewing the Day of the Month, &c. He also has for Sale, very good Eight-Day Clocks and Cases; Clock-Weights cas'd in Brass; Springs for Table Clocks; a good Assortment of Watch-Maker's Tools; and a Variety of other Articles in the Clock and Watch Way.—*Boston News-Letter*, Nov. 26, 1773.

RICHARD CRANCH, Watch-Maker, Hereby informs his Customers, That he has removed from his House near the Mill-Bridge, Boston, to a House in Braintree, nearly opposite the Rev. Mr. Winslow's Church, a few Rods South of Mr. Brackett's Tavern; where he proposes carrying on the Watch-Maker's Business as usual, And as he has a number of Watches in his Hands, belonging to his Customers, he desires such as cannot conveniently call for them at his House in Braintree, to leave a Line for him at the Shop of Messieurs Nathaniel and Joseph Cranch, who will convey the same and receive the Watches for the Owners as soon as they are finished.—*Boston News-Letter*, Apr. 13, 1775.

ISAAC DOOLITTLE.—We are informed that Mr. Isaac Doolittle, Clock & Watch-Maker, of New Haven, has lately compleated a Mahogany Printing-Press on the most approved Construction, which, by some good Judges in the Printing Way, is allowed to be the neatest ever made in America and equal, if not superior, to any imported from Great-Britain: This Press, we are told, is for Mr Goddard, of Philadelphia, Printer.—*Boston News-Letter*, Sept. 7, 1769.

——— ELWOOD.—The Granary of the Town of Boston was broken into and the Master of the Granary lost money and "a small old fashion'd Silver Minuet and Pendulum Watch, having an inside Chain and Brass Hands, part of the Head of the Cannon Pinnion broken off, it has a pretty thick Green String, and at the End of it, an old Key something bruis'd: Likewise a large Silver Watch, made by Elwood, being good work, has a Flower upon the Head of the Pillar and a Picture of a Man upon the inner part of the outside Case, with a three link'd Silver Chain, one of the Links is broke and mended with white Silk, with a triangular Steel Seal, hung upon a Wire."—*Boston News-Letter*, Feb. 1/8, 1732/3.

EDWARD TILLITT EMMETT, Clock-Maker; Informs the Publick, that he has just opened Shop upon the South Side of the Town-House, in King Street, in the Mansion House of *Gillam Phillips*, Esq.; where Clocks and Watches are repaired with Fidelity and Despatch.—*Boston Gazette*, July 16, 1764.

EDMUND ENTWISTLE.—Just Imported and to be Sold by Edmund Entwisle, at Mr. Fullen's in Cross-Street, Boston,—A Fine Clock, a Description of which is as follows, viz. It goes 8 or 9 Days with one winding up, and repeats the Hour it struck last when you pull it, the Dial is 13 Inches on the Square, and arched with a Semi-Circle on the Top., round which is a strong Plate with this Motto (*Time shews the Way of Life's Decay*) well engrav'd and Silver'd; within the Motto-Ring it shews from behind two semi-Spheres, the Moon's Increase and Decrease by two curious Painted Faces, ornamented with golden Stars between, on a blue Ground, and a white Circle on the outside divided into Days figur'd at every Third, on which Divisions is shewn the Age by a fixt Index from the Top, as they pass by the great Circle is divided into three Concentrick Collums, on the outmost of which it shews the Minute of each Hour, and the middlemost the Hours, &c. the innermost is divided into 31 equal Parts figur'd at every other, on which is shewn the Day of the Month by a Hand from the Dial Plate as the Hour and Hand is; it also shews the Seconds as common, and is ornamented with curious Engravings in the most fashionable Manner. The Case is made of very good Mahogony, with quarter Collums in the Body, broke in the Surface, and raised Pannels, with Quarter Rounds, Cross-Bands, and Strings; The Head is ornamented with gilded Capitals, Bases, and Frise, with new fashion'd Balls Composed of Mahogany, with gilt Laves and Flames. Also a new Silver Watch, and old large Ditto, etc.

As the said Mr. Entwisle don't intend to stay above three or four Days in Town, he will sell at low Prices.... The Ship that he goes in is so well repaired as to be able to proceed on her intended Voyage.—*Boston News-Letter*, Nov. 18, 1742.

JOSEPH ESSEX.—These are to give Notice to all Gentlemen, Merchants and Others, That there is lately arriv'd from Great Britain to this Place, Mr. Joseph Essex; who now keeps Shop in Buttler's Buildings, in King Street, Boston, and performs all sorts of New Clocks, and Watch works; viz. 30 hour Clocks, Week Clocks, Month Clocks, Spring Table Clocks, Chime Clocks, quarter Clocks, quarter Chime Clocks, Church Clocks, Terret Clocks, and new Pocket Watches, new repeating Watches; Likewise doth give any Gentlemen, &c. Tryal before Payment of either Clock or Watches, and after Payment for 12 Months will oblige himself to change either Clock or Watch, if not liked, or else return his

Money again; These Articles to be performed by the abovesaid Joseph Essex and Thomas Badley.—*Boston News-Letter*, Nov. 3/10, 1712.

CHARLES GEDDES, Clock and Watch Maker, and Finisher, from London, at his Shop below the Sign of Admiral Vernon, in King Street, Boston, Makes, mends, cleans, repairs, and finishes all sorts of Clocks and Watches, in the best and neatest Manner, and upon the most reasonable Terms.—*Boston News-Letter*, Oct. 14, 1773.

JAMES HAGGARS.—Lost on the 23d of October instant between Mr. Mower's and Winnisimmet, a small Silver Watch and Chain, of James Hagger's make, No. 383. Whoever shall convey the same to Mr. Joshua Cheever, at the North End of Boston, or to Mr. Mower of Lynn, or Mr Watts at Winnisimmet, shall be well rewarded for their pains.—*Boston Gazette*, Oct. 20/27, 1729.

JOHN HENRYSON.—Lost on 13th of August past, a Silver Watch with a Silver Chain and Seal, it has an Arch Dial Plate with Gold Stars in the half Hours, and the Maker's Name John Henryson of London. . . . Three Pounds Reward.—*Boston News-Letter*, Sept. 2/9, 1731.

——— KING.—Lost a few days ago, a middle siz'd silver watch with an enamel'd dial plate, maker's name KING, Salop — the Contrait wheel pinion has been broke and mended again, it had a cat-gut string, and one key, and looks like a new watch. Whoever will bring it to the printers hereof, shall have a GUINEA reward for their trouble.—*Boston Gazette*, Jan. 12, 1756.

——— KING.—Taken out of a House in Boston, on the Lord's-Day the 20th Instant, between 2 & 5 o'Clock in the Afternoon, a small Silver Watch, the maker's name King, LONDON. Whoever shall inform of the same, or bring it to the Printer, shall have five Pounds old Tenor Reward, and no Questions ask'd.— *Boston Gazette*, May 22, 1750.

W. KIPLING.—Three beautiful Silver Watches, to be Sold, cheap for the Cash, made in the most Modern Taste; one of them by that celebrated Workman, W. Kipling, London. Inquire of the Printer.—*Boston Gazette*, Sept. 25, 1753.

KNEELAND AND RELFAST.—Lost by Joshua House of Lancaster, . . . between Lancaster and Weston, A large Silver Watch, no Cristial, and a green Ribbon with a broken Key, made by Kneeland and Relfast, Moses Peck on the Paper in the Case. . . . Three Dollars Reward.—*Boston Gazette*, Aug. 14, 1758.

——— KOVER.—Lost in Boston, on Thursday last, a Silver Watch, with a scollapt Face, made by Mr *Kover* of London, a Silver Chain, and two Silver Seals, one of which has a Compass in the Seal; The Nubb of the Spring is broke off. . . . $3 reward.—*Boston Gazette*, Nov. 2, 1761.

——— LOVEDAY.—Lost last Wednesday Night . . . a small Silver Watch . . . on the Dial Plate mark'd Loveday and London, with a flowered yellow Ribbon and the Key. Reward £3.—*Boston Gazette*, Nov. 19/26, 1739.

DAVID MITCHELSON.—Watches, plain, skeleton and horizontal, in Gold, Silver and Pinchbeck Cases; in particular, a great Variety of Silver Watches, from ten Dollars to ten Guineas, some of which show the Day of the Month, and others with Seconds, are very suitable for Physicians; likewise Spring and Pendulum Eight-Day Clocks; also an Assortment of Tools and Materials used by Clock and Watch-Makers, To be sold by DAVID MITCHELSON, at the House of Mr. Benjamin Davis, Merchant, near the Mill-Bridge.—*Boston News-Letter*, May 26, 1774.

NATHANIEL MULLIKEN.—Monday Mr Nathaniel Mulliken, of Lexington, Clock-Maker, (who to all Appearance had been as well that Day as at any Time) as he was coming in at the Door of his House, instantly fell, and, notwithstanding all possible Endeavours for Relief, expired in a few moments, to the great Grief of his disconsolate Widow and seven Children. His Remains were inter'd on Thursday.—*Boston Evening Post*, Dec. 4, 1767.

JOHN NEWMAN, Clock and Watch-Maker; hereby informs the Town and Country, That he has lately opened his Shop opposite the North Door of the Court House in King-Street, *Boston*; where he makes and mends all Sorts of Gold & Silver Horozontal striking and repeating Watches, in the best and neatest Manner;

and extreme reasonable in his Demands, Seals, Keys, Glasses, &c. &c.—*Boston Gazette*, July 23, 1764.

ROBERT PEASELEY.—Whereas Twelve Watches are left in the *hands of* James Busby *Wine Cooper, at the Sign of the Duke of Marlborough's Arms in King-street* Boston, *by* Robert Peasely, *Watchmaker: This is to give Notice to all Persons to whom said Watches may belong, that they may have them paying Charges, a Memorandum whereof left by the said* Peasely *is as follows.*

No. 1. *Mr.* Hutchinson  2 Arthur Savage.  3. *Mr.* Parker of *Andover.*  4 *Mr* Goffe.  5. Tho. Savage.  6. Ruth Read.  7. Henry Wetherhead.  8 Tho. Lechmere.  9. Peter Prescot.  10. A Currier.  11. Michael Dalton of *Newbury.*  12. A Watch unknown belonging to one in the Country.—*Boston Gazette*, Aug. 11/18, 1735.

MOSES PECK, Watchmaker, on the South Side of the Town House, Boston, had on sale, tickets in the Philadelphia Lottery.—*Boston Gazette*, May 1, 1753.

MOSES PECK, on the South Side of the Exchange, King street, Boston, has Imported in Capt. *Hunter*, and to be Sold, a Number of good silver Watches; also an Assortment of Men's Watch Chains, Women's best ditto Gold Pattern, Cornelian and Chrystal Seals, Compass ditto with enamel'd Plates, Steel Keys with Hooks, Silk Strings, Lockets, Main Springs, fine Pendulum Wire, white Clock Lines, &c. &c.—Likewise has new and second hand Eight Day Clocks.—*Boston Gazette*, Apr. 25, 1763.

MOSES PECK Hereby informs his Customers and others, That he has to sell in his Shop in King Street, good Gold and Silver Watches made in London by *Samuel Toulmin*, and others.—Likewise good Eight Day Clocks, either with or without Cases—Also a good Assortment of other Articles in the Business.—*Boston Gazette*, Sept. 23, 1765.

——————ROBINSON.—Lost . . . in Andover, a good Silver Watch, Maker's Name *Robinson*, the Face Scollopt, a Stone Seal set in Silver, and Brass Key. . . . Two Dollars Reward, *Asa Foster.*—*Boston Gazette*, Jan. 12, 1761.

—————— ROGERS.—Left in a Shop in Cambridge, or lost on the

road from Cambridge to Charlestown, a best Silver Watch, with an enamel'd Dial Plate, Maker *Rogers*, No. 952, lately clean'd. . . . —*Boston Gazette*, Oct. 12, 1761.

JOHN ROULSTONE, Clock and Watch-Maker, Takes this Opportunity to inform those Gentlemen who favour him with their Custom;—That he has removed from the Shop he lately improv'd to a Shop three Doors Southward of that, and the third Door Northward of the White Horse Tavern; Where he does all sorts of Clock and Watch-Work as usual,—has all sorts of Watch Chains, Strings, Seals and Keys, &c. &c.—*Boston News-Letter*, May 12, 1768.

JOHN SINNETT.—WATCHES. As many People are put to Expense to no Purpose by those who undertake to repair their Watches, and many good Pieces of Work spoiled or damaged by unskilled Practitioners, *John Sinnett*, Citizen of London, and principal Manufacturer in England and Ireland, Inventor of, and Skeleton Watch finisher, continues to clean and repair at the same price as in London; and for the Convenience of Gentlemen in or near Boston, will pay the Carriage to and fro. for all Watches sent by Mr Noble's Stage, to me opposite Mr Staver's Tavern, Piscataqua, or Portsmouth. And as I intend to return Home next Summer, undertake as bespoke, to supply those of the Trade, Merchants, or private Gentlemen, with all manner of plain, horizontal or repeating Watches, and small ones for Rings; also plain, chime, machine, organ and astronomical Clocks. All Watches of the Name *Upjohn*, or *Story*, clean'd gratis.

☞ An Assortment of Gold and Silver Watches for Sale.—*Boston News-Letter*, Feb. 9, 1769.

MARMADUKE STORE.—Lost or stole in Charlestown, about five Weeks past, a small Silver Watch, having a Silver Chain, the maker's name wrote on the Dial Plate, *Marmaduke Store;* Whoever shall bring it to the Printer shall have Three Pounds Reward, and no Questions ask'd.—*Boston Gazette*, Jan. 19, 1742.

MARMADUKE STORR.—A genteel Gold Watch, made by *Marmaduke Storr*, to be Sold, inquire of the Printers.—*Boston Gazette*, Sept. 7, 1761.

TOMPION.—Lost between Warwick and Dr. Macsparren's House, in Narraganset, the 21st of this Current November, a large Gold Watch, the Maker's Name *Tompion*, the No. 4002; Whoever brings said Watch, shall have *Ten Pounds, Rhode Island* Currency paid him, by me JAMES MACSPARRAN.—*Boston Gazette*, Nov. 29, 1756.

ISAAC WEBB.—This is to give Notice that Isaac Webb, Watch-Maker and Clock-Maker, that formerly Liv'd next Door to the Royal-Exchange Tavern near to the East End of the Town-House in Boston, is now Removed over-against the West-End of the said Town-House in the High Street two Doors from Prison Lane, at the Sign of the Clock Dial that goes against the Side of the House; So that if any Person or Persons wants any Clock to be made, or any Old Clocks to be turned into Pendelums, or Watches and Clocks to be Mended, or Glasses, Keys, Springs or Chains of the best Sort; Let them repair to the said Webb, where they may be served on reasonable Terms.—*Boston News-Letter*, Mar. 29/Apr. 5, 1708.

———— WEST.—Lost on Christmas Day, between *Fiske's* of Lexington and Lancaster, a large Silver Watch, with a Steel Chain, the maker *West* of London. Whoever hath taken up Said Watch, and shall Convey it to the Printer, or to the widow *Prudence Prentice* at Lancaster, shall be honourably rewarded. P. S. Said Watch was wrapt in a brown Leather Glove.—*Boston Gazette*, Jan. 29, 1751.

JOSHUA WILSON.—Lost between Mr Hall's cordwainer in Roxbury, and Mr. Turner's Mill, a large Silver Watch, without a chain, that has a Bruise just where it opens, the Maker's Name is Joshua Wilson. Reward, forty shillings.—*Boston News-Letter*, Dec. 30/Jan. 6, 1736/7.

BENJAMIN WILLARD.—MUSICAL CLOCKS To be Sold Musical Clocks that go by Springs, also Musical Clocks that go by Weights, and play a different Tune each Day in the Week, on Sunday's a Psalm Tune. Inquire of *Benja. Willard*, Clock & Watch Maker in Roxbury Street near Boston, Where all sorts of Clocks are made in the newest Form and Warranted to go without

Variation, and many without Cleaning. Also Clock Cases are made at the same Place, in various Forms and in the best Manner, and cheaper than can be purchas'd in London. Also Convey'd with Clocks to any Part of the Country. All the Branches of this Business is likewise carried on at his Shop at Grafton.—*Boston Gazette*, Sept. 12, 1774 (*sup.*).

## Clocks and Watches

STRIKING WATCH.—A Good large striking Watch to be Seen and Sold at Mr. Adam Baeth, Cardmaker, his House near to the Star in Boston.—*Boston News-Letter*, Jan. 5/12, 1707/8.

A REPEATED CLOCK was advertised to be sold by Daniel Stevens at his Coffee House in Ann Street, Boston.—*Boston News-Letter*, Dec. 27/Jan. 3, 1714/15.

REPEATING CLOCKS.—Lately come from London, a Parcel of very fine Clocks, They go a Week, and repeat the Hour when pull'd; in Japan Cases or Wall-Nut. To be Sold by Mr. *William Gent*, and to be Seen at the House of Mr. *Peter Thomas* in Wings-Lane, Boston.—*Boston News-Letter*, Apr. 9/16, 1716.

HOUSE CLOCK.—"A fine House Clock" was advertised to be sold at Vendue at the Crown Coffee House, Boston.—*Boston News-Letter*, Dec. 28/Jan. 4, 1719/20.

STEEL SEAL.—Lost about a Fortnight since, a plain Silver Watch, with a plain Dial-plate, in a single Case on a black Ribbon, with a Steel Seal engraved three Mullets or Stars, and a Chevron Argent in a field Sable; the Crest a Demi-Blackmoor with a Dart in Hand: Whoever shall have taken up said Watch, and will bring it to the Post Office in Boston, shall have Forty Shillings Reward. —*Boston Gazette*, Aug. 2/9, 1731.

GOLD WATCH.—Taken out of the House of James Dolbear of Boston, on Monday the 7th of July, a Gold Watch with a Green String and Pearl Seal to it. Whosoever shall bring said Watch and Convict the Person that took it shall have Ten Pounds Reward paid by James Dolbear.—*Boston Gazette*, July 28/Aug. 4, 1735.

CALENDAR WATCH.—Lost some Days since in Boston, a Watch with a green String, and in the inside a Glass on the Pendelom or Ballance, and the Watch does not fill up the outer Case, and the Hinges of the outside Case cut off; and the Watch tells the Day of the Month. Whoever will bring the said Watch to the Printer hereof, shall have Three Pounds Reward, & no Questions ask'd. —*Boston Gazette*, May 1/8, 1738.

BRASS SEAL.—Left on board an old Sloop lying at the Wharff of Deacon Lee, on Saturday the 15th Instant, in the Forenoon, a Silver Watch, with a Silver three-braded Chain, a brass Seal, on the face of the Seal a Dove with an Olive Branch in her Mouth, also a Brass Key; and mark'd on the Dyal Plate Thomas. Whoever shall bring the above Watch to the Printer hereof, shall have Five Pounds Reward.—*Boston News-Letter*, Sept. 3/10, 1741.

A HANDSOME TIME-PIECE was to be sold at auction in Boston by John Gerrish, auctioneer.—*Boston News-Letter*, Jan. 10, 1745.

SILVER WATCH.—Lost or Stolen last Night at Mr. Webb's Meeting-House, a large Silver Watch, Tomlinson's make, London, No. 392. Reward Five Pounds, old Tenor, and no Questions asked. Apply to the Printer.—*Boston News-Letter*, Aug. 6, 1747.

STONE SEALS.—Drop'd in Boston last Evening, Part of a flat Chain of a Gold Watch, with a Key and two Stone Seals set in Gold, one of the Stones has a Coat of Arms engraven on it. Whoever will bring the same to the Printer hereof shall be well rewarded.—*Boston News-Letter*, Oct. 1, 1747.

LADIES' WATCHES.—For sale, . . . rich Chains, with Bottles, &c. for Ladies Gold Watches. . . . —*Boston News-Letter*, Nov. 5, 1747.

GOLD WATCH.—To be Sold, a Woman's Gold Watch, with a Gold Chain, a Man's Gold Watch, a pair of Diamond Earings, a Diamond Ring, 3 handsome Stone Rings; Inquire of the Printer. —*Boston Gazette*, Jan. 26, 1748.

TABLE SPRING CLOCK.—To be Sold a curious Collection of the Newest fashion'd Diamond Rings, Gold chased Watch and Chain, plain Ditto, Gold Seals, a neat Table Spring Clock, warrented, &c. Inquire of the Printer.—*Boston Gazette*, Oct. 23, 1750.

A HANDSOME CHIMEING CLOCK, was listed among the household furniture sold at publick vendue at the house of the late Joseph Scott, Boston.—*Boston Evening Post*, Mar. 9, 1751.

GOLD WATCH.—*Stolen*, from on board the *Endeavour*, James Nichols, master, at Boston, "a neat Chest Gold Watch, with a Shagreen Case and Pinchback Ladies Chain. It has an Enamel'd Dial Plate." Reward, £20. O. T.—*Boston Gazette*, Oct. 10, 1752.

ALARM CLOCKS.—Robert Jenkins and Son, near the Exchange, advertised among other items—"Jewellers Wares, the Particulars are too large to be here enumerated.—Also Hogsheads of Glass and Earthern Ware, handsom Eight Day and Alarm Clocks."—*Boston Evening Post*, June 17, 1754.

A PINCH-BACK WATCH, was offered at auction Sale in Boston.—*Boston Gazette*, Sept. 3, 1754.

A "NEW 8 DAY CLOCK, with a beautiful Japann'd Case," was advertised for sale at auction by Benjamin Church.—*Boston Gazette*, Dec. 17, 1754.

"A HANDSOME JAPAN'D CLOCK," was sold at publick Vendue Sept. 9, 1755, at the house of the late Ebenezer Holmes, King St. Boston.—*Boston Evening Post*, Sept. 8, 1755.

AN ALARM CLOCK was advertised for Sale at Public Vendue.—*Boston Gazette*, July 12, 1756.

PINCHBECK WATCHES.—Mr. Syberberg, of New York City, was robbed of two watches, one of Pinchbeck and the other Silver, as he was shutting up his shop. The thief "run his Hand thro' the Glass Window, and carried off the Watches" and got clear.—*Boston Gazette*, Jan. 10, 1757.

WATCH MAKER'S TOOLS.—"A parcel of Watch Maker's Tools," and watches, was advertised for sale at the vendue rooms of Benjamin Church, Boston.—*Boston Gazette*, Aug. 29, 1757.

SPRING CLOCK.—Samuel Smith, advertised for sale at his Vendue Room in Fore Street, at the North End, a variety of articles including, "a good 8 Day Clock, two silver Watches, a beautiful Spring Clock."—*Boston Gazette*, Oct. 8, 1759.

DIAMOND BEARINGS.—An excellent Silver Watch, that goes upon Diamonds, to be sold cheap for the cash: enquire of the printers.—*Boston Gazette*, Nov. 5, 1759.

SILVER WATCH.—Lost between Salem and Boston. . . . a midling siz'd Silver Watch, with a Iron Wier Chain, and the Inside glazed: . . . Three Dollars Reward.—*Boston Gazette*, Jan. 21, 1760.

A CHINA CLOCK, with household furniture, was advertised for sale at a vendue room in Boston.—*Boston Gazette*, Aug. 17, 1761.

WATCHES.—At the New Auction Room at the foot of Royal Exchange Lane, Dock Square, will be Sold at publick vendue, a great Variety of Silver and other curious Watches, warrented by *Merideth* and *Burnett*.—*Boston Gazette*, Nov. 28, 1763.

WATCHES.—At the New-Auction Room, will be sold a publick vendue a variety of articles including "A few new and exceeding good watches, one of £8, 10 s. Sterl. that goes on a Diamond."—*Boston Gazette*, Dec. 12, 1763.

WATCHMAKER'S MACHINES.—To be Sold at Colborn Barrell's store, near Treat's Wharf, Boston.

A few very neat Silver Watches, one extraordinary Watch suitable for a Physician, moving a Second Hand from the Center; also, two very fine Watchmaker's Machines, one for cutting Balance Wheels, and one larger for cutting all the various Wheels of a Watch, together with an Assortment of Watch Springs, Fusee Chains, &c. &c.—*Boston News-Letter*, Dec. 7, 1770.

SPRING CLOCKS.—"Two very handsome Spring Clocks" were advertised for sale at auction among the effects of the late John Apthrop, Esq.—*Boston News-Letter*, May 13, 1773.

PULL-UP CLOCK.—A "pull-up Clock" was advertised for sale at public vendue together with other furniture.—*Boston News-Letter*, Dec. 16, 1773.

# WALL PAPER

STAMPT PAPER.—John Phillips, bookseller, advertised "Stampt Paper in Rolls for to Paper Rooms."—*New England Journal*, Oct. 26, 1730.

HENRY STANBRIDGE, painter stayner, of Boston, settlement of estate.—*Boston Gazette*, Oct. 14/21, 1734.

"ROLL PAPER for Rooms, with most kinds of Stationary," for Sale by Samuel Eliot in Cornhill.—*Boston News-Letter*, May 6/13, 1736.

"ROLL PAPER for Rooms," with "most sorts of Stationary Ware" was advertised for sale by John Parker, over against the shop of Mr Dolbeare, Brazier, at the Head of the Town Dock in Boston.—*Boston News-Letter*, June 3/10, 1736.

"ROLL'D PAPER for hanging of Rooms" for sale by John Parker, bookseller, at the Head of the Town Dock.—*Boston News-Letter*, July 21/28, 1737.

PAINTED PAPER.—"Sundry sorts of Painted Paper for Rooms" were to be sold at public vendue at the Exchange Tavern in King Street, with other importations.—*New England Journal*, Aug. 29, 1738.

"FLOWER'D PAPER, or Paper Hangings for Rooms, to be Sold; Inquire of the Printer."—*Boston Gazette*, Feb. 2, 1742.

ARRAS HANGINGS.—"Beautiful Arras-Hangings for a Room," were advertised to be sold at public vendue by Benjamin Church. —*Boston News-Letter*, Aug. 22, 1745.

RICH HANGING.—"A Beautiful rich and good Hanging for a Room, to be Sold. Enquire of the Printer."—*Boston News-Letter*, Apr. 10, 1747.

PAPER HANGINGS.—"Handsome Paper-Hangings for Rooms" were advertised for Sale by Thomas Hancock at his Warehouse, 4 Merchants' Row.—*Boston News-Letter*, Feb. 18, 1748.

WALL PAPER.—To be sold at publick Vendue, a large commodious Brick Dwelling House, 3 Story high, 3 Rooms on a Floor,

WALL PAPER USED IN NEW ENGLAND

Reduced about one-half; probably used in 1775 or before. From originals owned by Walter Kendall Watkins

the Rooms well waistcoted, & newly painted, two of the large Chambers lately papered . . . situate at the lower End of Milk-street.—*Boston Gazette*, June 4, 1751.

LINING WALLS.—Andrew Hunter of Newport, Rhode Island, advertised to be sold "a very commodious House, well finished in the inside with Paint and Lining, four Rooms on a Floor."—*Boston Evening Post*, May 28, 1753.

"PRINTED PAPERS for Rooms" lately imported from London, for Sale by William Marchent, at his store opposite the Golden Ball on the Town Dock.—*Boston Gazette*, Apr. 9, 1754.

PAPER HANGINGS.—"A variety of Paper Hangings" were advertised to be sold by Jarvis & Parker, at their Store three Doors below Mr. Dowse's Insurance Office in King Street.—*Boston Gazette*, May 26, 1755.

PAPERED WALLS.—Ten dollars reward was offered for information as to who entered the house lately occupied by Mrs Campbell and tore the paper off the walls in two rooms and defiled the floors.—*Boston News-Letter*, Aug. 2, 1759.

PAPER HANGINGS.—Imported in Capt. Jacobson and to be Sold, Enquire of the Printer hereof: An Assortment of Paper-Hangings for Rooms, Blue Demi Paper, [various books] and Metzotinto Prints of the King of Prussia.—*Boston News-Letter*, July 31, 1760.

CHEAP HANGINGS.—"A great variety of cheap paper hangings," just imported from London in the *Jupiter* and for sale by Lewis Deblois.—*Boston Gazette*, Jan. 5, 1761.

PAPER HANGINGS.—Among other items advertised to be sold at public vendue at the New Auction Room, Dock Square, were:— 40 or 50 rolls of Paper Hangings.—*Boston News-Letter*, July 1, 1762.

PAPER FOR ROOMS.—Joshua Blanchard, at his Shop on Dock Square, hath imported in Capt. Jacobson, a new and large Assortment of Paper for Rooms.—*Boston News-Letter*, July 22, 1762.

PAPER HANGER.—Died. Mr Daniel Starr, of this Town, "who has been for many Years employed in Papering Rooms," Sept. 22, 1762.—*Boston News-Letter*, Sept. 23, 1762.

Paper Hanger.—Benjamin Russell, Informs his Customers and others, that he undertakes Papering Rooms and Stair-Cases in the best Manner, at a reasonable Rate,—Any Gentleman that has a mind to Employ him in the neighboring Towns, may be served by him (paying his Travelling Charges) at the same Rate as those in Boston,—Said Russell has a number of Window Sashes 10 by 8, 24 Lights in a Window, to Sell Reasonably for Cash,—they are made of the best of Pine. Said Russell lives the North-side of Bacon-Hill [*sic*] in Boston, opposite to Mr. Joseph Callender's, Baker.—*Boston Gazette*, Aug. 22, 1763.

Gothic Paper Hangings.—Just imported from London and for sale by Thomas Lee, a great variety of articles including: "a fine Assortment of Gothic Paper Hangings."—*Boston News-Letter*, May 17, 1764.

Cheap Hangings.—Joshua Blanchard at his Shop in Dock Square sold "a great Variety of Papers for Rooms, at lower Prices than ever:—Many of them as low as 20 s. and Half-a-Dollar a Piece."—*Boston News-Letter*, Aug. 16, 1764.

Gothic Paper Hangings.—A fine assortment of Gothick and other Paper Hangings, advertised by Thomas Lee, who designs for England in the Spring.—*Boston News-Letter*, Jan. 24, 1765.

"Paper Hangings for Rooms, one at 20 s. per Roll."—*Boston Gazette*, June 3, 1765.

Made in New York.—New York, Dec. 5, [1765]. At a numerous Meeting of the Society for promoting Arts, &c. in this Province . . . John Rugar produced several Patterns of Paper Hangings made in this Province. . . . The said Rugar has now a considerable Quantity on Hand, and lives in Bayard Street, next Door to Mr. Heyman Levi.—*Boston News-Letter*, Dec. 12, 1765.

Papers for Rooms.—Joshua Blanchard hath Imported from London and sells at his Shop on Dock Square:—Papers for Rooms, Chimney Pieces, Statues on Paper, fine India Figures for Screens, etc.—*Boston News-Letter*, May 14, 1767.

Copper Plate Paper.—Samuel Fletcher, at his Shop near the Draw Bridge, advertised among other articles; beautiful copper plate furniture Paper for Rooms, printed linens, 18 inch Pipes, japanned lacquer'd and Mohogony Ware, and a Variety of Baskets, all very neat; best cut and silverd Crewit Stands, Knives and Forks, gilt Buttons, all at a Very low Advance.—*Boston News-Letter*, Oct. 1, 1767.

PAPER HANGER.—"George Killcup, jun. Informs the Gentlemen and Ladies in Town and Country That he Paints Carpets & other Articles, and Papers Rooms in the neatest manner. He will take English or West India Goods as Pay.

"Said Killcup is ready to pay those he is indebted to, in Painting or Papering Rooms."—*Boston News-Letter*, March 17, 1768.

PAPER HANGINGS, a large and elegant assortment, To be Sold at Joshua Blanchard's Shop, Dock Square, Boston.—*Boston News-Letter*, Sept. 16, 1773.

PAPER HANGINGS.—William Gooch, at the Sign of Admiral Vernon, in King Street, advertised Painters Oil and Colours, a fine Assortment of Paper-Hangings, Window Glass of every size, Sheet Glass by the Crate, etc. etc.

N. B. Painting, Glazing, and Plumming, undertaken and done with Dispatch.—*Boston News-Letter*, May 5, 1774.

# FABRICS

INDIA CHINTS.—To be Sold by Mr *William Payne*, at his House in Queen-street Boston, Hollands for Shirting and Sheetings, fine Cambricks, India Chints, *&c*. By Wholesale or Retale at Reasonable Rates.—*Boston News-Letter*, Feb. 11/18, 1711/12.

GLAZED CHINCES, for sale at vendue.—*Boston News-Letter*, Nov. 17/24, 1712.

PRINTED LINNEN and Scotch Cloths.—*Boston News-Letter*, May 10/17, 1714.

INDIA COUNTERPANES, sold at vendue.—*Boston News-Letter*, Aug. 6/13, 1716.

LINENS, tickings and wool cards, just imported from Scotland. —*Boston News-Letter*, June 8/15, 1719.

GERMAN DUCK.—To be Sold, at Reasonable Rates, by Mr. Adam Leyland at his Ware-house in Merchants-Row on the Dock, in Boston, Boxes of Long Tobacco Pipes, Broad Cloth's, Kersey's, Shalloons and Tammeys of all sorts, flower'd & plain Ruffels, silk Belgrades, Three Quarter and Seven Eight Garlix, Checkquer'd Linnens, striped Hollands and Ticks Bunts for Beds, or bed-Ticks, White Demities, flower'd and plain Fustians, Buttons, Mohair, Quality bindings, and other Habedashey: All which were the last Goods Imported here, directly from Bristol and not yet op'ned to this date: Also German Duck, Course Ozenbriggs, Bed-Camblets, Cotton Quilts, and Deck Nails.—*Boston News-Letter*, Mar. 21/28, 1723.

QUILTS, Rugs and Wadings.—*Boston News-Letter*, June 22/29, 1727.

INDIA COTTONS.—To be Sold by Henry Caswall, at his Warehouse a few doors above the Crown Coffee-house, Cables, Cherryderies, Yorkshire & Spanish Broad-Cloths, Cotton, Romalls, Sooseys, Cheercoones, Muslins of all Sorts, Buttons and Mohair, fine Chints, Buckrams, Men's rolling Hose, Silk Attabanies &

Lungees, sundry Sorts of Stuffs, double and single Ginghams, white Callecoes, sundry sorts of Silks, Crocus, Wool-Cards, fine Rugs, silk Drugets, silk Grograms, Lemmanees, Dantzick Linnens, with sundry other European & India Goods.—*Boston Gazette*, June 16/23, 1729.

NEW ENGLAND DUCK.—To be Sold, by *Henry Caswall* at his Warehouse *in King-street*, viz. *Garlix, Yard wide, 7 8ths and 3 4ths, Gulix and Bag Hollands, Kentins, Cambricks & Lawns,* Dantizick *and* Russia *Linnens, brown and white Oznabrigs, Hollands,* Irish *and* New England *Duck, Dowlas, blue Garlix, small Duck and narrow Hammells, Cables, Broad Cloths and Kerseys, Men's and Women's Silk Hose, printed Handkerchiefs* & *Aprons, Haberdashery of several sorts, fine Imperial Green Tea, Powder blue, sundry sorts of Silks, with other* European *Goods, lately Imported.*—*Boston Gazette*, June 23/30, 1735.

SILKS AND DAMASKS.—For Present Money, Thomas Trowell, Sells Great Pennyworths of European Silks and Stuffs as, Rich Morrello Tabbies, Florence Satteens, A blue Ground Brocade, English Damasks, Handkerchiefs, Fine Norwich Mourning Crapes, Brilliants, Superfine Silk Camblets, Brocaded Stuffs, Cloth-coloured Padusoys, Italian Mantuas, Strip'd Ducapes, White English Pealong, Allamode, Bird's Eyes, Plain black-Thread Satteens, Burdetts, Black Bombazene, Callamancoes, &c. All of the very newest Fashion.

Likewise, Ladies short Cloaks, made of the very best Superfine light Cloth-coloured Cloth, with (or without) Gold Loops, and Riding Hoods of the best Silk Camblett, Good Stays to all Sizes, made of the very best Bone, and cover'd with Morello Tabby all over, Quilted Petticoats, the best Kidd Gloves, Fan Mounts upon Ivory, Ebony and Bone Sticks, Gentlemen's Night Gowns and Banjans, made of Worsted Damasks, Brocaded Stuffs, and Callamancoes.

And Rich Gold Lace for Shoes and Hatts, Turnery, Sadlery, Millenary, Gentlemen's fine Worsted hose, Glass, &c. To be Sold in any small Quantities, the Person intending to Return for Great Britain in 14 Days.

At Mr. William Walters against Mr. Lutwytche's House in King Street.—*Boston Gazette*, Mar. 18/25, 1734.

LACE AND RIBBONS.—To be Sold by Robert Jenkins on the North Side of the Town-House, in King-Street, Boston, a Variety of Haberdashery, consisting of Cambrick's Handkerchiefs, Threed, Fringe, Edgings, Silver Lace, black silk and snail Lace, Children's silver Peacks, Silver and other Flowers, Ribbands, Girdles, Fans, Necklaces, Ribband Roles and Wires, snail Bugles, Cadis Stay-Cord, Brade, Galloom, Mens Velvet Hunting Caps and others, Raw and Balladine Silk, Mantle Tossels, Masks, Pendants, Tapes, Shirt Buttons, Wig-Ribbands and Cauls, coarse Threads, some flowered Silks, two large Carpets, Cloath-Baskets, &c. Likewise choice Cheshire-Cheese: All lately Imported in the last Ships, and to be Sold Cheap for Ready Money.—*Boston News-Letter*, June 5/12, 1735.

FABRICS.—*TO be SOLD, by Clark and Kilby, at their Warehouse near the Swing-Bridge. Ticklingburgs, Oznabrigs, Dowlas, Kentings; Russia, Dantzick, Polonia and Pomerania Linnens, Yard wide, seven Eights, and three Quarter Garlix, Gulick and Bag Hollands, Lawns, Cambricks, Bed Ticks, Russia Duck, Men's short and long Worsted Hose, Red Shags, Scarlet Coatings, check'd Linnens, brown, dyed and strip'd Hollands, Scot's Linnen of various sorts; Handkerchiefs, Plads, Bengals, strip'd and plain Sattins, Bibles, Felt Hats, broad and narrow Diapers, narrow Ticks, Gables of 5, 6, 6 and half, 7, 7 and half, 8 and 11 Inches, and divers other European Goods.*—*Boston Gazette*, Aug. 11/18, 1735.

MILLINERY AND LACE.—Just arrived, and to be Sold Cheap, a Choice variety of Haberdashery, mostly consisting of Cambricks, spotted Lawns, Nun's Thread, Fringes, black bone Lace, Scarlet and Crimson Snale Lace, with Mantle Tossels, Snale and Bugles of all Colours, Gold and Silver Lace for Hats, Shoes and Trimings, Handkerchiefs, Ribbands, Girdles, Fans, Necklaces and Beads of all sorts, Hair Caps, Rolls, Sprigg Wiers, black Pendents, Velvet Masks, Children's Silver Peaks and Flowers, Laces, Cadisis, Quality's Tapes, Pins, Needles, Shirt-buttons, Crewels in

Shades, Dutch Prettys, Silk Cane and Watch Strings, light colour'd ballendine and raw Silk, Wigg-Ribbonds and Cauls, India Patches, flower'd Silk, Japan'd Tea Boards and Waiters, large Carpets, and sundry other Goods; with a variety of Cutlery Ware, Corks, Cloths, Flaskets, Cheshire Cheese, &c. by Robert Jenkins, on the North-Side of the Town-House in King Street, Boston.—*Boston News-Letter*, Apr. 15/22, 1736.

COUNTERPANE Stolen, "a Damask Counterpin of a Bed, one breadth, mark'd S. P. with a red & purple Chintz Border: from a Yard near Fort Hill," Boston. 20s. reward.—*Boston Gazette*, Dec. 20/27, 1736.

NARROW GOODS MADE.—All sorts of colour'd Threads, Gartering, Quality Binding, Tossels for Cabin Windows, Sashies, Swashies for Men's Night Gowns, with other sorts of narrow Goods, made and sold by Abraham Shelley, living under the Great Trees at the South End of Boston.—*Boston Gazette*, Aug. 29/Sept. 5, 1737.

BROCADED SILKS.—To be Sold, at the lowest Prices by John Phillips, at the Stationers Arms in Cornhill, near the Town Pump, A New Parcel of fine Brocaded Silks with White Grounds beautifully flower'd with lively Colours, rich Gold and Silver Laces, Looking Glasses of several Sorts, swinging Glasses with Draws and without, choice Bohea Tea and Coffee, fresh Spices of all Sorts, Lloyds best Garlets, Cambricks and Threads, wide and narrow Camblets, Velvet, scarlet Cloth, strip'd & plain Calamancoes, and a Variety of other Goods both Woollen and Linnen; also sundry sorts of Books and Paper.—*Boston Gazette*, Sept. 26/Oct. 3, 1737.

EAST INDIA CHINTS.—East India & English Chints, Long Cloths, Printed Linnens, & Handkerchiefs, Fine Cotton Romals, Colour'd Ginghams, and sundry sorts of Haberdashery. To be Sold at Warehouse No. Q in Butler's Row, Boston.—*Boston Gazette*, Feb. 13/20, 1738.

SCOTCH GOODS.—Lately imported from Glasgow a choice Parcel of Scot's Goods, viz. Chequed Linnens of several Breadths and Prices, Brown and Strip'd Hollands, Tartan or Plad for

Women's Gowns or Men's Night Gowns, white Linnen, Kersey, half Thicks, Shalloons, Cantaloons, Hats, Cordage of all sizes, Spikes and Nails, As also small & large Bibles, the former at the Rate of 11 Shillings and 6 Pence a piece taking one or more Dozen, the large at 42 shillings a piece ready Money. Sold by Samuel Bowman, the next Door to Col. Wendal's Warehouse, Belcher's Row, where may be had Leather Breeches at the rate of 15 Shillings a piece, and 18 Shillings a single Pair ready Money.
—*Boston Gazette*, May 1/8, 1738.

LACE AND TRIMMINGS.—Just Imported, and to be Sold at Robert Jenkins's on the North Side of the Town House, Boston. A Great Variety of China Ware of Bowls, Dishes, Plates, Tea and Coffee Sets, &c, and Choice Tea. Likewise in Haberdashery and Milinary Ware, Fine Lawns, Cambricks, Nuns Thread, Fringes, black Bone and snail Lace, with Snail of all Colours, Gold and Silver Lace for Hats, Shoe and Trimmings, and fine Brocade Silk and other Handkerchiefs, Silk Flowers and Children's Peaks, new fashion Silver and Silk Ribbons and Girdles of all Sorts; likewise Fans and Necklaces of all sorts, Mantel and other Tassels, Rolls, Children's Gloves and Mittens, worsted Shades, Masks, Wig Ribbons, Cauls, Raw and Ballandine Silk, fine Needles, Holland, Diaper and other Tapes and Sundry other Things in Millanary and Haberdashery Ware. Likewise, Grograms, Tiffenies, Lutestring and Alamode, Damask and Diaper Table Cloths, and Sortments of Cutlery Ware, with Corks, Cheese, Raisins, Dutch Tiles, and sundry other goods at the lowest Prices.
—*Boston News-Letter*, May 18/25, 1738.

HOSE AND MITTENS.—To be Sold, at Publick Vendue, by William Nichols, at the Royal Exchange Tavern, in King St. Boston, on THIS DAY, beginning (if the Company attend) precisely at 4 o'clock Afternoon, a Variety of Merchandize; which may be seen till the Sale begins, viz.

A curious and compleat double sett of Burnt China, Broad Cloths, Druggets, Shalloons, Cottons and long Ells, Buckrams, Scots Cloths, Dowlas, Garlixs, Hollands, Chintz, Patches, Qualities, Fine Nuns Threads, Garterings, Mens and Womens fine

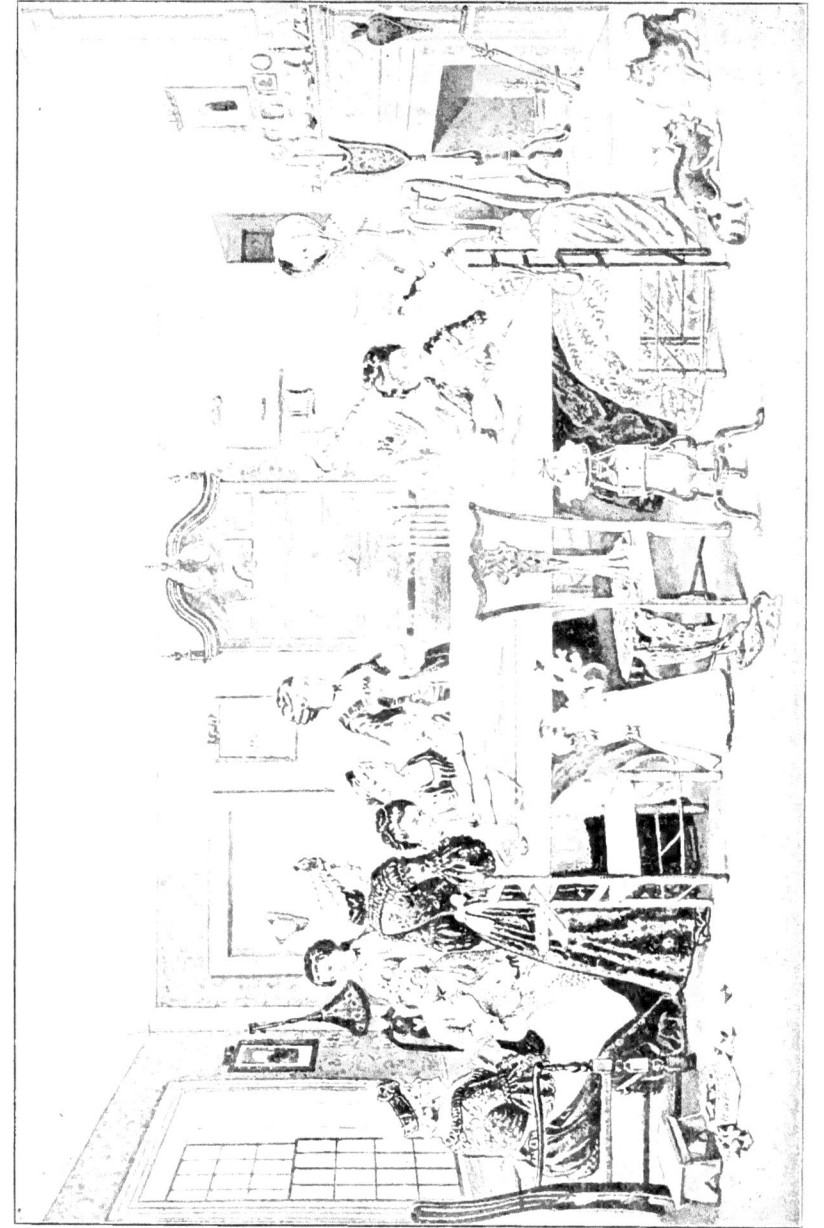

A Quilting Bee in the Olden Time
From a drawing by H. W. Pierce

Hose, Hatts, Caps, Wiggs Hankerchiefs, Womens fine Chiver'd Silk Hose, Mens superfine Silk Hose, fine Shirt Buttons, Womans superfine Mittens, yellow blue and Tabby, a Sattin Coverled, curiously embroidered with gold Lincey for Curtains, &c. Some Household Goods, such as Case of Draws, Tables, Chairs, Paints, Maps, Alabaster Effigies, China, &c. Sundry Suits of Mens Apparel, new and second hand; sundry very good Watches, Shoes, Boots, Green Tea, Chocolate, and Many other Things.—*Boston News-Letter*, May 18/25, 1738.

INDIA PICTURES.—Chinces, India Pictures, & handkerchiefs, fine brocade aprons, new fashion Ermine for gown trimmings, hoop petticoats, Nests of red Trunks.—*Boston News-Letter*, June 5/12, 1740.

INDIAN PATCHES, printed linens, hoop petticoats, Leg horn hats for women, gause handkerchiefs, Earings, women's trinkets for watches, boys pumps, morrocco Slippers, Barcelona & Scotch Handkerchiefs, Men's worsted and cotton caps.—*Boston News-Letter*, June 17/24, 1742.

WINTER AND SUMMER GOODS.—The Cream of all Sorts of the best Goods, just Imported in the very last Ship from London, by *Albert Dennie*. . . . He imports immediately from the maker, and has nothing but the Choicest of Goods, and has fresh supplies in every Ship constantly. He gives no Credit. . . . Said *Dennie* sells Black Taffetys the best Sorts at 22 l. a piece; fine Mohair newest Fashion Buttons at 12 d. per Doz. Buckrums finest Sort at 3 s. per Yard; India Chints at 8 s. per Yard; Broad Cloths superfine 6 Quar. wide, from 28 s. to 48 s. per Yard; Women's Fans at 2 s. a piece; Necklaces at 6 d. & 9 d. a piece; finest of Hollands at 15 s. per Yard; Garlix very good at 5 s. per Yard; and all Sorts of Winter and Summer Goods at the same Advance.

N. B. His Warehouse is upon *Dyer's* Wharff, near the New Market, his Name is wrote in Gold Letters over the Door Warehouse No. 3, next to *Mr. James Pemberton's*.—*Boston Gazette*, June 21, 1743.

ARRAS HANGINGS for a room, advertised.—*Boston News-Letter*, Aug. 22, 1745.

ENGLISH GOODS, *a great Variety imported from* London, *in the last Ships; and to be Sold* by *Albert Dennie,* By Wholesale or Retail, at his House on the Mill Bridge, upon the right Hand leading to Charlestown-Ferry, all for ready Cash, *viz.* Allum, Balladine sewing Silk, raw Silk, colour'd and waxed Threads, Pins, Ozenbrigs, India Dimetys, black Bombazeen and Alapene, silk Damask, Horse hair Buttons, Hair Shapes, Wadding, Linnen and Cotton Checks, Velvet, and Everlasting for Wastcoats, worsted Stuff plain and flower'd, worsted Damasks, Ruffels, Fearnothing Great Coats, Kerseys, Druggets, Swanikins, Broad Cloths, Serges, worsted & hair Plushes, Caps, Stockings, Cambricks, Shalloons, Camblets, Garlets, yard wide Linnens, bed Ticks, cotton Stockings, Chinces, Callicoes, Buttons and Mohair, Hats, Muslins, white Callicoes, Ribbands, Necklaces, Fans, Scots Snuff, Pewter, Nails, Buckles, Knives, Needles, Thimbles, short Cloaks, Taffieties, Persians, Velvets, Hangers or Cutlasses, Looking Glasses, Wigg Cauls, Shirt Buttons, Indigo, half Thick, bed Quilts, brass Wire, Horse Whips, bed Baskets, Saws, and sundry Sorts of brazery Ware, Paper for Room, Gloves, Sailors Cloths ready made, blue Callicoes.

*N. B.* Said *Dennie* has removed his Goods from his Ware house to his Dwelling House, as above.—*Boston Gazette,* May 27, 1746.

HANGING for a Room, "a Beautiful rich and Good Hanging for a Room," to be sold.—*Boston News-Letter,* Apr. 10, 1747.

PRINTED COUNTERPANES.—Lately Imported, and to be sold by William White in Arm Street, near the Head of the Town Dock, Boston, chiefly by Wholesail,

A Great Variety of Mens Worsted Caps, Mens Worsted, thread and cotton Hose, Tapes, Pins, Needles, Fans, Qualities, Gartrings, cotton Laces, Cambricks, Muslings, Linen, cotton and black Gauze Handkerchiefs, Cyprus, black Lutestrings, Silk Crapes, Calicoes, Buttons and Mohair, Lloyds, 3-4th, 7-ths and yard wide-Garletts, Nuns Hollands, mild Caps and Gloves, white Cord and Braid, Scarlet and Black Broad Cloths, black Bone Lace, Shapes, Wadding, Sieve Bottoms, printed Counterpins, flower'd Searge, rich green Tabby, Hair vallure for Mens Waistcoats, black and scarlet worsted Pieces for Breeches, fine Cotton and Worsted clouded Waistcoats, Capuchin Hatts, a fine Assortment of Looking Glasses, Horn and Ivory Combs, black Necklaces, Jews Harps, Knitting Needles, Case Knives and Forks, Pen Knives, Razors, Scizors, Shoe and Knee Buckles, Snuff Boxes, Mettle Buttons, Sleeve Buttons, Tea Spoons, Ink Cases, Ink Powder, Spectacles and Cases, Bibles, Psalters, Primers, &c.—*Boston Gazette*, Mar. 28, 1749.

STATIONERY.—Just Imported from LONDON in Capt Craige, and to be sold cheap for ready Money by Michael Dennis, at the corner of Scarlett's Wharf. A good assortment of Bibles and Common Prayer-Books of several sizes, West-India Pilots and other Sea Draughts, Mariner's Compasses and Kallenders, Atkinson's and Willson's Epitome of Navigation, a Complete Assortment of Books for the use of Grammar Schools, Testaments, Psalters, Primmers and Spelling Books, a good variety of Writing Paper, Marble, Blue and Cartridge Paper, Accompt Books large and Small, Brass Compasses, Gunter Scales, Slates in Frames, Pewter and Wood Ink Stands, Ink Powder, Sealing Wax, Wafers, Brass, Bone and Leather Ink Pots, Ivory and Horn Combs, best Dutch Quills, Spectacles of several Sorts, Pocket-Books, Ivory Books, Letter Cases, Cedar and Slate Pencils, Fountain Pens, Seals, Pen Knives, Jack Knives, Buckles, Snuff-Boxes, Scissars, and many other Articles.—*Boston Gazette*, May 9, 1749.

WHITE CALICO.—Two bredths of white Calico "drawn and partly work'd with blewish thread," advertised as lost.—*Boston Gazette*, July 25, 1749.

CLOTHING.—*Imported by* DAVID GAIRDNER, *from* Montrose *in* Scotland, *and sold by him at his Warehouse on* Belcher's *Wharfe, at the lowest Prices, viz.*

A Neat Assortment of Broad Cloths, Shalloons, Damasks, Callimancoes, Tammies, Hairbines Allapines, Poplins, Mantuas Creasses, silk and cotton Gowns, white and dyed Fustians, Velvets, black and colour'd velvet Shapes, Hatts, Wiggs, woollen, cotton and thread Stockings for Men and Women, and silk ditto for Men, frame Waste-Coats and Breeches, worsted & cotton Caps, Ribands, white Threads, white Chaple Needles, printed

Linnens & Cotton of all Kinds, white strip'd and check'd Linnens and Check Shirts, Oznabrigs, Sail Duck of all Numbers, Tyke, Tartanes, white & checker'd Handkerchiefs, flower'd plain & strip'd Lawns, Ruffles, sewing Silks, silk and hair Twist, mohair and metal Buttons, House and Ship Carpenter's Tools, with a Variety of Brass and Ironmongery Ware, single & double deck Nails, Spikes, halet and chink Rings, TakleHooks and Forelocks for Shipping, &c. rafree and plain bottleSnuff, some Shott, Lead and Gun Powder, large Iron Beams and Weights, a large Quantity of Mens and WomenShoes, and Boots, plain and gilded Bibles, common Prayer Books, and Books bound and ruled for Accomptants, Marriners Guides, playing Cards, *Hadley's* and other Quadrants, Brass and other Sea-Compasses, hand, depth and Logg Lines, Mahogany Tellescopes, Sand Glasses, speaking and sterding Trumpets, Buntin, Leather Breeches, Men and Womens Gloves, Ivory Combs, Ballast Shovells, Guns, Saddle Housings, with several other Goods.—*Boston Gazette,* Oct. 15, 1751.

MILLINERY.—*ELIZABETH MURRAY,* Millener, next Door to Deacon *Beautineau's* in Cornhill, imported in the last Ship from *London,* and sells at the most reasonable Rates the following Goods, *viz.*

*Caupuchin Silk, Waddings, black Bone Lace, and Fringes, Gauze Caps and Ruffles, Paris,Net, Cyprus Gauze, black Handkerchiefs, Fans & Gloves, Women & Childrens French Sattin Gloves & Mittens, Women & Childrens Worsted & Thread Hose,Women and Childrens Russel and Morrocco Shoes and Pumps, flower'd, spotted and clear Lawns, Hollands, Hooppetticoats Bone, Busks, Combs and Brushes, Neclaces, Stomachers, Patches, Ivory, Bone, Ebony, Fanns and Fannmounts, Ribbons, flower'd and plain Gauze for Shades and Hoods, Shades of Floss, Crewills & fine Silk, Mourning and other Pins, flowring and Scotch Threads, Tapes and Bobbing, Pearl & Coxcomb.*— *Boston Gazette,* Oct. 15, 1751.

GOLD LACE.—Just Imported and to be Sold by *Richard Martyn* in Union-Street, Gold and Silver Laces of the newest Fashion, also Silver and Gold Vellums, Cords, Threads & Buttons, colour'd

Velvets, Sattin Ribbons, Knee Garters, Mens Womens and Childrens Hose of all Sizes, at reasonable Rates.—*Boston Gazette*, Oct. 15, 1751.

HOLLANDS AND DRAWBOYS.—Dorcas Viscount, at her house in Back Street, offered for sale the following European goods, just imported:—Bag Hollands, Tandems and Callicoes, Cotton Caps, double and single worsted ditto, colour'd and Scotch threads, figur'd Drawboys, hooping Hollands, long and short Hoop Petticoats, Manchester ticking, London Shalloons, Pewter Water Dishes and Plates, a beautiful Set of Pictures, Grandurals for Mens or Womens wear, etc. etc.

The above Articles to be Sold in such Quantities as will best suit the Buyers, for which will take Pork or Beef in Payment, or any other Commodity that will answer.—*Boston Evening Post*, Jan. 6, 1752.

SCOT'S GOODS.—To be Sold by *William Hyslop*, at his Warehouse on the lower End of the South Side of the Town Dock. A Choice Assortment of *Scot's* Goods, just imported in the Snow *Glasgow*, viz. 3 4ths and 7 8ths Checks, 3 4ths & 7 8ths strip'd & check'd Hollands, 3 4ths and 7 8ths Bed Tick, broad and narrow Diapers and Toweling, Scots and Irish Hollands and Sheeting, Scots Handkerchiefs, white border'd ditto, blue Kilmarnock Caps, worsted ditto, Scotch Plad, white Threads of all Sorts, flower'd Lawns and Cambricks, Scotch Snuff, etc.

N. B., The above Goods will be sold very cheap for Cash, or for Rum or Molasses.—*Boston Gazette*, Feb. 13, 1753.

GAUZE, MUSLIN AND CAMBRICK.—Imported in the last Ship from LONDON, and sold very cheap, in Cornhill, *Boston,* as the Subscriber designs for London in fourteen days: A variety of silk Edge for Gause, Paris Net, plain and flower'd Gauze, Caps, Ruffles, Stomachers, Handkerchiefs, Gauze Ribbons, short Hoops, Umberallas, Horse-hair and straw Hats, Shoes, Clogs, plain & flower'd Lawn, Muslin, Cambrick, Holland, Capuchens, Wadding, bone Lace, Fringes, Capuchen silk, pink and black Persian, tan'd Kid, and all other sorts of Gloves and Mittens, silver Fringe, & Edge Flowers, Twitchers, Spangles, black & white Buggles,

Bags for Wiggs, black buggled Fringe, white ditto, silk Handkerchiefs, Firrits, Quality Binding, Ballandine Sewing Silk, Fan Mounts, Fans, Nuns Scots end Cotton Threads, London Trunks, &c. &c. by *Elizabeth Murray*.—Boston Gazette, Nov. 20, 1753.

TAPESTRY HANGINGS.—"A complete sett of Tapestry Hangings," for sale.—*Boston Gazette*, Nov. 27, 1753.

HOSE, GLOVES AND BUTTONS.—To be Sold by DANIEL MARSH in Cornhill, *Boston*, a good Assortment of worsted Cruels, well shaded, a variety of Mettal Buttons, Shoe and Knee Buckles, Ivory and Horn Combs, Scizars, Needles and Pins; also good Bohea Tea, Pepper, Nutmegs, Cloves, Cinnamon & Mace; also Chinces, Callicoes, Garlixs, Lawns, Cambricks, Mens, Boys & Womens Hose, Womens black silk Gloves, Mens and Womens white, black and colour'd Lamb Gloves; Womens white, black & colour'd Lamb Mittens; silk & hair & silk hair Buttons, & a variety of other Goods.—*Boston Gazette*, Oct. 1, 1754.

RUSSIA SHEETINGS.—To be Sold by Jarvis & Parker, at their Store three Doors below Mr. Dowse's Insurance-Office in King street. *Spanish* iron, hemp, cordage, *English* and *Russia* duck, starch, cod-lines, and hooks, nails, glass, brimstone, spanish white, broad cloths, german serges, sugathees, duroys, 3, 4 and 7, 8 garlix, Irish linnens, long lawns, *Irish* and *Russia* sheetings, tandems, cambricks, flower'd, spotted & clear lawns, chinces, callicoes, *India* patches, cotton hollands, cotton gowns, erminettas, chelloes, lutestring allimode gauze handkerchiefs, silk laces, shades, flower'd gauze, white jeans, corded dimothy, *Turkey* quilts, gloves, coca, bone and ivory stick fans, velvet masques, sewing silks, . . . shoe bindings, *Scotch* handkerchiefs, paistwork ditto, . . . sattins, damasks, persians, bandannoes, lemanees, silk romalls, buckrams, shalloons, tammies, durants, calimancoes, plain and strip'd camblets, gray and black allapens, russels, worsted and thread hose, Colchester bays, beaver coating, bearskins, Kerseys, and a variety of paper hangings. Also choice old *Jamaica* RUM.—*Boston Gazette*, May 26, 1755.

INDIA PATCHES.—To be Sold by John Phillips, opposite the Rev. Mr. Checkley's Meeting House; Rich Leather mounted

Fans, Fly-Caps, with Egrets, Drest Gauze Ditto, Pins, and white and blue and white Tobine Lutestrings, Pink and Straw Duiapes, Silk quilted Coats, India Patches and Ginghams, Holland tapes, Earrings, Ivory Combs, Womens and Girls Stays, Mens and Womens Kid and Lamb Gloves, Wiltshire Ale, long and short Pipes, Florence Oil and split Pease, plain and flower'd Wine and Beer Glasses, Salts, etc.—*Boston Evening Post*, July 14, 1755.

LAWNS.—To be Sold by Captain John Dobel, at the North End of Boston, near Dr. Cutler's Church, the following Goods, viz. Fine flower'd lawns for borders for caps and handkerchiefs for Ladies, flower'd lawn ruffles for gentlemen, fine spotted lawn, cross-barr'd and flower'd ditto for ladies capps, aprons or handkerchiefs, fine lawn aprons with flower'd borders for ladies, fine flower'd lawn ruffles for Ladies, all of the newest fashion—to be sold cheap for ready Money, either by the pieces or single.—*Boston Gazette*, Jan. 12, 1756.

GERMAN SERGES, shalloons, ¾ & ⅞ garlix, cambricks, lawns, caps, threads, sewing silk, mohair, quality, ribbons, neclaces, pins, combs, gloves, fans, tapes, horse-hair hats, crewels, English 4 thread, worsted, hour-glasses, half hour ditto, tea-chests, pepper-mills, cotton laces, boys, youths & mens felt and castor hats, all sorts of hatter's trimings, camel hair seives, mohair & metal buttons, shoe & knee buckles, case, clasp & pen-knives, japen'd waiters, bellows, hand-saws, allum, copperas, brimstone, rozin, log wood, red wood, white lead, spanish brown, English and best French gun-flints, fish hooks, round and square needles, nails, iron weights for windows, flat irons, fine light guns for hunting, swords & neat pistols, shot, snuff, fine and coarse salt, alspice, ginger, black bone-lace, velvet corks, flour, horn buttons, cart & chair boxes, horse-whips, spectacles, and many other sorts of cutlery, grocery and haberdashery wares; as also some blue and white china bowls, muggs, caps and lancers; to be sold cheap for the CASH, by *Nathaniel Loring*, at his Store near *Faneuil-Hall*.—*Boston Gazette*, May 10, 1756.

IRISH LINENS.—Just imported from *London* and *Bristol*, and to be Sold by *John, Robert* & *John Gould,* at their Store in Back-Street, viz.

Scarlet, crimson and cloth coloured broad cloths, Kerseys, german serges, blankets, stript and plain duffils, bayses, bearskins, ratteens, whitneys, plain and Knapt beaver coatings, everlastings, serge de Nims, mens and womens kid and lamb gloves and mitts, womens silk gloves and mitts, figured and plain allimode, black and white sarsinet, 3-4, 7-8, 4-4, 5-4, and 6-4 cotton checks, 3-4, 7-8 and yard wide irish linnens, crewells in shades, garlix, dowlasses, long lawns, pistol ditto, flower'd and plain do, taffaties, grograms, damasks, padusoys, lutestrings, ducapes, silk and linnen handkerchiefs, flower'd and spotted bandanno ditto, ribons of all sorts, a variety of new fashion stuffs, such as hungarian checks, barley corns, chevetts, silk maskerade venetians, silk bredaws, turynetts, dianetts, silk cords, tobine bezoarines, tobine, bendoarines, strip'd ditto, new changeable broglios, double berlins, new palmeritts, enamell'd dresdens and new pompey dones, &c. &c. And likewise Cutlery and Braziery ware, such as pewter, brass, steel, nails of all sorts, shot, lead, tin plates, lanthorn leaves, wire, small arms, cutlashes, knives, buckles, scissors, &c. &c. As also, copperas, allum, brimstone, pipes by the box, best raisons of the sun by the cask, cinnamon, mace, cloves and nutmegs, &c. To be sold cheap for cash or short credit.—*Boston Gazette,* Aug. 22, 1757.

UPHOLSTRY GOODS.—To be Sold by *Moses Belcher Bass,* at his Shop, just opened in Ann Street, near the Conduit, the following Upholdstry Goods, imported from London in one of the last Ships, viz.: 7-8, 3-4, and Nail-wide broad & narrow strip'd English Bed-Ticks, 6, 7, 8 and 9-4 Blanketts, 8, 9 and 10-4 Coverlids, 9 and 10-4 Bed Quilts, 9 and 10-4 Counterpins, Harrateen's, Chiney's Prints and Bindings, &c. also Chiney and Print Curtains ready made for sale, &c. &c.—*Boston Gazette,* Sept. 12, 1757.

FIFTY DOLLARS REWARD.—On the Night of the 2d & 3d of July 1758, the Shop of *William Morland* of Newbury was broke open, out of which the following Goods are Stolen, Viz. One Piece superfine Purple and red Chints, one Piece blue and white ditto, check'd Figure, two Pieces of coarser ditto, Purple and Red, two Pieces of Cotton and Linnen ditto, Purple and White, one Piece fine Cambrick, sundry Pieces fine Irish Hollands, one Dozen fine 3 thread white thread Stockings, 2 Dozen fine Worsted ditto, one Piece superfine Scotch Plaid red and green, sundry Pieces of fine wide black Bone Lace, sundry Pieces fine white Cap ditto, sundry Pieces wide new fashion Satten Ribbons, Sea-wave at Sides, with sundry other Figures, three Pieces fine 7, 8 Check Linnen, four Pieces of stript Holland, one Piece of London Shalloon, six Pair of Brass Candlesticks, one Piece of plain Lawn, one Piece long ditto, sundry Bundles of Sleeve Buttons, Glass set in Brass, one Card Bristol Stone sett in Silver, one Seal Ring with a Cornelion Stone, &c. &c. &c.

Whoever shall make Discovery of the Thief or Thieves, so as legally to convict them of said Theft, shall have FIFTY DOLLARS Reward, of me the Subscriber, WILLIAM MORLAND.—*Boston Gazette*, Aug. 14, 1758.

STRAW CARPET.—"A handsome Floor Straw Carpet," at auction.—*Boston Gazette*, Jan. 28, 1760.

WINDOW SCREENS.—"Wide yellow canvas for window screens."—*Boston Gazette*, June 23, 1760.

"SCOTCH FLOOR CARPETS, Counterpins, Bed Ruggs, . . . Scarlet and Crimson Check for Bed Curtains."—*Boston Gazette*, Sept. 1, 1760.

HUNT AND TORREY, have just imported from London, a Fine Assortment of Goods, to be Sold at their shop in Queen street near the Prison in Boston, at the Lowest prices for Cash or Treasurer's Notes.

Rich black, cloth and lead-coloured padusoys; damasks; sattins; lute-strings; persians; taffeties; grograins; alamodes; black silks & trimmings for cardinals and capuchines; muffs & tippets; broad-cloths; Kerseys; ratteens; beaver-coatings; German-serges; flower'd serges; corded druggets; whitneys; duffles; half-thicks; bays; flannels; swanskins; duroys; sagathees; blankets; bed ticks; shalloons; tammies; durants; calimancoes; camblets; camblet-teens; poplins; dresdens; dresdenetts; figur'd stuffs; worsted-damasks; everlastings; plush; shag; plaids; bombazeens; alapeens; grizets; silk crapes; hat and widow's crapes; tiffany; cherry-derrys; russels; dowlass; oznabrigs; garlets; Irish hollands; cambricks; long-lawns; muslins; clear, spotted and flower'd lawns; white gauze; callicoes; chinces; bengals; ginghams; chelloes; nicannees; Russia linens; diapers; table-cloths; cotton hollands; check'd cottons; cotton gowns; fustians; thicksetts; cotton velvets; velvet shapes for waistcoats; dimothies; velvet for capes; women's black velvet; worsted caps; men's, women's and children's worsted, thread & cotton hose; worsted pieces for waistcoats & breeches; silk knee straps; buckrams, buttons, silk & hair twist; sewing silks, white & coloured threads; needles, pins, tapes, qualities, fans, gloves, mittens, women's & children's stays; silk, linnen, cotton and gauze handkerchiefs; ferrets; gallooms; plain & figured ribbons of all sorts; garterings; cords, braids, white tabby; stay laces, masks, gimp edgings, fringes; worsted, cruel, black & white lace; combs; paper; women's shoes & clogs; women's chip hair & sattin hats; necklaces; stock-tapes; knives & forks; shears, scissars, razors, buckles; nutmegs, cinnamon, mace, cloves, Bohea Tea, pepper, starch, ribbons, silk & cauls for Wigs; linings, looping & buttons for Hatts, &c. &c. &c.

In the same column appears the advertisement of William Greenleaf listing importations from London and Bristol, among the items being:—

Devonshire Kerseys; Yorkshire plains; red, blue, green and drab frizes; red and blue duffils; blue and white bays; callamancoe and silk quilts; brocaded silk shoes; newest fashion feather muffs and tippets; bosom and head flowers; blue, white, & black pelong sattins; rich white sarsnet; white figured sattins for women's coats; black & white parisnet; cambrick & book muslins; silk and worsted sagathies; best London duroys; black serge denims; chinces, callacoes, and printed linnens; worsted knit patterns for waistcoats and breeches; ell-wide, yard-wide, 7/8 & 3/4 Irish linnens; tandems; gulix hollands; long lawns; shear lawns; spotted & flowered lawns; flowered lawn aprons & handkerchiefs; leather mount & ivory stick fans; 10/4 & 8/4 damask table-cloths; 12/4, 10/4, 8/4 & 6/4 diaper table-cloths; diaper napkining & towel-

COUNTERPANE OF QUILTED GALLOON
Made in Beverly, Mass., in 177- by Anne Cleaves

ing; cotton hollands; yellow hollands & canvas; 8/4 huckabuck; lettered garterings; scarff buttons; mohair; horn & ivory combs; pound pins & other pins; silver thimbles with steel tops; the best French wax necklaces & ears; stone necklaces & ears; black glass necklaces & ears; newfashioned solatiers & ears; a variety of white blond lace; stock tape; diaper tape; women's & children's cotton mitts; black silk fringe; black & white gauze handkerchiefs; ballandine sewing silk; 10 d, 8 d, 6 d, & 4 d nails; Cheshire cheese; a few canisters of the best Hyson Tea; fine flowered Mustard; China dishes, plates and sauce boats, &c. &c.

In another column appears the advertisement of Caleb Greenleaf listing importations "in Capt. Aitken," among the items being:—Blue, green & cloth colour ratteen; blue, scarlet, claret & cloth colour beaver serges; bearskins; embossed serges; blue whitney; missinets; bombazine & all sorts of mourning; blue, black & scarlet snail trimming; white watered tabby; blue and white & dark striped cotton hollands; nicanees; nuns & bag hollands; 3/4, 7/8 & apron Manchester checks; pistol lawns; clouting diaper; white & black silk hose; lungee romalls; bandannoes; red, blue & white paste handkerchiefs; Bilboa handkerchiefs; threads & ballendine silk; knee garters; knit breeches & waistcoats of most colours; tergedenim; black Genoa velvet; coloured velvet for capes; scarlet, crimson & white Jersey knit under-waistcoats; pink, yellow, white, green & blue sattin hats; gloves; furniture checks; scarlet, green & black hair plushes; women's quilted coats; cartridge, writing and printing paper; ink powder; sealing wax; clothier's press paper; etc.

In another column Johnathan & John Amory offer among many other importations in the same ship, the following:—Black, scarlet, crimson & cloth coloured India taffeties; black figured silk for capuchins & cardinals, with trimmings; also blue figured silk for ditto; superfine scarlet & blue drab Broadcloths for Men's roqueloes; green & blue Padua serge; green & red yard wide bayes; green hair shapes; bed ticks and bed bunts; blue & white and dark striped cotton gowns; English & India patches; broglioes; jeans; women's stays & jumps; black silk gloves; black, blue, green, buff, and cloth coloured knit waist coat shapes; black, blue, buff, scarlet, & crimson knit breeches shapes; gold & silver laces; striped, scarlet & green worsted caps; English soles; men's beaveret hats; knit under waistcoats; women's plain & chivered hose; silk breeches patterns; cypress; spotted & flowered India bandannoe handkerchiefs; flowered culgee ditto; checked & flowered linnin ditto; Men's Norway doe gloves; silk knee garters; Scotch carpets; a variety of paper hangings for Rooms, etc.

In another column, Daniel Jones, "at the HAT and HELMET in Newbury Street," offered:—Beaverett and Castor Hatts by the Box or dozen; English and French Felts by the Hogshead or dozen; French lace; Gold and Silver lace; also Beaver, Beaverett and Felt Hatts of his own make. N. B. Officers and Soldiers who have been in this Province Service may be supplied with any of the above Articles on Short Credit till their Muster Rolls are made up, as usual, the Soldiers being well recommended.—*Boston News-Letter*, Dec. 18, 1760.

COVERLETS AND QUILTS.—8; 9 & 10 q$^r$ Coverlids, 6, 7, 8, 9 & 10 q$^r$ Bed Quilts, 6, 7, 8, & 9 q$^r$ spotted Ruggs, good green & blue worsted and yarn ditto. 8, 9, 10 & 12 q$^r$ flowered Carpets, counterpins.—*Boston Gazette*, Dec. 29, 1760.

HOUSE FURNISHINGS, List Carpeting for Stairs, rich Persia Carpets, 3, 4 and 4 by 5 yards square for sale; also printed Carpets for tables and "a variety of silk and oyl cloth Umbrilloes for Ladies," a quantity of stout Carpeting both for Floors and Stairs, handsome oyl cloths for Tables, a suit of blue China Curtains and Counterpain, Cotton Copper Plate Furniture for beds, Wilton or Marble Cloths, "rich Persia Carpets, 3, 4 and 4 by 5 yards square, List Carpeting for Stairs."—*Boston Gazette*, Jan. 26, 1761.

NANKEENS.—Samuel Blodgett, at his Shop in Marlboro'-Street, advertised recent importations from London, including:—India and Manchester Nankeens; Seive bottoms; Dresdens Barlicorns; Loaf and Powder Sugars; Brown ditto per Cask; Tea, Coffee and Raisins; Violins; Looking Glasses in Dutch and English Frames; Fresh Figs by the Cask or frail; etc. etc.—*Boston News-Letter*, July 16, 1761.

ENGLISH CARPETS.—"A few English made Carpets, some very large Bed Quilts, and ready made Linceys and China Beds, etc. for sale by Lewis De Blois."—*Boston Gazette*, Oct. 5, 1761.

PRINTED CARPETS for Tables, for sale.—*Boston Gazette*, Apr. 5, 1762.

QUILTS AND RUGS.—Imported from London, and Sold by Moses Belcher Bass, at his Shop in Ann Street, near the Conduit: —6, 7, 8 & 9 Quarter Blankets, 6, 7, 9 & 10 Quarter Bed Quilts, 6, 8, 9 & 10 Quarter Coverlids, 6, 7, 8 & 9 Quarter Ruggs, . . . also, a good assortment of Looking-Glasses; Suits of ready-made Curtains.—*Boston News-Letter*, May 13, 1762.

SCOTCH GOODS.—Just imported from Glasgow, and to be sold by *John Crawford*, in Corn-Court, South side of Faneuil-Hall Market,— Mens and Womens Shoes and Pumps, *Glasgow* and Fyfe Checks, stript Holland, Bed Ticks, Tartans, white Linnen course and fine, Sheeting Diapers and Table Cloths, Stock Tapes, Leather Ink Potts, Leather Snuff Boxes, Paper ditto, bordered Handkerchiefs, Lawns, Mens and Womens Gloves, printed Clothes, Bed Covers, Garters, Tapes, plated Stocks, Silk Gauze, Women's Aprons, Carpets and Carpeting, *Kilmarnock* and *Stewarton* blue Caps . . . Mens and Womens Thread & Cotton Hose, Worsted Breeches of different Kinds, stript Waistcoats. . . — *Boston Gazette*, July 5, 1762.

PRINTED COTTONS.—Elegant printed Cottons for Bed Furniture a Variety of printed Cottons and Linnens; an assortment of Manchester Checks; Irish Linnens of all prices, just imported, etc. etc. for sale by *Nathaniel Rogers.*—*Boston Gazette*, Aug. 8, 1763.

AME & ELIZAH. CUMING, Inform their Customers, and others, That they have Removed from their Shop the Corner of Queen Street, to one lately improv'd by Mrs. *Anna Adams*, opposite the Old Brick Meeting House; *Where they have to sell just imported*, Yellow-ground Brocades, white figured Tabby; brown Padusoy; green mantua Silks; black, coloured, plain, flowered and spotted Sattens; pelong ditto; large fringed Barcelona Handkerchiefs; Ballandine Silk; Padusoy Satten; Sarsenet and figured Ribbons; Fans; newest fashion'd French Necklaces and Earings

Stone Earings and Necklaces; Garnet ditto; Sleeve Buttons, paste, shoe, knee and stock Buckles; stone Broaches; long knee Buckles; horn and Tortoishel Combs and Cases; Tooth Brushes; Wash Balls and Cases; French Chalk; Powder Boxes and Puffs; plain and scented Hair Powder; Almond Powder; Bags for Hair; Mens and Womens silk and worsted Hose; Men and Womens silk Gloves; Womens Kid and grained Lamb ditto; womens Lamb and Kid Mitts, Mens Buck and Dogskin Gloves; Velvet Masks; Silver Head Flowers; white and silver, purple and silver, and pink and silver Tippets; silk Trimings of all colours; grey Ermine, white and spotted with red and white and spotted with black ditto; Brussels Mecklin and Blond Lace, black bone Lace; Coxcomb Lawns; Cambricks, Threads, Pound Pins, Footings, Silk Laces printed Cambrick, Handkerchiefs, Cap Wire, Muslin Gauze, plain flowered and corded Catgut, chipt and Sattin Hatts & Bonets, flower'd Mode Patches, Court Plaister, Message Cards, Patch and Snuff Boxes, Silver Thimbles, Scissors black and white bugles Sattin and Stuff Shoes, Muffs and Tippets, Stock Tape—Hungaty Water, Salvolatile, Eau de Luce, Soughton's Elixer, Teeth Tincture and Powder, Tincture for the Tooth Ach—Tammies, Callimancoes, &c—*Boston Gazette*, Nov. 11, 1765.

UPHOLSTERERS' GOODS.—Just Imported from London, and to be Sold by JOHN SIMPKINS, at his Shop the North Side of the Mill-Bridge, fronting the Street that leads from Charlestown Ferry:—

Crimson, green and yellow Harrateens, Chaneys, Linceys, Trimmings of all Sorts, Quilts, Counterpins, Coverlids and Bedticks, Buckram, Looking Glasses, &c. Where may be had all Sorts of Curtains, Feathers, Easy Chairs, Cushions, or any sort of Upholsterers' Work done in the best Manner, at the lowest Rates.—*Boston Gazette*, June 17, 1765.

# COSTUME

SHOES.—Wooden-heel shoes were worn by a run-away servant of Rev. John Wise of Chebacco.—*Boston News-Letter*, Jan. 26/Feb. 2, 1712/13.

LACED SHOES.—Fine Womens and Childrens Lac'd Shoes, lately come from England, to be sold very cheap by *Joseph Thorn*, at his House in Trea-mount Street, Boston.—*Boston News-Letter*, Aug. 20/27, 1716.

SHOES.—Very good silk grass, lately imported, to make shoes, at 4 s. 6 d. per lb. and by the dozen, at 4 s.—*Boston News-Letter*, Nov. 23/30, 1719.

CALICO GOWNS.—Stolen from out of the Garden of the Governor's House, a "maid-servant's Callico-Gown turn'd up with White-Holland at the Sleeves, without any lining:" 10 shillings reward.—*Boston Gazette*, Oct. 3/10, 1726.

FANS.—George Harding lately from London, now at Mr. John Pitts, Confectioner, in Cornhill, Boston, Mounteth all Sorts of Fans, as well as any done in Old England: He likewise hath a large Sortment of curious Mounts which he will dispose of very reasonably, not purposing to stay long in these Parts.—*Boston News-Letter*, Aug. 8/15, 1728.

FROCKS, TROUZERS AND SHIRTS, part of the personal effects of William Davison, Taylor, in King Street, Boston, were advertised at Publick Vendue.—*Boston Gazette*, Oct. 20/27, 1729.

SERVANT'S CLOTHING.—The Stable of Mr William Stoddard of Boston was broken into and articles of clothing belonging to a servant were stolen, viz.:—1 drab coat with white mettle Buttons with a star in them, 1 light grey Duroy Coat trimmed with Black, 1 black Broadcloth Coat not trimmed, 1 pair grey Drugget Breeches, 1 pair black cloth breeches, 1 blew stript'd holland Waistcoat, 1 seersucker ditto, 1 Ozenbrige Jacket and Breeches, 1 light coloured Drugget Coat with brass Buttons, 2 pair white cotton hose, 1 pair blewish coloured worsted ditto, 1 Garlic shirt, 1 pair striptd

Cotton Bootlashes, 1 new Hat with Mourning hatband. £5 reward.—*Boston Gazette*, Jan. 18/25, 1731.

GREAT COAT.—Lost. dark blue Great Coat with light blue velvet cape and frosted Buttons.—*Boston News-Letter*, Nov. 20/27, 1735.

UNDERCLOTHES.—The corpse of a young man found in the Schuylkill river had "a pair of Drawers, Hat and Shirt, wrapt in another Shirt and tyed round his Neck."—*Boston News-Letter*, Aug. 11/18, 1737.

SHOES.—"Women's Callamanco and Brocaded Stuff Shoes, Women's Shamey Shoes, Clogs of all sorts, Goloshoes, Children's Shoes."—*Boston Gazette*, Dec. 19/26, 1737.

GREAT COAT.—Lost, a blue drab Great Coat & a boy's "Bever Hat, with a Mourning Weed in it."—*Boston News-Letter*, Sept. 21/28, 1738.

FANS.—Half mourning, Vaux Hall, and Gin Act mounts, for sale.—*Boston Gazette*, Nov. 6/13, 1738.

LEATHER BREECHES, lately imported from Scotland, at 20 s. and Felt Hats, at 8 s. 6 d. from Scotland.—*Boston Gazette*, Apr. 30/May 7, 1739.

FANS, ebony and ivory sticks, gold and silver brocaded aprons, velvet masks, men's velvet caps, pendants, earrings and beads, hat-band crapes, Japan teaboards and salvers, cloathes flaskets, voiders, china and other baskets, for sale by Robert Jenkins.—*Boston News-Letter*, May 17/24, 1739.

TROUSERS.—The corpse of a man found drowned at the mouth Roxbury creek wore a red shag great coat, a grey jacket, striped trousers and breeches underneath.—*Boston News-Letter*, Aug. 9/16, 1739.

SHOES.—Children's "scarlet Broad Cloth Shoes" mentioned, as stolen.—*Boston News-Letter*, Sept. 20/27, 1739.

HOOD.—The corpse of a woman was found on Gardiner's Island, dressed in a light striped Callaminco Gown, laced or tied with white Tapes, a white apron, shoes tied with white strings, and a hood of brownish color.—*Boston News-Letter*, June 14/21, 1739.

## Costume

BANJAN.—Lost in Roxbury a boy's Banjan, one side Plad, the other side striped Callamanco.—*Boston News-Letter*, June 3/10, 1742.

PUMPS.—Shop of Richard Manning, cordwainer, in King-street, Boston, broken into and stolen therefrom "One Pair of double channel Pumps not fellows, one of them stitched aloft, the other close stitched, one pair of sharp'd to'd Shoes, and one Pair of turn'd Pumps." £5. reward.—*Boston News-Letter*, July 8/15, 1742.

FANS.—Henrietta Maria East, from London, at the Sign of the Fan, up one pair of Stairs, over against Dr. Gibbon's in Marlborough Street, Boston,

Sells all sorts of Fans, mounts Sticks, and mounts Fans; likewise all sorts of Mellenary Goods, as Cambricks, flower'd or plain Gloves, Ribbons, Necklaces, Earings, Gause Handkerchiefs of all sorts, Girdles, Threads, Tapes, Pins, Needles, Ferrets, silk Laces, rich Shoes, and black Pumps, &c.

N. B. Ladies may have their Head-dresses, or Hoods, Mantelets, Pillerens, French Cloaks, Bonnets, made at reasonable Rates for Ready Money. —*Boston News-Letter*, Dec. 23, 1742.

SHOES.—"Stout Shoes for Servants," advertised.—*Boston News-Letter*, Jan. 3, 1743.

LEATHER BREECHES.—Philip Freeman, lately from London, makes and sells super-fine black Leather Breeches and Jackets, not to be discerned from the best super-fine Cloth: likewise makes Buff and Cloth Colour after the neetest Manner, also makes all sorts of Gloves by wholesale and retale. The said Freeman lives in Prison Lane, near the Town House in Boston.—*Boston Gazette*, June 21, 1743.

SHOES.—To be Sold by Isaac Cazneau in Water Street,—Women's Silk, Russel, and Ticken Shoes, Women's Black Morrocco Pumps, and all sorts of Children's Red Morocco Shoes.—*Boston News-Letter*, Apr. 30, 1747.

BEAVERET HAT.—Lost a Beveret Hat, which cost £7 old Tenor. —*Boston News-Letter*, June 11, 1747.

READY MADE BOY'S CLOTHES: also mens; lately imported from

London. Calico counterpins for Beds.—*Boston Gazette*, Aug. 4, 1747.

Fans.—Holley, Bone, and Ebony Stick Fans, best wax papered and black necklaces.—*Boston News-Letter*, Aug. 27, 1747.

Buttons.—Coat and Jacket Buttons, Bath Metal & other sleeve Buttons, chrystal ditto set in Silver, rich Chains, with Bottles, &c. for Ladies' Gold Watches.—*Boston News-Letter*, Nov. 5, 1747.

Shoes.—Just imported, women's fine, brocaded, flowered, russel, braided, and red morocco shoes; hand and toed clogs,—for sale.—*Boston News-Letter*, Nov. 5, 1747.

Red Cap.—John Coggin of Sudbury, a laborer, wore, a yellowish outside coat with Red Lining, a green Jacket, Goat-skin Breeches, and a red cap. He was suspected of theft.—*Boston News-Letter*, Oct. 27, 1748.

Hoop-Petticoats, of English make, advertised.—*Boston News-Letter*, April 6, 1749.

Embroidered Petticoat.—On the 11th of Nov. last, was stolen out of the Yard of Mr. Joseph Coit, Joiner in Boston, living in Cross street, a Woman's Fustian Petticoat, with a large work'd Embroider'd Border, being Deer, Sheep, Houses, Forrest, &c., so worked. Whoever has taken the said Petticoat, and will return it to the Owner thereof, or to the Printer, shall have 40 s. old Tenor Reward and no Question ask'd.—*Boston Gazette*, Dec. 19, 1749.

"Turkey Quilts fit for Lady's Skirts," for sale.—*Boston Gazette*, Mar. 12, 1751.

Frocks.—At the launch of a new brig at Halifax, N. S., "the Carpenters that built her were dress'd in clean white Frocks and Trowsers, Clean ruffle Shirts, and Gold-laced Hats."—*Boston Gazette*, July 2, 1751.

Lace and Clothing.—Just Imported and Sold by Peter Burn, in Fish-Street, next to Dr. Clark's, a choice percel of Flanders Lace of curious Patterns, high and low priz'd, a rich Bruxelles Lappet, Head Womans, best worsted Damask and everlasting Shoes, silk and velvet Clogs, Mens and Womens silk

Gloves, Mens silk Caps, Mens cotton Stockings, various sorts of Necklaces, flower'd & plain Ribands, clear Lawns, Cambricks, White border'd and mincanet Hankerchiefs, check ditto, long Cravats, Scots Thread, white chappel Needles, Irish Linnens, Waiste coats, flower'd velvet shapes of different Patterns, in-cut and flower'd Velvet, plain ditto, Mens shoes, a pair of pier Glasses gilt Frames with Branches.

N. B. The above mentioned to be sold at the very lowest Rates for Indian Corn, Maryland Pork, Bacon, Myrtle Wax, Hogshead and Barrel Staves, fit for the London Market.—*Boston Gazette,* June 11, 1754.

LEATHER STOCKINGS.—Made and Sold by Philip Freeman, at the *Blew Glove* next the Cornfields in Union Street; Leather Stockings of different Colours, viz. Black, cloth colour'd, and Yellow, made after the neatest manner.—*Boston Gazette,* June 25, 1754.

THE PETITION.
Artful Painter, by this Plan
Draw a Female if you can.
Paint her Features bold and gay,
Casting Modesty away;
Let her Art the Mode express,
And fantastick be her Dress;
Cock her up a little Hat
Of various Colours, this and that;
Make her Cap the Fashion new,
An Inch of Gauze or Lace will do:
Cut her Hair the shortest Dock:
Nicely braid her Forehead Lock:
Put her on a Negligee,
A short Sack or Sheperdee
Ruffled up to keep her warm,
Eight or Ten upon an Arm;
Let her Hoop extending wide
Shew her Garters and her Pride,
Her Stockings must be pure and white,

For they are seldom out of Sight.
Let her have a high heel'd Shoe,
And a glittering Buckle too;
Other Trifles that you find,
Make quite Careless as her Mind,
Thus equipp'd she's charming Ware
For the Races or the Fair.
—*Boston Gazette,* Mar. 15, 1756.

LEATHER CAPS.—For sale at publick vendue, with other goods "a Parcel of Leather Caps, very convenient for Soldiers."—*Boston Gazette,* Mar. 14, 1757.

STOCKINGS.—Part of the cargo of a French prize ship sold in Boston.—"Men's silk and worsted stockings, Men's, women's and Children's mill'd Stockings and Caps."—*Boston Gazette,* Aug. 22, 1757.

"QUILTED PETTICOATS from 4 to 9 Breadths, Hoop Petticoats of various Dimensions."—*Boston Gazette,* Aug. 22, 1757.

BUTTONS.—In the October 3, 1757, issue of the *Boston Gazette and Country Journal* are several advertisements containing the following references to buttons, viz.—"a great Assortment of White and Yellow mettle Coat and Breast-Buttons, Sleeve-Buttons." "A great variety of coat and breast buttons." "White and yellow mettle coat and breast buttons, white stone and other kind of sleeve buttons." "Best double gilt Regimental Coat and Breast Buttons, and a Variety of a cheaper Kind for the Country Sale, best London made Silver Sleeve Buttons, set with Brilliant Stones, and all other sorts of Sleeve Buttons."

ROQUELOE.—Andrew Oliver jr. of Boston advertised the loss of "two Scarlet Roqueloes, one the last Summer, the other the Summer before; which he supposes he left at some Friend's House after a shower, which occasion'd the Use of Them."—*Boston Gazette,* Oct. 17, 1757.

MUFF.—Lost, a Man's large Muff.—*Boston Gazette,* Dec. 12, 1757.

HOSE.—"Mens & womens worsted thread & cotton hose, mens white and black silk ditto, knit waistcoats and breeches of all colors . . . *Hose's* shoes clogs & galoshes, english soles, sattin and brocaded silk shoes."—*Boston Gazette,* Nov. 5, 1759.

MILITARY UNIFORMS.—To all who intend to engage in this Year's Expedition for the total Reduction of CANADA, Notice is hereby given, That Treasurer's Bounty-Notes will be taken without Discount; also Notes that are payable in 1760, 1761, and 1762, and the Interest allowed Thereon for any of the following Articles, where were imported in the last Ships from London, and are to be Sold at the lowest Rate by *Daniel Jones, at the Hat & Helmet, South End, Boston,* Uniform English Gold and Silver Lace for Hats, Lace suitable for Waistcoats, French Lace for ditto, scarlet, crimson, blue, buff, and cloth coloured Broad-Cloths, scarlet, green, blue, and cloth coloured Ratteens, Devonshire Kerseys, German Serge, Knit Patterns for Jackets and Breeches, Hair Plush, cut Velvet Patterns for Jackets, London and Bristol Shalloons, Durants and Tammies, with Trimmings of all Sorts for Men's Cloathing, black Cravats, Neck Ribbons, Cockades, Taffaty, Alamode, Sewing Silk, Silk, Linen, and Cotton Handkerchiefs, Cambleteens, Burgenell, check'd Hungarians, Callimanco, Damask and single Russell, Chinces, Cambricks, plain and long Lawns, flowered and spotted ditto, Worsted Stockings of most colours, white Thread ditto, a good Assortment of Yarn Stockings, Men's and Boy's Shoes, and Pumps, Women's ditto, &c. &c.—Also ready made Coats, Waistcoats, Breeches, ruffled Holland Shirts, Checked plain ditto, Baize wrapping Gowns—The best Beaver and Beaveret Hatts of his own make, which will be warranted; also, a great Assortment of English Beaver, Beveret and Castor Hatts, English and French Felts; likewise Felt Hats, the Manufacture of this Country, which will be warranted to wear at least Three Years with good Usage, Linings and Trimmings of all sorts for Hatts.—*Boston Evening Post,* Feb. 18, 1760.

HOSIERY.—In the advertisements in the *Boston Gazette* of June 23, 1760, are listed the following:—(a) "worsted hose of all sorts: cotton and thread ditto: Mens white and black, plain and ribb'd silk hose;" (b) "Mens, Womens and Childrens Cotton, Thread and Worsted Hose, Mens plain and ribb'd silk ditto;"

(c) "Mens and womens worsted, thread and cotton hose;" (d) "Men's black Hose;" (e) "mens and womens worsted, thread and cotton hose, boys and girls hose;" (f) "Mens, Womens and Childrens Thread, Cotton & Worsted Hose;" (g) "Superfine men's and women's worsted, cotton and thread hose;" (h) "plain and ribb'd white Hose;" (i) "Mens worsted hose."

HOSE.—"Mens plain & ribb'd worsted hose; mens plain & chiver'd ditto; mens thread and cotton ditto; plain and ribb'd white town china silk hose;" imported in the *Jupiter* and for sale by *Christopher Clarke* who has the above Goods from the first Hands in London.—*Boston Gazette*, Jan. 5, 1761.

HATS AND CLOAKS.—Joshua Blanchard, at the Bible and Crown, Dock Square, advertised importations from London, among which were:—Black trolly, and black & white Quebec for handkerchiefs; figured silvered paper hats; chipt hats; women's new fashioned black, white, pink & blue hats; new fashioned ready made cloaks; velvet masks; Scotch handkerchiefs; wire and horn-mould shirt buttons; women's Calamanco & fine durant petticoats; Hose's shoes, neat silk shoes, best of Lynn-made shoes; canvas for screens; paper hangings; chimney pieces; flower pots and urns; sea pieces, and neat painted India screens.—*Boston News-Letter*, Jan. 8, 1761.

STOCKINGS.—At the Royal Exchange, King Steet, will be Sold by Publick Vendue, on Wednesday next, A large Assortment of Men's knit and wove Stockings, (both Worsted and Yarn) in Lotts fresh imported. . . .

N. B. The Sale to begin on Wednesday aforesaid, at 11 o'Clock Forenoon, J. G.—*Boston Gazette*, Jan. 26, 1761.

HATS AND BONNETS.—Barnabas Binney imported from London and had on sale at his house in Summer Street:—Newly made black, pink, blue, and green callamanco quilted petticoats; plain and plaited black sattin hats; Prussian and Raneleigh bonnets; bags for gentlemen's hair; bosom flowers; newest fashion gauze caps; setts of round and oblong dishes, stone and Delph ware; Stone shoe, knee, stock, & bosom buckles; paste earings, stone rings; chrystal sleeve buttons in silver; brown ditto in gold;

chrystal seals; Moco rings & studs; French necklaces & earings; glass stands; etc.—*Boston News-Letter*, Jan. 29, 1761.

HOSE.—Imported from London, in the ship *Elizabeth*, Captain *Thomas Hulme*, and to be sold by JANE EUSTIS, at her Shop, next Door to Mr. *Kent's* Office, the North Side of the Town House, the following Goods Cheap for Cash, viz. . . . mens silk hose, mens, womens and childrens white thread & cotton ditto, mens plain & ribb'd worsted ditto, womens and childrens plain and Clock't ditto . . . —*Boston Gazette*, Feb. 2, 1761.

CLOGS, CAPS AND GLOVES.—Jane Eustis imported from London and had on sale at her shop on the North side of the Town House; a great variety of cloths, etc. and stampt sarsnet Shades, toed clogs, men's velvet caps, boy's sattin Jockeys and Feathers, new fashion thread blond lace for Gentlemen's Ruffles, white Kid Gloves and Mitts, Children's Stays, women's undress Stays, bugle solitier Necklaces, stone girdle and hat buckles, stone stay hooks, Robe royals, black Bags, Fan-hoops, India and Irish Bengals for Gentlemen's Jackets, Ladies gilt and bordered Message Cards, Ivory and Ebony Nutmeg Graters, Diamond Pencles, Ivory Patch Boxes, enameled China ditto, Wash balls and Cases, Paste Prints, a great variety of Toothpick Cases, silver pins for the Ladies Hair, Garnet Brasslets, Lavender Water, plain and perfumed Hair Powder, Pound and common Pins, Pomatum, Gold Rings set round with Garnet, new fashioned French Beed Solitier, chever de Frieze Earings, etc. etc.—*Boston News-Letter*, Feb. 12, 1761.

BUTTONS.—Lewis Deblois of Boston advertised a long list of fabrics and hardware just imported from London and Bristol, including "very great assortment of metal and breast buttons, black and coloured horn buttons, Mathewman's and Wild's ditto; All sorts colour'd stone sleeve buttons."—*Boston Gazette*, June 8, 1761.

HOSE AND HATS.—Jane Eustis, at her Shop opposite the north side of the Town House, Boston, advertised recent importations from London, viz: Mens black, white, marble, & Masqueraded Silk Hose; rose, cloth, & green Mantua Silk; Mens velvet Caps;

Boys Sattin Jockeys & Feathers; black Sattin Hats & Bonnetts; brocaded silk shoes; Childrens red Morocco ditto; black velvet clogs; black, Quebec, black and white ditto stampt Handkerchiefs; a great variety of enamelled Snuff & Patch Boxes; newest fashioned Egrets; black & bugle ditto; black & white Plumes for the Head; Umbrilloes, & Silk for ditto; Toothpick cases; Pricking irons; Ladies Court Plaister; Copper Plate Cottons; purple & White Bengals; Silver Girdles; Tammy & Calamanco Petticoats; feathered fillets; new-fashioned Book-Tea-Chests and Ink Stands; etc. etc.—*Boston News-Letter*, July 2, 1761.

SURTOUT.—"Joseph Tyler desires the Person that borrowed his Surtout to return it, if it is not worn out."—*Boston Gazette*, Nov. 2, 1761.

STOCKINGS.—"A very fine Assortment of Men's plain, mixt, motled, diced and peck'd Stockings, all very good: Men's thread Stockings:" imported in the Brig Betsey.—*Boston Gazette*, Jan. 25, 1762.

HOSE.—"Men's plain & ribb'd worsted hose; womens plain and white silk hose; mens black and white silk hose."—*Boston Gazette*, Feb. 1, 1762.

HATS.—Imported in Captains *Partridge* and *Hulme*, the last ships from London, and to be sold by *Thomas Handasyd Peck*, in Merchants Row, near the Golden-Ball; Superfine Linnen Linings for Beaver Hats, sundry sorts of Linings for Beaveret, Castor and Felt Hats: Tabby Linings, Mohair Luping and Bands: Silk Braid, round and flat Silk Lace for Button Lupes, Frog Lupes, plain and work'd Buttons, Gold and Silver Chain, yellow and white Buttons, large and small Bowstrings, hard and soft Brushes, Velures, Cards, Nuskin, Verdigreese, Coperas, Blockingline, Mens and Boys Felt Hats, Beaver, Beaveret and Castor Hats of his own Make; a few small Packs of Carolina Beaver; a quantity of French Gold Lace.—*Boston Gazette*, Feb. 1, 1762.

APRONS.—"Pink coloured short Aprons and Stomachers for Young Ladies."—*Boston Gazette*, Apr. 19, 1762.

MEN'S CLOTHING.—Imported from London, and for Sale by Wholesale or Retail, by Jolley Allen, at his Shop near the Draw-

Bridge; a large Assortment of English and India goods, fit for all Seasons.—Likewise ready made Cloathing of all Sorts for Men—Barcelona Handkerchiefs of all Colours—All Colours and Sizes of Women's best Callimanco Shoes, made by the neatest Workmen at Lynn, at 38s. O. T. Also the very best of Hyson Tea at 10 l. etc.—*Boston News-Letter*, Sept. 15, 1763.

SHOES.—"All sizes & colours of womens best Callimanco Shoes, made by the neatest workmen at Lynn, at 38 s. O. T. per pair.—*Boston Gazette*, Oct. 10, 1763.

MEN'S CLOTHING.—At public vendue:—"20 Suits London-made Claret & other Coloured Cloth Coats, Vests & Breeches," breeches patterns, all colours, bed counter-paines.—*Boston Gazette*, Dec. 5, 1763.

LEATHER CLOTHING.—A very great Number of the respectable Tradesmen of this Town, have come to a Resolution to wear Nothing but Leather for their Working Habits, for the future, and that to be only of the Manufacture of this Government.—*Boston Gazette*, Sept. 24, 1764. In the next issue of the *Gazette* is the advertisement of "*Adam Colson*, near the Great Trees at the South End, dresses all Sorts of Skins suitable for the Purpose above mentioned in the neatest and genteelest manner.—It is worth observing, that a Jacket made of Moos Skin, fit for Apprentices, will wear out at least seven Jackets made of Broad Cloth, and will wear handsome to the End."

MOURNING COSTUME.—Monday last were decently interred, the Remains of Mr. Ellis Callender, Son of the Late Minister of the Baptist Church. The Town had the Satisfaction of seeing in this Instance, a Funeral conducted conformable to an Agreement lately entered into by a great Number of the most respectable of its Inhabitants.—A long Train of Relations followed the Corpse (which was deposited in a Plain Coffin) without any sort of Mourning at all: Mr. Andrew Hall, the Chief Mourner, appeared in his usual Habit, with a Crape round his Arm; and his Wife, who was Sister and nearest Relative to the Deceased, with no other Token of Mourning than a black Bonnet, Gloves, Ribbons and Handkerchief. The Funeral was attended by a large Procession of Merchants and Gentlemen of Figure, as a Testimony of their approbation of this Piece of Occonomy and as a Mark of their Esteem for a Family who have shown Virtue enough to break a Custom too long established and which has proved ruinous to many Families in this Community.

☞ THE *Gentlemen and Ladies of the Town are informed*, That Bows and Roses of Ribbands for Gentleman, and Bonnets proper for Widows and other Ladies, are made in the genteelest Manner, and sold by ANNE and ELIZABETH CUMMINGS, at the corner of Queen-Street, near the Town-House. Where also may be had: Crapes for Gentlemen's Hats or Arms, and Handkerchiefs, Ribbands & Gloves for Ladies.

N. B. Bonnets for Funerals are either to be Let or Sold.—*Boston Gazette*, Sept. 24, 1764.

STOMACHERS.—Thomas Lee, at his store in Kilby Street, leading to Oliver's Dock, advertised a long list of fabrics and clothing, also; bags for the Hair, flowers, handsome silver Stomachers and flower'd ditto; a large Collection of Pictures, fram'd glaz'd, and in sheets; a fine assortment of Gothick and other Paper Hangings, very Cheap, sealskin and leather trunks, etc.—*Boston News-Letter*, Aug. 22, 1765.

MEN'S CLOTHING.—Benjamin Goldthwait, Taylor, Would Inform his Kind Customers and others, that he has just received by the Brig, Capt. Shayler, from London, the following Articles, viz. Very fine 6, 4 and 3 threaded black Breeches Patterns, uncommon large and good black, white and figured Silk ditto, very neat Tambore worked waistcoat Shapes, fine Nankeens, white and buff Kersemears, Corduroys, best silk striped Damascus, very fine corded Dimothy for Breeches, royal lastings, figur'd Tane, very neat, with many other Articles. The above goods are a consignment, and he will sell them at low as possible for the Cash, at his Shop just above the Concert-Hall. Embroider'd Holes in Gold, Silver and Twist, are done in the neatest manner at said Shop.—*Boston News-Letter*, May 19, 1774.

### Dress of Mechanics and Servants

SAILOR.—Ran-away from their Master, Capt. *Joseph Swadell*, Commander of the Lake Frigot, now in Boston, two Servant Men *viz David Rose* a North Britain, aged about 18 years, of a short stature, speaks broken English, short black Hair, Sailors Habit, viz speckled Shirt, dark Jacket and Breeches; he Ran away the 21st Currant.

And the other Servant an Apprentice, named *Joseph Riddell*, a South Britain; Ran-away the 23rd Currant, aged about 19 years, a tall man, pretty much pock broken, short black Hair, a black Wigg: with Sailoes Habit, a speckled Handkerchief, and divers sorts of Cloaths.

Whoever shall take up the said Runaway Servants, and them safely convey to their said Master, Capt *Swadell*, or to Capt. *Ebenezar Wentworth* at Mr. *David Jeffries*, Merchant, in Shrimpton's Lane, Boston, or can give any true Intelligence of them, so as their Master may have them again, shall have Thirty shillings Reward for David Rose, and Five Pounds Reward for Joseph Riddel, besides all necessary Charges paid.—*Boston News-Letter*, Apr. 21/28, 1712.

MAID SERVANT.—Ran-away from her Master *Thomas Moffet* of Boston Merchant, on Wednesday last the Tenth Currant, a Young Servant Woman, named *Mary Sutton*, of a Low Stature, light hair, has on a light Manto & Pettycoat lin'd with red, or a yellow & white mixt stuffe without lyning; she came over a Servant in the Ship Tiverton Gally from Briston, and is hereby advertised within three days from the Publishing hereof to return to her former Service, & she shall be forgiv'n, but if otherwise she does not return; Whosoever shall apprehend the said Servant and her safely convey to her abovesaid Master, or give any true Intelligence of her, so as her Master may have her again, shall be sufficiently rewarded besides all necessary charges paid.—*Boston News-Letter*, June 8/15, 1713.

SHIP CARPENTER.—William Netherton, a ship carpenter, absconded with tools and merchandise, from his ship lying at the

South Battery, Boston. He was "a man of middle stature, indifferent thin in Body and Face, short, Hair, of a Sandy color, wears an indifferent light Wigg, pretty long pale Visage, has on a light colour'd cloth Coat trim'd with black and Frogs of the Same, a Yellowish cloth Wastcoat, blue Breeches, a white shirt, black and white mix'd Stockings."—*Boston News-Letter*, Mar. 15/22, 1713/14.

PERRIWIG-MAKER.—Ran away from Mr. *Thomas Silby* in Boston, on the 25th of July last, a North Britain Man Servant, named *David Dowie*, a Perriwig-maker, of a middle Stature, fresh Colour, aged about 24 Years, wears a Perriwig, a Cinamon coloured Coat, Round to'd Shoes. Whoever shall apprehend the said Runaway, and him safely convey to his said Master, or give any true Intelligence of him, so as his Master may have him again, shall have Ten Pounds Reward.—*Boston News-Letter*, Aug. 20/27, 1716.

NEGRO SLAVES.—Ran away from Mr. *David Hillard*, of Stonington, a Negro Man, called *Mingo*, aged about Thirty one Years; with an Indian Squaw, called *Milly*, that ran from Mr. *John Swan* of said Town, both speak good English, the Negro Man is of a pale colour, he has on Home-spun Cloathes of a Russet colour. Whosoever takes up said Negro Man, and him safely keep, so that his Master may have him again, or give true Intelligence of them, shall have Three Pounds Reward, besides all necessary Charges paid.—*Boston News-Letter*, Aug. 20/27, 1716.

IRISH SERVANT.—Ran away, an Irish Servant: wore new frock & trowsers, short horse-hair bob wig, striped cap, old jacket patched with canvas. Ran away from a brigantine, at Boston.—*Boston News-Letter*, Jan. 6, 1725/6.

IRISH SERVANT.—Ran away frm. James Scotley in Boston, an Irish servant, Arthen Wade, aged 18 years, speaks good English, wore his own hair, a new Castor hat, light coloured coat, lined with Red, white Shirt, white Stockings & wooden heeled shoes. £5. reward.—*Boston Gazette*, May 16/23, 1726.

NEGRO SLAVE.—Ran away from Jeremiah Wilcox of Dartmouth, a negro man named Jack, aged 22 years, marked with small pox on his face, wore a Blew Cloth Coat, Home spun Woolen Breeches Black and White, Two Shirts, one checked Woolen and the other white Holland, Two Pair of Stockens one Black Silk and the other Grey Yarn, A New Pair of square toed Wooden Heel Shoes and old Castor Hat and a Red Silk Handkerchief. The said Negro is supposed to have a Counterfeited Pass with him. £5 reward.—*Boston Gazette*, June 27/July 4, 1726.

TALLOW CHANDLER.—Ran away, a young man, aged 22 years, from a tallow chander in Boston, hair cut close, worsted cap, white ozenbrigg wastcoat, dark fustian breeches, worsted stockings, pair pumps with silver buckles.—*Boston News-Letter*, Aug. 11/18, 1726.

COOPER.—Ran away, a negro man, aged 35 years, cooper by trade, leather jacket and breeches, yarn stockings, square-toed shoes, black double-breasted frize jacket, white flannel lining, good felt hat.—*Boston News-Letter*, Dec. 22/29, 1726.

SERVANT IN LIVERY.—John Davis, servant to Mr Okeden, formerly servant to Capt Austin, absented himself from service. He wears his own hair, a plain green Livery Coat with brass Buttons, buff colored jacket and breeches; took with him a brown fustian frock & pair of striped ticking breeches.—*Boston Gazette*, Mar. 11/18, 1727/8.

MAN SERVANT.—Nicholas Classon, servant of Andrew Bradford of Philadelphia, ran away, aged 21 years. "Much Pockfretten," wore grey Drugget Coat lined & trimmed with black, white Demity Jacket, white Fustian Coat with Mettle Buttons & faced in the neck with red Velvet, pair leather Breeches, pair striped Linnen home-spun Breeches, wore bob-wig.—*Boston Gazette*, June 17/24, 1728.

INDIAN WOMAN.—Ran away, an Indian woman, indented servant, tall lusty, wore narrow striped Cherrederry gown, turned up with a little flowered red and white callico, stript homespun quilted petticoat, plain muslin apron, & a suit of plain pinners, & a red & white flowered knot, pair green stone earings, white cotton stockings, leather heeled shoes.—*Boston News-Letter*, Aug. 15/22, 1728.

MAN SERVANT.—Ran away, a servant man, from Marblehead, aged 19 years, born in Marblehead, wore double-striped under Jacket, light colored drugget Jacket & breeches, new Castor hat, worsted stockings wooden heeled shoes.—*Boston News-Letter*, Aug. 22/29, 1728.

INDIAN WOMAN.—Ran away, from the Gray Hound tavern, Roxbury, an Indian woman, wore red flowered calico jacket & petticoat, quilted petticoat.—*Boston News-Letter*, Sept. 19/26, 1728.

CHAIR MAKER.—Ran away from a chair maker, an Irish man servant, aged 20 years, wore a dark colored pea jacket, lined with white flannel, dark colored breeches, felt hat, worsted stockings, round toed shoes.—*Boston News-Letter*, Mar. 6/13, 1728/9.

FELT MAKER.—Ran away, a man servant, felt maker, aged 30 years, wore a white shirt with a speckled one under it, Swansey striped jacket, dark colored cloth coat, narrow brim Castor hat, cut round the edges, his head being lately shaved hath a cap on.—*Boston News-Letter*, May 20/June 5, 1729.

HUSBANDMAN.—Ran away, an English man servant, aged 22 years, husbandman, wore a French Drugget coat trimmed with blue, small pewter buttons, brown breeches & jacket, white fustian jacket, short black hair.—*Boston News-Letter*, Sept. 4/11, 1729.

NEGRO SLAVE.—Ran away, a negro man, from Newbury, aged 23 years, wore a brownish colored homemade clothes, light colored jacket with pewter buttons.—*Boston News-Letter*, Nov. 14/21, 1729.

NEGRO SLAVE.—Ran away a negro man, from Newbury, branded on shoulder I. G. and a crow's foot (master's name was Victorious Lovby), "had on when he went away four Chains of a Scale Beam lock'd about his neck," cotton & linen shirt, black jacket, white Bays breeches, formerly a cooper in N. Y.—*Boston News-Letter*, Mar. 5/12, 1729/30.

NEGRO SLAVE.—Ran away, a negro man, wore cotton & linen shirt, mill'd cap, leather breeches, double-breasted pee jacket, with brass buttons, white woolen westcoat lined with brown ozenbrigs in the body, yarn stockings, leather heeled shoes.—*Boston News-Letter*, Nov. 12/19, 1730.

WEAVER.—Ran away, a Palantine, a weaver by trade, aged 27 years, wore dark colored cloth coat and breeches, buff leather wastcoat, chequer'd shirt & an old light perriwig.—*Boston News-Letter*, Nov. 12/19, 1730.

IRISH SERVANT MAN.—Ran away from Newton, from Rev. Cotton, aged 19 years, wore a "gray coat cuff'd up with black Velvet, narrow sleeves," striped holland Jacket, cotton & linen shirt, black callaminco breeches, felt hat and cap, hair short, & very much curled & reddish color, pair of new shoes, yarn stockings, with white over them, silk musling Handkerchief about his Neck, shaves well.—*Boston News-Letter*, Nov. 19/26, 1730.

IRISH SERVANT MAN.—Ran away from Newton, aged 20 years, wore a dark colored homespun coat, narrow sleeves, with brass buttons, jacket of the same with pewter buttons, fine shirt with silver buttons in the sleeves, light colored drugged breeches, a cap, new felt hat, yarn stockings, wooden heeled shoes, "pair of yarn Boots over his Stockings."—*Boston News-Letter*, Nov. 26/Dec. 3, 1730.

WEST COUNTRY MAN SERVANT.—Ran away at Newbury, aged 21 years, wore a fly coat, Cotton & linnen jacket, with blue and white stripes.—*Boston News-Letter*, Dec. 31/Jan. 7, 1730/1.

CORDWAINER.—Ran away, a negro man, a cordwainer, aged 25 y., wore a great loose coat of dark color, old blue jacket & leather breeches; reported to have been seen since "with a frock & trouzers on."—*Boston News-Letter*, Mar. 19/26, 1731.

WILLIAM EVERENDINE, aged 21 years, pretty fat and well set and Short, ran away from Mr. Pearson, Cooper, at the North end of Boston. He wore a black cloth coat lined with silk, a grey cloth wastcoat, with pewter Buttons; has lately cut his Hair and now wears a fair bobb Wigg. 40 s. reward.—*Boston Gazette*, May 10/17, 1731.

NEGRO SLAVE.—A negro man ran away from a ship master at Marblehead, aged 26 years, wore a light colored Duffel Coat, black buttons, and black velvet cuffs, strip'd linen jacket, & leather breeches, formerly belonged to Rev. George Pigot.—*Boston News-Letter*, Sept. 23/30, 1731.

JOHN HENDERSON, an Irishman, a servant of Ebenezer Eastman of Pennycook, N. H. aged 18 years, ran away. Wore home spun grey Clothes, leather breeches with a black wasteband, great blew coat, and beaver hat. 40 s. reward.—*Boston Gazette*, Nov. 29/Dec. 6, 1731.

MOLATTO BOY, aged 19 years, ran away from Boston; head close shaved; wore a worsted cap, brown suit of clothes; white strings to his breeches' knees; ring on one of his fingers.—*Boston News-Letter*, Feb. 10/17, 1731/2.

SPANISH INDIAN man Servant, ran away from Newbury, aged 26 years, wore dark coloured homespun pee Jacket, with round pewter buttons, a pair of long Trowsers over his leather breeches, felt hat, yarn stockings, and round toed shoes.—*Boston News-Letter*, Mar. 2/9, 1731/2.

A CONVICTED MURDERER escaped from jail at Newport, R. I. wore at the time brownish colored Duroy Coat, leather breeches and yarn stockings.—*Boston News-Letter*, Oct. 12/19, 1732.

SPANISH INDIAN SERVANT, ran away at North Kingston, R. I. aged 20 years, wore Beaver hat, silk muslin handkerchief, light grey cloth coat with long pockets, dark grey Camblet Jacket, Tow Cloth Breeches and Shirt and grey yarn stockings.—*Boston News-Letter*, Oct. 12/19, 1732.

IRISH MAN SERVANT, aged 24 years, ran away, wore checked woolen shirt, double-breasted Jacket, long trowsers, old shoes, old felt hat.—*Boston News-Letter*, June 14/21, 1732.

CHARLES DALY, an Irish Boy, ran away in Boston, wore "loose Blew Coat, a fustian Frock, blew Wastcoat, and black Breeches." —*Boston Gazette*, Dec. 11/18, 1732.

SAWYER.—Ran-away from *Joseph Lyn, Shipwright of Philadelphia, about 3 years past, a servant Man Named* Paul Raulisson, *a sawyer by Trade, about 33 Years of Age, he wore his own strait black Hair, tall of stature, white Looks. He had on when he went away, a good suit of black broad cloth full trim'd, good white shirt, good shoes, and stockings, good Hatt; he is suppos'd to be in NewEngland, and it is thought that his Wife is with him, her Name is* Sarah, *she wore a Green CallimincoGown, flour'd with white. Whosoever takes up the said servant and secures him so that his Master may have him again, shall have* Five Pounds *Boston Money Reward, and reasonable charges paid by*, Messr. John *and* Joseph Gooch, *in* Boston.—*Boston Gazette*, Nov. 18/25, 1734.

SPANISH INDIAN SERVANT.—Ran away from his master at Ipswich, a Spanish Indian servant, named Jack, aged 30 years, wore a Felt hat, orange coloured jacket, thick leather breeches, with a patch in the Crotch of shoe leather, checkered woolen shirt, light gray stockings, with tops sowed of another sort, and pretty good shoes. £5 reward.—*Boston News-Letter*, Oct. 2/9, 1735.

IRISH SERVANT, aged 21 years, ran away, wore light coloured Drugget Coat with Mohair buttons, Jacket of same with brass buttons, light colored broadcloth breeches, yarn stockings, took away a light old Bob Wig, a light Tail-Wig, and a dark brown Bob-Wig. £3 reward.—*Boston News-Letter*, Mar. 18/25, 1736.

NEGRO SLAVE.—Ran away from his Master, James Halsey of Boston, a negro lad aged about 18 years, wore a "blue Jacket trim'd with red and Brass Buttons, a Cotton and Linnen Shirt, a pair of Leather Breeches, a narrow-brimb'd Hat." 40 s. reward. —*Boston Gazette*, June 14/21, 1736.

RAN AWAY, "a Mustee man servant" belonging to Ebenezer Brenton of South Kingston, R. I. named Abel, aged 23 years, ("'tis supposed that his Father was a Dutch man, and his Mother a Spanish Indian") "shows something of white in his Complection" wore Grey Kersey Great Coat & Jacket, Linnen Frock & Trousers, new felt hat & new shoes.—*Boston Gazette*, Nov. 1/8, 1736.

ENGLISH MAN SERVANT.—Ran away from his Master in Roxbury, an English man Servant, aged about 20 years, short brown hair, wore a dark coloured homespun coat, Jacket & breeches, with metal buttons, a loose great red Coat with brass buttons, 2 shirts, a Garlick and a Cotton & Linnen one, 2 pr. stockings, one grey yarn, the other dark Worsted, small brimmed Castor hat, & a silk

Handkerchief about his neck, "goes shambling with his Feet, his Legs something turning out," 40 s. reward.—*Boston News-Letter*, Dec. 30/Jan. 6, 1737.

NEGRO SLAVE.—Ran away from her Master in Boston (but lately from Jamaica), a negro woman called Mimbo, aged 26 years, wore a dark coloured Bays gown, and over that a blue & white striped Holland Petticoat with a red one under it, took a striped Callimanco Jacket with a blue ferret round the bottom, & a pair of low heeled shoes, generally wears a handkerchief on her head, is marked K. L. on one of her shoulders. 40 s. reward.—*Boston News-Letter*, Apr. 21/28, 1737.

WORSTED COMBER.—*Ran-away from his Master Mr. Samuel Foster, of Boston, Clothier, on Tuesday the Third of this Instant May, at Night, an Irish Man Servant named Florence Carty, about 20 Years old, of a middle Stature, and fresh coloured. His Hair is cut off, and he wears a Cap, and he had on when he went away, a dark Blue Coat, a striped Jacket, Blue Plush Breeches and Yarn Stockings.*

N. B. *He is a Worsted Comber by Trade.*

*Whoever shall take up the said Servant, and bring him to his abovesaid Master living in* Newbury-Street *at the South End of* Boston, *or secure him and give Notice thereof so that he may be had again, shall have* Five Pounds *Reward, and all necessary Charges paid.*—*Boston News-Letter*, Apr. 28/May 5, 1737.

NEGRO SLAVE.—Ran away a negro servant man aged 27 years speaks French and Spanish, and fair English, wore blue jacket, 2 pr old "Trouzers" & a hat "painted of several Colours."—*Boston News-Letter*, Sept. 22/29, 1737.

WILLIAM COLEMAN, an English servant, aged 22 years, ran away from his master Mr Amos Wood of Unity Furnace, "in the Gore of Land between this Government and the Colony of Rhode Island," "had on when he went away a new Kersey Wastcoat of a light drab colour, with mettal Buttons, a pair of Deer Skin Leather Breeches, the colour changed by being daub'd with Tar in many places, a new worsted Cap lin'd with blue, a Felt Hat, also a good Broad Cloth Coat and Wastcoat, of a deep brown colour, an Oznabrigs Frock and Trowsers, and two or three white Shirts, his head lately shaved, and by Occupation a Gardner." George Blackmore, a fellow servant who ran away at the same time wore his "short dark curl'd Hair," and carried with him "a plush Coat with Gold Vellum button holes, and Gold wash'd Mettal Buttons." He also wore "a Frock and Trowsers" and a speckled Shirt. "They have with them a small Ticken Bed Sack for a Wallet." £3 reward for each.—*Boston Gazette*, Oct. 17/24, 1737.

NEGRO SLAVE.—Ran away from Andover, James Fry, master, a negro boy, aged 19 years, named Cuff, wore a brown coloured homespun coat, with Mettal Buttons, ditto breeches, with Knee Buckles, took a linen and a cotton shirt, 2 worsted caps and a felt cap, round toed shoes with large flowered pewter Buckles.—*Boston News-Letter*, Oct. 20/27, 1737.

BOAT BUILDER.—Ran away from Thomas Bently, boatbuilder, Boston, an English servant, aged 20 years, short hair, commonly wears a cap, old Kersey Jacket, "something patched," home spun Jacket with pewter buttons, dark drugget breeches, yarn stockings, round toed shoes, old felt hat painted red.—*Boston News-Letter*, Nov. 24/Dec. 1, 1737.

COOPER.—Ran away from Capt Luce of Boston, an Irish servant, aged 21 years, a cooper by trade; wore a hat, a worsted cap, snuff colored Fly coat, grey jacket without buttons but laced, speckled shirt, yarn stockings, double-soled shoes, took with him a cloth pea jacket, pair of trowzers and a frock. £5. reward.—*Boston News-Letter*, Dec. 22/29, 1737.

INDIAN WOMAN SERVANT.—Ran away, from Roxbury, an Indian woman servant, aged 22 years, named Ann Warwick, wore a homespun gown striped blue and grey, cotton and Linen shift, blue stockings & wooden heel shoes, also carried an English stuff gown stripped white, green and red. £3 reward.—*Boston News-Letter*, Jan. 26/Feb. 2, 1737/8.

IRISH LAD.—Ran away from Jonathan Pue of Roxbury, an indented Irish lad, aged 16 years, wears his hair; wore a good hat, double-breasted blue cloth coat with brass buttons & over that a great blue cloth coat, wore boots and took a gun with him.—*Boston News-Letter*, Mar. 9/16, 1737/8.

IRISH MAN SERVANT.—Ran away from his Master, James Sisson of Portsmouth, R. I. an Irish Servant named John Reynolds, about 22 years of Age, speaks pretty good English, has very short Hair, wore a worsted cap, old felt hat, "which had been bound, but the binding was rip'd off," red cloth Jacket, speckled shirt, blew great Coat & long Oznabrigs Breeches. £5 reward.—*Boston News-Letter*, Apr. 27/May 4, 1738.

WELSHMAN.—Ran away from his master, Ebenezer Moody of Farmington, a "heavy moulded" Welch-man named Lewis Williams, aged about 25 years, wore checkered cotton shirt, blue Duroy Vest, dirty colored cloth coat, linen trousers much patched, Yarn stockings footed with another Color, new felt hat, sharp toed shoes. £3.—*Boston News-Letter*, June 1/8, 1738.

WILLIAM BEAL.—Ran away from his father James Beal of Needham, aged 20 years, wore, grey Linsey-woolsey coat, dark home spun Coat, strippd Cotton & Linen jacket, linen breeches, blue yarn stockings, round toed shoes, new beaver hat. £3. reward.—*Boston News-Letter*, Oct. 19/26, 1738.

BRICKLAYER.—Ran away from his master Joseph Cundall of Portsmouth, R. I. Richard Comber, a bricklayer by trade. Had on when he ran away "a Frock & Trousers, and a Woolen Cap," aged 40 years. £5. reward.—*Boston Gazette*, Aug. 13/20, 1739.

MULATTO SLAVE.—Ran away, a mollatto man servant, at Scituate, wore an old felt hat, a worsted cap, blue broadcloth Coat, black & white flannel Jacket, white flannel shirt pair of trousers, etc.—*Boston News-Letter*, Nov. 23/30, 1739.

NEGRO WENCH.—Ran away from her master Andrew Sigourney, of Boston, a negro wench named *Janto;* wore on her head a speckled Handkerchief, a striped woolen jacket, a white oznabrigs petticoat, etc.—*Boston News-Letter*, Mar. 1/8, 1740.

TAILOR.—Ran away from Portsmouth, R. I. an English man servant, a taylor by trade, ruddy complexion and with a red beard; wore a blue strait Bodied Coat with black velvet buttons and black button holes, a bluish silk camblet Jacket, fine white shirt with ruffles at Bosome and Wrists, Cloth Breeches, worsted stockings, new calf skin shoes with Mettle Buckles, a blue shagg great coat, a Beaver hat and a linen Cap. A great drunkard. £10. reward.—*Boston News-Letter*, Mar. 12/19, 1741.

IRISH SERVANT.—Ran away from James Holt, of Co. York, Me, an Irish servant, aged 26 y. brown bushy Hair, high Nose; wore a broadcloth coat and jacket of a dark cinnamon color, pair orange-colored plush breeches and a good Beaver hat. £3. reward.—*Boston News-Letter*, Dec. 17/24, 1741.

SAIL-MAKER.—Ran away from his master, a Boston sail maker, a white servant lad, aged 19 years, wore a Pea-Jacket with large Plate Buttons; blew great Coat and a black Wigg. £5. reward.—*Boston News-Letter*, Feb. 25/Mar. 4, 1742.

TINKER.—Ran away from Gershom Flagg of Woburn, a negro servant, named Pompey York, indentured for 7 y. aged 35 years, speaks good English, had with him "two old cotton & Linnen Shirts, much patched, a grey Broad Cloth great Coat faced with Yellow, a blew Camblet Coat full trimmed, a blew Jacket made up of divers Pieces, light Cloth breeches patched with a brown Cloth in the Seat, two Pair of grey Yarn Stockings, a Pair of old Shoes which had a Patch upon each Side, an old Hat patched on the Crown. He had also a spoon and Dial Mould and other Tinker's Tools." 20 s. reward.

N. B. "The said Negro can read and write well, and is very deceitful, pretending to be a new Convert, and is very forward to mimick some of the Strangers that have of late been preaching about among us."—*Boston News-Letter*, Apr. 8/15, 1742.

INDIAN LAD.—Ran away, an Indian lad at North Kingston, R. I. aged 17 years, wore a thick Kersey cinnamon coloured jacket, black and white striped breeches, flannel shirt, new shoes, yarn stockings folded half way up his Leg, new felt hat. £6. reward.—*Boston News-Letter*, Dec. 16, 1742.

IRISH SERVANT.—Ran away from Dorchester, an Irish servant, aged 22 years, red short hair; wears cap, felt hat, dark Pea jacket, breeches of same color, pair of large Trowsers, strip'd under

Jacket, speckled cotton and wool shirt, freckled face. £10 reward.
—*Boston News-Letter*, Nov. 25, 1742.

SAILOR.—Ran away from the Ship *Leghorn-Galley* now lying at Long Wharf, an apprentice boy aged about 18 years, named John Lowder; wore a cinnamon coloured Coat, light coloured Velvet Cape and brass flat Buttons, leather Cap, dark coloured Wigg, light coloured Kersey breeches. £5 reward.—*Boston News-Letter*, Feb. 3, 1743.

NEGRO SLAVE.—Ran away from Sudbury, a negro man Sampson, aged 23 years, "has a pretty large Leg, walks light & spritely on the Ground." Wore a Castor hat, a Cap, dark coloured all wool Coat, with plain white metal buttons, a blue Cloth jacket, with brass buttons filled with Wood and Catgut Eyes, a cotton & linnen shirt, leather breeches, white cotton stockings, pair double-soled turned Pumps, dark coloured silk handkercchief. £5. reward.—*Boston News-Letter*, June 23, 1743.

NEGRO GIRL.—Ran away from Mrs Ann Phillips in Boston, a negro girl aged 14 years, named Violet, pretty lusty; wore a black linsey woolsey Coat and Jacket and a striped Callimancoe Petticoat under it; had also a new blew Bays jacket and a callico petticoat lined with a seersucker.—*Boston News-Letter*, Dec. 13, 1744.

INDIAN MAN.—Ran away from James Howell, Boston, an Indian Molatto Man aged 20 years, wore a green jacket and yellow leather breeches.—*Boston News-Letter*, May 23, 1745.

NEGRO SLAVE.—Ran away from Lebanon, Conn, a Negro man, aged 24 years, has a well proportioned leg; wore a dark coloured home spun Coat, light coloured fustian jacket with the sleeves cut off, tow cloth shirt and trowsers, yarn stockings, good shoes, carried in a yellow and white striped muslin handkerchief, a blue and white home spun checkered flannel shirt, and a pair of good cloth coloured Buckskin breeches, with a watch pocket in them, the buttons covered with leather. £3 reward.—*Boston News-Letter*, July 12, 1745.

NEGRO GIRL.—Ran away from her mistress in Boston, a negro girl, marked in her face with small pox; wore a white linnen jacket and large checked Petticoat.—*Boston News-Letter*, Aug. 8, 1745.

YOUNG LAD.—Ran away from Ship *Abigail* at Boston, Richard Acton, aged 12 years, wearing a cap or wig; wore "a blew freeze Coat with Brass Buttons, a pair of Trowsers and a strip'd worsted Cap." 20 s. reward.—*Boston News-Letter*, Aug. 15, 1745.

NEGRO SLAVE.—Ran away from the North End of Boston, a negro, aged 19 years, wore a green Ratteen Coat, Waistcoat, and Breeches, white metal buttons, cotton & linen shirt, ordinary worsted cap, grey yarn stockings; took with him a leather jockey cap and a new Oznabrigs Frock. £5. reward.—*Boston News-Letter*, Feb. 20, 1746.

MAN SERVANT.—A servant of Capt. Rimer of the Brigantine *Thomas*, ran away from his master. He was of low Stature and wore "Red Breeches, or Fear-nothing Trousers."—*Boston Gazette*, Dec. 22, 1747.

NEGRO SLAVE.—Ran away, a negro servant from Benauel Bower's Ship Yard in Swanzey, aged 35 years, wore double-breasted dark coloured Kerzey Pea Jacket, with yellow metal buttons, blue Devonshire Fly Coat, with large copper buttons, double-breasted without Lining.—*Boston News-Letter*, Jan. 29, 1748.

WOMEN'S CLOTHING.—Seized at Lebanon, Conn., from "a wandering Woman," as stolen goods; 4 Chince gowns, a Camblet gown, a quilt petticoat, a Hoop-petticoat, women's shifts and men's shirts, women's aprons, 9 women's neck cloths, 2 Pughoods, 2 night gowns, 4 women's Ruffles, an old Muff, a Portmanteau, 2 Malestrips, a riding skirt, etc. etc.—*Boston News-Letter*, Apr. 29, 1748.

NEGRO SLAVE.—Ran away from his Master, Timothy Stevens of Boston, a Negro Man named *Cato*, a tall well set Fellow, Aged about 25 Years, speaks English pretty well, has lost all his Toes by the Frost in Maryland, where he practiced runing away for some Years, his Way is to hide in the Day Time, and travel in the Night in the Woods, and Kill Fowls, Shoats, &c. for his Support. Had on when he went away, a red Kersey great Coat, Deerskin Breeches, yarn Stockings, double sol'd Shoes with Strings, double Worsted Cap, and Felt Hatt. Reward five Pound old Tenor, and all necessary Charges paid by *Timothy Stevens*.—*Boston Gazette*, Apr. 4, 1749.

ROPE MAKER.—Ran away from his Master Thomas Ivers, rope maker, of Stratford, Conn. a Prentice boy named Peter Hepbrow, aged about 17 years, wore "a light colour'd Cloth Pea Jacket, a blew Vest and Strip'd Waistcoat, and blew Camblet Breeches, and a Pair of Trowsers, wares a Wig or a Cap, a lusty rigged Lad of a swarthy Complection, with grey Eye;" reward, £20. old Tenor.—*Boston Gazette*, July 11, 1749.

BLACKSMITH.—A Transport man, Thomas Balderson, a blacksmith by trade, aged 35 years, ran away from his master William Johnson of Worcester; wore a cap, over his dark hair cut short, brown-coloured coat, with brass buttons, light coloured Jacket, new leather breeches, grey yarn stockings, pair of new pumps. £5. reward.—*Boston News-Letter*, July 27, 1749.

NEGRO SLAVE.—Ran away from Capt. James Forbes, a negro man named *Hercules*, has "a shaved spot on the crown of his Head" wore white shirt and Trousers, a handkerchief about his Head, no shoes, stockings, Jacket or hat. £5. reward.—*Boston News-Letter*, July 12, 1750.

ABSCONDED—Hugh Surrage, aged 18 years, wore "a striped homespun Jacket, Check Linnen Shirt, Leather Breeches, gray yarn Stockings, old Shoes, and a Felt Hat." Reward £5.—*Boston News-Letter*, July 12, 1750.

SCOTCH SERVANT.—Ran away *Charles Law* a Scotchman, aged 28 years, an indented servant of Sir Henry Frankland; wore a blue coat, dark coloured broad cloth breeches, a pair of sheep skin ditto red jacket, strip'd ditto, pair blue stockings, new double channel Pumps, brass buckles, wears Cap or Wigg. $5.00 reward.—*Boston Gazette*, Apr. 23, 1751.

SERVANT LAD.—"Ran away from his Master, Christopher Gardner of Boston, Mariner, a white Servant Lad, about 16 Years of Age, well set, brown Complection, black Eyes, and round

Face; Had on when he went away, a new light grey Forest Cloth Coat, with Metal Buttons, a blue Jacket, Pair of Trousers, check Shirt, black Stockings, and new shoes, and carried with him several other Sorts of Clothing." Reward £10. old Tenor.—*Boston Gazette*, June 4, 1751.

IRISH SERVANT.—"Ran away from his Master John Judkins, of Kingstown, N. H., blacksmith, a servant Man, came from Ireland, called Cornelius Lynes, is about 16 years of age, speaks pretty good English, is about 4 Feet and a half high, round shoulder'd; Had on when he went away a Bearskin Coat, the Body lin'd with red Bayes, and the sleeves with ozenbrig, brown Mohair Buttons, a Homespun Jacket, black and white stript, Wale woven, with flat Pewter Buttons on it, a Pair of Deerskin Breeches, Beveret Hat narrow brim'd, a Cotton and Linnen Shirt, blewish Stockings, a Pair of Pumps with Brass Buckles in them, a yellow Barcelona Handkerchief." £5. old Tenor, Reward.—*Boston Gazette*, Aug. 27, 1751.

IRISH MAID.—An Irish maid servant, aged 20 years, ran away from Francis Shaw, Boston, took with her "three Stuff Gowns, one blue, another green, and the other Birds Eye."—*Boston Gazette*, Sept. 17, 1751.

IRISH SERVANT.—Henry Jones, an Irish Servant lad, aged 18 years, ran away from his master, Israel Hersey of Boston, wharfinger. He wore "a good Hat, a white cloth Coat, blew Jacket without Lining, Buck Skin Breeches, worsted Cap, light coloured Stockings, and a Pair of Pumps." £5. old Tenor, reward.—*Boston Gazette*, Aug. 4, 1752.

JOHN MAYLAM, aged 19 years, a servant of Daniel Oliver of Boston, Peruke-maker, ran away. He wore a wigg, and had on "a Fly Cloth colour'd Coat and Breeches, a blew Jacket and grey rib'd Stockings." Reward, £10. old Tenor.—*Boston Gazette*, Feb. 20, 1753.

DAVID FITZ GARRALD, an Irish man servant of William Murray, Peruke-maker, in King street, Boston, ran away. Wore "a white Bearskin Coat, green Wastecoat, white Plush Breeches, gray yarn Stockings, and a Whitish Hatt much wore." Has sore eyes and short thick Legs. Reward £10. old Tenor.—*Boston Gazette*, Feb. 20, 1753.

NEGRO SLAVE.—Ran away from his Master, Capt. Benjamin Reed of Lexington, a Negro Man Servant, named *Sambo*, but calls himself Samuel Hanks, and pretends to be a Doctor, about 30 years of Age, speaks good English. Had on when he went away, a brown homespun Coat with brass Buttons, a brown Holland Jacket, new Leather Breeches, a pair of blue-clouded seam'd Stockings, a new course Linnen Shirt, and a Holland one, Trowsers, and an old Castor hat; has lost some of his fore Teeth, He carry'd with him a Bible, with (*Samuel Reed*) wrote in it, with some other Books. Reward, four dollars.—*Boston Gazette*, Sept. 18, 1753.

NEGRO SLAVE.—A negro man named *Cromwell*, aged 45 years, ran away from his master Henry Sherburne, jr, of Portsmouth, N. H., talks good English, can read and write and understands Husbandry work. He wore or carried away—"a blue Cloth Coat and Breeches, a Scarlet Cloth Jacket with Metal Buttons, and one pair of dark colour'd Plush Breeches, also some white Oznabrigs Jacket and Breeches, Linnen and Cotton Shirts, white Cotton and some Yarn Stockings, good Worsted Caps." Reward $8.—*Boston Gazette*, Oct. 22, 1754.

SPANISH INDIAN.—A Spanish Indian boy named *Jack*, aged 17 years, ran away from his master Capt. Wm Barber of Charlestown; wore short hair, a check shirt, dark jacket, black sheepskin Breeches, with a Frock and trowsers over them, dark yarn stockings, pair of half-worn shoes with brass buckles. Reward £2. —*Boston Gazette*, Nov. 24, 1755.

APPRENTICE LAD.—"Ran-away from his master Robert Macintire of Salem, on Monday the 3d Instant, an apprentice lad, named Benjamin Orne, jr., (who was lately impressed into Colonel Plaistead's Regiment) about 18 & ½ old, about 5 Foot high, a well sett, sturdy Fellow; Had on, either a blue Serge Suit, lin'd with black, or a gray Jacket with a spotted Flannel one under it, wears a cap, and had Pewter Buckles on his Shoes. Whoever shall take up said Apprentice, and convey him to his abovesaid Master in Salem, shall have ONE DOLLAR Reward, and all necessary charges paid by ROBERT MACINTYRE."—*Boston Gazette,* May 10, 1756.

NEGRO SLAVE.—Ran away from his Master, *Ebenezer Webster* of Bradford, a black slave, native of the East Indies, named *James:* speaks good English, about 21 years of Age, wears long bushy Hair . . . Had on a light Oznabrigs Coat, a brown homespun Jacket with brass Buttons, black plush Breeches, a pair of new Pumps, a new Felt Hat, and a white Linnen Shirt. . . . $3. reward.—*Boston Gazette,* June 13, 1757.

SERVANT MAID.—Mary Ingolson, aged 17 years, "a handsome brisk Girl" ran away from Pelitiah Man of Wrentham. She wore "a Linnen crossbarr'd Gown, a blue quilted Coat with divers other Cloathing." $1. reward.—*Boston Gazette,* June 13, 1757.

NEGRO SERVANT.—Ran away from James Dwyer of Portsmouth, N. H. truckman, a negro man servant named Scipio, aged about 35 years, born and brought up among the English, of a yellowish Complection; wore or carried away "a Saxon blue frize Jacket Lin'd with baize, slash sleeves and small Metal Buttons, a brown Fustian Jacket without sleeves, a pair of scarlet everlasting Breeches, a pair of Deerskin Breeches, yarn Stockings, a Pair of new Shoes, and new turned Pumps, one white cotton and Linnen and one Woolen check'd Shirt, an old Hat and Cap." 20 shillings sterling reward.—*Boston Gazette,* Aug. 8, 1757.

NEGRO SERVANT.—Toney, a negro, aged 30 years, ran away from Ichabod Chesley of Durham, N. H. He wore "a black and blue full'd Cloth round Tail Jacket, a stripped Cotton Jacket, grey yarn stockings, a Pair of new Pumps and Brass Buckles." £3. reward.—*Boston Gazette,* Aug. 29, 1757.

NEGRO SLAVE.—Joseph, a negro that spoke good French, but little English, ran away from his master Fortesque Vernon of Boston,—"has holes in both Ears, with several Turns of Brass Wire through them . . . wore a felt Hat, and a Handkerchief about his Head, a blue double-breasted Jacket, and a strip'd homespun ditto, a cotton and Linnen Shirt, brown Serge Breeches, a Pair of polished Steel Knee Buckles, and red Garters to be seen below his Breeches, speckled Yarn Stockings, and a Pair of work'd Shoe Buckles which looks like Silver;" carried with him "Blue cloth Breeches, broad check'd linnen Trousers, Oznabrigs ditto, a Frock, etc. Reward $2.—*Boston Gazette*, Oct. 10, 1757.

NEGRO SLAVE.—Ran away from Thomas Poynton of Salem, a negro aged 25 years, not very black, pitted with the small pox; had on "a dark colour'd Cloth Coat, lined with red Shalloon, with Mettal Buttons, a blue Sailor's Jacket, and a flowered German Serge Jacket, black Knit Breeches, a pair of grey Stockings newly stock'd, an old Beaver Hatt and an old Drap Great Coat;" well rewarded.—*Boston Gazette*, Feb. 11, 1760.

NEGRO SLAVE.—A negro man named *Abel*, ran away from his Master Capt. *Ephraim Holmes* of Halifax, in Plymouth Co., Mass., aged 21 years. He wore "a red Broad Cloth Jacket very fine, a white Holland shirt ruffled in the Slits, a Pair of Buckskin Breeches, greyish Stockings, and an Old Beaver hat." Reward £4. —*Boston Gazette*, June 8, 1761.

NEGRO SLAVE.—A negro man named *Peter*, ran away from his Master Ephraim Swift of Falmouth, Mass., aged 28 years. He wore, "when he went away a Beaveret Hat, a green worsted Cap, a close bodied Coat mill coloured with a green narrow Frize Cape, a Great-coat, a black and white homespun Jacket, a flannel check'd Shirt, grey yarn Stockings; also a flannel Jacket and a bundle of other Cloaths, and a Violin." Reward $5.—*Boston Gazette*, July 6, 1761.

NEGRO SLAVE.—Ran away from his master, John Lloyd of Stamford, Conn., a Negro servant named *Cyrus*, aged about 30 years, "long visaged, very black, active and ingenious in all sorts of country business, and is a good butcher, bred in the country, and speak good English" . . . "Had on when he went off, an iron collar riveted round his neck, and an chain fastened to it; carried with him a red cloth jacket, and another of brown frize, both considerably worn, black everlasting breeches almost new, tow trowsers, white stockings cotton or linnen, coarse tow shirt." . . . Reward £5.—*Boston Gazette*, Oct. 19, 1761.

NEGRO SLAVE.—Ran away, two mulattoes, from Fairfield,

Conn., *Titus*, aged 22 years, his hair cut off, wore blue flannel coat with flat pewter buttons, brown camblet vest with horn buttons, leather breeches and blue great coat with yellow metal buttons; *Daniel*, aged 16 years, "long black hair cut off on the top of his head," brown camblet coat with red lining, a white linnen vest, carried a gun and a forged pass.—*Boston Gazette*, Aug. 8, 1763.

NEGRO SLAVE.—A negro named Sambo, 30 y. old ran away from his master, Peter Bourn of Boston, and wore when he disappeard, "a check Woolen Shirt under a Frock, a pair of light reddish Breeches under a pair of Trowsers, and a blue mill'd Cap." $2 reward.—*Boston Gazette*, July 22, 1765.

NEGRO SLAVE.—Five Dollars Reward. Ran-away from his Master the 25th Day of November last, at North-Kingston, in the Colony of Rhode-Island, a well-set Negro Man Slave, named Isaac, about 5 Feet 6 or 7 Inches high, with a Scar on his Forehead, between 30 and 40 Years old, thick Beard, can play on a Fiddle, and loves strong Drink: had on and carried away with him a lightish-colour'd Thick set Coat, a blue Ratteen Jacket with Cuffs to the Sleeves, a blue Broad Cloth Jacket without Sleeves, Flannel Shirt, stript Flannel Trowsers, grey yarn Stockings, and single Channel Pumps. Whoever will secure said Slave in any of his Majesty's Goals, or deliver him to the Subscriber, his Master, shall have FIVE DOLLARS Reward, and necessary Charges paid. Per, Samuel Rose.

Masters of Vessels, and others, are hereby forbid carrying off or securing said Slave, as they would avoid the Penalty of the Law.—*Boston Gazette*, Dec. 5, 1768.

# ARCHITECTURE

## Houses and Buildings

TURRET ON THE ANCHOR TAVERN, BOSTON.—On Thursday the 24th, the Weekly Lecture being turned into a fast at the South-Meeting house, at the close of the the Forenoon's Sermon, broke out a fire in the Anchor Tavern (Near the Old-Meeting house) on the top of the Roof: occasioned by some unlucky Boys, who carried some Coals up to the Turret, to fire off a Pistol; which was by GOD'S good and signal Providence put out again, otherwise had proved of fatal consequence.—*Boston News-Letter*, Apr. 21/28, 1704.

LEAD ROOF ON HARVARD COLLEGE.—Cambridge, Octob. 29. About 1 of the Clock in the Morning there happened a fire in *Harvard College* occasioned by a foul Chimney which took fire, and the soot being blown into the Belfrey, fired some old Boards, and melted the Lead (wherewith the College was covered), and then fired the Planks; but one of the Tutors having the Key of the Scuttle which was lockt and barr'd was absent, wherefore 2 of the Students putting their backs to the Scuttle, forced it open, and threw water briskly, so that they quickly extinguished the Fire, which otherwise had been of very ill consequence.—*Boston News-Letter*, Oct. 30/Nov. 6, 1704.

WATCH HOUSE.—Rev. Andrew Gardner, minister at Lancaster, Mass. was accidentally shot and killed when coming out of "the little Watch house that was over one of the Flankers" of the garrison house, he probably coming out to warm himself. He was shot by an excited sentinel as he was "coming down out of the watch-house through a little Trap door into the Flanker."—*Boston News-Letter*, Nov. 13/20, 1704.

HOUSE CONSTRUCTION.—Lightning struck the house of Thomas Brooks at Newport, R. I. on Mar. 12, 1704-5, about noon, and "almost broke down the South-end of his House . . . broke several Windows to pieces and the Glass, broke the plank clear through

THE PARSON CAPEN HOUSE, TOPSFIELD, MASS.
Built in 1683. Note the overhang, drops and brackets, the leaded glass casements and the pilastered chimney top.

in several places of the sides, and tore the Clapboards off the sides three or four foot wide, broke down most of the tonnel of his Chimney . . . it started the shelter of the Cellar door three inches out of its Place." etc.—*News-Letter*, Mar. 19/26, 1705.

MEETING HOUSE CONSTRUCTION.—Lightning struck the Meeting House at Taunton and "split the wooden button on the top of the Vane Spindle . . . destroyed the biggest part of the Covering of the Terret boards." The roof of the meeting house was "almost flat" but shingled. Outside clapboarded; there was lath and plastering on the inside; "drove two of the Windows a little outward." "Several paynes of Glass are considerably shattered." The wheel of the bell somewhat shattered.—*Boston News-Letter*, Aug. 5/12, 1706.

PINACLE ON THE GABLE.—On Thursday last the lightning struck "upon the Pinnacle on the Gable end of Mr. Creese Apothecary his House, which run down the said Gable-end, rasping and shivering the Timbers and Clapboards as it went."—*Boston News-Letter*, July 14/21, 1707.

MANTEL-TREE.—Lightning struck the house of Robert Hazard in "the Narragansett Country," Rhode Island. Killed a negro man "that sat in the Chimney Corner," . . . "behind the Negroes head there was a hole made in the wall, the lime that came out of it struck on the Garret of the house and Mantle-tree, & the opposite Jamm of the Chimney like drops of Shot."—*Boston News-Letter*, Oct. 20/27, 1707.

MEETING HOUSE at Middletown, Conn., had upper and lower windows. A hurricane blew off its roof on Sunday, May 23, 1708. "The violence of the Wind drove the Rain through our tight and close Buildings to a very great degree."—*Boston News-Letter*, May 24/31, 1708.

LOW ROOM.—A Convenient Dwelling House, having a Cellar, Low Room, Chamber and Garret, in Pudding-Lane, Boston, to be Lett; Inquire at the Post Office in Cornhill, Boston, & Know farther.—*Boston News-Letter*, Oct. 4/11, 1708.

DOUBLE HOUSE.—The Lynn-Spring Farm between Salem and Lynn to be Sold on Reasonable Terms; It contains 20 Acres inclosed with a Stone Fence; Several other parcels of Land that are not fenc'd, good Pastorage, Maedow and Commonage: Having thereon a good double House, 4 Rooms on a Floor fit for an Ordinary, with a Barn and other Accommodations: Inquire of John Campbell Postmaster of Boston and know further.—*Boston News-Letter*, Mar. 17/24, 1707.

STONE HOUSE.—The Indians attacked a scouting party near Cape Neddick, Me., and the stragglers took refuge in "a Stone House where they bravely defended themselves till they were reliev'd from the Town."—*Boston News-Letter*, May 12/19, 1712.

GROUND CHIMNEYS.—A double house "with three Ground Chimneys, two Chamber Chimneys," advertised for sale by Capt. Nathaniel Hall of Hingham.—*Boston News-Letter*, Jan. 12/19, 1712/13.

SHINGLES.—On Wednesday last, while the General Court was sitting here, a Bonefire was made in King-Street, below the Town-House, of a parcel of Shingles (upward of Eight Thousand out of Ten thousand) found defective by the Surveyors both as to length and breadth prescribed by Law, which Shingles were rather Chips than Shingles, and to prevent the like for the future, both makers and sellers of shingles had best conform to the Law and prevent any more such Bonefires.—*Boston News-Letter*, Mar. 23/30, 1713.

SHINGLES.—By enactment of the General Assembly of the Island of Barbadoes, all shingles imported from New England must be not less than 18½ in. long, 5 in. wide and half an inch thick.—*Boston News-Letter*, Oct. 19/26, 1713.

BUILDING MATERIALS.—To be Sold by Capt. *Cyprian Southack* at his Hill, Sand for Plastering, Sand for Brick work, Mould and Gravel. Sand at One Shilling a Cart Load, Mould Two Shillings a Cart Load, and Gravel at Three Pence a Cart Load; their being Two very good Cart ways to fetch it, one over against the Bowling-Green [in Cambridge Street], and the other by Mr. William Young the Glasier's House.—*Boston News-Letter*, Mar. 12/19, 1715/16.

MARBLE HEARTHS, Marble Mortars, and Holland Wares, to be sold very reasonably by Capt. Arthur Savage at his House in

Brattle-Street, Boston.—*Boston News-Letter*, Nov. 26/Dec. 3, 1716.

SLATE.—A Parcell of Slate, ready Hol'd and Cut, fit to be Laid on Houses, to be Sold by Mr. Jarvis Ballard, either by Wholesale or parcels.—*Boston News-Letter*, Oct. 13/20, 1718.

HOUSE LAID IN OIL.—To be sold a large Dwelling House and Land, well finished and laid in Oil, with a Good Cellar, under both Ends, having a Chimney in one Part, a good Pump at the Door and a Garden, standing in Charter Street, Boston. . . . — *Boston News-Letter*, Apr. 23/30, 1722.

JIMMERS OF A HOUSE.—Lightning struck the house of Mr. Lyman in Boston, and "tore off the Slate & burst out of the cornish: and as it then run down the perpendicular sides of the House, it both broke the Windows & split their Frames, and began to melt both the upper & lower Ends of the Jimmers and the Heads of the Nails."—*Boston News-Letter*, June 23/24, 1726.

MEETING HOUSE AT READING.—A stroke of lightning "broke off the Vane and Spindle, broke the Turret in pieces, shivered off the clapboards on the West and South sides from the top to the bottom; shattered one of the Doors," etc.—*Boston News-Letter*, June 29/July 6, 1727.

MANTLE SHELF.—The house of Nathaniel Mason, jr, of Long Meadow, was struck by lightning "and the Cornish that was under the Mantle-tree-Shelve was beat off."—*New England Journal*, Sept. 11, 1727.

HOUSE FRAME.—Stoughton, Mar. 14, 1728, On Monday last, the Rev. Mr. Dunbar, our beloved Pastor had Ninety Men at Work for him, who cut & hew'd all the Timber needful for the Building his House; which we hope will be a motive to other Towns.—*New England Journal*, Mar. 18, 1727/8.

OLD SOUTH MEETING HOUSE BOSTON.—On Friday the 28th of Feb. last was kept as a Day of Fasting & Prayer by the South Church & Congregation in this Town, upon occasion of taking down their Old Meeting-House, & Building a New One of Brick, which is to stand in the same Place. The last Lord's Day the Second of this Instant, was the last time of Meeting in their Old

House, which has stood for Three-score Years the last January, since twas raised. On the Monday, the Workmen took down the Windows, the Pews, the Pulpit, and the Seats both below and in the Galleries. On the Tuesday in the Forenoon, they took down the Belfrey, the Porches, the Stairs and the Galleries themselves. In the Afternoon they drew off the Boards at both Ends and laid it open : and about Five a Clock, They turned over the whole remaining Part of the Building at one Draught into the Yard on the North side; in doing which, it fell all to pieces. Yesterday they employed in removing the Fragments. And when we came to examin the main Timbers, it was surprizing to see that the Bottoms of the Great Rafters which upheld the Roof, together with the hinder Beams which bore up the Galleries were quite decay'd with Rotteness: and the Ends of all the Summers, for Six or Eight foot were in a great measure turn'd to Powder; that nothing but the Kings posts and the other Frame above has for a long time kept them from tumbling down upon the People. And it seems to be a wonderful Providence, that the last Lords day especially, when it was so much crowded, that the whole Congregation was not buried in a heap of Ruins. For my own part I had always in my mind some difficulties about the Taking Down : But accounted it my Duty to yield to the superior Judgment of the Church: But now, I am intirely satisfied, as is every one who comes and sees, that there has been the merciful hand of a watchful Providence in this Affair, which requires our humble adorations and acknowledgments. The tumultuous Noise indeed, in Taking down with the increasing Desolation, grew more and more affecting : But it was a very grateful thing to hear no Prophane, or unbecoming word, and to see no Hurt received, throwout the whole Proceeding.—The Praise of all to GOD.

The Old Church having given them the Liberty of Assembling in theirs, in the Intervals of their Publick Worship, the South Church & Congregation are to begin to meet There the next Lord's Day at 11 a'Clock in the Forenoon, and at 4 in the Afternoon.—*Boston News-Letter*, Feb. 27/Mar. 6, 1729.

NEW HOUSE FOR SALE.—To be Lett or Sold, A new handsome

The Parlor of the Parson Capen House, Topsfield, Mass.
Built in 1683. The furniture is of the period

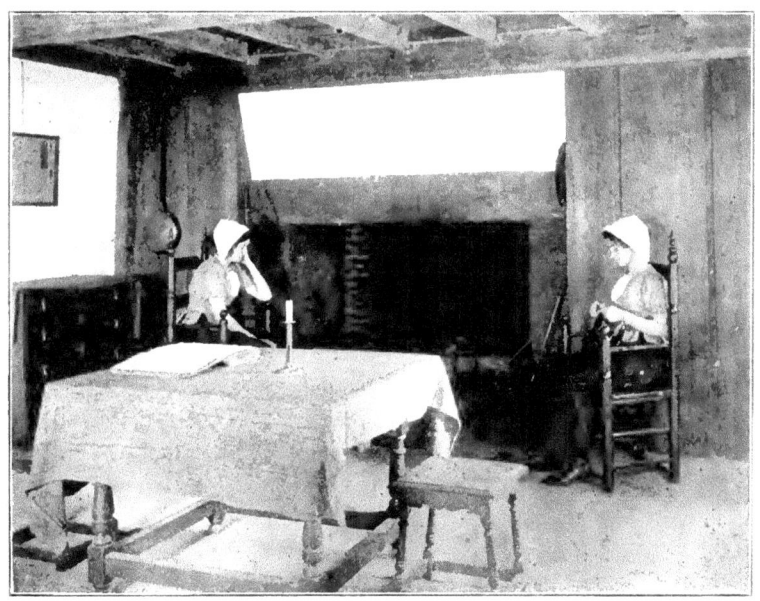

The Parlor of the John Ward House, Salem, Mass.
Built in 1684. The furniture and costume are of the period

well Built House, three rooms upon a Floor, Sash Windows and Window-Shuts, in all the Rooms, all nicely Painted, good Closets, two in most of the Rooms, a good large Dry Cellar, the Pump very near the Kitchen Door, a good Garden ready fit for House Keeping, having most sorts of Kitchen Seeds come up; Any Person that has a mind to Buy, may take any reasonable Time to pay the greatest part of the Money in. Inquire of John Staniford.—*Boston News-Letter*, May 13/20, 1731.

SHOP SIGNS.—Mrs. Hannah Boydell, wife of Mr. Boydell (Register of Probates for the County of Suffolk) Sells Bohea and Green Tea, Coffee, Chocolate, Loaf and Muscovado Sugars of all Sorts. . . . In a Shop adjoining to the Naval Office, & over against the Bunch of Grapes Tavern in King Street, Boston, ☞ N. B. Instedd of a Sign to the Shop, there's Placed before the Window, Canisters, Jarrs and Sugar Loaves.—*Boston News-Letter*, July 15/22, 1731.

DAMAGE BY LIGHTNING.—Last Lord's-Day the 2d Instant, a Thunder-Clap struck the House of Daniel Davis in Rutland and spent its force on a new Frame adjoining to the Dwelling-House. It ran along the ridge Pole . . . shivered the principal and corner post, . . . tore off the Cock-tenon of the Post. . . . moved the Mantle-tree a little, and split a Hearth-stone . . . melted a Carpenter's Square at two corners. . . . —*Boston News-Letter*, July 6/13, 1732.

BRICK OVEN FIRE.—A house of one Grant, near the ferry at Marblehead, was destroyed by fire, it was thought "the Fire took a Post of the House, thro' the defect of the Oven." The family before night had heated the oven and "fill'd the same with apples and a Pye" and went to visit a neighbor a quarter of a mile away leaving the house empty. The next morning after the fire "they drew out their Batch, and found it not too much Baked."—*Boston News-Letter*, Sept. 14/21, 1732.

EARLY SHELTERS IN CHARLESTOWN.—In the obituary of Dea. Bartholomew Green, the printer of the *Boston News-Letter*, who died Dec. 28, 1732, it is stated that his father, Capt. Samuel Green, who arrived in Charlestown in 1630, "upon their first coming ashore both he and several others were for some time glad to lodge in empty casks to shelter them from the Weather, for want of Housing."—*Boston News-Letter*, Dec. 28/Jan. 4, 1732/3.

BUNCH OF GRAPES TAVERN BAKERY.—On Oct. 11th the Anniversary of the King's Coronation was observed and "in the Evening a Great Number of curious Fire-Works were plaid off" they being thrown from the balcony of the Bunch of Grapes Tavern in King Street, Boston. Some on the balcony "bearing too hard against the Banisters, the whole Front fell down" and five or six men fell into the street and received broken limbs.—*Boston News-Letter*, Oct. 5/12, 1732.

HOUSE FOR SALE.—To be sold, the front part of a very good House Situated in the middle of Bristol, being two lower Rooms, two Chambers, and a large Garret or two, with sash Windows and well Painted, a Garden and two Entering ways, being part of the House the late Capt. Bragg lived in. Enquire of Samuel Howland in said Bristol.—*Boston Gazette*, Apr. 16/23, 1733.

OUTSIDE OVEN.—A fire broke out in the house of Gerardus Comfort, a cooper on the North River side in New York City, "occasioned by a Crack in the Oven, (which being then heating to bake Bread for the Family) thro' which the Fire took hold of a Fish Cart."—*Boston News-Letter*, Dec. 27/Jan. 3, 1733/4.

FASHIONABLE HOUSE.—To be Sold, a large Fashionable Dwelling-House, Consisting of Eight Fine Rooms, Two of which with Entries are very beautifully Wainscotted and laid in Oyl, and Four handsomely Painted, etc. etc. about 1¼ mile from Charlestown ferry.—*New England Journal*, Aug. 19, 1734.

DECORATIVE CARVINGS ON BOSTON HOUSE.—*Boston, November* 14. Last Wednesday we were alarm'd at the South End of the Town with the Cry of Fire; and by reason of the exceeding high Wind that blew, many were put into a great surprise by an Accident somewhat singular and remarkable:—About one o'clock a pretty high Chimney being on fire, a spark blew therefrom, and enter'd into the open mouth of one of the carved Lions, couchant upon the Top of the Brick Wall of the House which was the late Col. *Dyer's*, about a 100 feet distant from the said Chimney, on the other side of the Street; by the Force of the Wind the Fire soon enkindled, and the mouth of the wooden Beast discharging Smoke and Fire, it was presently discovered; and his Head being struck off at one or two Blows, tumbled into the Street all on a Flame, and broke in Pieces; and so further Damage was seasonably prevented.—*Boston News-Letter*, Nov. 6/14, 1735.

SLATE ROOF.—Brick house with slate covering, advertised for sale in Boston.—*Boston Gazette*, Apr. 26/May 3, 1736.

HOUSE FOR SALE.—To be Sold, a House & Land measuring in Depth 200 Feet, 45 Feet Front and Rear, the House thereon is a well built brick House, double Boarded and Slated, four Rooms on a Floor, and a Stair Case handsomely Wainscoted, also three of the lower Rooms, two Chambers in the first story hung with Scotch Tapestry, the other Green Cheney, the upper Chambers well Plaistered and white wash'd, a good Garret over the House 10 Foot high, with commodious Out Houses, a Barn, Stable, Chaise House &c. Any Person minding to purchase the same may do it, by paying 600 l. down, 600 l. more in 6 months, and the remainder on Interest with sufficient Security. Inquire of J. Boydell.—*Boston Gazette*, Nov. 8/15, 1736.

PLAN OR MODEL FOR A BUILDING.—At a town meeting held in Boston, it was voted to build a Work House and a Committee was appointed "to prepare and present a Plan or Model of the said House," at the adjourned meeting.—*Boston News-Letter*, Mar. 10/17, 1736/7.

GAMBERING ROOF.—To be Sold at publick Vendue, by Capt. Daniel Goffe, at the Exchange Tavern, on Thursday the first of December next, at three o'Clock Afternoon: Sundry parcels of land with Buildings thereon lying in Boston near Sudbury Street, viz: One Tenement two Stories upright, with a Gambering Roof, three Rooms on a Floor, a good Yard and Garden, being sixty foot on the street and sixty feet Rear, & about fifty-four feet deep. . . . —*Boston Gazette*, Nov. 21/28, 1737.

HOUSE STRUCK BY LIGHTNING.—The lightning struck the house of Mr. Jacob Hurd, in Atkinson Street, Boston, and first took off the top of the chimney at the south end of the house, split to pieces the corner balluster, then fell upon the roof and tore off abundance of shingles, and burst off the plastering into the Garret, then ran down the S.W. corner of the House, tore down the spout and rent off several clapboards, etc. etc.—*Boston News-Letter*, May 18/25, 1738.

AUCHMUTY HOUSE FOR SALE.—To be Sold upon one or two Years Credit paying lawful Interest, the House, Garden, & Out Houses of Robert Auchmuty, Esq., scituate in Essex Street at the South End of Boston: He purposing altogether to live at his House in Roxbury, and keep an Office in King Street.

N. B. The House is Wenscotted from the Garret to the Cellar, saving one Chamber, which is well hung, most of the Chimney Pieces are Marble, with Marble Hearths, and all with Glasses over them, as the Gardens are, and the Out Houses consist of back Kitchen, Coach House, Stable, Wood House, Cow House, Hen House, and three Coal Houses.—*Boston Gazette*, Nov. 27/ Dec. 4, 1738.

HOUSE FOR SALE.—To be Sold for ready Money, or on Credit with good Security. A Large new Dwelling House, very handsomely finished, with a fine Stair Case of 9 feet in the Middle, 3 Rooms on a Floor besides a large Pantree and an excellent good Cellar, painted throughout both within and on the outside, very well accommodated with good Water, handsome Yard & Pump in it, very Convenient for the Kitchen: Scituate in Braintree, opposite to the Rev. Mr. Miller's Church. Inquire of the Publisher and know further.—*Boston Gazette*, Feb. 19/26, 1739.

TRAMMEL STICK.—We hear from Liecester, That on Wednesday Evening last Week, a very sad accident happened in the Family of Capt. Daniel Denny of Liecester, viz. A large Kettle of boiling Water (or Wort) being over the Fire, and the Trammel-Stick happening to be burnt, the kettle fell down and split the Liquor upon Four Children who sat or lay upon the Hearth, (some of whom were asleep) which scalded them in so terrible a manner, that one died presently after, and another's Life is despaired of; but the other two, tho' much scalded, 'tis hop'd may recover.—*Boston News-Letter*, Nov. 25, 1742.

To be Lett, a convenient large House with Ten Fire-Rooms in it, with Stable, Coach-House, Warehouse, Gardens and Orchard, well stock'd with choice Fruit, and other Conveniences, late in the Occupation of Mr. *Edward Bromfield*, scituate in the Common, near Beacon-Hill in *Boston;* Inquire of *Alford, Vryling* and *Tyng.—Boston News-Letter*, Mar. 25, 1743.

Summer House.—Last Tuesday about Noon a Cloud arose from the S.W. . . . As it was passing over the Town, we had one very sudden and surprizing Clap with a sharp Flash of Lightning, which fell with great violence upon the Town Granary and the upper Summer-House in the Garden of Mr. John Jones, lately Peter Faneuil's, Esq. deceas'd. . . . The Summer-House was struck first in the King-Post under the Vane, and riping up the Lead of the Cupolo on the Southerly Part, descended and broke thro' the Roof, tore off the Cieling, split several Posts and Studs, Shatter'd the Window-Frames & Sashes, and broke all the Glass-Windows except about 10 or 12 squares; so that the Floor was covered with the Rubbish. . . . —*Boston News-Letter*, Aug. 4, 1743.

Lime and Sand.—To be Sold by *William Wheeler*, near Windmill-Point, Boston, About Six Thousand Bushels of good Stone-Lime, where may be had in a Month's Time, about 100 Hogsheads of the same: Also Sand, Slate, and Stone for Building: Likewise scouring Sand for Floors, all at a reasonable Price: The Larger the Quantity the less the Price.—*Boston News-Letter*, May 7, 1746.

Vassal House, Cambridge.—Friday Night last a Fire broke out at Cambridge in an Out Building belonging to Mr *Henry Vassal*, and improved by Mr. *Eyres* of this Town, Carpenter, who was finishing Mr. Vassel's House there; the Building was entirely consumed, by which 'tis said Mr. *Eyres* lost in Tools, &c. to the Value of three Hundred Pounds, old Tenor.—*Boston Gazette*, Nov. 11, 1746.

Sand for Floors and Scouring.—Whereas there are some Ill-minded Persons designing to hurt me in my Business, and personate my People who sell Sand, fine Salt, &c. pretending they belong to me, and so impose on some of my best customers, to my great Disadvantage; To prevent their mischievous Designs, I have set my Name on the sides of my three carts, with the Parts of the Town they are to supply, strictly charging my People to be very obliging to every Customer, the Sand I sell for six advantage old Tenor for what it is sold for out of the Sloops, and the Salt for one Shilling:

Gentlemen and Ladies; You shall have a constant Supply; and altho' I am engaged in the War, there is none would more chearfully embrace, or more faithfully improve an opportunity to serve your Interest, than your humble Servant, *James Fairservice*.—*Boston Gazette*, May 19, 1747.

BREW HOUSE.—The Brew House in Brattle Street, near Dr. Colman's Meeting-House, formerly in the Occupation of Calder & Torrey, being finely fitted up with a fine new Copper, and all other proper Utensils, is again opened: where Gentlemen and others may be supply'd with Beer for their Families, and Merchants for their Shipping, by Wm. Calder.—*Boston News-Letter*, Aug. 27, 1747.

LIME.—Men from the blockhouse at Fort St. George, Me. "going to work at the Lime Rocks," were ambushed by Indians.—*Boston News-Letter*, Sept. 17, 1747.

STOVE ROOMS.—A letter from a correspondent in Philadelphia informs of a period of extreem heat during which the thermometer reached 100° at 4 P. M. on Sunday. He continues—"How warm our Stove-Rooms seem in Winter! and yet the highest they ever rais'd my thermometer was to 56°."—*Boston Evening Post*, July 17, 1749.

MARBLE SLAB.—A large Philadelphia Marble Slabb for a Hearth, to be sold by Mary Johnson.—*Boston News-Letter*, June 6, 1751.

BRICK DWELLING.—To be Let, a commodious Brick Dwelling House, 3 story high, 3 Rooms on a Floor, the Rooms well wainscotted and newly painted, two of the large Chambers lately paper'd, etc. etc. scituate at the Lower end of Milk Street.—*Boston Evening Post*, July 1, 1751.

FRONTIER SETTLERS HOUSE.—Six thousand acres of Province land lying south of Charlemont, Mass., were advertised for sale to the highest bidder, to be set up at three shillings per acre, the purchaser to give bonds to settle fifteen families on said land and "to build an House 18 feet Square and 7 feet Stud, and to clear up 6 acres fit for Mowing and Tillage, and stock the same with English Grass, or Grain for each Family."—*Boston Gazette*, Feb. 27, 1753.

HOUSE FOR SALE.—To be Sold, By Andrew Hunter of Newport, a very commodious House, well finished in the inside with Paint and Lining, four Rooms on a Floor, etc. etc.—*Boston Evening Post*, May 28, 1753.

FIREPLACE IN THE CELLAR.—To be Lett, a large Brick House in Dassert's Lane (so called) in Queen Street, formerly the Estate of Capt. Robert Harris, deceased, three Rooms on a Floor, and nine Fire Rooms in the House, well finish'd, with a Cellar the same Bigness of the House, with a Fire Place in the same, and also a good Well & Pump.—*Boston Gazette*, Sept. 11, 1753.

GEORGE TILLEY'S HOUSE.—George Tilley of Boston, having failed in business, transferred to trustees, representing his creditors, his dwelling house on Pleasant street, Boston, near the Hay-Market, described as follows: "with eight Rooms in it, seven of which are fire rooms, with a Number of convenient closets and a good Cellar, four of the said Rooms is cornish'd, and the House is handsomely painted throughout, one of the Rooms is painted Green, another Blue, one Cedar and one Marble; the other four a Lead colour, the Garrets are handsomely plaistered; the House has twenty Sash-Windows to it."—*Boston Gazette*, Sept. 18, 1753.

WOODEN CHIMNEY.—A small house about seven miles from Annapolis, Maryland, which had a wooden chimney, took fire while the occupants were away and burned down.—*Boston Gazette*, Feb. 19, 1754.

HOUSES TO LET.—David Collson, Jr. advertised "To be Let opposite to the Elm-Trees, at the South End, a large commodious well-finish'd House, suitable for a Gentleman, having nine Fire Rooms, in it, with a large Pantery, a Plank Cellar of sixty Feet long, a good Paved Yard, a choice well of water, a Cistern that holds ten Hogsheads of Rain Water, a good Garden," etc., etc. Another house "just above" with six Fire Rooms, etc. "with the Out-housen."—*Boston Gazette*, July 23, 1754.

BARRACK AT CASTLE WILLIAM, BOSTON.—A Barrack of 200 feet long, 36 feet wide and 14 feet studd, to have 16 Rooms on each Floor, 4 main Entries, 4 stacks of stairs, and Cabbins sufficient to lodge 700 men; the outside to be rough boarded, with feather-edg'd Boards, and clapboarded; the inside to be lined with Boards planed and feather edged or groved; also to have 6 double and 4 single stacks of Chimneys, and the whole Building to be well under-pinned, is proposed to be built forthwith at *Castle William*, . . . proposals in writing to be submitted before March 7th to John Osborne, Esq. . . . —*Boston Gazette*, Mar. 4, 1755.

WHITE HORSE TAVERN, BOSTON.—To be sold, by Johnathan Dwight; the White-horse Tavern in Boston, the land adjoining to the street leading from the state-house to the fortification, measuring 108 feet front, and 314 feet back, in all about an acre; a garden full of all sorts of fruit; Said tavern has more room than any inn in town, and will with the three shops adjoining, rent for above l.200 old tenor a year. Also a barn 60 feet long, a woodhole, cole-house and stables 120 feet long, with as good a well and pump as any in town, being shaded with two green elm trees, and the water as cool as if in an ice-house; inquire of said Dwight, living in the said house.—*Boston Gazette*, July 7, 1755.

LEANTO.—John Wheelock of Leominster, advertised for sale a farm of 45 acres, well accommodated for a tavern, the house having two stories, with two cellars under it, "with a Backlento, comfortably finish'd with two smoaks from the Bottom."—*Boston Gazette*, Mar. 21, 1757.

KITCHEN IN CELLAR.—A Fine Large Dwelling House at Newport [R. I.], for Sale, 42 feet Square, with four spacious Rooms on a Floor, and a large Kitchen in the Cellar, and every appartment is finished in the genteelist Manner, etc. etc.—*Boston Evening Post*, Apr. 11, 1757.

PAINTED HOUSE.—Thomas Britt advertised the opening of a

THE WILLIAM CLARK MANSION, BOSTON, MASS.
Built in 1715 by a wealthy merchant and after his death occupied by
Sir Harry Frankland and Agnes Surriage

school for Children, young Men and Women, to be kept "in the white House nigh the Stone Cutters, Draw Bridge," Boston. —*Boston Gazette*, May 2, 1757.

CROSS-BAR OF THE CHIMNEY.—A dwelling-house in Bridgewater caught fire at about four in the afternoon during the absence of the family "supposed to be occasioned by the Cross-Bar of the Chimney's taking Fire and burning thro' to the wooden work."— *Boston Gazette*, May 29, 1758.

BRICKS.—To be sold very reasonable, about Forty Thousand best large siz'd well-made Bricks, with a proportionable Number of Sand Bricks, Water Tables and O G's; inquire of the Printers hereof.—*Boston Gazette*, June 18, 1759.

FREE-STONES FOR FIREPLACES.—Just imported a fine assortment of Free-Stones for Hearth-Jambs, Steps, and all other Kinds of Stone-Cutter's Work; manufactured in the best manner . . . by Henry Christian Geyer, near the South Fish Market.— *Boston News-Letter*, Oct. 2, 1760.

SLATE AND STONE WORK.—Wanted a Person that understands cutting slate to cover Houses; . . . who will agree for one month, or as many Days as he will work this Fall, and pay him Forty Shillings Old Tenor, for Four Shillings Sterling per Day, he finding himself: and if he wants to Board he may agree very reasonable at the Tenants who lives nigh the Works; . . . the subscriber will agree to provide this Fall upon proper Encouragement; also Stones for building or any sort of stone proper for filling up Drains, or filling Bridges, they may have them brought to any Place not exceeding six miles from the Work at Cambridge, by agreeing with me at my House near the King's Chappel, between the Hours of Eleven and Twelve in the Forenoon. J. JONES. —*Boston Gazette*, Nov. 3, 1760.

HOUSE FOR SALE.—To be Sold; a House within a Hundred Rods of the Meeting House in the First Parish in Woburn. It has three large Rooms on a Floor, two Stories high, all finished and painted within and without, etc. etc. Inquire of Mr James Fowle, Innholder in Woburn.—*Boston News-Letter*, Feb. 12, 1761.

HOUSE OF EDMUND QUINCEY.—For Sale, the Farm, Mansion-House and Farm Houses, formerly belonging to Edmund Quincey, Esq., situate in Brantree, about a mile from Rev. Dr. Millers' Church. The Mansion House has 4 Rooms on the lower Floor, besides a Dairy Room, 11 good Chambers on the two upper Floors, 7 convenient Fire Places besides the Kitchen, several of which are handsomely tiled. Three of the lower Rooms and three of the Chambers, with a large Entry and Stair Case are well painted, and two of the Rooms hung with painted Canvas. A deep Cellar runs under the whole House, the walls of which are laid in Lime Mortar, with three good Arches, one large enough for a Winter Dairy Room. . . . —*Boston Gazette*, Mar. 2, 1761.

STONE LIME.—Best of Eastward Stone lime, in Hogsheads, sold by Saunderson West, Part of it being at the South End is very convenient for the Country.—*Boston News-Letter*, July 30, 1761.

IRON WEIGHTS for windows, advertised.—*Boston Gazette*, Sept. 21, 1761.

FANEUIL HALL CELLAR.—Any Person or Persons inclined to undertake the digging and making a Cellar at their own Charge, under *Faneuil Hall*, for doing which they are to be allowed a Lease of the same for such a Term of Years, as shall be equivalent to the Expense they are at, are desired to send in their Proposals as soon as may be to the Selectmen.—*Boston Gazette*, Sept. 28, 1761.

SETTLERS HOUSES IN MAINE.—The Proprietors of the Kennebeck Purchase advertised the laying out of townships west of the Kennebeck river near Fort Western (now Augusta) settlers to be granted 200 acres of land "on Condition that they each build an House not less than twenty Feet square, and seven Feet stud." . . . and dwell on their premises for seven years.—*Boston Gazette*, June 6, 1763.

THE LEFFINGWELL BRIDGE, at Norwich-Landing, Conn. over the Shetucket river, was raised June 20th, 1764, and is the most curious and compleat piece of architure, of the kind, ever erected in America. It is 124 feet in length, 28 feet from the water, and the water 30 feet deep; having nothing underneath between the butments to support it, but is entirely supported by the geometry work above, and is supposed to be strong enough to bear 50 ton weight. The work was performed by Mr John Bliss of Norwich, said to be one of the most curious mechanicks this age has produced.—*Boston News-Letter*, July 19, 1764.

Mr Kilbourn of Litchfield, Conn. was the master workman in the Frame and Mr Easton of Pittsfield, the Master joiner, in the construction of Christ Church, Great Barrington (*see account*).—*Boston News-Letter*, July 19, 1764.

Rough Cast House.—To be Sold, a New House, two Rooms on a Floor, not half a Mile East of the Meeting-House in *Marlborough*, late in the Occupation of Mr. Munning Sawen, (with a good Well and Barn, and about a Quarter Acre of Land) a south Front and in a very pleasant Situation; as the inside is not thoroughly finished, it can be made to accommode any Gentleman who may incline to retire from Business; or as it is, it will do for any Tradesman, the outside being rough-cast, and very warm: The Price will be so low as 90 l. Lawful Money. For further Particulars enquire of the Printers.—*Boston News-Letter*, Feb. 7, 1765.

English Architect.—A Person lately from England, and well acquainted with the present *London* Method of Building, which for Eloquence [*sic*] and cheapness exceeds anything as yet heard of, would carry up any Building, or find Materials on the most reasonable Terms; Plans of Estates and Houses done in the neatest manner, and surveying in all its Branches. Any Person who Pleases to favour the Advertiser with their commands, shall be duly attended to by a Line directed for A. B. to be left at Mr. *Draper's* Printing Office.

N. B. A Carpenter's Shop for about 5 or 6 Benches is wanted, with a small Piece of Ground, direct as above.—*Boston News-Letter*, Mar. 10, 1768.

Building Materials.—WANTED, For building a New Meeting-House in Brattle-Street, Boston, the materials following:

Good Stones for the Foundation and Cellar, Stones for two or three Courses above Ground, to be hammered to a good Face, each one Foot in height, and not less to go into the Wall.

Free Stone, or other kind of Stone of a light Colour, that will answer for Rustic Quoins, &c.

800 Thousand Bricks eight Inches long four wide and two thick, to be made of tough well-tempered Clay, and well burnt, one quarter Part of them to be struck in Sand for the outward Face of the Building.

Four Thousand Sand Bricks for outside Arches, nine Inches long four & half wide and two & half thick.

One Thousand Water-table Bricks made in Proportion to the Others.

One & half Thousand O G Bricks for Facias, 8, 4 & 2.

Three hundred & thirty Hogsheads of the best Stone Lime.

Five Hundred Cart Loads of Sand of a good Grit and free from all Loom.

Oak Timber for the lower Floor of the proper Scantlings.

Pine Timber for the Roof, Galleries, &c. of proper Scantlings.

A Quantity of seasoned clear Boards.

A Quantity of seasoned Merchantable Boards.

A Quantity of Plank.

A Quantity of Joist.

Slate for the Roof.

Such Persons as incline to contract to supply the Materials abovementioned (all which must be such as shall be approved by the Committee and warranted good in their kind) are desired to write and seal up their Proposals (in which they are requested to describe the Quantity and Quality of the Articles they would supply them, also the lowest Price for the Money) and deliver their Proposals at the Shop of Mr *Timothy Newell* in Dock Square, Boston, by the Eleventh Day of *March* next at farthest: After which Time, as soon as may be, there will be a Meeting of the said Committee to open and consider of the Proposals; and the Preference will be given to such as shall appear best calculated to answer the Purpose and Interest of the Society. It is intended that the Building should be undertaken as soon as Materials can be had."—*Boston News-Letter*, Feb. 20, 1772.

BRICK HOUSE.—The large brick house, fifty feet in length, of the late Isaac Gridley of Boston, was to be Sold at public auction on Sept. 5, 1771. The house contained thirteen rooms, three lower rooms being "genteely finished with Tapestry Hangings," etc. situated near Fort-Hill.—*Boston News-Letter*, Aug. 1, 1771.

### BOOKS ON ARCHITECTURE

SALMON'S "Builder's Guide," advertised.—*Boston Gazette*, May 28, 1754.

*Scammozz's Architecture*, with other books just imported from London, was advertised for sale by Philip Freeman, in Union Street near the Corn-Fields, Boston.—*Boston Gazette*, Dec. 3, 1754.

The following new books were advertised for sale by the Printer, in the *Boston News-Letter* of Mar. 13, 1760, viz:—

Ware's "Paladio, or 4 Orders of Architecture," fol.

Ware's "Complete Body of Architecture," adorn'd with Plans, Elevations, &c. with some Designs of Inigo Jones, never before published, fol.

Halfpenny's "Architecture," not bound, fol.

Langley's "City and Country Builder's and Workman's Treasury of Designs," 4to.

Twelve Designs for Country Houses.

The Printer of the *Boston News-Letter* advertised for sale among importations in the last vessel from London, many books, including:—

"London Art of Building," 4to.

Prices "British Carpenter," 4to.

"Builder's Vade Mecum," 8vo.

Hudson's "Art of Drawing in Water-Colours and in Miniature."

Metzotinto Prints of the King of Prussia.

Prints and Drawings.

Trunks.

Paper Hangings. —*Boston News-Letter*, July 16, 1761.

At Mr Holbrook's House in the Common, Boston, were offered for Sale a large importation of books, among which were:—Halfpenny's Architecture, fol:, ditto Perspective Made Easy; Hoppus's Architecture, fol.; Langley's Builder's and Workman's Treasury of Designs, 4to.; ditto, Golden Rule; ditto, Builder's Jewel; ditto, Builder's Assistant, or Library of Arts & Sciences for Builders, &c. 2 vol. 8vo, with 100 Copper Plates; London and Country Builder's Vade Mecum; Morris's Architecture, 4to.; Practical Measurer, or plain Guide to Gentlemen and Builders.—*Boston News-Letter*, Feb. 18, 1762.

Lately Imported, and to be sold the following Books, &c. Among which are a variety upon Architecture.—Enquire of the Printers. . . . Art of Drawing in Water Colours, Cuts;—ditto in Miniature, Cuts; Le Cleve's Architecture, 2 vols in 1; De Piles on Painting; Halfpenny's Modern Architecture; fol.; Halfpenny's Architecture in Perspective; Hoar's Builder's Companion; Handmaid to the Arts, 2 vol.; London and Country Builder's Vade Mecum; London Art of Building, 4to.; Leadbeaters Dialling; Langley's Treasury of Designs, 4to.; Langley's Builder's Jewel; Langley's Golden Rule; Langley's Builder's Assistant; Murray's Ship Building, 4to.; Morris's Architecture; Ware's compleat Body of Architecture, fol.:—*Boston Gazette*, Nov. 30, 1761.

New Books imported by Rivington & Miller, at the London Book Store, North Side of the Court House, Boston, included:—Swan's British Architect or Builders' Treasury of Stair-Cases.—*Boston Gazette*, Dec. 5, 1763.

For sale at Timothy White's Shop, a little above the *Market*; various books including— Compleat Body of Architecture, Folio, Langley's Designs, 4to, Langley's Builder's Assistant 22 vols. 8vo, Hoppus Builder's Repository, Hoar's Builder's Companion, . . . —*Boston Gazette*, Dec. 10, 1764.

Cox and Berry—Arrived from London, in the *John Galley*, Captain Blake, Beg leave to acquaint the Publick, That they have just opened at the Store of the late Messirs. *Green & Walker*, opposite the Rev. Mr. *Cooper's* Meeting-House, an Assortment of

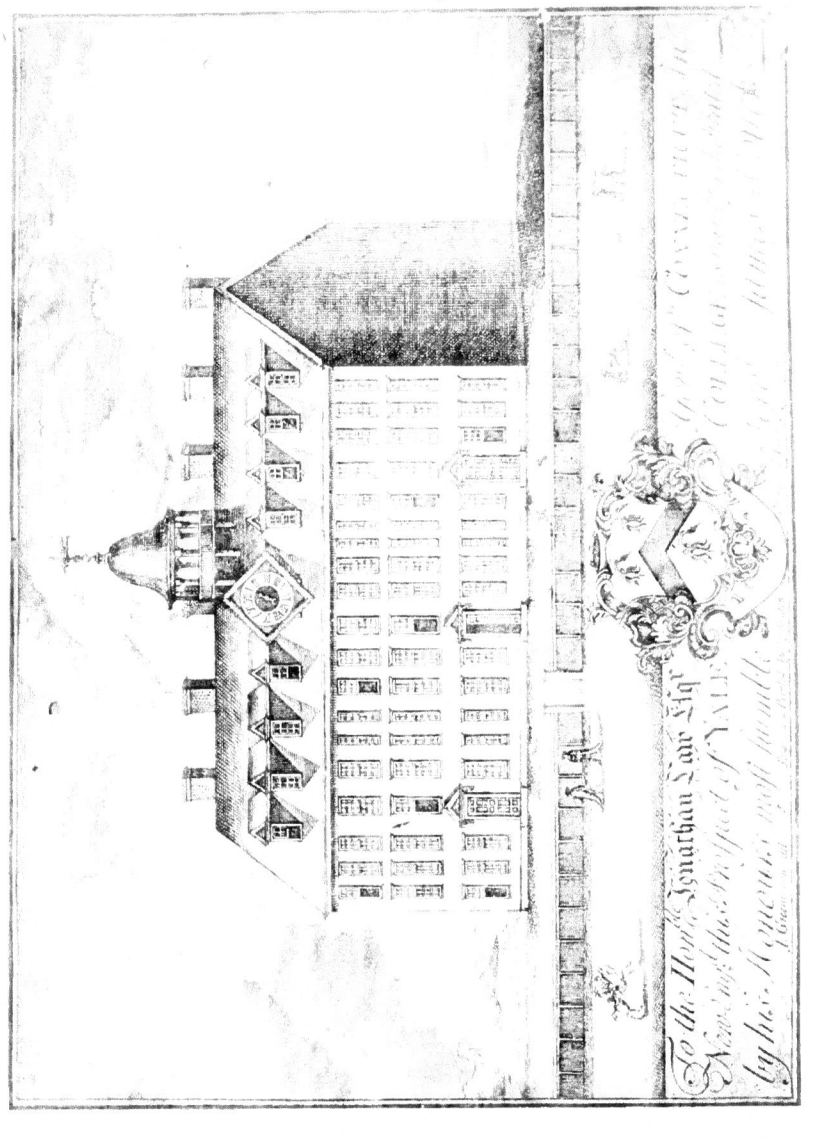

PROSPECT OF YALE COLLEGE IN 1749

From an engraving by Thomas Johnston, after a drawing by J. Greenwood

Plate, Jewellery, Gold and Silver Lace. Also modern Books of all kinds . . . including

Garrett's Designs and Estimates for Farm-Houses.

Every Man a complete Builder, or easy Rules and Proportions for Drawing and Working the several Parts of Architecture.

The Cabinet and Chair-Maker's real Friend and Companion, containing upwards of 100 new and beautiful Designs of all sorts of Chairs.

Crunden's Joiner and Cabinet-Makers Darling, containing 60 new and beautiful Designs for all sorts of Frets for Freezes, Impost, Architraves, Tabernacle Frames, Tea-stands, Stoves, Fenders, and Fan-lights over Doors.

The Manner of Securing all sorts of Buildings from fire.

The Carpenter's Companion, containing 32 new and beautiful Designs for all sorts of Chinese Railings and Gates.

Crunden's Joiner and Cabinet-makers Darling, containing 60 Gothic Railing.

The Smith's Right Hand, in all its Branches.

Barretti's new Book of Ornaments very useful for Cabinetmakers, Carvers, Painters, Engravers, Chasers, &c.—*Boston News-Letter*, Jan. 1, 1767.

The Printer's of the *Boston News-Letter* advertized for sale among other books, the following:—

*Langley's* Builder & Workman's Treasury of Designs.

*Langley's* Golden Rule.

Builder's Pocket Companion.

Builder's Vade Mecum.—*Boston News-Letter*, Jan. 8, 1767.

# HARDWARE

NAILS AND TOOLS.—To be Sold by Messieurs *Andrew* and *Jonathan Belcher*, at their Ware-house in Boston, being all of the best make from Sir *Ambrose Crowley*, Knight and Alderman of the City of London: *Viz*. Nails from 2 *d*. to 24*d*. Brads from 2 *d*. to 6 *d*. Hammers of sundry sorts & sizes, Spring & StockLocks, Chest ditto, & Padlocks of several sorts. Steel Hand-Saws, & other Joyners & Coopers Tools. Hinges of several sorts. Whipsaws of sundry sizes. Curtain Rods for Beds. Steel Spades. Frying-Pans of all sizes. Scythes of the best long sorts. Rubstones and Grindstones of all sizes. Steel in Fagots. Sweeds Iron of all sizes. Crepers and Grapnells. Anchors from 100 to 23 Hundred Weight. And many other sorts of Iron Ware.—*Boston News-Letter*, Feb. 11/18, 1711/12.

TOOLS AND IRONWARE.—To be Sold by Messieurs *Andrew* & *Jonathan Belcher* at their Ware-house in Boston: being all the best make from Sir *Ambrose Crowley* Knight and Alderman of the City of London. *viz*. Nails from 2d. to 40d. Spikes of several sizes. Brads from 2d to 6d. Iron Bolts for Ships of several lengths & sizes. Smiths Anvils, Sickles, Gridirons, Bellows, Frying pans of all sizes, Scythes, short & long. Whipsaws of several sizes. Curtain rods for Beds. Steel Spades, Iron shod Shovels, Steel handsaws, and other Joynours & Coopers Tools. Hinges of all sorts, Padlocks and Springlocks. Hammers of all sorts & sizes. Creepers & Grapnels of all sizes. Anchors 1 hundred to 23 hundred weight. Steel in Fagots very fine & good. Sweeds Iron of all sizes. And many other sorts of Iron Ware.—*Boston News-Letter*, June 8/15, 1713.

WOOD AXES made by Wallis' Pattern, scythes long and short, hatches, corn mills, curtain rods, hand screws, locks, etc. imported from London.—*Boston News-Letter*, Oct. 11/18, 1714.

WINDOW GLASS and drinking glasses, Pipes of all sorts, "Nails from a Spick to a Joyners Bradd."—*Boston News-Letter*, Apr. 25/May 2, 1715.

HOLLAND STOVE, for sale.—*Boston Gazette*, Oct. 7/14, 1723.

GRATE.—"Large Kitchen Grate to burn Coals in," at auction, with other household goods.—*Boston News-Letter*, May 6/13, 1731.

GRATE.—"A fine Chamber Grate" sold with other household items.—*Boston News-Letter*, Mar. 23/30, 1732.

KNIVES AND FORKS.—To be sold by Amos Wood at his Warehouse at the Head of Belcher's Wharf, the very best of Firkin Butter at 18 pence per pound, Cheshire Cheese at 15 pence per pound by the Quantity, White Earthen, Delph and Flint Ware, and fine Salt in Baggs; all lately imported in a vessel from Liverpool, as also Maple and Horn Case Knifes & Forks, Scythes and Guns, with sundry European Goods at reasonable Rates.—*Boston News-Letter*, May 17/24, 1733.

BRASS FOUNDER.—JAMES JACKSON, Founder, *At the Sign of the Beacon Head in Cornhill* Boston makes and sells all sorts of Founder's Wares, also Mends, Tinns, Buys or Exchanges all sorts of Cooper, Pewter, Brass, Lead or Iron by wholesale or retail Likewise a two Wheel'd Chaise well finish'd, and lin'd with Scarlett broad Cloth, with a good Harness, also a Chair lin'd with red Morocco Leather, with a good Harness, and both new, to be Sold reasonably by said *Jackson*.—*Boston Gazette*, June 23/30, 1735.

BRAZIERS' WARES.—Mary Jackson, at the Brazen-Head, in Cornhill, makes and sells all sorts of Brass and Founders Ware, as Hearths, Fenders, Shovels and Tongs, Hand-Irons, Candlesticks, Brasses for Chaises and Saddles, of the newest Fashion; all sorts of Mill Brasses; Mortars, Cocks, large and small; all sorts of polish'd Brazier's Ware, at reasonable Rates. A Quantity of large Brown Paper fit for sheathing ships, to be Sold: Likewise buys old Copper, Brass, Pewter, Lead and Iron.—*Boston Gazette*, Sept. 27/Oct. 4, 1736.

GRATE.—"A fashionable Chamber or Parlour Grate" for sale. —*Boston Gazette*, Dec. 6/13, 1736.

BRAZIERS' WARES.—William Coffin, at the Ostrich, near the

Draw-Bridge, makes and sells Mill Brasses, Chambers for Pumps, Brass Cocks of all Sizes, Knockers for Doors, Brasses for Chaises and Sadlers, Brass Doggs of all Sorts, Candlesticks, Shovels and Tongs, small Bells, and all sorts of Founders ware. Also, all sorts of Braziers and Pewterers ware, small Stills and worms, and all Sorts of Plumbers work; likewise Buys old copper, Brass, Pewter, and Lead.—*Boston News-Letter*, Feb. 17/24, 1736/7.

CUTLERY AND HARDWARE.—Just Imported from London, and to be Sold at Warehouse No. 3 in Butler's Row. A Choice Variety of all Sorts of Cutlary and hard Ware, viz. Case, Clasp, Silver handle Knives and Penknives, Sleeve and Coat mettal Buttons, and Buckles of divers sorts and of the newest Fashion, Ivory and Horn Combs, Thimbles, Razors, Spoons, Hinges and Locks, smoothing Irons, Gimlets, Compasses, Steel Instruments, Cases, Scizers, and Snuff Boxes the newest and best Fashions; with many other things for common use, all very Cheap.—*Boston Gazette*, Nov. 28/Dec. 5, 1737.

CUTLERY AND BUTTONS.—To be sold at Public Vendue at the Royal Exchange Tavern, in King Street, Boston: Sundry large and small Looking Glasses, sundry sorts of Painted Paper for Rooms, a large assortment of Sleve Buttons and Shoe Buckles, Stay Hooks, sundry sorts of Knives, Tobacco Boxes, Ivory Combs, Tea spoons, Tooth Brushes, Razors, Sissars, Shears, Tin Pots with Sand, Coat and Jacket Buttons, Horn Combs, etc. Also some Pictures and Household goods.—*New England Journal*, Aug. 29, 1738.

BRAZIERS' SHOP.—Thomas Russell, Brazier, near the Draw-Bridge in Boston, Makes, Mends, and New-Tins, all sorts of Braziery ware, viz. Kettles, Skillets, Frying-Pans, Kettle-Pots, Sauce Pans, Tea Kettles, Warming Pans, Wash Basins, Skimmers, Ladles, Copper Pots, Copper Funnels, Brass Scales, Gun Ladles, &c. makes all sorts of Lead Work for Ships, Tobacco Cannisters, Ink Stands, &c. and buys old Brass, Copper, Pewter, Lead and Iron.—*Boston News-Letter*, Oct. 30/Nov. 6, 1740.

IRON STOVE, very neat Guns, & Pistols, Brass hilted Swords, Looking Glasses, &c. &c. were advertised by John Gerrish to be sold at Publick Vendue at the house of Joseph Lewis, Tobacconist, on Dock Square, Boston.—*Boston News-Letter*, Dec. 9, 1742.

DOOR LATCHES.—Brass knobed latches for doors, hand fire skreens, bed bunts and short aprons, for sale.—*Boston News-Letter*, Aug. 26, 1744.

STOVES.—New-fashioned Fire-Places or Stoves from Philadelphia, to be sold by *Thomas Wade*.— *Boston News-Letter*, Jan. 31, 1745.

JUST PUBLISHED.—An account of the new-invented Pennsylvania Fire-Places: Wherein their construction and manner of operation is particularly explained; their Advantages above every other method of warming Rooms demonstrated; And all objections that have been raised against the Use of them, answered and obviated. Sold by *C. Harrison*, over against The Brazen-Head in Cornhill. —*Boston News-Letter*, Feb. 7, 1745.

SHEFFIELD CUTLERY.—To be SOLD by GILBERT DEBLOIS. At his Shop in Queen-Street, near the Town-House, opposite to the Post-Office, *Boston*. *All Sorts of Iron-mongers, Founders and Brazery Goods; with all Sorts of* London, Sheffield *and* Birmingham, *Cutlery Ware*, viz. Brass Kettles, Skillets, Warming-Pans, Chaffing-Dishes, Copper Tea-Kettles, Coffee-Pots and Sauce-Pans, best London Pewter Dishes, Plates, Basons, Porringers, Spoons, Pint and Quart Pots, Hardmetal Pint and Quart Cans, Tea Pots, Bed Pans, London Nails of all Sizes, Tacks and Battins, Bellows, Saws, Hammers, a large Assortment of Locks and Hinges, Gimblets, Bolts, Latches, Pulleys and Pins, Dripping and Frying Pans, Assortment of Sadler's Ware, Carpenter's Chizels, Compasses and Rules, Lathing Hammers and Stone Trowels, tin'd Tax, Bullions, Handles and Squares for Coffins, London Scythes, Sickles, Rub-Stones, Glew, Wool-Cards, English Steel, Powder and Shot, Brass Handles, Scutchions and all other Materials needed by Cabinet-Makers, the best Sorts of Knives, Scissors, Lancets and Razors, Coat and Breast Buttons, Thimbles, Pins and Needles; All sorts of Fishing-Tackle for Sea or Fresh Water, walking Canes, Horn and Ivory Combs, Brushes of all sorts, Assortment of Men's and Womens Buckles, Brass, Horn and Leather

Ink-Pots, Spurrs, Gun Flints, Necklaces, Memorandum Books, Pencils; all sorts of Shoemaker's Tools, Files, Iron Wire, Scales, Snuff Boxes, Sleeve Buttons and sundry other sorts of hard Ware, sewing Silks, fine Cambricks, Cotton Handkerchiefs, an Assortment of single and double worsted flower'd Caps, with the best Bohea Tea, and Loaf Sugar, &c.

*N. B.* Said *Deblois* gives ready Money for old Brass and Pewter.—*Boston News-Letter*, Mar. 7, 1746.

SILVER HANDLED KNIVES and forks, and wormed wine glasses. —*Boston News-Letter*, Mar. 13, 1746.

KNIVES AND FORKS.—Just imported and to be sold by D. Gookin, at his Shop next to the Governor's House: Maple, horn & buck haft Table Knives and Forks, Pocket Knives, Pen-Knives, Scissars, Sheers, Pins, Needles, Brass and Leather Ink Potts, Wood Ink Standishes, Ink and Sand Glasses, Ivory Memorandum Books, Horn & Ivory Combs, &c., &c.—*Boston News-Letter*, Dec. 1, 1748.

BRASS JACK.—Among the effects sold at vendue at the house of Joseph Marion in Boston were:—a brass jack, a large Coffee Mill, a Chocolate Mill, a Mill to break Nuts, a snuff Mill, a mourning Sword, etc. etc.—*Boston News-Letter*, Feb. 1, 1750.

BRAZIERS' WARES.—To be sold by Publick Vendue this Afternoon, at 3 o'Clock, at the House of the late Mr. Stephen Apthrope, Brazier, deceas'd, Codlines, Match, Warming-Pans, Frying-Pans, Kettle-Potts, Brass-Kettles, Pewter Plates, Dishes, Spoons, &c. Locks of several Sorts, Jacks, Knives of several sorts, Hinges of several sorts, Snuff Boxes, Buttons, Trowells, Shod Shovels, Fire Shovel and Tongs, Lanthorn Leaves, Brass Candlesticks, Chaffin-Dishes, Horn-Combs and Wire with a great Variety of other Articles.—*Boston News-Letter*, May 31, 1750.

BRAZIERS' WARES.—Mary Jackson, at the Brazen-Head, Cornhill, Boston, advertised by Wholesale and Retail, Brass Kettles and Skillets, etc. "N. B., Said Mary makes and sells Tea-Kettles, and Coffee-Pots, Copper Drinking Pots, Brass and Copper Sauce-Pans, Stew-Pans, and Baking-Pans, Kettle-Pots and Fish-Kettles.—*Boston News-Letter*, June 21, 1750.

WINDOW PULLIES were mentioned in an advertisement of tools and hardware in *Boston News-Letter*, Aug. 2, 1750.

KITCHEN GRATE and Fender, also a good Jack, at auction.—*Boston Gazette*, Oct. 22, 1751.

BRASS AND PEWTER.—Gilbert and Lewis Deblois, at their Shop in Queen Street, Sold: All Sorts of Brass, Pewter, and Nails, with a large Assortment of London, Sheffield and Birmingham hard Ware, very neat figur'd China Plates and Dishes, Bowls, Mugs, &c., Holland Toys, etc. etc. Choice Coffee at 8 s. 6 d. by the Dozen, the best of Chocolate at 9 s. 6 d. and cheaper by the Hundred weight.—*Boston Evening Post*, Oct. 23, 1752.

CUTLERY AND STATIONERY.—Just Imported from London and Sold by THOMAS RAND, opposite to the Town Pump in Corn Hill; a large Assortment of Stationary and Cutlery Wares, viz. best Writing Paper, Press Boards, large & small, Holman's Ink Powder, best Dutch Quills, Receit and account Books, Slates large and small, Pencils, English & Latin Dictionarys, Lexicons, Most sorts of Latin books, a great Assortment of Histories, Plays, Mariners Compass and Kallenders, Epitomy, Quarter Wagoners, Seaman's Compasses, Scales and Dividers, Case Knives & Forks, Pen-Knives, Jacknives, Ivory Haft, Pocket Butcher's and Shoe Knives, long Stag Cutos, Thimbles, Jews harps, Shears & Scizars, Razors, brass Ink Pots with Penknives, Horn ditto, Shoe & Knee Buckles, sleve Buttons, new fashion Breast ditto, Snuff Boxes, Ivory & Horn Combs, Forehead ditto, Ivory Books, Temple and Common Spectacles, new fashion Canes, Iron & Ivory head ditto, Whips, Violins & Strings, Wigg Cauls & Ribons, Straps, Hones, & Pipes, raw Silk, Tea Pots & Kittles, gilt Trunks in whole or half Nests, some with brass Locks, Brushes of all Sizes, Mops, Wooll & Cotton Cards, best white Chappel Needles & Common, Hour Glasses, Children's Toys of all sorts.

Where may be had the French Convert and the Church Primer and Catechism.—*Boston Gazette*, May 7, 1754.

HOUSE HARDWARE.—Imported from *London* and *Bristol*, and to be Sold by *Mary* and *William Jackson*, at the Brazin-Head in Cornhill, by Wholesale and Retail. And as ready money is a great Inducement, they will sell cheap for Cash, Viz. . . . nails, brads, stock locks, egg nob locks, and other door locks, H & HL hinges, pew hinges, hooks and hinges, and garrets, chest hinges, door latches, . . . screws, square butts, . . . —*Boston Gazette*, Aug. 2, 1756.

In the same issue of the *Gazette*, *Gilbert Dublois* advertised for sale: copper nails and tacks, London nails, tacks and brads of all sizes, . . . all sorts of locks, hinges, bolts, latches, brass knockers, box pulleys and pins, sash lines, brass and steel chimney hooks, brass and iron wire. . . .

HOUSE HARDWARE.—Just Imported and to be Sold by Edward Blanchard, at his Shop, late in the Occupation of Mr. Byles, opposite the Conduit, Boston, cheap for Cash; . . . all sorts of Nails, Brads and Tax, Hinges of all Sorts, Sash Lines and Pulleys, Thumb Latches, Brass Knobb Latches, Locks of all Sorts. . . . —*Boston Gazette*, Feb. 14, 1757.

BRAZIER AND IRONMONGER.—The late Mr. *Edward Jackson's* stock in Trade, consisting of a great variety of Articles in the Braziery and Ironmongery Way, in larger or smaller Lots as will best accommodate Customers,—Lead, Shot, bloomery, brittle, refined and Guinea Iron, Hollow Ware, best heart and clubb German Steel, best London Steel in half Faggots, Blowers' best Wool Combs, Iron Hearths for Ships, a Copper Furnace for ditto, Cannon Shot, Iron Backs, Deck, Sheathing and Drawing Nails, Newcastle Coals, &c. &c. Inquire at the House where the Deceased's Family dwells, or at his Shop.—*Boston Gazette*, Sept. 12, 1757.

LOCKS AND TOOLS.—Imported from London and Bristol and to be sold by *Mary & William Jackson* at the Brazen Head in Cornhill:—[A great variety of articles including] double and single spring chest locks, chest handles, stock locks, egg-nob locks and other door locks, H & HL hinges, pew hinges, hooks and hinges and garnets, chest hinges, door latches, compasses, hammers, turning gouges, firmers, plain irons, gimblets and tap borers, hand-saws, plows, hollow and rounds, augers, rules, plastering and brick trowels, splinter and black pad locks, . . . desk

HANDWROUGHT IRON WORK FORMERLY ON ST. STEPHEN'S CHURCH,
EAST HADDAM, CONN.
Presented to the Morgan Memorial, Hartford, by Morgan B. Brainard

and bookcase furniture, viz. handles and scutcheons of various sorts, desk and bookcase locks, bookcase hinges, scutcheons and bolts, prospect hinges, scutcheons and locks, desk buttons, brass pins, clock-case hinges, brass and iron table ketches, London glue, screws, brass and iron desk hinges, rule joint table hinges, square butts, dovetails. . . . —*Boston Gazette*, Oct. 3, 1757.

NAILS.—Sheathing and Deck Nails at 44s. per Hundred, 3d or Lath Nails at 2s. & 2d. per thousand, Orr's best Scythes at 40s. per Dozen, hard Metal Dishes [pewter] at 1s. 8d. per lb, for sale at the Shop of the late *Edward Jackson*, near the Head of the Town Dock.—*Boston Gazette*, Nov. 14, 1757.

GRATE.—"An Iron Grate with a Brass Face," at auction.—*Boston Gazette*, Jan. 30, 1758.

COFFIN FURNITURE.—To be sold by Arthur Savage Tomorrow Evening at his Vendue Room, about 50 sett of neat Polished Coffin Furniture, consisting of Breast-plates, Angels, Flowers, Posts, etc.—*Boston Gazette*, May 29, 1758.

WINDOW WEIGHTS.—Nathaniel Loring, at his store near Faneuil Hall, advertised for sale among many other items:—Iron window weights, Stone lime, chair boxes, white and red lead.—*Boston News-Letter*, Aug. 24, 1758.

BRAZIERS' WARE.—Mary Jackson and Son, have open'd their Shop, since the late fire, a few Doors from the Court House, opposite Deacon Phillip's in Cornhill; where their customers may be supply'd with following articles, viz:—

Brass kettles, skillets, warming-pans, frying-pans, iron pots, kettles and skillets, powder, lead and shot of all sizes, London dishes, plates and basons, tankards, quart and pint cans, quart and pint pots, tea pots, of all sizes, cream pots, spoons, pewter measurers, porringers, bed and closestool pans, turrenes, copper coffee pots, brass and copper sauce pans, copper drinking-pots, andirons, shovels and tongs, fire pans, brass & iron candlesticks, iron chafin dishes, flat irons, bellows & box-irons, nails, brads, tack & hob nails, coffin bullions, tin tacks, double & single spring chest locks, stock locks, egg nob locks & and other door locks, H & HL hinges, pew hinges, hooks, & hinges and garnets, chest hinges, door latches, compasses, hammers, firmers, gimlets, hand saws, augres, rules, plaistering & brick trowels, splinter & black padlocks, brass nails, post pepper mills, brass cocks, an assortment of files, desk & bookcase furniture, viz. handles & scutcheons of various sorts, desk & book case locks, book case hinges, scutcheons & bolts, prospect hinges, scutcheons & locks, desk buttons, brass pins, clock case hinges, brass & iron table ketches, London glew, screws, brass & iron desk hinges, rule joint table hinges, square butts, dovetails, three bar'd and plain stirrup irons, white sets, black buckles, saddle heads, tarf nails, bridle bitts, rings & staples, girt web, Sadler's buttions, jobents, spurs, &c. case knives and forks, jack-knives and pen-knives, cuttoc and clasp knives & forks, and Butcher's knives, coat and sleeve buttons, swords, hangers & belts, brass and leather ink-pots, shoe and knee buckles, Scissors & shears, London needles, ivory & horn combs, razors & hones, Dutch spectacles, brass & iron thimbles, bath metal thimbles with steel tops, fountain pens, brass, iron, steel & japan'd snuffers, black glass necklaces, stay-hooks, snuff-boxes, powder flasks, pewter tea-spoons, flints, money scales and weights, jews-harps, fish lines & hooks, gun locks, guns and gun barrels, an assortment of Shoemaker's tools, knives, hammers, sowing and pegging aul-blades, and hafts, rasps & knippers, tacks, spinnel, white wax, with a great variety of other London, Birmingham & Sheffield cutlary wares.—*Boston News-Letter*, May 15, 1760.

CUTLERY AND TOOLS.—Just Imported By Edward Blanchard, and to be Sold at his Shop in Union-Street, near the Conduit, By wholesail or retail, cheap for Cash.

London pewter dishes, plates, basons and porringers, quart and pint pots, quart and pint hard metal cans, quart tankards, tea pots with and without feet, hard metal breakfast bowls, tea and table spoons, best large bed-pans, hard metal dishes and plates.—Brass kettles, skillet and warming pans, shot and flints, English and German steel.—Nails, brads and tacks, frying-pans, line and hooks of all sizes, Shoe-makers tools, brass furniture for desks, &c. Guns and gun locks, box & flat irons, Carpenters tools, files and rasps of all sorts, brass and iron candlesticks, augers, latches of all sorts, locks and hinges, brick and plaistering trowels, lathing, shingling and all other sorts of hammers.—Steel, brass and brass head dogs, steel, brass and iron head tongs, and shovels, bed screws, knitting needles, bellows of all sizes, neat chamber belows with brass noses, large and small fire-pans, iron wire, tea-kettles.—London wool, cotton and Clothiers cards, chalk lines, sail and boltrope needles, palms, twine, tin'd tacks and bullens, T P hobs, trunk nails, scupper nails, handsaws of all sorts, and cross cutsaws, gimblets, tap borers and bung borers, dowling-bitts, Coopers vises, marking irons, caulking and marking irons.—Best London glew, sash pullies and lines, chest locks and hinges, horse locks, box iron grates, iron ladles, shoe spinnel, fish skins, sickles, hour, half hour, minute and ¼ minute glasses, Sadler's ware, Curriers knives, lanthorn leaves, Blacksmiths' vises, &c.—Brass scales and weights, scale-beams, money scales and weights, and money weights, pins, sheers and scissars, very neat scissars in sheaths, case knives and forks, cutteaus and all sorts of clasp knives, horn and ivory combs, neat silver plated spurs, quart and pint japan'd mugs, hearth brushes, sieve bottoms, coat and breast buttons, shoe and knee buckles, silver plated shoe buckles, chaise whips, whole and half hunters, switches and twig whips, womens brass and bath thimbles, neat japan'd waiters, tea chests, nail nippers, white wax necklaces, brass and other ink pots, &c. &c. Felt and castor hats, Bristol short pipes by the box, boxes of glass ware well sorted.—*Boston News-Letter,* July 17, 1760.

HOUSE HARDWARE.—John Townley, takes this Method to acquaint his Customers, &c. That he is Remov'd from the *Wheat Sheaf,* Hanover Street, the corner of Wings-Lane, to the *Wheaf Sheaf* (opposite the Drum-Makers, North of the Draw-Bridge) Ann Street, where he is selling off Wholesale and Reatil . . . as he is going Home this Season. . . .

A Variety of Hard Ware, as Drawer Locks, Door and other Locks, Hinges, Screws, new fashion curious Brass spring Sash-fastenings, Racks and Springs for reading Desks, a curious sett of large 3 Wheel Casters or Bed Runners, &c. Escutchions, Bolts, Curtain Rings, Brass Curtain Hooks, large smoak Hooks, Brass

Clock Hinges, Iron Hooks and Eyes, Fire Screen Springs, &c. &c. —*Boston Gazette*, July 28, 1760.

BRASS KNOCKER.—A Guinea Reward for any one who shall give information to the Printer, of the Person or Persons that stole a Brass Knocker from off the Door of a House at the Westerly Part of Boston, last Tuesday Night.—*Boston News-Letter*, Oct. 30, 1760.

HINGES AND TOOLS.—Just imported in the ship *Jupiter*, from London, by Capt. Samuel Bull:—

Nails, locks, hinges, and all sorts of carpenter's tools: glass lanthorns and tin ware; prepared colours of all sorts, boiled linseed oil and paint brushes; sconce looking glasses of different sizes; mohogany tables and chairs; setts of pictures glazed and framed; images in plaster-appalas, water-colours and pincles; gold lace and plain hatts; soldiers' shoes; ships colours and bunting, etc. etc.—*Boston News-Letter*, Dec. 25, 1760.

TIN AND LATTIN WARES.—*Hardware*. Imported in the last ships from London and Bristol and to be Sold by Timothy Newell, at his Shop on Dock Square, Nails by the Cask of all sizes, London Hard Metal and common Pewter of all Sorts, Brass Kettles and new-fashion Tea-Pots, Maple, Horn, Buck, and Ivory handle Case Knives and Forks, Tinn'd Knife Baskets, Spring and Cutteau Knives, Brass & Leather Ink Pots, Iron Chafing-Dishes, . . . Long & Short Pipes, Tin Plates, Lanthorn Leaves, Lattin Brass, Wier of all Sorts, &c. &c.—*Boston Gazette*, June 22, 1761.

TIN PLATES AND WIRE.—Joshua Blanchard, at his shop in Dock Square, advertised as recently imported from London a great variety of fabrics, etc. also; tinplates and wire, white and red lead, crimson, blue and white bunting, 4 d. 10 d. 20 d. nails, 6 x 8, 7 x 9, 10 by 8 glass, paper sheathing, cartridge & press papers, papers for rooms, neat chimney pieces, stone statues, India screens. —*Boston News-Letter (postscript)*, Nov. 11, 1762.

CUTLERY AND STATIONERY.—Just Imported and to be Sold by *Rivington & Miller*, Head of King-street, North Side of the Court House, Boston.

A very great Variety of the finest Pinchbeck Shoe and Knee Buckles, single and double gilt:—a fine Assortment of Silver Buckles, the newest and most fashionable Patterns; fine paste and stone Shoe & Knee buckles; elegant garnet and paste Broaches; Gold seals; fine Gold Lockets for Lover's Hair; Scotch Peble Buttons; Goggles worn in Riding to prevent the Eyes being hurt by the Dust; fine Walking Sticks, with Gilt Heads; neat Switches with Ivory Tops; fine Turkey Leather Pocket Books; with Silver Clasps; steel spring Spurs; fine steel Nail Nippers; silver Pencil cases; steel and double gilt Watch Keyes; silk and buff Sword Belts, with Buckles & Locks; Battledores and Shittlecocks; Baggamon Tables compleat, Chessmen; a great choice of Barlow's Pocket and Penknives, with one, two or four Blades, also with Saws, Pickers, Mohawks, &c. Very fine Toothpick Cases; Mahogony and Leather Shaving Equipages; the finest London made Ivory Handle Chinese Fashion Table Knives, with swelled Bosom Forks.—Also, a fine Assortment of Stationary, Consisting of Writing Paper, gilded and plain, best Writing Parchment, Dutch Quils, best London made Pens, Sealing Wax, Wafers, Ink-powder, and blank Books for Accounts.—*Boston Gazette*, Dec. 5, 1763.

KITCHENWARE.—Imported from Bristol and London by William Jackson and sold at his Shop at the Brazen-Head, next the Town House, a great variety of articles including:—Chaffing-dishes, box and flat-irons, roasting jacks, card wier, brass handles, escutcheons, locks, etc. knives & forks, best fine pinchbeck, bath-mettal, white-mettal, block-tin, steel and mourning, and stone-set knee buckles, plated shoe buckles and spurs, gun hammers, key rings, tooth drawers, wooden punch ladles; metal, steel, silver and china seals; china, enamell'd, painted and paper snuff-boxes; patch ditto, with glass tops; china, ebony, a paper picktooth cases; temple and other spectacles; etc. etc.—*Boston News-Letter*, Sept. 27, 1764.

CUTLERY, BUCKLES, etc.—Rivington and Miller Inform their Customers and others that they have removed to the Store where Mr *Savage* lately kept his Insurance-Office, about the Middle of King-Street, North-Side, two Doors above the British Coffee-

House, and opposite to Colonol *Ingersol's* Tavern; . . . A fine Assortment of Penknives, 2, 3 & 4 Blades, made by the best hands in England; Chinese Ivory handled Knives and Forks; a great Variety of Walking-Sticks; Battledore and Shittlecocks; Paste buckles, finest Pinchbeck Buckles, double gilt; Steel Knee Buckles for broad Straps; Muco Buttons; a variety of Breast Buckles; Gold Lockets; Nail Nippers; Rasors with Tortoise-shell Handles; neat steel Watch Chains and Keys; Ivory Memorandum Books; Prospect Glasses; neat Leather Bottle Stands; a Variety of fine German Flutes, Tutors for ditto; Soap Boxes for Shaving; finest Strasburg Snuff; Essence of the Balm Gilead, a sure Cure for Coughs and Consumptions; Turlington's Balsam of Life, &c. &c. —*Boston Gazette*, Jan. 21, 1765.

# PAINT

PAINTER'S COLORS, most sorts of, with lancets, Lockyer's Pills, spices, tea, pomcitron, wet sweetmeats, raisins, snuff, etc. were to be sold by Zabdiel Boylston.—*Boston News-Letter*, Mar. 5/12, 1710/11.

"Painter's Colours" were advertised in the *Boston News-Letter*, Mar. 17/24, 1711/12.

All Sorts of Paints and Oyl to be Sold, by Wholesale and Retayle by Nehemiah Partridge *Japanner* upon the Mill Bridge, Boston, likewise all Sorts of *Japanning*, Painting, and all Sorts of Dials to be made and done by the said Partridge at reasonable Rates.—*Boston News-Letter*, Sept. 21/28, 1713.

Painter's colors and tea, condemned at the Court of Admiralty to be sold at public vendue.—*Boston News-Letter*, Aug. 2/9, 1714.

Painter's colors of all sorts, advertised by Robt. Gibbs, apothecary, in Cornhill.—*Boston Gazette*, Feb. 6/13, 1720/1.

Just arrived from London, all sorts of Colours for Painting, and Linseed Oyl. To be Sold by Whole-Sale or Retail at Reasonable Rates, at a Ware-house joining to Mr Salter, the Cooper's Shop, at Pooles Wharff by Olivers Bridge, Boston.—*Boston News-Letter*, July 18/25, 1723.

Just Arrived from London & Sold by John Howard in a Warehouse Joyning to Mr Callender's Sen. at the North side of the Swing-Bridge, Boston, Colourman's Wares, with all Sorts of Colours ground in Oyl, fit for Painting, by Wholesale or Retail, at Reasonable Rates.—*Boston News-Letter*, June 4/11, 1724.

John Howard who sells all Sorts of Colours & Oyl fit for Painting is removed from the Swing-Bridge to the middle of King-Street in Boston, where all Persons may be supplied as usual.—*Boston Gazette*, July 12/19, 1725.

John Howard, late of Boston, "colourman," estate settled, colors ground in oil or dry continued to be sold by his widow.—*Boston Gazette*, June 21/28, 1731.

John Adams, of Marblehead, painter, his estate settled.—*Boston Gazette*, June 19/26, 1732.

Mr. Stanbridge, painter, died in Boston.—*Boston Gazette*, July 8/15, 1734.

Painters' Tools, Paint Oyles and Colours & dyewoods sold by Capt. Joseph Majory at his house in Marblehead.—*Boston Gazette*, May 24/31, 1736.

John Merritt, at the Three Sugar Loaves and Cannister in King Street, near the Town House, Boston, advertised "Painter's Colours and Gums of every Kind, for House-painting, Face-painting and Water Colours, Linseed Oil, Nut Oil, Oil of Terpentine, Varnish; all Sorts of Tools and Brushes."—*Boston News-Letter*, Sept. 16/23, 1736.

Painter's Colours, Oyles, etc. sold by John Merrett, in King St. Boston, viz: White lead, Red lead, Spanish white, Spanish brown, Spruce yellow, Fine Smalts (3 sorts), Vermilian Red, Indian Red, Ruddle, Terraumber, Leaf Gold, Leaf Brass, Carmine and other Fine Colours (16 in Number) for Oyl or Water, Shell Gold, Silver and Brass, Gold Litherage, Lamb black, Printer's black, Black Led, Chalk, Ivory and Blew black, White Vitriol, Indian ink, Powder Gold, Zint, all sorts of Hair Pencils, Gumbouch, Arabac, Sandrach, Allemy, Splatum, Seedlach, Borax, Linseed Oyl, Nut Oyl, Turpentine Oyl, Varnish, and Glasses, Cannisters and other Utinsils, Also, Sugar Candy, Power Blew, Copperas, Madder, Nut Galls, Argal, Redwood, etc.—*New England Journal*, May 9, 1738.

Samuel Hely of Boston, painter-stainer, settlement of estate.—*Boston Gazette*, Jan. 30, 1750.

Isaac Foster, in Charlestown, sold complete sets of rigging for Ships, gunpowder, Painters Colours and Oil, Earthen Ware and Glass, etc.—*Boston Evening Post*, Feb. 17, 1752.

Shrimpton Hutchinson advertised that his Shop in King Street, shut during the Prevalency of the Small Pox, is again opened and supplied with a fresh Assortment of Grocerys, Painters Colours and Dyers Wares.—*Boston Evening Post*, Oct. 30, 1752.

Hutchinson and Brinley, at the *Three Sugar-Loaves* and *Can-*

*nister* in King street, sold, white lead, red lead, Spanish brown, Spanish white, smalts, verdigreese, lynseed oil, leaf gold, leaf silver, and all other Painters Colours, oils, brushes, and tools.— *Boston Evening Post,* June 4, 1753.

Imported in the last ships from London, and to be Sold by Benjamin Church, jr., at his Shop Next Door to Mr. Drapers' Printing Office in Newbury Street.

A choice assortment of Drugs and Medecines, Chymical and Galenical.—Also, allum, Nutgalls, Argoll, Madder, Ground-Redwood, Spanish White, white and red Lead, Venetian Red, Spanish Brown, Yellow Oker, Vermillion, Umber, Sugar of Lead. . . . Also, the genuine Lockyer's and Anderson's Pills, British Oyl, Bateman's and Stoughton's Drops, Daffy's Elixir, etc. etc.—*Boston News-Letter*, Sept. 18, 1760.

Lately imported from *London* by John Gore, Painter; and sold cheap for Cash, at the Painter's Arms in Queen Street, viz. *White Paints*—White Lead, Flake White, Spanish White. *Red,*—Red Lead, Vermillion, Carmine, Drop Lake, Rose Pink, Venetian Red, Indian Red, Spanish Brown, Umber. *Yellow*—Kings Yellow, Naples Yellow, Spruce Yellow, Stone Yellow, Orpiment pale and deep, Dutch Pink, Brown Pink. *Blue*—Ultramarine, Prussian Blue of various sorts, Calcin'd Smalts, Strowing ditto, Blue Verditer, Powder Blue. *Blue*—Ultramarine, Prussian Blue of various sorts, Calcin'd Smalts, Strowing ditto, Blue Verditer, Powder Blue. *Green*—Verdigrease, Distill'd ditto, Sap Green, Green Verditer. *Black*—Franckfort Black, Ivory Black, Blue Black, Lamp Black, India Ink. *Oils*—Linseed Oil raw & boiled, Oil Turpentine, Nut Oil. *Varnishes*—Hard Varnish white and brown, Picture Varnish, Common ditto, Lacker, Large Painters Knives, small ditto, Pallett ditto, Crayons and Water Colours, &c. Leaf Gold, Leaf Silver, Dutch Mettal, White French Chalk, Bronze pale and white, Brushes, Tools and Pencils of all Sorts, white Coperas and Litharge of Gold, Colours ready prepared for House and Ship Painting, Whiting by the Hogshead, and Rozin by the Barrell or smaller Quantity.—*Boston Gazette,* Mar. 9, 1761.

Just Imported from London, and to be Sold by John Gore, at his Shop at the Sign of the Painter's Arms in Queen Street: OILS. Linseed, by the Barrel or smaller quantity, Boiled oil, Nut oil, Oil Turpentine, Turpent, Varnish. PAINTS, *White*, White Lead, Flake white, Spanish white, French Chalk. *Reds*, Red Lead, Spanish Brown, India red, Venetian red, Vermillion, Drop Lake, Carmine, Umber, Rose pink. *Yellows*, King's yellow, Princess yellow, Naples yellow, Spruce yellow, Stone yellow, English Oaker, Orpiment pale & deep, Dutch pink, Brown pink. *Blues*, Ultramarine, Ultramarine Ashes, Prussian blue of various sorts, Calcined Smalt, Strowing ditto, Verditer blue, Powder blue. *Greens*, Verdigrease, distilled ditto, Sap Green, Green Verditer. *Blacks*, Frankfort black, Ivory black, Blue black, Lamp black, India Ink. *Varnishes*, Hard Varnish, white & brown, Picture Varnish, Common Varnish, Lacker.

Brushes, Tools, and Pencils of all Sorts; half-length Cloths, Kitt Katt and three quarters ditto; large Stone Knives, Pallet ditto, white coperas and Litharge of Gold, Leaf Gold, Leaf Silver, and Dutch Metal; Colours prepared for House and Ship Painting, Whiting by the Hogshead, and Rozin by the Barrel or small quantity. The Best of London Crown Glass for Pictures; with an Assortment of Metzotinto Prints, Watercolours ready prepared in shells, &c. &c.—*Boston News-Letter*, Nov. 25, 1762.

New York City, Sept. 17. On Monday last, Mr Daniel Carter, Painter and Glazier in this City, as he was painting the house of Charles Ward Apthorp, Esq. fell down with the Ladder and is very much hurt.—*Boston Evening Post*, Sept. 24, 1764.

Thomas Crafts, recently removed from Capt. Cunningham's to his Shop at the Sign of Raphael's Head, southward of the Great-Trees, opposite the House of Hon. Samuel Welles, advertised at wholesale or retail recent importations from London, including; paints (34 different colors named); colors prepared for House and Ship painting; Glass of all dimensions, as 14 and 10, 10 by 8, 7 by 9, and 6 by 4; also an Assortment of Metzotinto Prints.—*Boston News-Letter*, Oct. 4, 1764.

Imported in the ship *Devonshire*, Capt. Hunter, and to be sold

Cheap for Cash, By WILLIAM GOOCH, Glasier, at the Sign of Admiral Vernon, in King Street.

Painter's Oyl and Colours, White and Red-Lead, Spanish Brown, Spruce and Stone Yellow, blue Smalt, and Prussian Blue, Verdigrease, Vermillian, white Vitriol, raw and boil'd Oyl, and Colours ready prepared for House and Ship Painting, &c. &c.

N. B. Where may be had *Bristol* Crown Glass, of all sizes, and Sheet Glass by the Crate; Glasier's Diamond, Ship Tausells, Bar and Sheet Lead, Rozin, Spirits of Turpentine, Varnishes, Paint and Brushes of all sizes, &c.—*Boston News-Letter*, Apr. 4, 1765.

Just Imported from London in Captain Bruce, and to be Sold by John Gore, at his Shop at the Sign of the Painter's Arms in Queen Street, Wholesale and Retail, at the very lowest Rates.

Linseed Oil by the Barrel, or smaller Quantity, Boiled Oil, Nut Oil, Turpentine Oil, Turpentine Varnish.

Paints, White, White Lead, Flake white, Spanish white, French halk.

Reds. Red Lead, Spanish brown, India red, Purple red, Venetian red, Vermillion, Drop Lake, Carmine, Umber, Rose, Pink.

Yellows. King's yellow, Princess yellow, Naples yellow, Spruce yellow, Stone yellow, English oaker, Orpiment pale & deep, Dutch pink, Brown pink.

Blues. Ultramarine, Ultramarine Ashes, Prussian blue of various sorts, Calcined smalt, Strowing ditto, Verditer blue, Powder blue.

Greens. Verdigrease, distill'd ditto, Sap Green, Green Verditer.

Blacks. Frankfort black, Ivory black, Blue black, Lamp black, India Ink.

Varnishes. Hard Varnish, white & brown, Picture Varnish, Common Varnish, Lacker.

Brushes, Tools, and Pencils of all sorts; Crayons in Sets; half-length Cloths; kitt-katt* and 3-quarters ditto, large Stone Knives, small ditto, Pallet ditto, white Copperas, Litharge of Gold, Leaf-Gold and Dutch Metal; Colours prepared for House and Ship Painting, Whiting by the Hogshead, and Rozin by the Barrel or

* 36 inches by 28 inches. — *Oxford Dictionary*.

small Quantity. The best of *London* Crown Glass for Pictures; with an Assortment of Mezzotint Prints, Water Colours ready prepared in Shells, &c. &c.—*Boston News-Letter*, Jan. 23, 1766.

John Gore, at his Shop the Sign of the PAINTER's-ARMS in Queen Street, advertised a great variety of paints and supplies; also "Coach & Carpet Painting done in the best and cheapest Manner."—*Boston News-Letter*, May 7, 1767.

Thomas Craft, jr., at his Shop near the Liberty Tree advertised Painter's Oyl and Colours, also Carpet and all Sorts of Painting. —*Boston News-Letter*, May 21, 1767.

George Killcup, jun. Informs the Gentlemen and Ladies in Town and Country, That he Paints Carpets & other Articles, and Papers Rooms in the neatest Manner: He will take English or West India Goods as Pay.

Said Killcup is ready to pay those he is indebted to, in Painting, or Papering Rooms.—*Boston News-Letter*, Mar. 17, 1768.

Just imported from London, and to be Sold by John Gore, at his Shop at the Sign of the Painter's Arms in Queen Street, Wholesale and Retail, at the very lowest Rates,

White Lead, flake white, Spanish white, French chalk, red lead, Spanish brown, India red, purple red, Venetian red, drop lake, carmine, rose pink, umber, King's yellow, Naples yellow, spruce yellow, stone yellow, English oker, orpiment pale and deep, Dutch pink, brown pink, ultramarine, Prussian blues of all sorts, calcin'd smalt, strowing ditto, verditer blue, powder blue, verdigrease, distill'd ditto, verditer green, Franckfort black, blue black, lamp and ivory black, hard varnish, white & brown lacquer for silver or brass, brushes, tools and pencils of all sorts, crayons in sets, kitt-katt and 3 qr cloths, large and small stone knives, pallet ditto, white copperas, letheredge of gold, leaf gold, silver and Dutch metal, gum arabick, fandriac, seed and shell lac:—Colours prepared for House and Ship painting, whiting by the hogshead, rozin by the barrel or smaller quantity, the best of London Crown Glass for pictures, with an assortment of metzotinto Prints, water colours ready prepared in shells, Glazier's diamonds, Chariot glasses, genteel Looking glasses, Wilton carpets, &c. Coach and carpet painting done in the best and Cheapest manner.—*Boston News-Letter*, Oct. 13, 1768.

George Kilcup, Painter, Living in Black-House Lane; Hereby informs the Public, That he stands ready to wait on any Gentlemen and Ladies, in Town or Country, who will favor him with their Custom, in any Branch of the Painting and Gilding Business, if they chuse to hire by the Day, and will instruct any young Ladies the Art of Gilding Picture Frames and other Articles.— *Boston News-Letter*, July 6, 1769.

John Gore, at his Shop the Sign of the Painter's Arms, in Queen Street, among other items advertized: Very good red, black and yellow Paints the produce & manufacture of North-America; Three very beautiful rich Wilton carpets, three yards square each; also Coach and Carpet painting done in the best and neatest Manner.—*Boston News-Letter*, Dec. 21, 1769.

Francis Green, at his Store lower End of King Street, advertised Red Lead in Casks qt. one Hundred Weight each, ground White Lead in Casks of half a hundred each, dry white Lead and Lump Whiting in small Casks—also Paper Hangings, Looking Glasses, Carpets, etc. etc.—*Boston News-Letter*, June 6, 1771.

William Fullerton, painter, died at Piscatqua, N. H.—*Boston News-Letter*, Sept. 26, 1771.

## WINDOW GLASS

WINDOW GLASS.—"Window-Glass and Lead" lately come from London were advertised in *Boston News-Letter*, Oct. 15/22, 1711.

Window Glass, Window Lead, Time Glasses, Manchester Ware, Earthen Ware, Printed Linen Huckaback, and Ready-made Cloaths, with many other articles were advertised to be sold at Publick Vendue or Outcry at the House of Stephen North, at the Sign of the Star in Hanover-Street, Boston.—*Boston News-Letter*, Feb. 25/Mar. 3, 1711/12.

"Window glass," sold at vendue.—*Boston News-Letter*, Nov. 10/17, 1712.

"24 Chests of Window Glass, three cases of Drinking Glasses, and other sorts of Glass ware" to be sold a Vendue.—*Boston News-Letter*, Feb. 9/16, 1712/13.

Any Person that hath occasion to or is disposed to buy good Sash Glass, with Lead Lines, Rolls and Pins fitting for the Same, the Glass being framed ready to put up, being to be sold at a reasonable Rate: enquire at Mr. Alexander Trotters in Union Street, Boston, where they may have further Information.—*Boston News-Letter*, Mar. 11/18, 1716/17.

In a satirical communication on the extravagant expenditures of New England wives appears a list of expeditures, one of the items being—"To new Glazing the House with new fashion'd Square Glass, . . . 057.09.08."—*New England Courant*, Mar. 19/26, 1722.

Good New Castle Glass by the Box, viz. Sixes and Fours and Tens, and Diamonds to cut Glass withal; To be Sold by Mr. Moses Peirce, near the Old North Meeting House, Boston.—*Boston News-Letter*, Aug. 22/29, 1728.

"Common Glass, 6 by 4," sold by Joseph Brandon, on the Dock.—*Boston Gazette*, Jan. 27/Feb. 3, 1728/9.

"Good Newcastle Glass, viz. 6 and 4es and 10es, by the Box or half Box, also good Diamonds to cut Glass withal, to be Sold by Moses Peirse, near the old North Meeting House."—*Boston Gazette*, June 23/30, 1729.

Good Newcastle Glass, viz. 6 and 4es and 10es by the Box or half Box, also good Diamonds to cut Glass withal to be Sold by Moses Peirse near the Old North Meeting House.—*Boston Gazette*, June 30/July 7, 1729.

To be Sold by Messieurs Clark & Kilby at their Warehouse near the Swing Bridge, Crown & Common Sheet Glass in Crates & Boxes of 6 & 4, and Diamond cut Common Glass.—*Boston Gazette*, July 19/26, 1729.

Crown and Common Sheet Glass in crates and boxes of 6 x 4 and diamond cut common glass, advertised in *Boston Gazette*, June 21/28, 1731.

To be sold by Messieurs Clark & Kilby at their warehouse near the Swing Bridge, Crown & Common Sheet Glass in Crates & Boxes of 6 x 4 and Diamond Cut Common Glass.—*Boston News-Letter*, July 1/8, 1731.

A very good Glaziers vise, lately from London; Also glaziers Diamonds, choice velvet corks, and glass of divers sorts: To be sold by Moses Pierse, near the old North Meeting House.—*Boston News-Letter*, Jan. 27/Feb. 3, 1731/2.

"Crates of Glass, Lead," etc. just arrived from New Castle.—*Boston News-Letter*, July 20/27, 1732.

The House & House—Lot of Capt. Thompson Phillips late of Plymouth, Marriner, Deceased; being a large House with Sash Glass, in Plymouth, aforesaid: To be Sold on reasonable Terms.—*Boston News-Letter*, Feb. 8/15, 1732/3.

John Alford, Esq., at his Warehouse on the Town Dock, or at his House near Beacon Hill, advertised for sale by Wholesail or Retail, several sorts of London and Bristol Glass and Lead, also Imperial Tea, Persion and Herba Taffities, Turkey Burdetts, Dunjarrs, and a parcell of newest Fashion Rich Brocaded Silk from 30 to 75 s. per yard.—*Boston News-Letter*, Dec. 13/20, 1733.

Nathaniel Cunningham [Boston merchant] advertised "New Castle Window Glass, viz. 8 by 10, 6 by 4, and Diamond.—*Boston Gazette*, Mar. 25/Apr. 1, 1734.

Jacob and John Wendell and Company [Boston] advertised among many other items—"Window Glass and Lead."—*Boston Gazette*, Mar. 25/Apr. 1, 1734.

Nathaniel Cunningham [Boston], advertised among many other items—"Diamond Glass in Cribs and Boxes, and 6 and 4 in Boxes."—*Boston Gazette*, June 14/21, 1736.

"Window Glass in Boxes 6 by 4, and Diamond & Bristol Diamond in Cribs," for sale.—*Boston Gazette*, Mar. 28/Apr. 4, 1737.

Crown glass, also Glass in Squares, 10 by 8, 9 by 7, 7 by 5.—*Boston Gazette*, Apr. 24/May 1, 1738.

To be sold by Alexander Middleton at Warehouse Number 3, in Butlers' Row, Crown Glass in Cases uncut, Ditto in Chests cut in Squares, ordinary ditto cut in squares per the Chest, Bar & Sheet Lead, white & brown Earthen ware, Glass Bottles, Quarts & Pints, bottled Ale in Hampers, . . . Pipes, glaz'd and ordinary ditto. And best Sunderland Coal on board the ship *Betty*, William Foster, Commander, lying at the North side of the Long Wharff.—*Boston Gazette*, June 4/11, 1739.

To be Sold by Nathanael Cunningham, Merchant in Boston, Best Crown Glass, Diamond, 6 and 8, 7 and 9, 8 and 10, and Sheet Ditto, Common Glass, Diamond and 6 & 4, in Boxes, Crates of very fine Crown Glass for Pictures, Lead, and all sorts of Shot, etc. etc.—*Boston Evening Post*, Sept. 28, 1741.

Taken on board a Medford boat, about the 15th of November last from Clark's Wharff, a Crib of *Bristol* Crown Glass, and a Box of drawn Lead, mark'd W. F. and not yet delivered according to Direction. . .—*Boston News-Letter*, Apr. 14, 1743.

Lightning struck a house in Weston, Mass. and "a cap of one of the Lower Windows was thrown off, and the Lead melted in several Places."—*Boston News-Letter*, Aug. 11, 1743.

Just Imported from London and Bristol and to be sold by John Rowe, etc. London and Bristol Pipes, Crown Glass of all Sizes, 10 by 8, 7 by 9, 8 by 6, 7 by 5, 6 by 4, Sheet Glass, Boxes of Glass Wares Assorted, Gill Glasses, etc. etc.—*Boston Evening Post*, Jan. 9, 1743/4.

Nathaniel Cunningham advertised Crown Glass in sheets, and Boxes of 8 and 10, 7 and 9, 6 and 8, and common Glass in Sheets, Diamond in Boxes and Cribs, and 6 and 4 Boxes, etc. etc.—*Boston Evening Post*, May 7, 1743/4.

On Aug. 16, 1744 the house of Johnathan Smith of West Haven, a parish of New Haven, Conn. was struck by lightning which "melted a pretty deal of Lead in the Windows," and killed Mrs. Smith as she was going "to fasten the windows."—
—*Boston News-Letter*, Sept. 6, 1744.

To be sold by Gershom Flagg, in Hanover Street near the Orange Tree, viz. Spanish Whiten, and choice Diamonds fit for Glazier's use, English Sole Pieces for Shoes and Boots, fine Jelly Glasses and Crewits of double Flint, all sorts of Coffin Gear, silvered, plain and lackered, and sundry other Articles.—*Boston Gazette*, Aug. 6, 1745.

Glass of the following Sizes, viz. Crown and Green Diamond 10 by 8, 6 by 8, 7 by 5, Crown Glass, etc. etc. advertised by Jones and Griffin, King Street, Boston.—*Boston Evening Post*, Feb. 3, 1746.

"A Glasier's Diamond and Vice," with appurtenances, To be Sold.—*Boston News-Letter*, Mar. 26, 1747.

Lately lost in Boston, a Glazier's Diamond. Twenty Shillings Reward paid by Nathaniel Brown, Glazier.—*Boston Evening Post*, Jan. 26, 1747.

In Dec. 1747, James Buck offered a reward of £3. for the return of his Glazier's Diamond.

Broken glass bought by Stephen Whitney of Boston.—*Boston Gazette*, Sept. 20, 1748.

"Cribs of Green Crown & Diamond Glass, Boxes of Crown Square Glass," for sale.—*Boston Gazette*, June 5, 1750.

To be Sold by James Griffin:—various articles, including Glass, 6 by 4, 6 by 8, 7 by 9, 8 by 10, and Diamond, etc.—*Boston Evening Post*, May 27, 1751.

To be sold by Jonathan Bradish in Charlestown near the Sign

of the Buck, sundry sorts of Window Glass, viz., 8 by 10, 8 by 6, 7 by 9, etc. Also Painters' Colours and Linseed oyl.—*Boston Gazette*, Nov. 12, 1751.

Thomas Savage, at his Warehouse No. 13 on the Long Wharf, sold cheap for ready money, Window Glass in sizes from 10 by 8 to 6 by 4, long and short Pipes, a variety of Glass including Apothecary's Phials, Bottles to prove Rum with, Bristol Beer in Bottles, Delph and Dutch Ware in Hogsheads and Crates, Crates of Marble and Yellow Ware (hollow and flat), Carolina sole leather, Cases of 12 and 15 Bottles, Philadelphia Flour, etc. etc. —*Boston Evening Post*, Jan. 13, 1752.

James Griffin, at his store in King Street, sold recently imported Window Glass, 10 by 8, 9 by 7, 8 by 6, 7 by 5, 6 by 4, Sheet Glass, and Diamond Glass, etc. etc.—*Boston Evening Post*, Jan. 6, 1752.

A choice assortment of Window Glass, viz., 10 by 8, 7 by 9, 8 by 6, 7 by 5, 6 by 4, Diamond Ditto, Sheet Ditto, Bar Lead, White Ditto, Spanish Brown, Ditto Whitten, Glaziers' Diamonds, by Wholesale or Retail. Also a Choice Glazier's double Vice.—*Boston Gazette*, Dec. 12, 1752.

To be sold by Arthur Savage, To-morrow Evening, at his Vendue-Room on the North side of the Town Dock. Twelve Crates of Knot Glass of various sizes, large and small Looking Glasses, . . . Leather Breeches, Desks, Tables, etc. Also, a Camera Obscura with Prints.—*Boston Gazette*, Jan. 24, 1757.

New-Castle Coal, New-Castle Crown-Glass, and Quart-Bottles in Hampers; to be sold by John Scollay, at his shop in the Head of the Town-Dock.—*Boston Gazette*, May 23, 1757.

"A large Glass Lanthorn for an Entry Way."—*Boston Gazette*, Dec. 12, 1757.

"Two setts of Glass in Frames for Hot-Beds, with Iron Bars." —*Boston Gazette*, Jan. 30, 1758.

Rev. Mr. Haven's meeting house at Portsmouth, N. H., was struck by lightning and "the Glass Windows in the Steeple all broke; two Casements next the Post that was split to Pieces [at the Westerly Corner], were stove quite into the House; most of

DIAMOND-PANE, LEADED GLASS, DOUBLE SASH
Period of 1675-1725: in Museum of the Society for
the Preservation of New England Antiquities, Boston

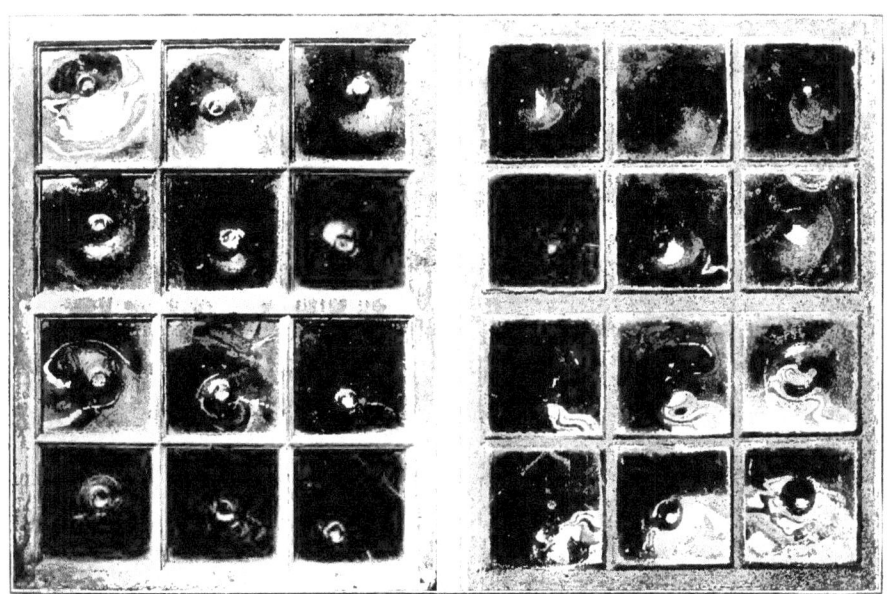

CROWN GLASS WINDOW SASH
Period of 1725-1750: in Museum of the Society for the Preservation of New England Antiquities, Boston

the Glass in the Westerly End was broke; and some on the South side."—*Boston Gazette*, May 14, 1760.

To be sold Cheap, Enquire of the Printer; A number of good Glass Casements, suitable for Hot Beds, or any other Use.—*Boston News-Letter*, May 7, 1761.

Henry Lloyd at his Warehouse, No. 5 Long Wharf, offered for sale among other items:—London Crown Window-Glass, 7 by 9 & 8 by 10.—*Boston News-Letter*, May 14, 1761.

Caleb Champney announced that he had reopened the shop of Nathaniel Brown, glazier, deceased, where he proposed to carry on "the Glazing and Plumming Business."—*Boston News-Letter*, Dec. 24, 1761.

John Hurd, at his store in King Street, advertised recent importations from Bristol, England, including:—Nails, 4 d. 10 d. 20 d. Boxes of Glass and Sheet Glass, Bristol Beer, etc.—*Boston News-Letter*, July 29, 1762.

Robert Gould, at his Store opposite the *Crown and Septre*, in Back Street, near the Mill Bridge, advertised an importation from Bristol, including Window Glass, 6 by 8, 7 by 9, and 8 by 10; Stone and Delph Ware by the Hogshead or smaller Quantities; Crates of Yellow Wares, single and double flint Glasses by the Box, short and long Pipes, &c. . . . —*Boston Gazette*, Oct. 4, 1762.

Window Glass, 6 by 8, 7 by 9, and 8 by 10, was advertised by John Savage at his Store on the Long Wharf.—*Boston News-Letter*, Nov. 11, 1762.

Thomas Hancock & Co. advertised as just imported from London and Bristol; Crown Glass, 10 by 8, 7 by 9, 6 by 8, 7 by 5 and 6 by 4; Nails, 2 d. 4 d. 6 d. 8 d. 10 d. 20 d. 24 d. 30 d. 40 d. etc. etc.—*Boston News-Letter*, May 26, 1763.

John Quill, at his store in Wing's Lane, advertised "Sheet Glass & 7 by 9."—*Boston News-Letter*, June 9, 1763.

"Window Glass, 6 by 8 at Eight Dollars; 7 by 9 at Nine Dollars; and 10 by 8 at Ten Dollars per Box," also Wine Glasses, Proof Glasses and Cases with Bottles, advertised for Sale by John Savage at his Store No. 13, on the Long-Wharff.—*Boston Gazette*, Oct. 17, 1763.

John Savage, at No. 13, Long Wharf, advertised for sale; Window glass, 6 by 8 at Eight Dollars; 7 by 9 at Nine Dollars; and 10 by 8 at Ten Dollars per Box.—*Boston News-Letter*, Oct. 27, 1763.

Imported from Bristol and to be Sold by William Gooch, at the Sign of Admiral Vernon, in King Street; The Best Crown Window-Glass of all Sizes; also Newcastle Crown Sheet-Glass; the best London white Lead—Spanish Brown—red Lead—stone and Spruce Yellow; English and Dutch Glazier's Diamonds; Whiteing, by the hogshead or hundred; the best Prussian-blue; Colours ready prepar'd for shipping or Houses; also Glazing done with Dispatch.—*Boston News-Letter*, Dec. 9, 1763.

Thomas Crafts, jr. advertised a great variety of paints and oils, etc. also "glass of all dimensions, as 14 and 10, 10 by 8, 7 by 9, and 6 by 4."—*Boston News-Letter*, Sept. 27, 1764.

Crown Window Glass, 6 by 4, 7 by 5, 8 by 6, 9 by 7, 10 by 8, 11 by 9, and 12 by 10, Crates of Flint Glass, hardware and jugs, just imported from England, were advertised by Richard Baker, in King-Street, Boston.—*Boston Gazette*, Aug. 13, 1764.

William Gooch, advertised a variety of painter's colors and also "box Glass of all sizes: sheet and diamond Glass," etc. etc.—*Boston News-Letter*, Nov. 20, 1766.

A Number of Windows set in lead with strong Frames, suitable for Hot-Beds, &c. To be sold: Enquire of the Printer.—*Boston News-Letter*, Feb. 11, 1768 (*sup.*).

A Number of Windows set in Lead, suitable for Hot-Beds. To be Sold. Enquire at Draper's Printing Office.—*Boston News-Letter*, Feb. 23, 1769.

Josiah Waters & Son, at their Shop in Arm Street, near the Draw-Bridge, among other items advertised: Painter's oyls & colours of all kinds, prepared (or otherwise) in the best Manner, for House or Ship-Painting, 15 & 18 Inch London T D Pipes, by Box or less, large and small Bowl, Hunter ditto per ditto, Taylor's 10 by 8, 9 by 7, and 8 by 6 Window-Glass, Putty, Coarse and fine Sieve Bottoms, Sieves made up, &c.—*Boston News-Letter*, Oct. 24, 1771.

William Gooch, at the Sign of Admiral Vernon, in King Street, Boston, advertised Painter's oil and colours of every sort, ready prepared for House and Ship Painting, the best London Crown Glass as large as 24 by 19 Inches, down to 10 by 8, a Handsome Assortment of Mezetinto Prints and Engravings, the best Bristol Crown Sheet Glass, Taylor's make, and Box Glass of every size, Diamond Quarreys by the Cribb, Glazier's Diamonds, Sixty different sorts of Paper Hangings, etc. etc.—*Boston News-Letter*, Oct. 1, 1772.

# TRADES AND OCCUPATIONS

ANVIL SMITH.—Samuel Bissel, anvil smith, lately come from England, living at New-Port on Rhode Island, makes all sorts of Black-smiths and Gold-smith's anvils, Brick-irons and stakes and new Faces old ones, at reasonable Rates, and may be spoke with or wrote to, at his House or Shop near the Topsaile Street in said Town.—*Boston News-Letter*, Mar. 4/11, 1716/17.

APOTHECARY.—To be Sold by Mr. Zabdiel Boylston, at his Apothecary's Shop in Dock Square, Boston, *Viz.* All Sorts of Fruit, and Spice, Ginger, Rase and Ground; The finest white, and other Powder, and Household Sugars; All Sorts of Snuff, either Brazil, Barcelona, or Spanish, Perfum'd or Plain; Fine Green, and ordinary Tea, Sweetmeats, Rice, Chocolate; The finest Spanish Powder-blew, Starch, and Indigo, Painter's Colours, allum, Copperas; Good Eating Oyl, Choice Hungary, and the Royal Honey Water, an Excellent Perfume, good against Deafness, and to make Hair grow, as the directions sets forth, 1 *s.* 6 *d.* the bottle, and proportionably by the ounce. The Spirit of Benjamin, sweet Powder, Oyl and Pomatom for Hair, A Powder to refresh the Gums, and whiten the Teeth, pr. 6 *d.* the Paper. The True and famous Lockyer's Pills, with Books of directions: Nut-Galls, fresh Anniseed at 2 *s.* Carna at 1 *s.* 6 *d per* Pound, Choice Almonds at 3 *s.* and French Barly at 12 *d. per* Pound. The Best Elixir Salutis in Bottles, or by the Ounce, Spirit of Scurvy-grass, Golden and Plain. The Bitter Stomach Worm Drops, Potions for Children, with directions; And all sorts of Cordial Waters, Cupping-glasses, Nipple-shells, Urinals, Lancets, Plaister-boxes, Salvatory's and most other Sorts of Surgeons Instruments. Fresh druggs, and Medicines, both Galenical, and Chymical, by the last Ship (Capt. *Carnock*) from *London*. And in the same ship had come over a Journey-man Apothecary, who for any ones particular occasion can make Dr. *Salmon's* Medicines, or other Preparations in Chymistry.—*Boston News-Letter*, Mar. 17/24, 1712.

APOTHECARY.—Just imported from London, and to be sold by *John Peck*, At his Shop opposite Dr. Austin's. A choice Assortment of Druggs and Medicines, Chymical and Galenical, with all Kinds of Grocery, cheap for Cash or short Credit. Also most kinds of Surgeon's Instruments; Turlington's Balsam, Stoughton's and Daffy's Elixir, British Oyl, Bateman's Drops, Hooper's, Anderson's & Lockyer's Pills, Golden Spirits, Scurvey Grass, Lavender and Hungary Water, Hill's Balsam of Honey, Brimstone, Verdigris, Copperass, Logwood, Redwood, &c. N. B. Smelling Bottles of all Sorts.—*Boston Gazette*, Nov. 18, 1765.

APOTHECARY.—*William Coffin*, jun. next door to the Governor's, has to sell by wholesale or Retail, a general Assortment of Drugs, and Medicines, Salt-Petre in Casks of 100 wt. . . . Country Doctors and Traders may be supplied by Letter, with the usual Fidelity and Dispatch, as if present themselves.—*Boston Gazette*, Dec. 2, 1765.

APOTHECARY.—Imported in Capt. Scott from London, and to be Sold by *Oliver Smith*, at his Shop the third Door South of the Old-Brick Meeting-House in Cornhill, Boston;

A Compleat and Fresh Assortment of Drugs and Medicines, Chemical and Galenical, with most Kinds of Groceries, Painter's Colours, and Dye-stuff, viz. Finest Florence Sallad Oil in large Flasks, Cinnamon, Mace, Cloves & Nutmegs, Choice Turkey Figs, Raisins, Currants, Prunes & Almonds, Pepper, Allspice, Race & Ground Ginger, Red Lead, White Lead, Spanish Brown, Verdegrease, Vermillion, Allum, Copperas, Madder, Ground Red Wood, Argoll, Otter, &c. &c.

The following Patent Medicines Imported in Capt. Davies are directly from the Original Wholesale Warehouse kept by Dicey and Okell in Bow Church, London, are just come to Hand and Warranted Genuine, viz. Turlington's Original Balsam of Life, Bateman's Pectoral Drops, Betton's True and Genuine British Oil, Anderson's Scotch Pills, Hooper's Female Pills, Lockyer's Pills, Godfrey's General Cordial, Walker's Jesuit's Drops, Essence of

Pepper Mint, Golden Spirits of Scurvy Grass, and Swinsen's Electuary, being a certain safe Medicine for the speedy Cure of the *Stone* and *Gravel*, and is taken without any particular Regimen or Confinement and is now in Great Reputation in London.

A few cases of Surgeon's Pocket Instruments, and Instruments for extracting Teeth, made by the best Workmen in London, and warranted; Anodine Necklaces, for the easy breeding of Children's Teeth, Court Plaister, best French Hungary, and finest Lavender Water, Daffy's Elixir Salutis, Soughton's Elixir, &c. Those who favor him with their Custom may depend upon being waited on AT ALL TIMES in the readiest and most grateful Manner.—*Boston News-Letter*, Apr. 25, 1771.

AQUÆDUCTS.—For the Publick Good, aquæducts made & sold by Rowland Houghton which Instrument being properly applyed to the outside of a Pump Tree, prevents said Pump from freezing tho' scituate in the most bleak Place & sharpest Season.

Said Houghton has lately improv'd on his New Theodolate, by which the Art of Surveying is rendered more plain & easy than heretofore.—*Boston Gazette*, Jan. 17/24, 1737.

ASSAYER.—If any Persons desire to know the true value of ores, minerals or metals, of what kind soever, may have them justly essay'd on reasonable terms, by Robert Baden, at Mrs. Jackson's, Founder, at the Brazen Head in Cornhill, Boston.—*Boston Gazette*, Sept. 27/Oct. 4, 1736.

BAKER.—Any Persons wanting good brown Bisket fit either for the Fishery or for Shipping Off, may be supplyed by *Lately Gee* at the Sign of the Bakers Arms in Hannover Street, at the following Rates, *viz*. If Wheat be at 6 *s*, per Bushel, then Bread at 22 *s*. per Hundred, if at 7 *s*, then 25 *s*, and if at 8 *s*, then Bread at 28 *s*, and so proportionable either for money or Good Wheat at the Prices above said.—*New England Courant*, Sept. 10/17, 1722.

BAKER.—Whereas in the Courant of the 17th Instant, an Advertisement was publish'd by *Lately Gee* of Boston, Baker, offering brown Bisket at lower Prices than usual. These are to give Notice, That Bread of the same Courseness with the said *Gee's*, and with the same Quantity of Bran remaining in it, may be had for the same Prices at other Bakers in Town; but they being willing to avoid the Curse of the Common Sailors, those employ'd in the Fishery, etc. generally make their Bread better, and sell it for a better Price.—*New England Courant*, Sept. 17/24, 1722.

BARBER.—To be Sold by Publick Vendue at the Sun Tavern in Boston, on Tuesday next the 30th Instant at 4 of the Clock, P.M. Sundry Goods belonging to the Estate of James Wright, Barber, deceased, viz: Wiggs, Hair on the Pipes, Sash Lights and Shutters fitting for a Barber's Shop, and also sundry other Goods.—*Boston Gazette*, Oct. 20/27, 1729.

BARBER.—To be Let in a pleasant Country Town on the Post Road to Portsmouth, a Barber's Shop with proper Implements or Utensils for that Business, where there is enough to keep two Hands employ'd. Inquire of the Publisher.—*Boston Gazette*, May 7/14, 1739.

BARBER'S UNION IN 1724.—Boston, Dec. 7, on Tuesday the first of this Instant in the Evening, Thirty-two Principal Barbers of this Place, assembled at the Golden Ball, with a Trumpeter attending them, to debate some important Articles relating to their occupations; where it was propos'd, that they should raise their Shaving from 8 to 10 s. per Quarter, and that they should advance 5 s, on the Price of making common Wiggs and 10 s. on their Tye ones. It was also propos'd, that no one of their Faculty should shave or dress Wiggs, on Sunday Mornings for the future, on Penalty of forfeiting 10 Pounds for every such Offence: From whence it may fairly be concluded, that in times past such a Practice has been too common among them.—*New England Courant*, Nov. 30/Dec. 7, 1724.

BELL FOUNDER.—This is to give notice to all Persons that have occasion for a Bell or Bells in Churches or Meeting-houses, that in New York they may be supplyed with New Bells, or if they have any old Bell broke they may have it new cast at a reasonable Price, and warranted good for Twelve Months, that if it Crack or Break it shall be new Cast for nothing: And all New Bells shall be made of better mettal than any other that comes out of Europe for Churches or Meeting-houses. All Persons that have Occasion may apply themselves to Joseph Phillips who is now building a Furnace for that purpose, and hath already agreed with some Persons, and is ready to do the same with any that are disposed.—*Boston News-Letter*, June 10/17, 1717.

BELL FOUNDER.—John Whitear, of Fairfield [Conn.], Bell-Founder, makes and sells all sorts of Bells from the lowest size to Two Thousand Weight.—*Boston Gazette*, May 29/June 5, 1738.

BELL FOUNDER.—Last Week was raised and fix'd in the State-house Steeple [Philadelphia, Pa.], the new great Bell, cast here by PASS & STOW, weighing 2080 lb. with this Motto, *Proclaim Liberty throughout all the Land, unto all the Inhabitants thereof:* Lev. XXV, 10.—*Boston Gazette*, June 19, 1753.

BELL FOUNDER.—Caleb and Robert Barker in Hanover; Casts Bells for Meeting-Houses and other Uses, from a smaller to a greater, even to one of two Thousand Weight; cheaper than they can be Imported; By whom all Persons may be supplied on reasonable Terms.—*Boston Gazette*, Dec. 11, 1753.

BELL FOUNDER.—Robert Barker of Hanover, in the County of Plymouth, Hereby informs the Public, that he makes BELLS of any size suitable for Meeting-Houses, at *Two Shillings* per Pound.—*Boston Gazette*, July 29, 1765.

BELLOWS MAKER.—Joseph Clough near the Charlestown Ferry in Boston, makes and mends all sorts of Bellows for Furnaces, Refiners, Blacksmiths, Braziers and Goldsmiths; and also Makes and Mends all sorts of House Bellows after the best Manner; where all Gentlemen, and others, in Town and Country may be served at very reasonable Rates.—*Boston Gazette*, Dec. 15, 1741.

BLACKSMITH.—This is to give Notice, that there is one William Bryant, Blacksmith, that now keeps a shop adjoining to the Presbyterian Meeting House in Long Lane, Boston, who makes and mends Glaziers' Vises, Cloathers' Screws, and worsted Combs, and makes, grinds and setts Cloathers' Shears; he also makes and mends Smiths' Vises, Ship Carpenters', Blockmakers', Tanners', Glovers' and Coopers' Tools, Braziers' and Tinsmens' Shears, and makes House work, with many other things too tedious to mention here. He will make and engage his work to any of his Employers according to the value of them.—*Boston News-Letter*, July 6/13, 1732.

BLACKSMITH AND LOCKSMITH.—Made and Sold by Robert Hendry, on Scarlet's Wharff in Boston, Horse Shoeer, Spinning Wheel Irons after the best Manner, at *Ten Shillings*, old Tenor per sett: Also all sorts of Locks are made and mended by the said Hendrey, who keeps a Man that served his Time to the Lock Smith's Business.—*Boston Gazette*, Dec. 10, 1751.

Four months later he also advertised "fine White-Smiths Work; Also Spades, and the best sort of Steel Shod Shovels made very reasonably.—*Boston Gazette*, Apr. 21, 1752.

BOOKKEEPER.—Mr. *Brown Tymms* Living at Mr. *Edward Oakes* Shopkeeper in Newbury Street, at the South End in Boston, keeps Merchants & Shopkeepers Books, also writes Bills, Bonds, Leases, Licences, Charterparties, &c. for any Person that may have Occasion, at reasonable Rates. And likewise teacheth Young Men Arithmetick and Merchants Accounts.—*Boston News-Letter*, Feb. 17/24, 1717/18.

BRAZIER AND IRONMONGER.—The late Mr. *Edward Jackson's* Stock in Trade, consisting of a great variety of Articles in the Braziery and Ironmongery Way, in larger or smaller Lots as will best accommodate Customers.—Lead, Shot, bloomery, brittle, refined and Guinea Iron, Hollow Ware, best heart and clubb German Steel, best London Steel in half Faggots, Blowers' best Wool Combs, Iron Hearths for Ships, a Copper Furnace for ditto, Cannon shot, Iron Backs, Deck, Sheathing and Drawing Nails, Newcastle Coals, &c. Enquire at the House where the Deceased's Family dwells, or at his Shop.—*Boston Gazette*, Sept. 12, 1757.

BUCKRAM.—Any Person that has occasion to have any Linnen Cloth made into Buckram, or to buy Buckram ready made, or Callendring any Silk, Watering, Dying or Scouring: they may apply themselves to Samuel Hall, lately from London, and Thomas Webber near the New North Brick Meeting House, or at their Work-house near the Bowling-Green, Boston.—*Boston News-Letter*, June 25/July 2, 1722.

BUTTON MAKER.—Thomas Thornton, button maker, died in Boston.—*Boston Gazette*, Apr. 22/29, 1728.

BUTTON MAKER.—A Person came Passenger with Capt. Jenkins [who arrived in Boston, Nov. 24, 1772] who carried on the Button-making Business, and has bro't over the Materials for making all sorts of gilt Buttons.—A Manufacture not known by any in America.—*Boston News-Letter*, Nov. 26, 1772.

CALICO PRINTER.—Francis Gray, Callicoe Printer from Holland; Prints all sorts of Callicoes of several Colours to hold Washing, at his house in Roxbury near the Meeting-House.—*Boston Gazette*, June 16/23, 1735.

CALICO PRINTER.—To be Sold, very cheap for Cash, by the Person who Prints the dark Callicoes, an excellent Sett of Prints for the Same. ☞ The Person who has them to dispose of, would Instruct the Purchaser in the Use of them if required. Enquire of the Printer.—*Boston News-Letter*, May 13, 1773 (*sup.*).

CARDMAKER.—Imported in the *Wilmington*, and to be Sold in School Street by Joseph Palmer, Cardmaker from London, at his House next above the French Meeting House, viz. Broad Cloths, the best steel Wire, Exeter Fish Hooks, Buckles, Mettal & Horse Hair Buttons, Tinplate Ware of several Sorts, and other Goods; Also the best Wool and Cotton Cards are there made (as good as any brought from England) by the said Palmer, and Sold by Wholesale or Retail. N. S. The said Palmer wants a Servant Maid and a Negro Boy.—*Boston Gazette*, Nov. 25, 1746.

Joseph Palmer advertised that he intended for England in the early spring.—*Boston Gazette*, Feb. 28, 1749.

CARD MAKER.—Joseph Palmer & Richard Cranch From England, at their House in South School-Street, Boston, Make very good CHOCOLATE, at 12 s. per Pound, and a superfine Sort for 14 s. per Pound, with large Allowance by the Dozen. They also continue to make best WOOL-CARDS & COTTON-CARDS. At the same place are to be Sold, several Pair of Woman's best Tabby Stays.—*Boston Gazette*, Mar. 12, 1751.

CAULKERS.—Whereas the Caulkers in general within the Port

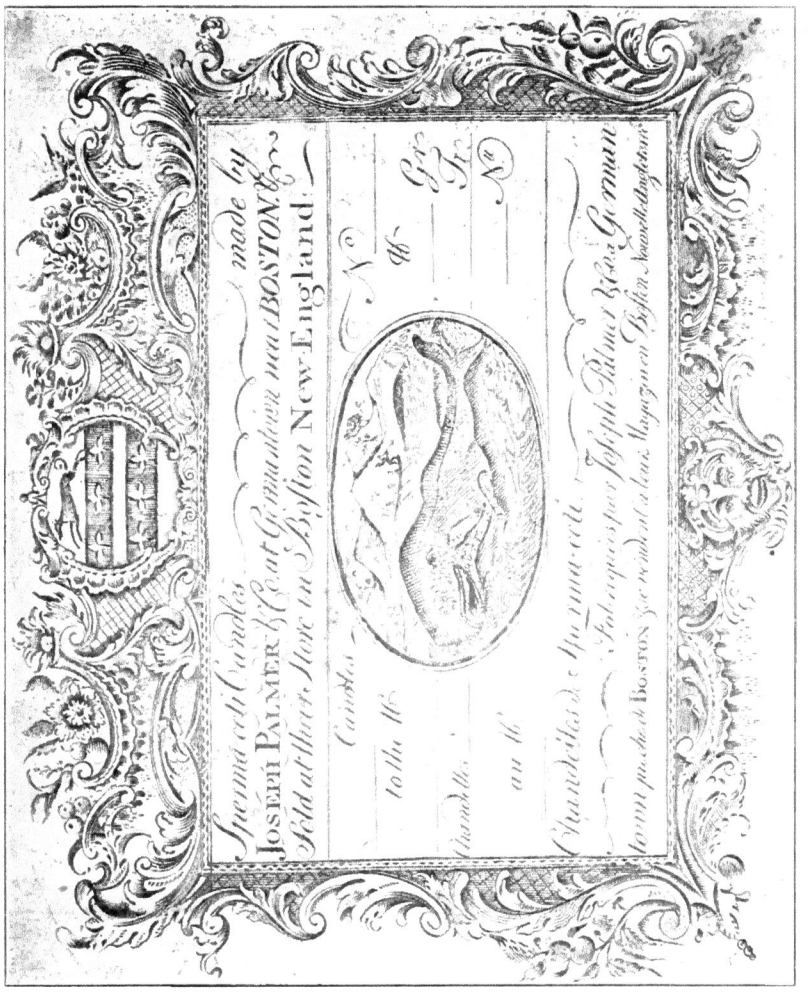

Price Sheet of Joseph Palmer & Co., Chandlers
Engraved about 1765 by Nathaniel Hurd

of Boston, have for many years past, laboured under great Inconvenience, and have suffered much Damage, Wrong and Injury in receiving their Pay for their Work, by Notes on Shops, for Money and Goods; and thereby have greatly Impoverished themselves and Families . . . they have entered into an agreement . . . that they will take no other Pay for their Service, than good lawful publick Bills of Credit, Manufactory Bills, or Merchant's Notes, Corn, Wheat or other Grain, Pork, Beef or other Provisions, Rum, Sugar, Molasses, or other West India Goods, at the Price Current, or Market Price.—*Boston News-Letter*, Feb. 12/19, 1741.

CHANDLER.—To be sold on Minot's T. by James Clemens, Sperma Ceti Candles, exceeding all others for Beauty, Sweetness of Scent when extinguished; Duration, being more than double Tallow Candles of equal size; Dimensions of Flame, nearly four Times more, emitting a soft easy expanding Light, bringing the Object close to the Sight, rather than causing the Eye to trace after them, as all Tallow-Candles do, from a constant Dimness which they produce.—One of these Candles serves the Use and Purpose of three Tallow Ones, and upon the whole are much pleasanter and cheaper.—*Boston News-Letter*, Mar. 30, 1748.

CHANDLER AND SOAPBOILER.—To be sold by *Edward Langdon*, in Fleet Street, near the Old North Meeting House, A Quantity of Hard Soap by the Box, soft Soap by the Barrel, and good old Candles both Mould and Dipt, fit for Shipping or Families, also Mould Candles of Bayberry Wax, all by the Box or by Retail.—*Boston Gazette*, July 24, 1750.

CHANDLER.—Bay Berry candles for Sale. "large & small, plain & flower'd;" also dipp'd Candles at 4/6, by single pound, half Dozen or Dozen, "also sells green Wax and Mould Candles, plain & fluted."—*Boston Gazette*, Feb. 20, 1753.

CHANDLER.—Made and Sold by Edward Langdon & Son, in Fleet Street, near the old North Meeting-House, Sperma-Ceti Candles, Bayberry Wax Candles, mould and dipp'd Tallow Candles—also refin'd Sperma-Ceti Oil, by the Barrel or smaller Quantities for Lamps.—*Boston Gazette*, May 25, 1761.

CHANDLER.—Sperma-Cæti Candles, Warrented Good, are made by *Richard Cranch* and *Company*, at *German-Town*, and sold by *William Belcher*, at his Store on the South-Side of the Town-Dock, in Boston; where also may be had the best *Sperma-Cæti* Oil by the Cask.—*Boston Gazette*, Jan. 11, 1762.

CHANDLER.—John Sweetser, Jun. Just opposite to Deacon Church's Vendue, sells best Ship and Family *Candles*, at 5/6 d. per lb. per Box and Dozen, neat Mould Candles plain and fluted, Tallow by the Barrel, Hard Soap by the Box, warranted.—*Boston Gazette*, Jan. 24, 1763.

LAMP OIL.—A New England vessel having "30 Tons of Lamp Oyl" on board was captured by French and Indians in Newfoundland.—*Boston News-Letter*, Oct. 2/9, 1704.

LAMP OIL.—Best Refin'd Sperma-Ceti Oil for Lamps, to be sold next Door to the *Salutation*, near the North Battery.—*Boston Gazette*, July 17, 1758.

CHAPMAN OR PEDDLER.—"On Thursday last Dyed at Boston, James Gray, That used to go up and down the Country selling of Books, who left a considerable Estate behind him."—*Boston News-Letter*, Apr. 9/16, 1705.

CHIMNEY SWEEP.—Ran away on Thursday last, from his Master James Fairservice of Boston, a Servant Lad, named Wm. Thomas, about 17 Years old, small of his age, short black Hair, black Eyes (he often brings the same to the Grief and Damage of his Master,) was bred a Chimney-sweeper, and has been employ'd in that Service, and went away in and with his Sweeper's Gears, had on two dark Jackets pretty sutty; chews Tobacco plentifully, and chuses the best sort. Whoever shall take him up & bring him to his Master, shall have two Dollars, and necessary charges.

All Masters of Vessells are caution'd against carrying him off; for he cost me 250 Pounds old Tenor 6 Months Ago. JAMES FAIRSERVICE.—*Boston Gazette*, Nov. 14, 1752.

CHOCOLATE MILL.—Salem, Sept. 3. By a Gentleman of this Town is this Day bro't to perfection, an Engine to Grind Cocoa; it is a Contrivance that cost much less than any commonly used; and will effect all that which the Chocolate Grinders do with their

Mills and Stones without any or with very Inconsiderable Labour; and it may be depended on for Truth, that it will in less than six Hours bring one Hundred weight of Nuts to a consistance fit for the Mold. And the Chocolate made by it, is finer and better, the Oyly Spirit of the Nut being almost altogether preserved, and there is little or no need of Fire in the making.—*Boston Gazette*, Sept. 5/12, 1737.

COOPER.—John Henry Dyer, Cooper, lately arriv'd from ——
———, living on Mr. Henshaw's Wharffe, near the South Market House in Boston; makes all sorts of Cooper's Ware, after the best manner, as Rum Hogsheads, Barrels, Caggs, little Tubs and Trays, as cheap and good as any in the Town.—*Boston Gazette*, July 30, 1751.

COUNTERPANE STAMPER.—Whereas a certain Person, who followed the Business of stamping Counterpanes, is going out of the Country, and has intirely dropt that Business here: These are to inform all Shopkeepers and others, that they may have Counterpanes and Curtains, &c., stampt after the same Manner, and at the same Rates that the Said Person stamp'd them, at the House of John Williams in King Street.—*Boston Evening Post*, Nov. 16, 1747.

CURRIER.—The Trade of a Currier is very much wanted in *Middletown* the Metropolis of Connecticut: any Prudent person that is Master of that Trade may get a pretty Estate in a few Years.—*Boston Gazette*, Nov. 6, 1758.

DYER.—This is to give notice, that there is lately arriv'd here from England *George Leason*, who with *Thomas Webber* of Boston, Cloathier, have set up a Callendar-Mill and Dye-House in Cambridge-street Boston near the Bowling-Green: Where all Gentlemen Merchants and others may have all sorts of Linnens, Callicoes, Stuffs or Silks Callendar'd; Prints all sorts of Linnens; Dyes and Scowers all sorts of Silks, and other things, and makes Buckrames; and all on very reasonable Terms.—*Boston News-Letter*, Apr. 21/28, 1735.

DYER.—*EDWARD CARTER*, Silk Dyer and Scowrer from *London*, at the *Rainbow and blue Hand in Wing's Lane* Boston:

*Dyes and Scowers all sorts of Brocades, Velvets, Silks, Stuffs, Linnen and Woolen,* as in his former Advertisements, *withCare and Expedition.*

*The said* Carter *has Apparrel by him belonging to a number of People, desiring they would fetch them away paying for the same, and for the future has determined to keep no Books for private Families, but to be paid for every Parcel at the Delivery.*

Note, *He's ready to give his Attendance to his Customers for their Work, but desires they would send for it when finished and pay for the same.* Edward Carter.—*Boston Gazette,* June 23/30, 1735.

DYER.—Alexander Fleming, Dyer, lately from Great Britain, has set up said Business in Boston, in a House of Mr. Arthen's near Dr. Gardner's in Marlborough street, on the same side of the Way, who can dye all sorts of Colours, after the best Manner and cheapest Rate, viz. Scarletts, Crimsons, Pinks, Purples, Straws, Wine Colours, Sea-Greens, Saxon ditto, common Blues, shearing, dressing and watering of cloths: Also he can dye linnen Yarn either red, blue, green, yellow or cloth colours, and all Colours on silks, and cleaning of Cloths.—*Boston Gazette,* May 14, 1754.

DYER.—Notice is hereby Given, That *John Hickey* living at the South End of Boston, next House to the Sign of the White-Horse, has furnished himself with all sorts of Utensils fit to carry on the Business of silk or Cloth dying, scouring of any Colour, and Prints Linnens with true Blues and Whites, and takes all Manner of Stains out of Silk or Cloth; dyes Thick setts, Cotton or Linen of any Colours: *Price for Cash,* Coats scoured for 2 s. and dyed for 4 s. Silk Gowns for 6 s. Riding hoods for 5 s. Linnen or Cotton per lb. blue 1 s. and all other Goods in Proportion: and engages to his Work as well as if sent to London.—*Boston Gazette,* Sept. 1, 1760.

FIRE ENGINE.—To be sold, a Large and extraordinary good Copper Fire-Engine, newly fixed, that works well, and will be of excellent Use in Time of Fire, in any populous Place. Enquire of Mr. James Read, Blockmaker, near Oliver's Bridge in Boston.—*Boston News-Letter,* Feb. 19/26, 1735/6.

HAND ENGINES.—Hand Engines made after the best manner, fitted with Brass Clappers, very useful in all Families, convenient for extinguishing Fire in Chimneys, or in any Room in a House; Also very proper for Coasters to carry to sea to wet the Sails in small Winds to preserve them from Mildews; said Engine throws Water with ease 40 Feet perpendicular. Sold by Rowland Houghton, on the North side of the Town House at 25 s. each.—*Boston Gazette*, June 10/17, 1734.

WATER ENGINE.—There is newly erected in the Town of Boston, by Messieurs John and Thomas Hill, a Water-Engine at their Still-house, by the Advice and Direction of Mr. Rowland Houghton, drawn by a Horse, which delivers a large quantity of Water twelve Feet above the Ground. This being the first of the kind in these Parts, we thought taking Notice of it might be of Publick Service, inasmuch as a great deal of Labour is saved thereby. —*Boston Gazette*, Jan. 15/22, 1733.

FISHERMEN.—Capt. Robinson, who arrived here last Tuesday from London, has brought a Number of Families from North-Britain, to carry on the Fishing-Business, and settle at the Eastern Parts of this Province.—*Boston News-Letter*, Nov. 1, 1764.

GLOVER.—To be sold by the Maker, Ph. Freeman, who arrived in the last Ship from London, at Mr. Irish's in Bridge's Lane near Mr. Welsteed's Meeting-House, A Large Parcel of Gloves of all Sorts, viz. Men's and Women's Buck and Doe, Kid and Lamb, for Mourning and all other Sorts.—*Boston News-Letter*, Sept. 30/Oct. 7, 1742.

GLOVER.—Just Imported and Sold by Philip Freeman, Norway Doe Gloves, and Makes and Sells Winter Gloves, for Men and Women: and lines Gloves with Fur, after the best Manner. —*Boston Gazette*, Nov. 26, 1754.

GROCER.—To be Sold by John Merrett, at the Three Sugar Loaves, and Cannister in King-Street, near the Town House in Boston; Super-fine Chocolate, Coffee, raw & roasted, very choice Teas, viz: Bohea Tea from 22 s. to 28 s. per Pound, Congou Tea, 34 s. Pekoe Tea, 50 s. per Pound, Green Tea from 20 s. to 30 s. per Pound, fine Imperial Tea from 40 s. to 60 s. per Pound, with proper Abatements, by large Quantities; Double refin'd and single Loaf Sugars; All sorts of fine clay'd, powder & muscovado Sugars, from 12 d. to 3 d. per Pound; Sugar-Candy, Citron, Pepper, Pimento or Alspice, Cayan Pepper, white Pepper, Mace, Nutmegs, Cloves and Cinnamon, race Ginger, grin'd or powder Ginger, Raisins of the Sun, new Currants, Figs, Prunes, fine Jordan Almonds, Rice, Pearl Barley, French Barley, Sago, Starch, English Hair-Powder, Indigo, Powder Blew, Isonglass; Annis, Corriander & Carriway Seeds, Salt Peter, roll Brimstone, flower of Brimstone; Havanna, Scott, Tobacco, plain Spanish, sweet scented and fine Spanish Snuff; Rozin, Bees wax, Tamarins, Hungary Water, Castile Soap; fine Florence Oil, by the Chest, by the Flask, and by Retale, out of Jarrs; Olive Oil in small Jarrs; fine Leghorn Anchovies; Choice White Wine Vinegar, Allum, Copperas, Logwood, Brazeleto or Redwood, ground Redwood, Madder, Potash, English & Flemish, Argol, Nutgauls, and other Dyers Wares; Painters Colours of every Kind, for House-painting, Face-painting, and Water Colours, Linseed Oil, Nut Oil, Oil of Turpentine, Varnish; all sorts of Tools and Brushes; Choice Velvet Corks from 5 s. to 12 s. per Gross.

N. B. He has received fresh Supplies of most of said Goods by the last Ships.—*Boston News-Letter*, Sept. 16/23, 1736.

GUNSMITH.—To be sold by John Pim of Boston, Gunsmith, at the Sign of the Cross Guns, in Anne-Street near the Draw Bridge, at very Reasonable Rates, sundry sorts of choice Arms lately arrived from London, viz. Handy Muskets, Buccaneer-Guns, Fowling pieces, Hunting Guns, Carabines, several sorts of Pistols, Brass and Iron, fashionable Swords, &c.—*Boston News-Letter*, July 4/11, 1720.

GUNSMITH.—Newly imported, and sold by Samuel Miller, Gunsmith, at the Sign of the cross Guns near the Draw-Bridge, Boston: Neat Fire Arms of all sorts, Pistols, Swords, Hangers, Cutlasses, Flasks for Horsemen, Firelocks, &c.—*Boston Gazette*, May 11, 1742.

GUNSMITH.—Made by John Cookson, and to be Sold by him at his House in Boston: a handy Gun of 9 Pounds and a half weight; having a Place convenient to hold 9 Bullets, and Powder for 9 Charges and 9 Primings; the said Gun will fire 9 Times distinctly, as quick, or slow as you please, with one turn with the Handle of the said Gun, it doth charge the Gun with Powder and Bullet, and doth prime and shut the pan, and cock the Gun. All these Motions are performed immediately at once, by one turn with the said Handle. Note, there is Nothing put into the Muzzle of the Gun as we charge other Guns.—*Boston Gazette,* Apr. 12, 1756.

GUNSMITH.—All sorts of BAYONETS for Muskets, made and sold by *John Cutler,* at the Lion and Bell in Marlborough street, Boston; where may be also had Silk Umbrellas for Ladies, made in the neatest Manner.—*Boston Gazette,* June 27, 1757.

HATTER.—Daniel Jones, at the *Hat & Helmit,* South-End, Boston, . . . makes and sells Beaver, Beaveret, and Castor-Hats: and has also a good Assortment of English Castor and Beaveret Hats, English and Felt ditto; Hat Linings and Trimmings of all sorts: Red Wool, Coney Wool, Camels Hair: Logwood by the 100 Wt. by Wholesale or Retail, cheap for Cash or Treasurer's Notes.—*Boston Gazette,* Dec. 10, 1759.

HOSIERY MANUFACTORY.—"There has lately been made and sold at Mr. Beall's Stocking Manufactory at Annapolis, Maryland, a Quantity of Thread Stockings, with this Device in Place of the Clock, A-M-E-R-I-C-A."—*Boston Gazette,* Sept. 3, 1764.

HOUR GLASSES.—All sorts of Hour-Glasses to be made or mended on Reasonable terms, by *James Maxwell,* at his House in Water Street, near the Town House in Boston.—*Boston News-Letter,* Sept. 17/24, 1716.

IRON FOUNDRY.—Any Person that has occasion for Forge Hammers, anvils, or Plates, Smiths' Anvils, Clothiers' Plates, Chimney Backs, Potts, Kettles, Skillets, Cart Boxes, Chaise Boxes, Dog-Irons, or any other Cast Iron Ware, may be provided with them by Richard Clarke, at his Furnace in the Gore, giving speedy Notice (of the Sizes and Quantity they want) to him there, or to Oliver, Clarke, and Lee, at their Warehouse in King Street, Boston; where they may be supplied with Swivel Guns.—*Boston Gazette*, July 13/20, 1741.

IRON FORGE.—To be Sold a good Penniworth, a Slitting Mill compleatly finished and furnished, scituated in the middle of near 20 Forges in the Compass of 12 Miles, with a well built Forge with Two Fires, and conveniency for a third; together with a well built and well accustomed Grist Mill, all standing on one Dam; on as constant a stream as this Land affords; with accommodations for other Water Works; A good Dwelling House, Coal House, and above 6 Acres of Land, and a good Orchard upon it, said Works stand on Namasket River in Middleborough, 13 Miles from Plymouth, and 10 from Taunton. All finely scituated for a Country Seat; and now Lets for 379 Pounds per Annum. Any Person or Persons minded to purchase the same, may inquire of the Rev. Mr. Peter Thacher of Middleborough aforesaid, or of the Printer hereof, and know further.

N. B. The Reason of this Sale is because the Person wants the money for it, and intending to leave off that Business.—*Boston Gazette*, May 11, 1742.

IRON MONGER.—To be sold by *John Winslow*, at his Warehouse, in Newbury-Street, near Summer Street: Best refined and blommery Iron, Ploughshare Moulds, Anchor Palms, Coohorns, Swivel Guns, Ten Inch Mortars and Shells, 6, 4, & 3 pound Swivel and Grape Shot.—*Boston Gazette*, Apr. 25, 1757.

JACK-MAKER and Trader, Joseph Essex of Boston adjudged a bankrupt.—*Boston News-Letter*, Jan. 17/24, 1714/15.

ROASTING JACKS.—To be sold by John Jackson, Jack-maker, at his shop, being the corner shop at the Draw bridge, in Boston, all sorts of Jacks, reasonably, and makes, mends and Cleans all sorts of Jacks; also makes & mends Locks, Keys, and Ironing Boxes, at a reasonable rate.—*Boston Gazette*, May 2/9, 1737.

JAPANNING.—Whereas John Waghorne, has lately Receiv'd a fresh parcel of materials for the new Method of Japaning, which was Invented in France, for the Amusement and Benefit of the Ladies, and is now practised by most of the Quality and Gentry in Great-Britain, with the greatest Satisfaction; He is also

QUILL WORK SCONCE

Of twisted paper, wax, mica and silver wire, in contemporaneous walnut frame. One of a pair made about 1720 by Ruth Read of Boston. From the Francis Hill Bigelow Collection

remov'd from the South End, to the House that was lately tennanted by Mr Leblond, in Queen Street; for the Convenience of his Scholars; and such Ladies as desire it, he will attend at their own Houses, but to make the Expence less to others, he designs a School at Five Pounds for each Scholar, and to begin on Friday the 30th of this Instant, Boston, May 24th.

N. B. The said Waghorne will attend to teach any Ladies out of Town, so that he may have a suitable Encouragement for so doing, and for the future all Persons may be by him, supplyed with the best of Turnery Ware of Mehoganey &c. for their Use here, or to send abroad.—*Boston Gazette*, May 19/26, 1740.

JAPANNING.—Whereas John Waghorne has lately received a fresh Percel of Materials for the new invented Method of Japaning; this is therefore to acquaint the Ladies that he purposes to begin his School for this Season on Monday June 8, at his House in Queen street, Boston, New England, 1741.—*Boston Gazette*, June 1/8, 1741.

JAPANNING.—Drawing, Japanning, and Painting on Glass, taught by Mrs. Sarah Morehead, at the Head of the Rope-Walks, near Fort Hill.—*Boston Evening Post*, Apr. 18, 1748.

JAPANNING.—This is to inform the Publick, That David Mason, Jappanner, has open'd a Shop under Messieurs Edes and Gill's Printing Office: where all Sorts of Painting, Japanning, Gilding and Varnishing are done; Coats of Arms, Drawings on Sattin or Canvis for Embroidering; also Pictures fram'd after the neatest Manner. ☞ And as he has been employ'd in the Service to the Westward for three Years, and was one of the unhappy sufferers at Fort William Henry, he hopes the Gentlemen of the Town will be kind enough to favour him with their Custom, as he shall endeavour to give general Satisfaction.—*Boston Gazette*, Dec. 18, 1758.

LIME KILN.—To be Sold a good Pennyworth; A good Lime-Kiln, a Lime-House, a good Well, a Wharf, and a piece of Ground, being near the Bowling-green, Boston; Inquire of Mr. Walter Browne at the Sign of the Blue Anchor in King-Street, Boston, and know further.

N.B. There is very good Limejuice to be sold by the aforesaid Browne at his House.—*Boston News-Letter,* Mar. 28/Apr. 4, 1723.

STONE LIME.—To be sold by the Hogshead or Bushel, the best eastward Stone Lime, by John Blowers of Boston, Mason, in School Street.—*Boston Gazette,* Mar. 31, 1747.

LINEN PRINTER.—The Printer hereof Prints Linens, Callicoes, Silks, &c. in good Figures, very lively and durable Colours, and without the offensive smell which commonly attends the Linnens Printed here.—*Boston Gazette,* Apr. 18/25, 1720 (*sup.*).

LINEN PRINTER.—The Printer hereof having dispers'd advertisements of his Printing Callicoes, etc. a certain Person in Charlestown, to rob him of the Benefit of said advertisements and impose upon strangers, calls himself by the Name of Franklin, having agreed with one in Queen Street, Boston, to take in his work. These are to desire him to be satisfyed with his proper Name, or he will be proceeded against according to Law.—*Boston Gazette,* May 2/9, 1720.

STAMPED LINEN.—These are to Inform the Publick, that I the Subscriber propose to come once more to Boston; if any Person or Persons have old sheets or Linnen to stamp, they are desired to leave them at the House of *James Nichol* in School Street, next door to the French Meeting House; and if they send them in four Weeks from this Date, they shall have them in March next without fail. As Witness my Hand, *Sarah Hunt.*—*Boston Gazette,* Dec. 22, 1747.

LINEN MANUFACTURE.—Publick Notice is hereby given, That sundry Looms for Weaving of Linnen, of all Sorts, are set up at the Linnen-Manufacture House in the Common below Thomas Hancocks' Esq; where all Persons may have their Yarn wove in the best and Cheapest Manner, and with the utmost Dispatch. At the same Place, money will be given for all Sorts of Linnen Yarn.

And whereas the setting up and establishing the Linnen Manufacture is undoubtedly of the utmost Importance to this Province: It is propos'd by a Number of Gentlemen, very soon to open several Spinning-Schools in this Town, where children may be taught Gratis. And it is to be hop'd, that all Well-wishers to their Country will send their children, that are suitable for such Schools, to learn the useful and necessary Art of Spinning; and that they will give all other proper Countenance and Encouragement to this Undertaking.—*Boston News-Letter*, Dec. 13, 1750.

LINEN MANUFACTORY.—The Massachusetts General Court at its session held in the summer of 1753, passed an "Act for granting the sum of Fifteen Hundred Pounds To encourage the Manufacture of Linnen," providing for a tax on every "Coach, Chariot, Chaise, Calash and Chair" for the term of five years, the Governor, Lieutenant Governor, the President of Harvard College, and the settled ministers in the Province, being excepted from its provision, at the following rates: each Coach, ten shillings annually, Chariot, five shillings, Chaise, three shillings, Calash, two shillings, Chair, two shillings. The several sums received from Time to Time were to be paid to a committee of ten appointed by the Act, "to be applied to the purchasing a Piece of Land, and building or purchasing a convenient House within the Town of *Boston*, for carrying on the Business of Spinning, Weaving, and other necessary Parts of the Linnen Manufacture." This legislation was instituted because of "the great Decay of Trade and Business the Number of Poor is greatly increased, and the Burden of supporting them lies heavy on many of the Towns within this Province, and many Persons, especially Women and Children are destitute of Employment."—*Boston Gazette*, Aug. 7, 1753.

LINEN PRINTER AND DYER.—John Hickey, linen-printer and dyer, from Dublin, is now settled in this town, at the linen manufactory, where he follows the business of blue and white printing, and silk or cloth dying; and takes all manner of spots out of silk or cloths, cleans gold and silver lace, and scarlet cloth, dyes linnen and cotton of a blue or London red, and all manner of country stuffs, worsteds, camlets, tammies, or leather; he dyes blacks so as they shall be sound and clean as any other colour; also dyes ribbons and makes them up again as well as ever, and English thick sets after they have been worn or faded, and blue yarn for one shilling a pound. N. B. as there has been several who have imposed upon this country in telling that they were printers; I engage myself that if my colours be not as good and as lasting as any that comes from Europe, to satisfy my employers with all charges or damages that shall be justly laid against me.

All the above articles done with expedition at the most reasonable price, by JOHN HICKEY.—*Boston Gazette*, May 7, 1759 (*sup.*).

LINEN PRINTER.—"*Extract of a Letter from Baltimore, January 16, 1772.* We learn that a person who has for many years past been a master in several large manufactories for linen, cotton and callicoe printing, likewise cutting and stamping of the copper plates for the same, intends some time this month to leave England for America, with six Journeymen, and all materials for carrying on the said business, previous to which, and unknown to the English manufacturers, he has shipped sundry machines, some of which will spin ten, and others from twenty to one hundred threads at one time, with the assistance of one hand to each machine.—These machines are not allowed at home, and so inveterate are the common people against them, that they burn and destroy not only them, but the houses wherein they are found. The Americans being able to purchase cotton to more advantage than the Europeans, a manufactory of this kind will doubtless be properly encouraged by the well-wishers to America."—*Boston News-Letter*, Feb. 20, 1772.

MANUFACTORY-HOUSE, BOSTON.—At the Manufactory-House, in Boston, is made and to be sold by *John Brown*, plain, check'd and striped Linnens; Bed Ticks; Handkerchiefs; Diapers; Coatings; Furniture Checks; the very best of Spinnel, and Shoe Thread.—*Boston Gazette*, June 21, 1762.

LINEN MANUFACTORY.—At the Linnen Manufactory in *Boston*, there has been made within these last three Months, 400 Yards of Bengals, Lilleputias and Broglios, which have been bought by some of the principal Ladies in this Town, for their own and their children's wear. . . . JOHN BROWN. N. B. The said *Brown* has now to sell several sorts of Winter and Summer Manufactory Goods.—*Boston Gazette*, Jan. 14, 1765.

LINEN WHITENER.—The whiting of Linnens is carried on as usual, and all spots, stains, Iron Moulds, Milldews and Yellowness taken out of Linnens, Lawns and Cambricks, by *John Brown*, at the Manufactory in *Boston*.—N. B. None will be received after the 20th of June next.—*Boston Gazette*, May 28, 1764 (*sup.*).

LOCKSMITH.—This is to inform my Customers, that I have remov'd from Middle-street, to the Bottom of Cross street, where I continue to mend all sorts of Locks, also to fit Keys to Locks, mend all sorts of Kettles, as Brass, Copper, Pewter, &c. at a very reasonable Rate, by *Reuben Cookson*.—*Boston Gazette*, Apr. 23, 1754 (*sup.*).

MATHEMATICAL BALANCEMAKER.—Jonathan Dakin, Mathematical Balance maker, at the Sign of the Hand & Beam, opposite to Dr. *Colman's* Meeting House, makes all sorts of scale Beams, and likewise mends all that can be mended; where all Gentlemen may be supplied with Beams ready adjusted and scaled, as the Law directs.—*Boston Gazette*, Nov. 12, 1745.

MATHEMATICAL INSTRUMENTS.—Stephen Greenleaf, Mathematical Instrument-Maker, in *Queen Street*, Boston, opposite to the Prison, Makes and Mends all Sorts of Mathematical Instruments, as Theodolites, Spirit Levels, Semi circles, Circumferences, and Protractors, Horizontal and Equinoctial Sun Dials, Azimuth and Amplitude Compasses, Eliptical and Triangular Compasses, and all sorts of common Compasses, drawing Pens and Portagraions, Pensil Cases, and parallel Rulers, Squares and Bevils, Free Masons Jewels, with sundry other articles too tedious to mention.

N. B. He sets Load Stones on Silver or Brass, after the best manner.—*Boston Gazette*, June 18, 1745.

MILITARY EQUIPMENT.—On Thursday the 6 of February at three of the clock Afternoon, will be sold by Publick Vendue at the Exchange Tavern, about one hundred Canvice & Ticken Tents, Poles, Mallets, and Pins to them, about five hundred Pick-Axes, fifty Axes and Hatchets, about eight hundred Tomhawks or small Hatchets, about three hundred Spades and Bills, a parcell of Shovels, Wheelbarrows, Handbarrow's, Baskets of Speaks and Nails, all to be put and sold in Lots, and to be seen at the place of sale the Morning before the Sale begins: Also a very fine Negro Woman.—*Boston Gazette,* Jan. 27/Feb. 3, 1728/9.

MILITARY EQUIPMENT.—Extract from the *Act for Regulating the Militia:*—Every listed Soldier, and other Householder shall be always provided with a well fixt Firelock Musket, of Musket or Bastard-Musket bore, the Barrel not less than three Foot and an half long, or other good Fire Arms to the satisfaction of the Commission Officers of the Company; a Cartouch Box: one Pound of good Powder: Twenty Bullets fit for his Gun, and twelve Flynts; a good Sword or Cutlass; a Worm, & priming Wire, fit for his Gun, on Penalty of six Shillings."—*Boston News-Letter,* Feb. 7/14, 1733/4.

HALBERTS.—A Set of Halberts for a foot Company to be sold on reasonable Terms, by Nicholas Boone Bookseller, to be seen at his House near School-House Lane, Boston.—*Boston News-Letter,* Apr. 22/29, 1706. "A Set of New-Halbards" were offered for sale in the June 3/10, 1706, issue.

PISTOL.—Lost between Salem and Ipswich, a Pistol dropt out of the Holster, the barrel having on it the Tower mark, all the other work (except the stock of Maple, and the Lock made by *R. Lawrence*) being handsomely wrought with silver and the London Goldsmith's Hall mark on it. Thirty shillings reward.—*Boston News-Letter,* July 14/21, 1712.

MUSTARD MAKER.—John Ingram, the Original Flower of Mustard Maker, from Lisbon, now living at the House of Mrs. Townsend, near Oliver's-Dock, Boston, Prepares Flower of Mustard to such Perfection, by a Method unknown to any Person by himself, that it retains its Strength, Flavour and Colour Seven Years; being mix'd with hot or cold water, in a Minute's Time it makes the strongest Mustard ever eat, not in the least Bitter, yet of a delicate and delightful Flavour, and gives a most surprizing grateful Taste to Beef, Pork, Lamb, Fish, Sallad, or other Sauces. It is approved of by divers eminent Physicians as the only Remedy in

PETIT POINT PICTURE WORKED IN 1765 BY MISS DERBY OF SALEM
Contemporaneous frame. From the Dwight M. Prouty Collection

the Universe in all nervous Disorders, sweetens all the Juices, and rectifies the whole Mass of Blood to Admiration. If close stopt it will keep its Strength and Virtue Seven years in any Climate. Merchants and Captains of Ships shall have good Allowance to sell again.—*Boston Gazette*, Sept. 19, 1752.

NAILMAKING TOOLS.—To be Sold by Edward Jackson of Boston, Sundry sorts of Nailer's Tools, as Bellows, Stakes, Hammers and Nail-Tools: Also a very good new Bell of near Five hundred Weight.—*Boston Gazette*, Feb. 26/Mar. 5, 1739.

NAILMAKING.—Any Gentleman that hath a mind to set up the nailing Business, which may be done to very great Advantage in this Country, may by inquiring of the Printer be informed of a Man that will carry it on to Perfection for him.—*Boston Gazette*, Mar. 2, 1742.

NEEDLE MAKER.—Simon Smith, Needle maker from London, is removed from the Rainbow and Dove in Marlborough Street, now in Union Street near the Corn fields; continues to make and sell all sorts of white Chapple Needles, and all other sorts round and square.—*Boston News-Letter*, Apr. 15/22, 1742.

NEEDLEWORK AND MILLINARY.—This is to give Notice, That at the House of Mr. *George Brownell*, late School Master in Hanover Street Boston, are all sorts of Millinary Works done; making up Dresses, and flowering of Muslin, making of furbelow'd Scarffs, and Quilting, and cutting of Gentlewomens Hair in the newest Fashion; and also young Gentlewomen and Children taught all sorts of fine Works, as Feather-Work, Filegre and Painting on Glass, Embroidering a new way, Turkey-Work for Handkerchiefs two ways, fine new Fashion Purses, flourishing and plain Work, and Dancing cheaper than ever was taught in Boston, Brocaded-Work for Hankerchiefs and short Aprons upon Muslin, artificial Flowers work'd with a Needle.—*Boston News-Letter*, Aug. 20/27, 1716.

NEEDLEWORK AND MILLINARY.—Lately come from London, Mrs E. Atkinson, Who designs the making of Mantos and Riding dresses after the newest fashion, the taking in of all sorts of Millinary Work, teaching Young Ladies all Sorts of Works, and dressing of Heads and cutting of Hair. Now living with Mrs Edward Oakes's in Cornhill Street, Boston, near the Brick Meeting House.—*Boston News-Letter*, Mar. 27, 1729.

NEEDLEWORK AND EMBROIDERY.—All sorts of Drawing for Embroidery, Childrens quilted Peaks, drawn or work'd; Caps set for Women and Children; or any sort of Needle Work, done by Mrs. Mary Sewall, Widow, near the Orange Tree.—*Boston Gazette*, Sept. 26/Oct. 3, 1737.

EMBROIDERY.—To be had at Mrs Condy's near the Old North Meeting House; All sorts of beautiful Figures on Canvas, for Tent Stick; the Patterns from London, but drawn by her much cheaper than English drawing; All sorts of Canvas, without drawing; also Silk Shades, Slacks, Floss, Cruells of all Sorts, the best White Chapple Needles, and every thing for all Sorts of Work.—*Boston News-Letter*, Apr. 27/May 4, 1738.

WORSTEDS.—Shaded Crewells, blew, red, and other colours of Worsteds.—*Boston News-Letter*, Apr. 28, 1743.

EMBROIDERY PATTERNS.—A Variety of very beautiful Patterns to draw by, of the late Mrs. *Susannah Condy*, deceas'd, any Gentlewoman or others disposed to improve and purchase the same, which will be very much to their Advantage, may inquire of *Elizabeth Russel*, Daughter of the deceas'd, near the Draw Bridge.—*Boston Gazette*, Dec. 15, 1747.

NEEDLEWORK.—At the Bottom of Cold-Lane in Boston. All Manner of Instruments in Writing, and Conveyances in the Law, now in Use and Practice, are carefully drawn and ingross'd, Also young Gentlemen and Ladies may be boarded and educated, and taught English, Writing & Arithmetick, both Vulgar and Decimal; with several other Branches of the Mathematicks, after a very easy and Concise Method.     By GEORGE SUCKLING.

Also young Ladies may be taught plain Work, Dresden, Point (or Lace) Work for Child Bed Linnen, Crosstitch, Tentstich, and all other kinds of Needle Work.     By BRIDGET SUCKLING.
—*Boston Gazette*, July 2, 1751.

NEEDLEWORK.—Elizabeth Hinche, living in a House of Mr. Jonathan Clark's, in Long Lane, does plain Sewing, Irish stitch,

Ten Stitch, Sampler Work, Embroidery and all other Sorts of Needle Work, also Painting on Glass; Likewise any Person may be supplyed with Chimney Flowers, Branches for Jams, or Sconces very Cheap.—*Boston News-Letter*, July 24, 1755.

EMBROIDERY.—To be taught by *Jean Day*, at Mrs Cutler's up William's Court, opposite the Brazen-Head in Cornhill, viz. Dresden, Embroidery with Gold and Shell-work, Coats of Arms, Tent stich, and Variety of other Work, all in the neatest & newest Fashion. N. B., The above Mrs *Cutler* takes in young Ladies to Board.—*Boston Gazette*, May 16, 1757.

EMBROIDERY.—"Yellow Canvas and Canvas Pictures ready drawn, a Quantity of worsted Slacks in Shades."—*Boston Gazette*, Aug. 8, 1757.

EMBROIDERY.—Taught by Eleanor M'Glvaine, opposite the Governor's, Dresden painting on Glass, Shell Work, Tent Stitch, and other Works proper for young Ladies.—*Boston Evening Post*, Mar. 27, 1758.

EMBROIDERY SCHOOL.—*To the Young Ladies of Boston.* Elizabeth Courtney, as several Ladies has signified of having a desire to learn that most ingenious art of Painting on Gauze & Catgut, proposes, to open a School, and that her business may be a public good, designs to teach the making of all sorts of French Trimmings, Flowers, and Feather Muffs and Tippets, and as those arts above mentioned (the Flowers excepted) are entirely unknown on the Continent, she flatters herself to meet with all due encouragement; and more so, as every Lady may have a power of serving herself of what she is now obliged to send to England for, as the whole process is attended with little or no expense. The Conditions are *Five Dollars* at entrance, to be confin'd to no particular hours or time: And if they apply constant, may be compleat in six weeks. And when she has fifty subscribers, school will be open'd, as not being designed to open a school under that number, her proposals being to each person so easy, but to return to those who have subscribed their Money again, and keep the business to herself.

*N. B.* Feather Muffs and Tippets to be had; and Gauze wash'd to look as well as new.

Please to inquire at Mr. *Courtney's*, Taylor, four Doors below the Mill-Bridge, North-End.—*Boston Gazette*, Oct. 19, 1767.

NEEDLEWORK SCHOOL.—Eleanor Druitt, takes this Method of Informing the Publick, That she has opened School at the House of Mr. William Pritchard, Cooper, near the Quaker Meeting-House, Boston, where she intends teaching French and English with the following Needle Works, viz. Point, Brussells, Dresden, Sprigging, Embroidery, Cat-Gut, Diaper, and all Kinds of Darning, French Quilting, Marking, Plain Work and Knitting.—*Boston News-Letter*, Oct. 17, 1771.

EMBROIDERER.—Barnard Andrews, Embroiderer, makes all Sorts of Embroidery for Men and Womens Ware, either Gold, Silver or Silk; also cleans Gold and Silver Lace, and Silk Work; —Paints upon Glass; Likewise, Feathers driven in old Beds when matted, in four different Sorts, which makes the Bed as good as if new Feathers;—Tossels, Fringes, &c. work'd with either Gold Silver or plain Silk in the genteelest Mode;— He also makes Paper Works, Hat, Bonnet, Patch, and Millenery Boxes in the neatest Manner.

☞ If any Gentleman and Ladies have an inclination to learn the above Business, they shall be waited on at their Houses, or at his Lodgings at Mrs *Geyer's*, Flower-Maker, in Pleasant-Street, Boston.—*Boston News-Letter*, July 2, 1772.

NEEDLEWORK SCHOOL.—Ruth Hern, hereby informs the Public, that she intends to open SCHOOL the 20th of March, in Orange Street, South End, against the Sign of the Swan; where she will endeavor to Teach young Misses all the various Arts and Branches of Needle-Work; Namely, Needle-Lace-Work, Needlework on Lawns and Muslins, flowering with Crewel-working Pocket-Books, with Irish-stitch, drawing and working of Twilights, marking of Letters, and Plain-sewing, etc. Learning young children to Read.—*Boston News-Letter*, Mar. 9, 1775.

PAPER MILL.—Whereas some Gentlemen design to set up a Paper-Mill in New England, if a supply can be had to carry on that Business: These are therefore to give Notice, that James Franklin, Printer in Queen Street, Boston, buys Linen Rags, either coarse or fine, at a Peny a Pound.—*New England Courant*, June 1/8, 1724.

STATIONER AND PAPER MAKER.—This is to give Notice, That Richard Fry, Stationer, Bookseller, Paper-maker, and Rag Merchant, from the City of London, keeps at Mr. Thomas Fleet's Printer at the Heart and Crown in Cornhill, Boston; where the said Fry is ready to accommodate all Gentlemen, Merchants, and Tradesmen, with sets of Accompt-Books, after the neatest manner; and whereas, it has been the common Method of the most curious merchants in Boston, to Procure their Books from London, this is to acquaint those Gentlemen, that I the said Fry, will sell all sorts of Accompt-Books, done after the most accurate manner, for 20 per cent. cheaper than they can have them from London.

I return the Publick Thanks for following the Directions of my former advertisement for gathering of Rags, and hope they will continue the like Method; having received seven thousand weight and upwards already.

For the pleasing entertainment of the Polite part of Mankind, I have Printed the most Beautiful Poems of Mr. Stephen Duck, the famous Wiltshire Poet; It is a full demonstration to me that the People of New England, have a fine taste for Good Sense & Polite Learning, having already sold 1200 of these Poems, Richard Fry.—*Boston Gazette*, May 1/8, 1732.

PAPER MILL.—Wanted Rags of Linnen, course and fine, old Sail-Cloth, Cotton or Checks, pretty clean dry. Those that will bring them to Mr. Alexander Boyce, on Mr. Gould's Wharf, near Mr. Hallowell's Ship-Yard, or to Mr. Kneeland's opposite to the Prison in Queen-street, Boston; or to the Milton Paper Mills; or Salem, Marblehead, Newbury, or Portsmouth, shall receive Five Pence a Pound Old Tenor, or One Dollar one Cwt; and half that money for old Rope;—And as a further Encouragement to Industry: They that will gather and bring the greatest Quantity of Rags between this Day and the 29th May, 1762, to any of the mentioned Places, shall receive a premium of 12 Dollars and the second Quantity 8 Dollars, and the third Quantity 4 Dollars. May 7, 1761.—*Boston Gazette*, May 25, 1761.

PAPER MILL.—The Public are once more requested to save their linnen, and cotton-and-linnen RAGS, all that is White and finer than Oznabrigs, two Coppers a pound will be given; and for coarse Whites and cheques, one Copper a pound.—They are taken in at Mr. Caleb Davis's, Merchant, at the Fortifications, and at Mr. John Bois's, near the South Battery, Boston; or at the Paper-Mill in Milton. Any Person that brings one Cwt. of fine Rags to the Mill at one Time, shall have over the Payment *Ten Shillings* old Tenor.—Half a Dollar the Cwt. is given for Rope and Junk.

Choice Press-Paper to be sold at Mr. Davis's abovementioned, and at the Mill, at two Guineas per Groce.—*Boston Gazette*, Feb. 18, 1765.

PLUMBER.—Caleb Champney, begs leave to acquaint the Customers of Mr. Nathaniel Brown, Glazier, deceas'd, That he has opened the shop lately occupied by said Brown, and should be glad to serve them in the Glazing and Plumming Business.—*Boston Gazette*, Dec. 14, 1761.

POWDER MAKER.—Any Gentlemen, Merchants or others, that have any damnifyed Powder, or dust of Powder, either to sell, or to be made of New, They may repair with the same unto Walter Evenden, Powder-maker, at his House in Dorchester, who will either buy it or make it of New for them, on reasonable terms.—*Boston News-Letter*, Nov. 25/Dec. 2, 1706.

PUMPS.—Pumps erected or altered after a new and Easy Method, whereby they will deliver more Water, and with less strength, not being apt to loose water, not at all liable to Freeze, tho' fixed in the most Bleak Places; by the Directions of Rowland Houghton.—*Boston News-Letter*, Sept. 14/21, 1732.

SADDLER'S WARES.—Lately Imported from London, and to be sold by *Isaac Cazneau*, at his House in Water Street, by Wholesale or Retail; All sorts of Sadler's Ware, viz. Cannon-pad Bits, large and small, Snaffle and Trench Bits of all sorts, large and small white Setts, Girth and Straining Webb of all sorts, fine twist Webb, Buckles of all sorts, Lace and Fringe of all Colours,

Women's Reins, all sorts of Whips and Bridles, and Tuff Nails, &c. Also choice *Bohea Tea*, All at a very reasonable Price for ready Money.—*Boston Gazette*, Mar. 2, 1742.

SCALES.—All Sorts of Weights and Skales of the best sort for weighing Money or other Merchandize. Made and Sold by Caleb Ray, Chief Skale-maker of New England; or Skales to be new strung and mended; at the sign of the Skales and Weights in the Alley near to Governours Dock in Boston, at reasonable Rates.—*Boston News-Letter*, Apr. 26/May 3, 1708.

SCALES AND BALANCES.—Jonathan Dakin, Mathematical Balance-maker, at the sign of the Hand & Beam opposite to Dr. Colman's Meeting House, Makes all Sorts of Scale Beams, and likewise mends all that can be mended; where all Gentlemen may be supplied with Beams ready adjusted and sealed as the Law directs.—*Boston Gazette*, Nov. 26, 1745.

SCALE MAKER.—Made and sold by Jonathan Dakin, Mathematical Ballance-maker, at the sign of the Hand and Beam, below the Mill-Bridge in Middle street, Boston. All sorts of Scale Beams ready prov'd and seal'd as the Law directs: likewise Money Scales with Weights, such as Ounces, Penny Weights and Grains; where all Persons in Town or Country, may be supply'd at the lowest Rates for ready Money.—*Boston Gazette*, Aug. 7, 1753.

SCHOOL MASTER.—This is to acquaint the Publick that there is a private school open'd in Boston, near the Orange Tree; wherein is taught the Latin & Greek, (both to young Gentlemen & Ladies) Arithmetick, and divers sorts of Writing, viz. English, German, and Church Texts, the Court, Roman, and Italian Hands. . . . Children sent to said School for their education, shall have the Utmost Care & Diligence used therefor, by the Master thereof: James Hovey, A.B.—*Boston Gazette*, Sept. 7, 1742.

SCHOOL MASTER.—Any Country Town that is destitute of a School-Master, may be supplied with one, on Custumary terms, that has been used to the Business, and will be faithful. Inquire of the Printer.—*Boston Gazette*, Dec. 17, 1754.

SCHOOL MASTER.—This is to give Notice, That there is a School open'd in the White House nigh the Stone Cutters, Draw

Bridge, where Children, young Men and Women, are taught Reading, Writing, Vulgar and Decimal Arithmetick, and French, by THOMAS BRITT.—*Boston Gazette*, May 2, 1757.

SWISS SERVANT MAID.—Ran away from her Mistress *Sarah Warton* of Boston, a Swiss Servant Maid, named Anna Maria Barbarie Collier, aged about 20 years. . . . She commonly us'd to wear on her head a black velvet Cap, after the Dutch mode. . . . —*Boston News-Letter*, Jan. 28/Feb. 4, 1711/12.

SERVANTS.—Tradesmen of all Sorts, and very likely Boys, lately arrived in a Ship from Bristol, all whose time is to be disposed off by Mr. *Thomas Moffatt* in Merchants-Row, Boston.—*Boston News-Letter*, May 17/24, 1714.

IRISH SERVANTS.—Arrived from Ireland per the Globe, Capt. *Nicholas Oursell*, Commander, and to be disposed of by him, the following Protestant Servants—viz. Men, Anchor & Ship Smith, House Carpenters, Ship Joyners and Carver, Cooper, Shoemakers, and Pattoun Maker, Naylors, Lock-Smiths, Currier, Taylor, Book Printer, Silver-Gold Lace Weaver, Silver Smith. And Women, Milliners, Ribband & Lace Weavers, Button Maker, Earthen Ware Potter Maker, House Keepers, Washer Women and Cooks. —*Boston News-Letter*, June 18/25, 1716.

SCOTCH SERVANTS.—"A number of Indented Servants, viz. Weavers, Taylors, Coopers, men and Maid Servants, to be disposed of for a certain Time:—For Terms, inquire on board the Ship *Douglass*, Captain *Montgomery*, from *Ayre* in *Scotland*, now lying at the Long-Wharff in *Boston*."—*Boston Gazette*, Oct. 31, 1763.

SNUFF MAKER.—To be sold, at the Dwelling-House of Peter Barbour, Wing's-Lane, in Boston, the best Snuff by the Pound, Bottle or any greater or lesser Quantity: made from Tobacco of the best Quality: by a Master Workman, who was late foreman to the famous Keppin of Glasgow, and worked with him many years, this Snuff, upon Trial, will be found to be at least as good, and much cheaper than any Foreign Snuff, and it is at the same Time a Manufacture of our own. It is therefore presumed that private Interest, as well as a Regard for the Publick, will give it the Preference to any that is Imported from Abroad. At the same Place, Money or Snuff will be given for Bottles.—*Boston Gazette*, Aug. 16, 1756.

CROWN SOAP.—Made and Sold by *Elizabeth Franklin*, at the Post-Office, the best sort of Crown Soap; also hard soap by Wholesale or Retail, at the lowest Rate.—*Boston Gazette*, Aug. 23, 1756.

SOAP.—William Frobisher, hereby informs his Customers and others, That he is removed from his shop opposite the Governor's, opposite the Blue Ball at the Head of Union-Street, leading to the Green Dragon, Boston: Where he has to sell by Wholesale and Retail, viz. CROWN SOAP warranted as good as any in Town, by Box or Dozen, at 40 s. Old Tenor, choice Hard Soap by Box at 4 s. 6 d. and 5 s. per single pound, soft ditto at 6 d. Also, camphireated and scented Wash-Balls, at Six Coppers each, which are judged to be as good as those from London.—*Boston Gazette*, June 24, 1765.

SPINNING WHEELS.—"New-fashion linen wheels."—*Boston News-Letter*, Mar. 10/17, 1719/20.

SPINNING ON BOSTON COMMON.—On Wednesday an excellent sermon was preached before the *Society for encouraging Industry and employing the Poor*, by the Rev. Samuel Cooper, after which £453, old Tenor was collected and in the afternoon near 300 Spinners, some of them children of 7 or 8 Years old and several of them Daughters of the best Families among us, with their Wheels at Work, sitting orderly in three Rows, made a handsome Appearance on the Common:—The Weavers with a Loom and one at work, on a Stage made for the Purpose, attended with Musick, preceeding the Society as they walk'd in Procession to view the said Spinners. Several thousand Spectators assembled on this Occasion.—*Boston Gazette*, Aug. 14, 1753.

SPINNING SCHOOL.—The Managers of the Spinning School in Charlestown, give publick Notice, that they are ready to employ two good Weavers: such as are disposed to engage in their Service, shall find suitable Encouragement by applying to them at Charlestown aforesaid.—*Boston Gazette*, Aug. 20, 1754.

SPINNING SCHOOL.—Notice is hereby given that the Spinning School in the Manufactory House in *Boston* is again opened: Where any Person who inclines, may learn to Spin grates, and be paid for their spinning after the first three Months; and a Premium of Eighteen Pounds old Tenor will be paid to the four best spinners either in School or Town, by JOHN BROWN.—*Boston Gazette*, Sept. 16, 1762.

SPINNING WHEELS.—These may inform the Publick, that *Wm. Nelson* of *Boston*, makes Spinning Wheels and Reels after the best Manner, near the Salutation, at the North End, with Fidelity and Dispatch.—*Boston Gazette*, Oct. 22, 1754.

FLAX HECHELS.—James Yuill of Boston, advertised that he had furnished himself with a complete set of Hechels for dressing Flax, and a Man from Scotland, bred to that business, and sold flax dressed for spinning at 10 s. old Tenor, to 30 s. per pound. Had "Hechels two sizes finer than any in the Province."—*Boston Gazette*, Oct. 16, 1753.

WOOL CARDS.—On Thursday the 31st Currant, at 5 a Clock in the afternoon, will be exposed to Sale by Inch of Candle at the Coffee-House of Robert Guttridge in Boston, a Parcell of old Woollen Cards, about 22 Dozen, more or less, to be put up at 3 Shillings per dozen; to advance 3 Pence each bidding, and to be seen at the Warehouse of Mr. John George, Merchant, at the Dock.—*Boston News-Letter*, Jan. 21/28, 1705/6.

STATIONARY, SPECTACLES, ETC.—Just Imported from London, and to be sold by *John Perkins*, at his shop in Union Street, nearly opposite to Deacon Grant's . . . All kinds of stationary ware, writing, printing, cartridge, brown and whited brown paper, Spanish pocket-books, pocket ivory memorandum books, temple spectacles, Conrad Windows ditto, green glass ditto, ink and ink powder, Dutch quills, sealing wax and wafers, pocket looking-glasses, large folio demi paper cases, slates and slate pencils, case knives and forks, razors, fine dander combs, horn do, buckling ditto, toupee ditto, with and without cases, account books of all sizes, painted wood ink chests, pewter and lead ditto, ink stands and pots, glass round and square for ditto.—A large and compleat

GRAVESTONE OF MRS. SUSANNAH JAYNE OF MARBLEHEAD
Made by Christian Geyer of Boston

assortment of Paper Hangings for rooms; a general assortment of small books for children.—*Boston Gazette*, June 13, 1763.

STONE CUTTER.—Henry Christian Geyer, Stone Cutter, hereby informs his Customers, and all other Gentlemen, That he has just imported a large Assortment of Stones fit for all sorts of Architect Work; The said Geyer manufactures them in the best Manner; he also has to sell one Marble Hearth, and several Marble Tables, worked by him, etc.—*Boston News-Letter*, Aug. 19, 1762.

STONE CUTTER.—Henry Christian Geyer, hereby informs his Customers, and all other Gentlemen, that he has a large assortment of all Sorts of Stones by him, as follows, viz. for hearths, jambs, steps, tombs, paving, sinks, spouts, and all other sorts of *Connecticut* Stones; he has also a large assortment of Slate-Stones, fit for hearths or graves; Likewise about 120 feet of *Chegnecto* [Nova Scotia] Stone for underpinning: and all other Sorts of Stones, which said *Geyer* manufactures in the best manner.—*Boston News-Letter*, Mar. 17, 1763.

STONE CUTTER.—Henry Christian Geyer, stone cutter, advertised a fine Assortment of Free-stones, slate and marble Stones for Hearths and Jambs; underpinning Stones; marble Frontispieces; marble Tables; slate hearth; gravestones, and all sorts of Stones for architect Work. Also Braintree Stones for underpinnings, fences, or front Walls.—*Boston News-Letter*, Feb. 14, 1765.

STONE CUTTER.—Henry Christian Geyer, near the Tree of Liberty, South End, Boston, Hereby Informs his Customers and all other Gentlemen, all Commissioners, and all Masters of Vessels far and near, That he has by him a considerable Assortment of *Connecticut* Free Stones fit for architect Work, Tomb-Stones, Hearth, and Fire Stones, some Frontice-Pieces work'd in with some the compleatest Mouldings of any in this Town. Spout Stones, Stone Mustard Mills, which will grind Mustard equal to that imported, with little labour, and has been approv'd of in this Town.—Also, a Number of *Connecticut* and *Nova-Scotia* underpining Stones, Slate Hearth Stones, Grave Stones, Drean Stones,—and does all other Sorts of Stone Work too numerous to mention here, he has likewise some fine Marble Slabs for Tables, he Cleans, Polishes and Mends old broken Marbles, all in the best and neatest Manner, and at the most reasonable Rate for Cash or short Credit.—

N. B. Said *Geyer* also makes Stone Coverts either of Marble, Slate or Free Stones, which may be erected in any convenient place in a Gentleman's House, in order to preserve any sort of Provision or Liquor from Spoiling, and are very convenient for Gentlewomen to preserve their Milk, Cream and Cold Victuals.—*Boston News-Letter*, Aug. 13, 1767.

STONE CUTTER.—Henry Christian Geyer, Stone Cutter, near Liberty Tree, South End, *Boston*, Hereby informs his Customers, and other Gentlemen and Ladies, that he carries on his Stone Cutting Business as usual:— . . . The said *Geyer* has thought it necessary to erect the Art of Fuser *Simulacrorum*, or the making all sorts of Images, Birds, Cats, Dogs, & all other sorts of curious Animals, all of Plaster of Paris: He has opened a Shop opposite the South Fish Market, where constant attendance is given, and where Gentlemen and Ladies may depend upon being well used. The said Animals will be sold reasonable for Cash only.—*Boston News-Letter*, Mar. 10, 1768 (*sup.*).

STONE CUTTER.—Henry Christian Geyer, Stone-Cutter, near Liberty-Tree, South-End, Boston, Hereby informs his Customers, and other Gentlemen and Ladies, that besides carrying on the Stone Cutting Business as usual, he carries on the Art and Manufactory of a fuser Simolacrorum, or the making of all sorts of images, viz.

1st. Kings & Queens; 2d. King George & Queen Charlotte; 3d. King & Queen of Denmark; 5th. King & Queen of Sweden;— Likewise a Number of Busts, among which are, Mathew Prior, Homer, Milton, &c.—Also a number of Animals, such as Parrots, Cats, Dogs, Lions, Sheep, with a number of others, too many to enumerate:—Said Geyer also cleans old deficient Animals, and makes them look as well as new, at a reasonable Rate. All the above mentioned Images, Animals, &c. are made of Plaister of Paris of this Country Produce, and Manufactured at a reasonable

## Trades and Occupations 285

Rate by said Geyer, who cleans, mends and polishes Marble of all sorts.

N. B. All Merchants, Masters of Vessels, Country Traders, Shopkeepers, &c. may be supplied with what Quantity of Figures they may have occasion for by giving timely Notice to said Geyer.—*Boston News-Letter*, Feb. 1, 1770.

STONE CUTTER.—A monument has been cut in this Town by Mr. Henry Christian Geyer, Stone-cutter at the South End, to be sent to Connecticut: it is executed in the Composite Order with twisted Pillars, and the other proper Ornaments, having a Cherub's Head on Wings, and the following Label from his Mouth, Rev. XIV. 6, 7. The inscription follows. [This was a monument to Robert Sandeman who died at Danbury, Conn. Apr. 2, 1771.]—*Boston News-Letter*, July 30, 1772.

STAY MAKER.—Women's and Children's Stays, made and Mended after the best and neatest Manner, a Quarter Part cheaper then can be done in Town, for the sake of ready Money, with Fidelity and Dispatch; Opposite to Mr. *Martin's* near the Cornfields, at the Sign of the Stay, by JOHN BANKS.—*Boston Gazette*, Oct. 1, 1754.

STAY MAKER.—John Greer, Stay-Maker, hereby informs his Customers, that he has remov'd from Marblehead to Boston, and lives in the next House to Capt. Sigourney's Distill-House in Blackhorse Lane, near Charlestown-Ferry where he makes stays of the newest Fashion at a reasonable Price. The said John also at any Notice will wait on the Ladies his former Customers, or any other in Town or Country, who please to favour him with their Commands.—*Boston Gazette*, July 17, 1758.

TANNER.—To be sold, at a Tan Yard formerly belonging to Elder Bridgham, deceas'd, by Nathaniel Gardner & Matthew Adams, Washleather and Cloth Coloured Buck Skins for Breeches, and Breeches ready made; Red & Purple Calf Skins for Shoes, Washleather & Shammy Gloves, Sheeps wool & White Leather; all of the best Sort, and kept at such a Distance from any Dwelling-House, that Persons in the Country may be supplyed without the least Danger of Infection from the Small Pox.—*Boston News-Letter*, June 4/11, 1730.

TINMAN'S TOOLS.—To be sold by Savage & Winter at their Vendue House in Wing's Lane, on Wednesday Evening: A compleat set of Tinmen's Tools, large Cranes, Bottle Cranes, and other Tin Ware, a large Pewter Crane, etc.—*Boston Gazette*, Apr. 12, 1756.

TOBACCONIST.—Snuff, Role, Twist, Piggtale and Cut Tobacco, Manufactured the same way as done in Scotland, To be sold at the Sign of the Barber's Poll, on the Long-Wharffe, at a Reasonable Rate.—*Boston News-Letter*, Jan. 14/21, 1730/1.

TOBACCONIST.—Mrs Mary Pelham, (formerly the Widow *Copley*, on the Long Wharff, Tabacconist) is removed into *Lindel's* Row, against the Quaker's Meeting House, near the Upper End of King Street, Boston, where she continues to sell the best Virginia Tobacco, Cut, Pigtail and spun, of all Sorts, by Wholesale or Retail, at the cheapest Rates.—*Boston Gazette*, July 12, 1748.

TOBACCONIST.—Andrew Gillespie, Tobacconist, from London, near Doctor John Clark's, at the North End of Boston; Manufactures and sells by Wholesale and Retail, all sorts of Tobacco, viz. Tea, Cut, Shag and Square Cut; also fine Pigtail, black Role, large Role, and Leaf Tobacco, &c. N. B. Gentlemen or Shopkeepers in the country, shall be served by a Line, as if Present.—*Boston Gazette*, Sept. 17, 1759.

TRANSLATORS SHOP.—These are to give Notice, That Samuel Stebbins, has set up a Translators Shop at the lower End of King-street, Boston, where all Persons may have Boots, Shoes, Pattoons, or any thing belonging to that Trade mended.—*Boston News-Letter*, Oct. 10/17, 1715.

TRUCKING IN BOSTON.—Bylaws were adopted by the Town of Boston in 1727, regulating Trucks and Carts and were in force in 1744, providing that no truck should be driven through the streets and lanes, "whose Sides exceed the length of Sixteen Feet"; nor "with more than Two Horses at a Time"; nor carrying "more than One Tun weight at a Load"; and every driver

WAX FIGURE MADE BEFORE 1748 BY A DAUGHTER
OF REV. JOSHUA GEE OF BOSTON

In the Museum of the Society for the Preservation
of New England Antiquities

should "go by the side of the Thilhorse, with his Halter in his Hand."—*Boston News-Letter,* Mar. 22, 1744.

UMBRILLOES.—All sorts of SILK UMBRILLOES for Ladies, Made in the Neatest and newest Fashion: to be sold at the *Lion & Bell* in Marlborough-street, Boston.—*Boston Gazette,* May 31, 1756.

UMBRILLOS.—Silk Umbrilloes for Ladies, made in the neatest Manner, to be sold at the *Lion* and *Bell* in Marlborough Street, Boston.—*Boston Gazette,* May 15, 1758.

UMBRILLOS.—Umbrillos of all sorts made and sold at the Golden-Cock, Marlboro' Street, Boston. Ladies that have silk by them, may have it made up at said Place.—WANTED a Lad of 14 Years, as an Apprentice to the Braziers Business.—*Boston Gazette,* May 25, 1761.

UMBRILLOES, with Ivory or Bone Sockets and Sliders, and Mehogany Sticks, made in the neatest Manner by *Isaac Greenwood*—Ivory Turner, next Door to Dr. John Clark's at the North End of Boston. He also covers Old sticks at a reasonable Rate.—*Boston Gazette,* June 20, 1763.

WAX WORK.—This is to give Notice, That there is to be shewn by Mr John Dyer, at the Head of Love's Lane, near the New North Meeting House, Boston, a very curious set of Wax Work, being a lively Representation of Margaret, Countess of Heininburg, who had 365 Children at one Birth, occasioned by the rash Wish of a poor Beggar Woman, who is represented asking her charity. Price 6 Pence.—*Boston News-Letter,* Nov. 30/Dec. 6, 1733.

WAX WORK.—The Royal Wax-Work is to be seen at the House of Mr. Thomas Brooks Shopkeeper, in Draw Bridge-street, near the Town-Dock, Boston.—*Boston Gazette,* May 7/14, 1739.

ROYAL WAX-WORK.—Last Week died in Concord, aged upwards of a Hundred Years, Mrs *Sarah Brigs,* formerly a noted Shop Keeper in Boston, and Proprietor of that curious Piece of Workmanship, call'd the Royal Wax-Work.—*Boston Gazette,* Feb. 10, 1747.

WAX WORK.—This may inform young Gentlewomen in Town and Country, that early in the Spring, Mrs Hiller designs to open a Boarding-School at the House where she lives, in Fish street, at the North End of Boston, where they may be taught Wax Work, Transparent and Filligree, Painting upon Glass, Japanning, Quill-Work, Feather-Work, and Embroidering with Gold and Silver, and several other sorts of Work not here enumerated, and may be supplied with Patterns and all sorts of Drawing, and Materials for their Work.—*Boston Evening Post*, Feb. 15, 1748.

WAX WORK.—This Notifies the Public, that the Wax-work shown in this Town formerly by Mrs Briggs, and lately by Mrs Brooks, but has been out of Town this eight or ten years, is now to be shown (with a considerable Addition of Images and Dress) by Mrs Hiller, in Cambridge-Street, leading to West Boston, at Six Pence a piece, Lawful Money, for Men and Women, and Four Pence for Children; where also young Gentlewomen are taught Wax-work, Filligree, Transparent, &c. &c. and boarded or half boarded as they see Cause.—*Boston Evening Post*, Apr. 22, 1751.

WAX WORK.—This is to notify the Publick, that there is a fine Sett of Wax-work, consisting of Kings, Queens, &c. at full-Length; to be shown by Mrs. *Hiller* in *Cambridge-Street*, leading to West *Boston*, at *Six Pence* a Piece, Lawful Money, for Men and Women, and *four* Pence for Children; where is also to be taught Wax-work, Painting upon Glass, Quill-work, Feather-Work, Filligree and Transparent, Tentstitch and other fine Works; And young Ladies boarded or half boarded.—*Boston Gazette*, Apr. 30, 1751.

WAX WORK.—Abagail Hiller, hereby gives Notice, that she is removed to a House in Hanover-street, next Door to Mr Gersham Flagg's, near the Orange-Tree, where she still continues to Board young Ladies, and also teach them Wax-Work, Transparent, Filligree, Feather-Work, Quill-Work, Japanning upon Glass, Embroidering, Tent Stitch, &c. Where also may be seen Kings, Queens, &c. in Wax Work as formerly.—*Boston Gazette*, June 11, 1754.

WAX WORK.—This is to give notice, That Mrs. Hiller still

continues to Keep School in Hannover-Street, a little below the *Orange-Tree*, where young Ladies may be taught Wax work, Transparent and Filligree, painting on Glass, Quill work and Feather work, Japanning, Embroidering with Silver and Gold, Tenstich, &c. Likewise the *Royal Family* to be seen in Wax work. Also Board and Lodging to be had at the cheapest Rate.—*Boston Gazette*, May 26, 1755.

WAX WORK.—This is to give NOTICE, That Mrs Hiller keeps school to learn young Ladies all sorts of Work, and likewise board and half-board; The Wax work to be seen new drest; any Gentlemen or Ladies that incline to see it must come quickly, for it is soon to be mov'd out of Town; Drawing of all Sorts to be done at the cheapest Rate.—*Boston Gazette*, May 24, 1756.

WAX WORK.—Whereas the Curious Waxen Images, shewn by Abigail Hiller in Hanover Street, will soon be removed out of Town; Notice thereof is hereby given to such as are desirous of seeing them, that so they may not loose the opportunity of gratifying their Curiosity.—*Boston Gazette*, Aug. 29, 1757.

WAX WORK.—"New York, June 10. On Monday evening, about 8 o'clock, a Fire was discovered in the House of Mrs. Wright, the ingenious artist in Wax-Work, and proprietor of the Figures so nearly resembling the life, which have for some time past been exhibited in this City to general satisfaction. The accident happened when Mrs. Wright was abroad, and only Children at home, and was occasioned by one of them accidentally setting fire to a curtain inclosing some of the Figures, which soon communicated to the cloaths, and the wax of which they were composed. The neighbours immediately assembled, and gave all possible assistance in removing and preserving the household Goods. The fire engines play'd into the House and soon extinguished the flames; But, tho' most of the Wax-Work was destroyed, amounting to several hundred pounds, yet she was so fortunate as to save the curious Piece of the Rev. Mr. Whitefield, the Pennsylvania Farmer, and some others."—*Boston News-Letter, June* 20, 1771 (*sup.*).

WAX WORK.—The *Mercury Packet*, Capt. Dillon, sailed from

New York for London, on Feb. 3, 1772, in which went passenger "the ingenious Mrs. Wright, whose skill in taking likenesses, expressing the Passions, and many curious Devices in Wax Work, has deservedly recommended her to public Notice, expecially among Persons of Distinction, from many of whom we hear she carries Letters to their Friends in England."—*Boston News-Letter*, Feb. 13, 1772.

WEAVING.—TEN GUINEAS Are deposited in the Hands of the Printers to be disposed of in the following PREMIUMS. 1st. For the best Piece of CLOTH of 12 Yards long and seven Quarters wide, that shall be made in this Province and offer'd to Sale at the Printing Office the last Week in *April* next; the Fineness, Dressing and Colour, all to be considered in the Determination, FOUR GUINEAS. 2ndly. For the best Piece of GERMAN SERGE (so called) of 30 Yards long and one Yard wide; Fineness, Dressing and Colour, as before, TWO GUINEAS. 3dly. For the best Piece of SAGATHY 30 Yards long and half-ell wide; Fineness, Dressing and Colour as before, TWO GUINEAS. 4thly. For the best Piece of SHALLOON 30 Yards long, and one Yard wide; Fineness, Dressing and Color as before, TWO GUINEAS.

The several Articles are to be offer'd for Sale at the Office of the Printers of this Paper, the last Week in *April* next. The PREMIUMS to be determined by three Gentlemen, who will be desired to attend for that Purpose.—*Boston Gazette*, Oct. 16, 1769.

WEAVING.—On Tuesday next, at Ten o'Clock in the Morning, will be sold by PUBLIC VENDUE, at the Province Manufactory House, all the Looms, Warping, Twisting and other Machines, Dying Presses, &c. belonging to the Estate of *William Molineaux*, deceased. R. GOULD, Auctioneer.—*Boston News-Letter*, Dec. 16, 1774.

WHITE SMITH.—Nathaniel Cape, White Smith from London, living near the New Brick Meeting House.—Makes Smoak Jacks that will go with the Smoak or Draught of a Chimney, that will roast any Meat under 60 weight, without any Weights or Trouble in winding: and other Sorts of Jacks; also mends and cleans old

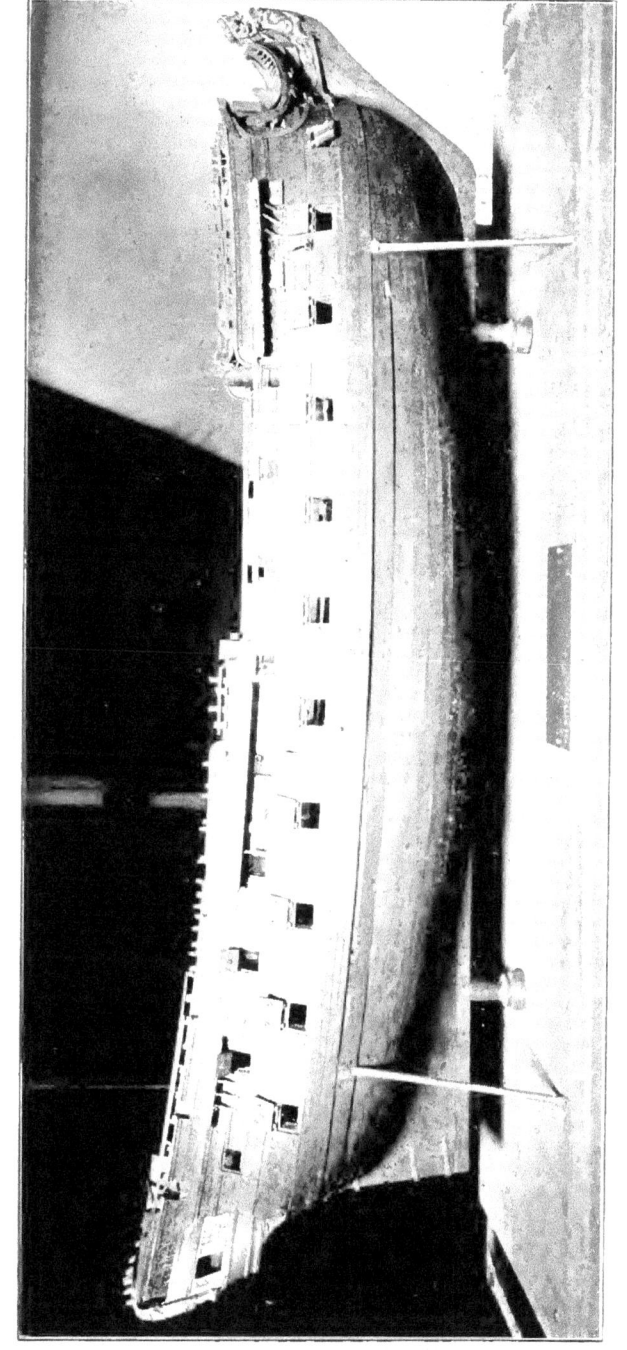

Model of H.M.S. "America," 44 guns, built at Portsmouth, N.H., in 1749
Model in the Portsmouth Athenæum, Portsmouth, N.H.

Jacks: Any Gentlemen that will favour him with their Custom, may depend on being well served, by NATHANIEL CAPE.—*Boston Gazette*, Aug. 15, 1757.

WIG MAKER.—Made by James Mitchell, at his Shop in King-street, next door to Richard Dana, Esq: After the best and newest Fashion: Tye Wiggs, full bottom Wiggs, Brigadiers, Spencers, Cues, Bag Wiggs, Albemarles, Scratches, cut and curl'd Wiggs; also black Bags, and Rambilees for Wiggs: And has all sorts of Pomatum. He also cuts and dresses Hair after the London, French, Spanish, or Italian Fashion. And makes all sorts of Gold, Silver, or Common wire Wiggs. The said Mitchell has lately visited and work'd at the most noted Cities in Europe.—*Boston Gazette*, Dec. 18, 1753.

WIG MAKER.—John Tucker, next below the Golden Fleece in King-street, Boston: Makes in the best and neatest Manner, and sells at a moderate Rate, all sorts of Wiggs, as Cues, Ramilies, Brigadiers, Scratch-Curls, Scratch-Cutt, ditto, Cut and Bobs, and all Sorts of Campaign Wiggs. Said Tucker has just Imported the newest Fashion Bags of all sizes, and Pins for Gentlemen's Hair of all Colours: where all Gentlemen may be supplied cheap for Cash.—*Boston Gazette*, Apr. 18, 1757.

WOOD CARVER.—William Shute, carver, of Boston, settlement of estate.—*Boston Gazette*, June 3, 1746.

WOOD CARVER.—*Isaac Dupee*, Carver, Advertises his Customers and others, that since the late Fire (on Dock Square) he has opened a Shop the North side of the Swing-Bridge, opposite to *Thomas Tyler's*, Esq; where Business will be carried on as usual with Fidelity and Dispatch.—*Boston Gazette*, Feb. 9, 1761.

## SWEETMEATS AND PROVISIONS

CONFECTIONARY.—Wet sweetmeats, pomcitron, raisins, spices, tea and snuff were sold by Zabdiel Boylston, as his Shop at the head of Dock Square, Boston.—*Boston News-Letter*, Mar. 5/12, 1710/11.

ANCHOVIES (Gorgona) and Cases of Pickle.—*Boston News-Letter*, May 9/16, 1715.

SWEETMEATS.—Mackeroons of Geneva by the Pound, sweet waters for the Ladies. Orange Flower Butter, best Levant Coffee, Bohea Tea, Calmaco by the Bottle or Doz., and Red Herrings by the Hundred or Barrell, to be sold very reasonably by Capt. Arthur Savage, at his House in Brattle-Street, where is to be shewn by William Nichols, a Lyon of Barbary, with many other Rarities, the like never before in America.—*Boston News-Letter*, Nov. 26/Dec. 3, 1716.

SUGAR, double-refined, advertised at 3 s. per lb. by the loaf.—*Boston News-Letter*, Apr. 16/23, 1724.

SUGAR, single-refined loaf, advertised at 2 s. per lb.—*Boston News-Letter*, Apr. 2/8, 1725.

CANDY.—To be Sold at Mr. James Smith's Sugar Refining House adjoining to Mr. Colman's Meeting House, all Sorts of Loaf Sugar, Powder Sugar, White & Brown Candy, Fine & Course Syrrups, Molasses, & all sorts of Brown Sugar by the Hogshead or Barrell.—*Boston Gazette*, Apr. 11/18, 1726.

CONFECTIONER.—John Pitts, "confectioner," mentioned.—*Boston News-Letter*, Aug. 1/8, 1728.

BOHEA TEA advertised at 45 s. per pound.—*Boston News-Letter*, Dec. 25/Jan. 1, 1729/30.

GROCER.—JOHN MERRETT, Grocer. *At the Three Sugar Loaves and Cannister near the Town-House*, Boston. SELLS Cocoa, Chocolate, Tea, Bohea and Green, Coffee raw and roasted, all sorts of loaf, powder and Muscovado Sugar, Sugar-Candy brown and white, candy'd Citron, Pepper, Pimienta or Alspice, white Pepper, red Pepper, Cinnamon, Cloves, Mace, Nutmegs, Ginger race and powder, Raisins, Currants, Almonds sweet and bitter, Prunes, Figgs, Rice, ground Rice, pearl Barley, Sago, Starch, Hair-Powder, powder Blue, Indigo, Annis, Corriander & Carraway Seeds, Saltpetre, Brimstone, flower of Brimstone, all sorts of Snuff, Allum, Rozin, Beeswax, Tamarines, Castile Soap, fine Florence Oyl, Vinegar, Capers, Olives, Anchovies, and fine English pickled Wallnuts, Icing-Glass, Hartshorn Shavings and burnt Gums, &c.

Also Painters Colours, Oyls and Tools, Dye Woods and other Dyer's Wares, Cotton, by wholesale & retail at very reasonable Rates.

N. B. *The said* John Merrett *has lately Imported fresh Supplys of all sorts.—Boston News-Letter*, Dec. 7/14, 1732.

GROCER.—John Merrett, Grocer, *At the Three Sugar-Loaves and Canister in King-street, near the Town-house Boston Sells Cocao, Chocolate, Tea Bohea and Green, Coffee raw and roasted. All sorts of Loaf, Powder and Muscovado Sugar, Sugar Candy brown and white, Candid Cittron, Pepper, Pimienta or all Spice, white Pepper, red Pepper, Cinamon, Cloves, Mace, Nutmegs, Ginger Race and Powder, Raisins, Currants, Almonds sweet and bitter, Prunes, Figs, Rice, ground Rice, Pearl and French Barley, Sago, Starch, Hair-powder, Powder-blew, Indigo, Annis Corriander and Carraway Seeds, Saltpetre, Brimston, Flower of Brimston. All sorts of Tobacco and Snuff, Rozin, Bee's-Wax, Tarmarins, Castille Soap, Olive Oyl, Fine Florence Oyl, Capers, Anchoves*, &c.

Also *Painters Colours, Oyls and Tools, Dye-woods, Allum, Copperas and other Dyers Wares,* &c. *by Wholesale and Retail at reasonable Rates.—Boston Gazette*, Nov. 18/25, 1734.

FIGS, at £3. 10s. per hundred.—*Boston News-Letter*, Dec. 26/Jan. 2, 1734/5.

SUGAR CANDY.—To be Sold by John Merrett, at the Sign of the Three Sugar Loaves & Cannisters, near the Town House in King-Street in Boston: . . . Sugar Candy, Spices, . . . Hair Powder, Brazelleto, Logwood, Madder, ground Redwood, Nutgauls, Potash English and Flemish, Argol, all Sorts of Gums; Also, all Sorts of Painter's Colours, Water Colours, Linseed Oyl, Nut Oyl, Oyl of Turpentine and Varnish, Brushes & Pencils; by Wholesale & Retaile at Reasonable Rates. . . . —*Boston Gazette*, Oct. 31/Nov. 7, 1737.

CHOCOLATE.—Italian Chocolate ready prepared with sugar, for sale.—*Boston Gazette*, Mar. 5/12, 1739.

DRIED FRUITS.—To be Sold, at the cross'd Pistols in Fish Street, by Obadiah Cookson, Raisins, Currants, Turkey Figgs, Prunes, Sugars of most Kinds, Loaf and Muscovado, Coffee, Chocolate, Green and Bohea Teas, Sago, French and Pearl Barley, Citron, preserv'd Ginger, Race and Ground Ginger, Pepper, Alspice, Nutmegs, Cinnamon, Cloves, Mace, the very best Indigo, Figg-Indigo, Red-Wood, Log-Wood, Salt-Petre, Allum, Copperas, Brimstone, Rozin, Starch, Rice, Flower, Oatmeal, best Scots Snuff, by the Dozen, single Bottle or Ounce, best Plain, Jews, and other Snuff, Hair-Powder, Kyan Pepper, and other Grocery's, neat Dutch Pipes, Hempseed for Birds, Bay and Rock Salt, by the Hogshead or Bushel, most sorts of Bottles from four Gallons to half Pints by the Groce, &c. best Velvet and other Corks very cheap by the Sack, Cotton Wool, Wool Cards by the Groce or Dozen, Card-Wire, and Tacks, Blew Melting Pots, &c. —*Boston News-Letter*, Oct. 7/14, 1742.

PRICE CURRANT of Provisions in the Town of Boston, December, 1748: Beef, per Quart. 18 *d.* to 22 *d.*; Pork, 2 *s.* 6 *d.*; Mutton, 18 *d.* to 2 *s.*; Veal, 2 *s.* 6 *d.* to 3 *s.* 6 *d.*; Turkeys, 3 *s.* to 4 *s.* 6 *d.*; Geese, from 15 *s.* to 20 *s.*; Dunghill Fowls, 6 *s.* to 10 *s.*; Butter, 6 *s.* to 6 *s.* 6 *d.*; Cheese, 3 *s.* 6 *d.* to 4 *s.*; Milk, 2 *s.* per quart; Eggs, 5 *s.* per Dozen; Apples, 30 *s.* to 40 *s.* per bush.; Potatoes, 20 *s.* to 30 *s.*; Indian Meal, 23 *s.* per bush.; Cyder, 3 *l.* to 5 *l.* per bar.; Charcoal, 3 *s.* to 4 *s.* per bush.; Wood, 3 *l.* 10 *s.* to 5 *l.* per load; faggots, 3 *l.* to 3 *l.* 15 *s.* per load.—*Boston Evening Post*, Jan. 11, 1748.

CANDY.—White and Brown Candy, sold at James Smith's Sugar House, Boston.—*Boston Gazette*, June 4, 1751.

CURRANTS.—Any Person that has a mind to take a walk in the

Garden at the Bottom of the Common, to eat Currants, shall be Kindly Welcome for Six Pence a piece.—*Boston News-Letter*, July 10/17, 1735.

BOHEA TEA, from India House, London, at 5/4 per lb.; French indigo, at 8/1 per lb.—*Boston Gazette*, Feb. 6, 1758.

OYSTERS.—"Caggs of Pickled Oysters, also Pickled Cucumbers and Peppers, and Ketchup by the bottle," advertised.—*Boston Gazette*, Oct. 1, 1759.

DRIED FRUITS.—Green & Walker, at the North Corner of Queen Street, advertised recent importations, including: new raisins in casks, jar raisins, Turkey figs, Jordan Almonds, Durham & Young's Mustard, a great variety of spices, white and red lead, Spanish brown and whiting, ground Madder, Argot, nutgalls, verdegrease, Indigo, Poland and common starch, 15, 18 and 22 inch London pipes, a few sets of Money scales, etc.—*Boston News-Letter*, Nov. 18, 1762.

SPICES.—Just Imported, Poland Starch by the Cask, 15 and 18 Inches, London Pipes per Box, Spices of all Sorts, new Currents per Cask, Allum, Copperas, Isinglass, Crates Apothecaries Phials, French Indego, Powder and Stone Blue, Bohea & Hyson Tea, Turkey Figgs, Boxes Young's & best Durham Mustard, Kippen's Snuff, Saltpetre, neat Mahogany Trays, Tea boards and Tea Chests, Tea Kettles and Lamps, very handsome Knives and Forks, Buckles, Candlesticks, &c. —. Pins No. 4 & 12, a fine Assortment of japann'd Ware, China and Knife Baskets, Chimney Tile, Sets Glass Salvers—WINES in Quarter-casks.—English Duck, Cordage, Stone Lime per Hogshead, House-brushes—and a very large and compleat assortment of China and Glass Ware, too many Articles to enumerate—Nests of Sugar-chests, chests Florence Oil, Writing Paper per Ream, &c. and Sold Cheap by SAMUEL FLETCHER, near the Draw-Bridge, Boston.—*Boston News-Letter*, July 17, 1766.

LEMONS.—To be Sold by John Crosby, Lemmon Trader near the Sign of the Lamb, Fresh Lisbon Lemmons at 12 s. per dozen; also a number pairs double flint cut Salts, at sterling cost 5 s. pair; beautiful Paper for Rooms of many sorts; also enamell'd Snuff

Boxes made of Copper in Imitation of Hogs—Dogs—Lions—Wolves—Tygers—Birds—etc.—*Boston News-Letter,* Apr. 28, 1768.

CONFECTIONER.—PETER LORENT, Confectioner and Distiller from London, At Mr Piemont's in King-Street, Boston, Takes this Method to acquaint Gentlemen and Ladies, that he will preserve a Great Variety of Fruits, and also make Cordial and Syrup every Thing in as great Perfection as in Europe, having worked in England, France, and Italy,—Cakes of all Kinds,—Maqueroons, canded Fruits and dried in their Colours, Rock-candy upon them, Syrup of Capilary & Orgat, Lemons and others, at the most reasonable Rates. Sugar confect and Sugar Plumbs of all sorts wholesale and retail.

He will give a reasonable Price for Angelico, Pepper-Mint, Fennel and Fruits of all Kinds, Plumbs, Pears, Peaches, and Apricots, before they are ripe.—*Boston News-Letter,* July 13, 1769.

## MUSIC AND MUSICAL INSTRUMENTS

MUSICAL INSTRUMENTS.—This is to give Notice that there is lately sent over from London, a choice Collection of Musickal Instruments, consisting of Flaguelets, Flutes, Haut-Boys, Bass-Viols, Violins, Bows, Strings, Reads for Haut-Boys, Books of Instruction for all these Instruments, Books of ruled Paper. To be Sold at the Dancing School of Mr *Enstone* in Sudbury-Street near the Orange-Tree, Boston. *Note*, Any Person may have all Instruments of Musick mended, or Virgenalls and Spinnets Strung and Tuned at a reasonable rate, and likewise may be taught to Play on any of these Instruments abovementioned; dancing taught by a true and easier method than has been heretofore.—*Boston News-Letter*, Apr. 16/23, 1716.

VIRGINALS, pair of, for sale.—*Boston News-Letter*, Nov. 26/Dec. 3, 1724.

CONCERT OF MUSIC.—On Thursday the 30th of this instant December, there will be performed a Concert of Musick on sundry Instruments at Mr. Pelham's great Room being the House of the late Doctor Noyes near the Inn Tavern. Tickets to be delivered at the place of performance at Five Shillings each, the Concert to begin exactly at six a Clock, and no Tickets will be delivered after Five the Day of Performance. N. B. There will be no admittance after Six.—*Boston News-Letter*, Dec. 16/23, 1731.

PSALMODY AND JAPANNING.—Whereas John Waghorne, now resident in Boston, has been often requested by some of the principal Gentlemen of this Town, to instruct their Children in vocal Psalmody, with a Promise of Encouragement: And he having now a suitable House for the purpose, therefore this is to Inform such Persons who think proper to send their Children, that said Waghorn intends to instruct Youth in the Gamut and Measure of Notes, &c. according to the Method of the famous Dr. Crafts, late Organist and Composer to his Majesty's Chappel, and will attend on Monday, Wednesday, and Friday, from 4 to 6 o'clock in the Afternoon.

He also will teach Ladies to Japan in the newest Method invented for that Purpose, which exceeds all other Japaning for Beauty.

He has had the Honour to teach several Ladies of the first Quality in England, who all did express the greatest Satisfaction for that agreable and delightful Art.

N. B. The said Waghorn is to be treated with at his dwelling House, opposite to the great Trees, at the South End of this Town, and purposes to begin his undertaking when he has a suitable Number of Subscribers, in order to make the Learning easy to each scholar.—*Boston Gazette*, July 9/16, 1739.

SINGING LESSONS.—Any Person minded to learn the Art of Psalmody may apply themselves to *Josiah Carter*, living in Union street, Boston; by whom they may be instructed at 40 s. old Tenor, a Quarter, paying at Entrance the first Quarter.—*Boston Gazette*, May 3, 1748.

MUSIC TEACHER.—Notice is hereby given to the Publick, That JOHN RICE, lately from New-York, & Organist of Trinity-Church in this Town, proposes to teach young Gentlemen and Ladies, Vocal and Instrumental Musick, viz. Spinnet, or Harpsicord, Violin, German Flute, &c. and is to be spoke with at Mrs Harvey's, behind Capt. Tyng's, in Rows' Lane.—*Boston Gazette*, Nov. 27, 1753.

ORGAN AND HARPSICORD.—Lewis Deblois of Boston advertised for sale "a curious Ton'd, double key'd, new harpsicord, just imported in Capt. *Millard* from London. Is esteem'd the Master Piece of the famous *Falconer*. Also has for Sale, an Organ, made by Mr. *Thomas Johnston* of this Town, formerly made Use of in Concert-Hall, and can be recommended.—An abatement of Ten Guineas will be made, (from the real Value of said Instrument) if bought and made Use of for any Congregation in this Town.— *Boston Gazette*, June 27, 1763.

ORGAN made by Thomas Johnston for sale, also a harpsicord. —*Boston Gazette*, July 25, 1763.

MUSICK, & INSTRUMENTS, To be disposed of by a Gentleman from *LONDON*; A Large and curiousCollection of it inManuscript, (warranted correct) and in Print, viz Italian and English Opera's and Songs in Score, and the prettiest of 'em transpos'd into easy Keys for the German Flute, Violin, or Harpsicord, &c to accompany the Voice; they may be play'd either as Lessons, or with the thoro'Bass in theNature of Venetian Ballads in two Parts; they are by Leo, Pergolese, Hasse, Galuppi, Handel, &c. Concerto's; by Vivaldi, Tessarini,Rugere Alberti, Corbets, 35 grand ones (which imitates the Tastes of all Nations in the World) Hasse, Boismortier, &c. McGibbon and Carusi's famous and easy Trios; likewise Corelli's, Hasse's, Granom's, Bessossi's, Dotzel, Figlio, Humphreys &c. Camini andGerardi very pretty and easy Duets; likewise Seiss, Dotzel's 12Nocturals. The 55 new Militia Marches, Burney, Nandot, Putti, Musicæ Spiritus by Handel; 40 Tattoos and Night Peices for serenading (18Divertimenti and the delightful Pocket Companion, 2 Books for 2 Guittars) &c. GreatVariety for 2Violoncello's, Col Reid's pretty and easy Solo's, 2 Vols. likewise Corelli, Hasse, Castrueci 2Vol. Geminiani, Quants, Oswald's 4Seasons in 2 or 3 Parts; Veracini, Pepusch, L'æeillet, &c. All the old and new Scotch Songs and Tunes, with their Variations and Words by Messirs. Rutherford, Oswald McGibbon and Bremner in 27 Vols. Polly (and otherOperas) by Mr. Gay, with 71 Songs accompanied with the Harpsicord, or any Instrument, at 30s O. T. The merryMountebank, viz. humourous Songs for theVoice and Harpsicord, &c. at 15s. O. T. Pasquali's new Art of fingering the Harpsicord, likewise his Rules for learning the thoroughBass without a Master; Handel, Smith and Roseingraves Lessons, Handel and Felton's Organ Concerto's, Lampes 60 musical Magaz with the Harpsicord with vast large and most beautiful Copper Plates to each Song, a great Collection of old and new printed English single Songs with their Musick; the Fiddle new modell'd (with 25 copper plates) or rules to play it well without a master; old and new country Dances, Minuets, Scots Reels, Marches, Hornpipes, &c. in different books at 10s. O. T. each. Tutors for Singing and for all Instruments singly, and for transposing Musick into proper Keys for your Instrument, by Rutherford, Johnson and Thompson; pocket and large rul'd books for the Harpsicord, &c. some of the pocket ones are almost filled with wrote Songs, Solo's, Duets, Marches, Jigs, Minuets, &c. some good German Flutes at 3 Dollars apiece, others with 2 or 3 middle pieces to lower the pitch to accompany the Voice, or any Wind Instrument, and a Voice Flute; common Flutes of all sizes at a Dollar each, and upwards, some of 'em exceeding good; Hautboys & Reeds; Fiddles, lined & corner stopt, to strengthen 'em, and to prevent their unglewing in hot, or moist weather, from 3 Dollars and upwards, some of 'em are the best made in London; a Tenor Violin; a fine 6 string Bass Viol for a Girl, with its Case; Fiddle Bows (and Giardini's new invented ones) of all lengths, from 20s. O. T. and upwards, and spare Nuts; Fiddle (& Bass Viol) Bridges, well season'd, at 40s O. T. per Doz. Pegs, Tail-pieces & Breechpins; Fiddle & Bass Viol Strings of all sizes and prices, from 30s. O. T. a bundle (viz. 30 strings) and upwards; with a great many other things in the musical way. The above mostly collected for his own use, in his Travels thro' Italy, Germany, France, Spain, and elsewhere; and now disposing of, as he is to return soon to England. A new Map of Virginia and Maryland, with part of the Jerseys, Pennsylvania, and North Carolina, on 8 sheets, with the Waggon Roads up to Pittsburg, and the cross Roads; very useful for those who travel to the southward.—N. B. He lodges at Mr. *Richardson's*, the bottom of Cold Lane, by Hanover street.—*Boston Gazette*, June 28, 1764.

SPINET (new) made by Hitchcock sold at auction.—*Boston Gazette*, Aug. 12, 1765.

HARPSICHORD MAKER.—John Harris, who arrived in Capt. Calef [from London], begs leave to inform the public, that he makes and sells all sorts of *Harpsichords* and *Spinnets*. Likewise mends, repairs, new strings, and tunes the said instruments, in the best and neatest manner. Any Gentlemen and ladies that will honour him with their custom, shall be punctually waited upon. He lives at Mr Gavin Brown's Watch-maker, North-side of King Street.—*Boston Chronicle*, Nov. 14, 1768.

HARPSICHORD MAKER.—It is with pleasure we inform the Public, That a few days since was shipped for Newport, a very curious Spinnet, being the first ever made in America, the performance of the ingenious Mr John Harris, of Boston (Son of the late Mr Joseph Harris, of London, Harpsichord and Spinnet Maker), and in every respect does Honour to that Artist, who now carries on Business at his House, a few Doors Northward of Dr Clark's, North end of Boston.—*Boston Gazette*, Sept. 18, 1769. [This instrument was in the possession, in 1877, of Miss Catharine Crook, 111 Spring St., Newport.]

FRENCH HORNS.—Just Imported from London, per Captain Lyde, and to be sold by Gilbert Deblois, at his Shop opposite the Bottom of School-street, only for ready Money.

French Horns, Bassoons, Hautboys, Fifes, Drums, English & German Flutes, Violins, Roman strings, Bows, Space Reeds, with *Tutors* for each sort of Instrument, which are so very plain & easy as the Learner may soon make himself Master of it.—also

A great Assortment of *Gold* and *Silver* Regimental & Train of Artillery Laces, Bindings, Shoulder Knots, Apaulets, Hat Loops, &c. with a few genteel Gold and Silver Spangled Laces, and Coat & Waistcoat Frogs or Loops, with Buttons, &c—Likewise Swords, Hangers, Belts and very neat Powder Flasks.—*Boston News-Letter*, Sept. 9, 1773.

# MOVING PICTURES

THE ITALIAN MATCHEAN, or Moving Picture, wherein are to be seen, Wind-Mills and Water Mills moving round, Ships sayling on the Sea, and several curious Figures, very delightful to behold, to be daily shewn by Mr. *Nehemiah Partridge*, at his House in Water-Street, Boston, at the Head of Oliver's Dock, for Twelve Pence a Piece.—*Boston News-Letter*, Mar. 7/14, 1714/15.

PICTURE MACHINE.—Whereas there is lately arrived from Holland a certain Machine by which is presented to the sight a Prospect of Landskips, beautiful Seats, Water Works, Alcoves, Groves, and Sea Pieces; a Curiosity most accurately done, and represented in such a beautiful Manner, as will attract the Minds of the ingenious, and delight the Fancy most agreeably.

Therefore this serves to advertise the Curious, and such as are disposed to view the said Machine consisting of fourteen distinct Pieces taken (from Things Real) That at the Dwelling House of Mr Hubbert the Carver in Common Street near the Granary in Boston.

Attendance will be given on Mondays, Wednesdays, and Fridays, from three a Clock to six in the Afternoon of the said Days weekly, each Person paying One Shilling and Six Pence for the View of the whole Set of Prospects.—*Boston Gazette*, Apr. 7/14, 1740.

ELECTRICAL EXPERIMENTS.—This is to give notice to the curious, that the Electrical Experiments with Methodical Lectures, exhibited last Winter near the Blue-Ball, are now exhibited in Orange-Street, a little below Concert-Hall, in the House where the Wax-Work is shewn: Price, One PISTARENE. By JOSEPH HILLER, *Jeweller*.

☞ All who would attend these LECTURES, are desired to improve every dry Evening for this purpose; because the Season for these Experiments will continue but a few Weeks: They are also desired to send for Tickets in the Morning.—*Boston Gazette*, Feb. 23, 1756.

THE MICROCOSM.—To be Seen (for a short Time) at the House of Mr. *William Fletcher*, Merchant, *New-Boston*; That ELABORATE AND MATCHLESS PILE OF ART, Called, THE MICROCOSM, Or, The WORLD in MINIATURE.

*Built in the Form of a* Roman *Temple, after Twenty-two Years,close Study and Application, by the late ingenious Mr.* HENRY BRIDGES, *of* London; *who, having received the Approbation and Applause of the Royal Society,* &c. *afterwards made considerable Additions and Improvements; so that the Whole, being now compleatly finished, is humbly offered to the Curious of this City, as a Performance which has been the Admiration of every Spectator, and proved itself by its singular Perfections the most instructive as well as entertaining Piece of Work in* Europe.

*A* PIECE *of such complicated Workmanship, and that affords such a Variety of Representations (tho' all upon the most simple Principles) can but very imperfectly be described in Words the best chosen; therefore 'tis desired, what little is said in this Advertisement may not pass for an Account of the* MICROCOSM, *but only what is thought meerly necessary in the Title of such an Account,* &c.

ITS *outward Structure is a most beautiful Composition of Architecture, Sculpture and Painting. The inward Contents are as judiciously adapted to gratify the Ear, the Eye, and the Understanding; for it plays with great Exactness several fine Pieces of Musick, and exhibits, by an amazing Variety of moving Figures, Scenes diversified with natural Beauties, Operations of Art, of humanEmployments and Diversions,all passing as in real Life,* &c.

1. SHEWS all the celestial Phænomena, with just Regard to the proportionable Magnitudes of their Bodies, the Figures of their Orbits, and the Periods of their Revolutions, with the Doctrine of JUPITER's Satellites, of Eclipses, and of the Earth's annual and diurnal Motions, which are all rendered familiarly intelligible. In Particular will be seen the Trajectory and Type of a Comet, predicted by Sir ISAAC NEWTON, to appear the Beginning of 1758; likewise a Transit of VENUS over the Sun's Disk, the Sixth of

*June* 1761; also a large and visible Eclipse of the Sun, the First of *April* 1764, *&c.*

2. ARE the nine Muses playing inConcert on divers musical Instruments, as the Harp, Hautboy, BassViol, *&c.*

3. Is ORPHEUS in the Forest, playing on his Lyre, and beating exact Time to each Tune; who, by his exquisite Harmony, charms even the wild Beasts.

4. Is aCarpenter's Yard, wherein the variousBranches of that Trade are most naturally represented, *&c.*

5. Is a delightful Grove, wherein are Birds flying, and in many other Motions warbling forth their melodious Notes, *&c.*

6. Is a fine Landskip, with a Prospect of the Sea, where Ships are sailing with a proportionable Motion according to their Distance. On theLand areCoaches, Carts and Chaises passing along, with their Wheels turning round as if on the Road, and altering their Positions as they ascend or desend a steep Hill; and nearer, on a River, is a Gun-powder-Mill at Work. On the same River are Swans swimming, fishing, and bending theirNecks backwards to feather themselves; as also the Sporting of the Dog and Duck, *&c.*

7. AND lastly, Is shewn the wholeMachine in Motion, when upwards of twelve Hundred Wheels and Pinnions are in Motion at once: And during the whole Performance it plays several fine Pieces of Musick on the Organ and other Instruments, both single and in Concert, in a very elegant Manner, *&c.*

IT *will be shewn every Day, exactly at Eleven o'Clock in the Morning, and again at Three and Five in the Afternoon, at* Four Shillings & Six Pence *each, and Children under Twelve Years of Age, at* Three Shillings (*Lawful Money*) *thoughPrice quite inferior to the Expence, and Merits of this Machine.*

N. B. ANY Person subscribing *Thirteen Shillings and Six Pence*, will be entitled to see the MICROCOSM at the above Hours, during its Stay at *Boston*.

☞ TICKETS *to be had of* Edes *&* Gill *in* Queen-Street, *and at the above Mr.* Fletcher's.—*Boston Gazette*, May 17, 1756.

TO BE SOLD at auction, "a beautiful Instrumentum Proferendi Lucim."—*Boston Gazette*, Jan. 29, 1759.

## GARDEN SEEDS AND FLOWERS

GARDEN SEEDS.—Fresh Garden Seeds of all Sorts, lately imported from London, to be sold by Evan Davies, Gardener, at his house over against the Powder House in Boston; As also English Sparrow-grass Roots, Carnation Layers, Dutch Goose-berry and Current-bushes.—*Boston Gazette*, Feb. 29/Mar. 7, 1719.

GARDEN ROOTS.—Richard Francis, Gardener in Long-lane, has got several sorts of Garden Roots, viz. Cabbages, Carrots, Turnups, Patatoes, Onions, Sallery and Endiff, and all sorts of Sweet Herbs, necessary for all Masters of Vessels, if they want, may apply to the above Francis & be supplied at reasonable Terms.—*Boston Gazette*, Sept. 19/26, 1737.

GARDEN SEEDS.—Lately Imported in Capt. Shepperdson, and to be Sold by John Little, in Milk Street, Choice good Windsor and Sandwich Beans, hot spur, & marrow fat Peas, Dwarffe, and Norman Hots, Raddish Seed, Spinage, Orange Carrot, Sweet Marjoram, Colliflowers, and hard Time Seeds, large Summer Cabbage Seed, Golded Purslan, Cabbage, Lettice, Parsnip, and double Marygold Seed; all of the best Sort, and at a very reasonable rate.—*Boston Gazette*, Apr. 10/17, 1738.

GARDEN SEEDS.—To be Sold by Elizabeth Decoster, at the Sign of the Wall-Nut Tree in Milk Street, Boston, a little below Dr. Sewall's Meeting-House: English Pease, Windsor Beans, Garden Seeds, Flower Seeds, lately imported. Flower Roots, Parsnips at Ten Shillings a Bushel, pickled Pepper and Beans at five Shillings a Pound.—*Boston News-Letter*, Apr. 12, 1744.

GARDEN ROOTS.—To be Sold by Richard Francis, Gardiner, living at the Sign of the Black & White Horse, at the South End [Boston].

All Sorts of Garden Roots and Seeds, as follows, Windsor Beans, Sandwich and Hotspur Beans, early hotspur Pease, marrowfat, rouncival, sugar, dwarf, egg blue-rouncival and grey-rose Pease, early Dutch cabbages, sugarloaf and batticey Cabbages, Savoy and large English Cabbage, white cross Lettice Cabbages, Siletian imperial and brown Dutch Lettice, short top London Reddish, Sandwich Reddish, round Spinnage, orange and yellow Carrot, white and red Spanish onion, double Parsley, Sallary, Thyme, sweet Marjoram, and Collyflower Seeds, Asparagrass Roots and several other sorts, too many to be enumerated here: all Fresh and new Imported from London.—*Boston News-Letter*, Mar. 14, 1746.

In the spring of 1748 he advertised the following additional items:—smooth and long parsnips, Strasburg and Welsh onions, London leck, endef Sallet, Hyssop, Sage, Balm, Dubett, Parsley and Parsley Dubett, Pepperglass, single Mustard, Cucumbers, Musmellon, Watermellons, and all Sorts of the best Flower Seeds.

GARDEN SEEDS.—To be Sold by *Richard Francis*, Gardner, living at the South End, at the Sign of the black and white Horse, fresh and new imported in the last ships from London, all Sorts of Garden Seeds as follows. Windsor Beans, Sandwich and Hotsper Beans, long Hotspur Pease, Ormants, Hotsper Pease, Marrafatt, Rouncival Nonpareil Rams horn Crooked Sugar, Dwaf Egg grey Pease, early Dutch Cabages, Battersy Sugar Loaf, large English Rusey white Heart and Red Cabages, Yellow and Green Savory, white cross Lettas, green cross Cabages, imperial Silitia, brown Dutch & curl'd Lettas, oring and yellow Carrots, early Dutch Turnips Green and Yellow Turnips, smooth and long Parsnips, White Spanish Strasburg and Welsh Onion, London Leek, short top London Redishes, Sandwich Redishes, Round Leaf Spineges, Colle Flowers, endef Sallet, sweet Margoram, Time, Summer Savory, Hyssop, Sage, Balm, Dubett, Parsley, and Parsley Dubett, Peppergrass, and single white Mustard, Cucumbers, Musmelion, Watermelions, and all Sorts of the best Flower Seeds. All Gentlemen, Masters of Vessels and others, may be supplied with good Seed to send to Sea to any Parts, at the lowest Price by the abovesaid *Francis*.—*Boston Gazette*, Feb. 16, 1748.

GARDEN SEEDS.—To be Sold, by Richard Francis, Gardner, living at the sign of black and white Horse at the South End of Boston, fresh and new imported in the last ships from London, all sorts of Garden Seeds, as follows: Windsor, Sandwich, & Hotspur Beans; long Hotspur, Ormats, & Hotspur Pease; Marrafat, Rouncival, Nonpariel, Ramshorn, crooked Sugar, Dwarf, Egg, & grey Pease; early Dutch Cabbages; Battersy Sugar-Loaf, large English, Russian, white Heart, and Red Cabbages; Imperial, Silesia, brown Dutch, & curl'd Lettice; orange & yellow Carrots; early Dutch Turnips; green & yellow Turnips; smooth & long Parsnips; white, Spanish, Strasburg, & Welsh Onions; London Leek; Short-top London, & Sandwich Reddishes; round leaf Spineges; Colley-flowers; endef Sallet; sweet Marjoram; Thyme; Summer Savory; Hyssop; Sage; Balm; Dubett; Parsley; & Parsley Dubett; Pepper-grass; & single white Mustard; Cucumbers; Musmellon; Watermellons; and all Sorts of the best Flower Seeds.—*Boston News-Letter*, Mar. 3, 1748.

MARKET PRICES.—Price Current of some of the most Saleable Commodities in Boston,—Geniton Pears, as sold on the Dock, 3 a Penny, 4 by the Quantity. N. B., Katterns are not yet come to Market, Green Apples, 4 for 6 Pence, Hurtle-Berries, 2 *s.* a Quart, and falling, Black Berries, 3 *s.* ditto, Cherries, none, Young Cock-Robbins, 5 *s.* Old ones, if tame, 15 *s.*, Bob-Lincolns, 4 *s.*, Squirrels, 10 *s.* Flying ditto, 3 *s.* Ground ditto, 2 *s.* Rum at the Retailers, 12 *d.* a Jill, brisk, Toddy, 3 *s.* a Mug, ditto, Flip, dull, Punch at the Taverns, 4 *s.* a Nip, brisk, Lemmons, 12 *d.* to 1 *s.* 6 *d.* a Piece. There is to be a fine Crop of Peaches this Year. N. B. The above Prices are in Old Tenor.—*Boston News-Letter*, July 19, 1750.

GARDEN SEEDS.—Imported in the last Ship from London, and to be sold by ANNA JOHNSON, at her Shop at the Head of Black-Horse Lane, leading up from Charlestown Ferry:

A Fresh assortment of GARDEN SEEDS, Peas and Beans, among which are, early charlton, early hotspur, golden hotspur, large and small dwarf, large marrowfat, white rouncevals, rose and crown, crooked sugar, and grey Pease; large windsor, early hotspur, early Lisbon, early yellow, six-weeks long podded, and white Kidney

Beans; early Dutch, yorkshire, sugar-loaf, battersea, savoy, and large winter Cabbage; early and late Colliflower; early orange, scarlet and purple Carrots; best swelling Parsnips; Endive; Cellery; Asparagus, and Pepper; early prickly, long and short cluster, white and green turkey Cucumber; Thyme and Sweet majoram; Balm, Hyssop and Sage; London short and Salmon Raddish; Lavender; green and white goss, green and white silesia, imperial, cabbage, tennis-ball, marble, and brown dutch Lettice; ripe canary Seeds; red and white Clover; herd's Grass; red top and tye-grass Seeds; also a Parcel of curious Flower-Seeds.

☞ As said *Johnson* has no Person in her Family who is subject to the Small-Pox, any Person sending to her from the Country may be supplied without Danger, as great Care will be taken to keep the above Articles free from any Infection.—*Boston News-Letter*, Apr. 5, 1764.

FRUIT TREES.—Sarah Dawson, widow of Joseph Dawson, Gardner, in Cambridge Street, at the Cold Bath,—has got, a large Collection of grafted and inoculated English Fruit-Trees of all sorts where Gentlemen may have their Choice among three or four hundred which will be ready to be removed this Fall; also, Goose berries and Currant-Bushes; also, a large Number of Pares and Plumbs from 7 to 3 Years graft, of 9 or 10 different sorts of the best of English Fruit; also, Garden Seeds suitable for the West Indies, and all sorts of young Shrubs, dried Sweet Herbs and Celery by the Hundred.—*Boston News-Letter*, Oct. 22, 1772.

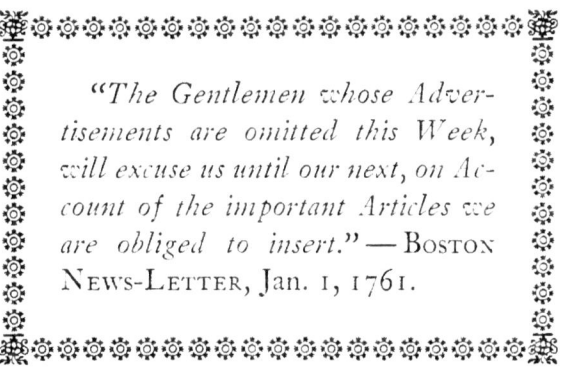

"The Gentlemen whose Advertisements are omitted this Week, will excuse us until our next, on Account of the important Articles we are obliged to insert." — BOSTON NEWS-LETTER, Jan. 1, 1761.

# INDEX

Abbot, Mrs. Rebecca, 97.
Account books, 29.
Acton, Richard, 197.
Adams, Mrs. Anna, 171.
   John, 238.
   Matthew, 285.
Alabaster effigies, 39, 159.
Alford, John, 245.
Allen, Jeremiah, 80.
   Jolley, 182.
Amory, Jonathan & John, 169.
Andrews, Barnard, 276.
   Benjamin, 130.
Anthony, Isaac, 41.
Anvil smith, 252, 265.
Apothecary, 252, 253.
Apothecary, *see also* Drugs.
Appleton, Priscilla, xxiv.
Apthorp, Charles Ward, 240.
   John, 126, 149.
   Stephen, 228.
Architect, English, 219.
Architecture, xxiii - xxvi.
Architecture, Books on, 221-223.
Arnold, Ann, 34.
Arras hangings, 150, 159.
Asby, James, 132.
Assayer, 254.
Atkinson, Mrs. E., 273.
   James, 133.
Auchmuty, Robert, 212.
Austin, ———, 41.
   Nathaniel, 73.

Bacon, Pierpont, 105.
Baden, Robert, 254.
Badely, Thomas, 133-141.
Badger, Joseph, xxi, 1.
Baeth, Adam, 146.

Bagnall, Benjamin, 133.
Baker, John, 55.
   Richard, 250.
Baker, 254.
Balderson, Thomas, 198.
Baldwin, Capt. David, 65.
Ball, John, 41.
Ballantine, William, 87.
Ballard, Jarvis, 207.
Banks, John, 285.
Barber, Nathaniel, 54.
   Capt. William, 200.
Barber, 255.
Barbour, Peter, 280.
Barker, Caleb & Robert, 256.
Barnard, John, 107.
   Jonathan, 110.
Barnes, Henry, 87, 98, 99.
Barnsley, Capt. Henry, 29.
Barre, Col. Isaac, 6.
Barrell, Colborn, 133.
   Joseph, 101.
Bass, Moses Belcher, 128, 166, 171.
Bath metal, 79.
Batterson, James, 134.
"Bay Psalm Book," xxvii.
Beal, James, 194.
   William, 194.
Beall, ———, 265.
Bed screws, 107.
Berkeley, Dean, xx.
Belcher, Andrew & Jonathan, 224.
   William, 104.
Bell, William, 85.
Bell founder, 255, 256.
Bellows maker, 256.
Bently, Thomas, 193.
Bernard, Gov. Francis, 124-126.
Bibles, 158.

311

Bichaut, James, 134.
Billings, Richard, 79.
Binney, Barnabas, 180.
Bissel, Samuel, 252.
Blackburn, Joseph, xx, 1.
Blackmore, George, 193.
Blacksmith, 256, 257.
Blanchard, Edward, 79, 230, 232.
 Joshua, 91, 151-153, 180, 234.
Bliss, John, 218.
Blodgett, Samuel, xix, 23, 170.
Blowers, I., 41.
 John, 268.
 Pyam, 110.
Bois, John, 278.
Bonner, Capt. John, 27.
Bookkeeper, 257.
Books, 124, 126, 157, 158, 161, 162, 221-223, 229.
Boone, Nicholas, 272.
Boston Massacre, xvii, 39.
 Plan of, 17, 27, 28.
 Prospects of, xv, xvi, xxv, 15-18, 22.
 View of Court House, 22.
Bottles, 99-101, 104.
Bourn, Peter, 203.
Bower, Benauel, 197.
Bowes, William, 79, 129.
Bowman, Samuel, 158.
Boyce, Alexander, 277.
Boydell, Hannah, 209.
 J., 110.
Boyer, Daniel, 66.
 James, 69.
Boylston, Zabdiel, 237, 252, 292.
Bradford, Andrew, 187.
Bradish, Jonathan, 247.
Brand, John, 134.
Brandon, Joseph, 244.
Brattle Street Meeting House, Boston, 219.

Bray, George, xxii.
Braziers' wares, 73-80, 103, 108, 109, 115, 117, 120, 122, 135, 150, 225-235, 257.
Bread, 254.
Breadnig, Philip, 88.
Brenton, Ebenezer, 191.
Bricks, 217, 220.
Bridge building, 218.
Bridgham, Ebenezer, 94, 95, 285.
Brigden, Michael, 82.
 Zechariah, 41, 42.
Briggs, Mrs. Sarah, 287.
Britt, Thomas, 216, 280.
Brocas, John, 105.
Bromfield, Edward, 213.
 Thomas, 36.
Brooker, ———, 59.
Brooks, Thomas, 204, 287, 288.
Brown, John, 270, 271, 282.
 Nathaniel, 247, 249, 278.
 William, 60.
Browne, Gawen, 134-137, 300.
 Walter, 267.
Brownell, George, 273.
Bruleman, John, 42.
Bryant, William, 256.
Buck, James, 14, 21, 22, 28, 34, 35, 247.
Buckles, 42, 44.
Buckram, 257, 261.
Bull, Capt. Samuel, 234.
Burgis, William, xvi, 15.
Burn, Peter, 128, 176.
Burnet, Governor, furniture, 108, 109.
Burr, Thaddeus, 68.
Burrill, S., 42, 46.
Busby, James, 143.
Bushell, J., 14.
Butler, John, 42.
 Samuel, 61.

Buttons, 75, 153, 159, 160, 165, 167, 176, 178, 181, 182, 226, 235, 258, 280.

Cabinetmakers, 105, 106.
Calder, William, 214.
Calico printer, 258.
Callender, Ellis, 183.
    Joseph, 152.
Calvinism, xi.
Camera obscura, 25, 35, 248.
Campbell, ———, 1, 151.
    John, 58.
    Mrs. Susannah, 58.
Candles, 114, 117, 259, 260.
Candlesticks, 71.
    Glass, 91, 95.
Cape, Nathaniel, 291.
Capen house, Topsfield, xxiv.
Cardmaker, 258.
Caricatures, xvii, 8, 25.
Cario, William, 69.
Carnes, John, 73.
Carpet painting, 242, 243.
Carpets, 92, 110, 113, 114, 116, 118, 119, 121, 122, 124, 126, 127, 128, 153, 156, 157, 167, 170, 171, 242, 243.
Carter, Daniel, 240.
    Edward, 261.
    Josiah, 298.
    William, 61.
Carty, Florence, 192.
Casey, Samuel, 42.
Caswall, Harry, 154, 155.
Cazneau, Isaac, 175, 278.
Chairmaker, 105, 106.
Chaise, 108, 115, 123, 225, 269.
Champney, Caleb, 249, 278.
Chandler, 259, 260.
Character blanks, 19-21.
Chariot glass, 99.

Charts, 17, 26-33.
Checkley, Rev. John, 6.
Cheever, Joshua, 141.
Chesley, Ichabod, 201.
Chimney sweep, 260.
China, *see* Earthenware.
China, Enamelled, 84, 86, 89-91.
China stove, 121.
Chocolate, 258.
Chocolate mill, 260.
Church, Benjamin, 6, 63, 112, 113, 115, 120, 122, 150.
    Benjamin, Jr., 239.
Clagget, William, 137.
Clark, James, 63.
    Dr. John, 286, 287.
    Jonathan, 274.
    Thomas, 137.
    William, xxv, xxxi.
Clark & Kilby, 245.
Clarke, Christopher, 180.
    Richard, 1, 265.
    Sukey, 1.
    Thomas, 43.
Classon, Nicholas, 187.
Clemens, James, 259.
Clements, Timothy, 30.
Clocks, 121, 127, 129, 132-149.
Clothing, 109, 131, 155, 158, 159, 160, 161, 168, 171, 173-203, 244, 285.
Clothing, *see also* Costume.
Clough, Joseph, 256.
Coburn, John, 43.
Cockle, Thomas, 25.
Codner, William, xxxi.
Coffin, Ebenezer, 77, 78.
    Nathaniel, 101.
    William, 105, 225, 253.
    John, 176.
Coins, Hoard of, 60.
Coit, Job, 105.

Coit, Joseph, 176.
Coleman, William, 192.
Collier, Anna Maria Barbarie, 280.
Collins, Daniel, 105.
   Elijah, 137.
Collson, David, Jr., 215.
Colman, Rev. ———, 18.
Colson, Adam, 183.
Comber, John, 73.
   Richard, 194.
Comfort, Gerardus, 210.
Condy, Mrs. Susannah, 110, 274.
Coney, John, xvi, xxix, 43.
Confectionery, *see* Sweetmeats.
Conway, Hon. H. S., 6.
Cookson, John, 264.
   Reuben, 271.
Coolidge, Joseph, Jr., 69.
Cooper, Rev. Samuel, 281.
   Rev. William, 34.
Cooper, 261.
Copler, John, 134.
Copley, Mrs. ———, 286.
   John Singleton, xvii, xviii, xxii, 1.
Coral, 42.
Coram, Thomas, 124.
Costume, 115, 123, 127, 128, 131, 154-203, 301.
Cotton, Rev. ———, 189.
Counterfeiting, 9, 13, 47.
Counterpane stamper, 261.
Counterpanes, 154, 157, 160, 166, 167, 170, 172, 176.
Courtney, Elizabeth, 275.
Coverly, John, 43.
Cowell, ———, 58.
   John, 43.
   Rebecca, 43.
   William, 43.
Cox & Berry, 67, 68, 132, 222.
Crafts, Thomas, 240, 242, 250.
Cranch, Joseph, 139.

Cranch, Nathaniel, 139.
   Richard, 138, 258.
Cranch & Co., Richard, 260.
Crawford, John, 171.
Creese, ———, 205.
Crosby, John, 95.
Croswell, Nathaniel, 43.
Crowley, Sir Ambrose, 224.
Cudworth, Lydia, 54.
Cummings, Anne, 171, 184.
   Elizabeth, 171, 184.
Cundall, Joseph, 194.
Cunningham, Capt. ———, 240.
   Nathaniel, 246, 247.
Currier, A., 143.
   David, 73.
Cutler, John, 78, 265.
   Dr. John, 64.
Cutlery, 71, 161, 165, 166, 226, 227, 229-236.

Dakin, Jonathan, 271, 279.
Dalton, Michael, 143.
Daly, Charles, 190.
Dana, Richard, 135, 291.
Dancing, 9-12.
Dancing Master, 69.
Dancing Schools, xviii, xix.
Davies, Evan, 305.
Davis, Benjamin, 142.
   Caleb, 278.
   Daniel, 209.
   John, 105, 187.
   Nicholas, 83.
Davison, William, 173.
Dawson, Joseph, 308.
   Sarah, 308.
"Day of Doom," xxvii.
Deblois, Gilbert, 227, 230, 301.
   Gilbert and Lewis, 76-78.
   Lewis, 151, 181, 298.
   Stephen, 63, 116.

De Bruls, Michael, 6.
Decoster, Elizabeth, 305.
Delph ware, 84, 85, 87-90, 92-96, 98, 102, 103.
Dennie, Albert, 20, 159, 160.
Dennis, Michael, 161.
Denny, Capt. Daniel, 212.
Dentist, 55.
Dentists' extractors, 126.
Deshon, Moses, 65, 120, 122.
Dexter, John, 70.
Dials, 237.
Diamonds, 50, 62, 133, 147.
Dixwell, John, 44.
Doane, John, 44.
Dobel, John, 99, 165.
Dolbear, James, 146.
Dolbeare, ———, 150.
Dolhonde, Dr. Lawrence, 59.
Doolittle, Isaac, 139.
Dorothy, John, 15.
Douglass, Dr. William, 30.
Dowie, David, 186.
Dowsing, William, xiii.
Draper, John, 31.
 Richard, 31, 83.
Drugs and Medicines, 239, 252, 253.
Druitt, Eleanor, 275.
Duck, 154, 155, 164.
Dumb-Betty, 116.
Dumerisque, Philip, 12.
Dummer, Jeremiah, 44.
Dunbar, Rev. ———, 207.
Dunbibin, Daniel, 31.
Dupee, Isaac, 291.
Dwight, Jonathan, 216.
Dwyer, James, 201.
Dyeing, 257.
Dyer, Col. ———, 210.
 John Henry, 261.
Dyer, 261, 262, 269.

Earthenware, 75, 81-96, 98, 120.
East, Henrietta Maria, 175.
Eastman, Ebenezer, 190.
Easton, ———, 219.
Edwards, Benjamin, 62.
 John, 44.
 Joseph, Jr., 44, 45.
 Samuel, 45.
 Thomas, 42, 44, 46.
Electrical experiments, 302.
Electric machine, 114.
Eliot, Benjamin, 18.
 Samuel, 150.
Elwood, ———, 139.
Embroidered bed, 108.
Embroidered petticoat, 176.
Embroidery, 274-276.
Emmett, Edward Tillitt, 139.
Emmons, Nathaniel, xxi, 1.
Engravings, 14-26.
Engraving on copper, xvi-xix, 6-37.
Engraving on wood, xv, 37-40.
Enstone, ———, 297.
Entwistle, Edmund, 139.
Erving, George, 137.
Essex, Joseph, 140, 266.
Eustis, Jane, 181.
Evans, Lewis, 30, 31.
Eveleth, James, 9.
Evenden, Walter, 278.
Everendine, William, 189.
Eyres, ———, 213.

Fabrics, 154-172, 257, 258.
Fabrics, *see also* Costume.
Fairservice, James, 260.
Faneuil, Peter, 213.
Faneuil Hall cellar, 218.
Fans, 173-176.
Feke, Robert, xx.
Fenter, ———, 46.
Fire engine, 262, 263.

Fishermen, 263.
Fishing rods, 80.
Fitzgerald, David, 199.
Flagg, Gersham, 61, 195, 247.
    Josiah, 13.
Flax hechels, 282.
Fleet, Thomas, 277.
Fleming, Alexander, 262.
Fletcher, Samuel, 90, 91, 100, 152, 295.
    William, 303.
Floor cloths, 127.
Flower maker, 276.
Food, 109, 112, 119, 126, 137, 156, 158, 170, 225, 252-254, 263, 292-296.
Forbes, Capt. James, 198.
Foster, ———, 8.
    Benjamin, 83.
    Edward, 46.
    Isaac, 238.
    John, xv.
    Samuel, 192.
    Capt. William, 246.
Fowle, James, 217.
Francis, Richard, 305, 306.
Frankland, Sir Harry, xxv, xxxi, 198.
Franklin, ———, 268.
    Benjamin, xxviii.
    Elizabeth, 281.
    James, 277.
    John, 47.
    Josiah, 47.
Freeman, Philip, 133, 175, 221, 263.
Frobisher, William, 281.
Fruit, 100, 158, 170, 252, 253, 264, 293-295, 307.
Fry, James, 193.
    Richard, 277.
Fullerton, William, 105, 243.

Furniture, xxviii, xxix, 17, 23, 83, 105-131.

Gairdner, David, 161.
Gallop, Mary, 100.
Games, 162, 235.
Garden glasses, 125.
Garden seeds and flowers, 305-308.
Gardner, Rev. Andrew, 204.
    Christopher, 198.
    Nathaniel, 285.
Gardner & Co., Joshua, 79.
Geddes, Charles, 141.
Gee, Lately, 254.
Gent, William, 146.
Gerrish, John, 147, 226.
    Samuel, 14, 18, 27.
Geyer, Mrs. ———, 276.
    Henry Christian, xxxi, xxxii, 217, 283-285.
George, Cornelius, 20.
    John, 282.
Germantown (Braintree) Glass Works, 103, 104.
Gibbons, Thomas, 105.
Gibbs, Robert, 237.
Gilbert & Deblois, 114.
Gilding, 243.
Gillespie, Andrew, 286.
Glass, Broken, 21.
    Cut, 102.
    Painted, xiii.
    Painting on, 12, 25, 32, 34, 37, 128, 275, 288.
    Shop window, 23.
    Table, 84-87, 90-104, 244, 247, 249.
    Window, 124, 224, 240, 241, 244-251.
Glass Works at Germantown, 103, 104.
Glasses, Garden, 125.

Glazier, 244-250, 256.
Glover, 263.
Gloves, 166.
Goddard, ———, 139.
Goffe, ———, 143.
　Daniel, 107, 110.
　Capt. Daniel, 211.
Goldsmith, see Silversmith.
Goldthwait, Benjamin, 184.
　Joseph, 46.
Gooch, John & Joseph, 191.
　William, 153, 241, 250, 251.
Gookin, G., 228.
Gould, John, 39, 124, 128, 166.
　R., 290.
　Robert, 249.
Gordon, ———, 122.
Gore, John, 239-243.
Grant, Joseph, Jr., 118.
Grate, Kitchen, 130.
Gravestones, xxxi, 283-285.
Gray, Francis, 258.
　James, 260.
　John, 46.
　Samuel, 95, 101, 102.
Green, Bartholomew, 27.
　Dea. Bartholomew, 209.
　Francis, 243.
　James, 78.
　Nathaniel & Benjamin, 90.
　Capt. Samuel, 209.
Green & Walker, 91, 119, 222, 295.
Greene, R., 46.
Greenleaf, Caleb, 169.
　Stephen, 271.
　William, 69, 89, 90, 92, 168.
Greenwood, Isaac, 287.
Greer, John, 285.
Gridley, Isaac, 221.
　Richard, 28, 34.
Griffin, James, 247, 248.
Griffith, David, 46.

Griggs, Jacob, 30.
Grocer, 263, 292-295.
Gruchy, James, 117.
Gun, Air, 114.
Gunsmith, 264-266.
Guttridge, Robert, 282.

Haggars, James, 141.
Halberts, 272.
Hale, Samuel, 81.
Haley, Samuel, 112.
Halifax, View of, 29.
Hall, Andrew, 183.
　Giles, 79.
　Jonathan, 81.
　Capt. Nathaniel, 206.
　Samuel, 257.
Halsey, James, 191.
Hamock, Charles, 127.
Hancock, Thomas, 18, 123, 150, 268.
Hancock & Co., Thomas, 249.
Hangings for rooms, 119, 120.
Hanks, Samuel, 200.
Hannah, George, 47.
Hanners, George, 47.
Harding, George, 173.
Hardware, 162, 165, 224-236.
Harris, ———, 29.
　John, xvi, 300, 301.
　Joseph, 301.
　Capt. Robert, 215.
Harrison, C., 227.
Harvard College views, xvi, 18, 20, 28.
Harvey, Rev. James, 35, 36.
Hastier, John, 47.
Hats, 159, 163, 165, 168-170, 172, 174, 175, 178-181, 265.
Hatter, 265.
Hawding, Thomas, 112.
Hazard, Robert, 205.

Hazro, John, 93.
Healey, ———, 47.
Hely, Samuel, 238.
Henchman, Daniel, 18, 27.
Henderson, John, 190.
Hendry, Robert, 257.
Henryson, John, 141.
Hepbron, Peter, 198.
Hern, Ruth, 276.
Hersey, Israel, 199.
Hickey, John, 262, 269.
Highmore, Joseph, 35.
Hill, John & Thomas, 263.
Hillard, David, 186.
Hiller, Mrs. Abigail, xxx, 288, 289.
    Joseph, 70, 302.
Hinche, Elizabeth, 274.
Hitchcock, ———, 300.
Hogarth, William, xix, 25, 32, 36.
Holbrook, ———, 222.
Hollis, Thomas, 35.
Holmes, Ebenezer, 113, 148.
    Capt. Ephraim, 202.
    William, 47.
Holt, James, 195.
Hose, 154, 155, 156, 158-160, 162, 164, 168, 177-182, 265.
Houghton, Rowland, 254, 263, 278.
Hour glasses, 265.
House, Joshua, 142.
Household furnishings, xiv.
Houses and buildings, 204-221.
Houses, Types of, xxiii-xxvi.
Hovey, James, 279.
Howard, John, 237.
Howe, Rev. Perley, 61.
Howell, James, 196.
Hubbard, N., 61.
    Thomas, 75.
    Rev. William, xv.
Hubbert, ———, 302.
Hudson, Dr. Seth, xvii.

Hulme, Capt. Thomas, 181.
Hunt, Francis, 105.
Hunt, Sarah, 268.
Hunt & Torrey, 167.
Hunter, Andrew, 151, 215.
Hurd, Jacob, 47, 48, 211.
    John, 47, 249.
    Nathaniel, xvii, 8, 37.
Hutchinson, ———, 143.
    Shrimpton, 238.
    Gov. Thomas, 123, 124.
    William, 107.
Hutchinson & Brinley, 238.
Hyslop, William, 163.

Inch, John, 71.
India china, 85, 87, 88, 95.
India cottons, 154-172.
Indian screens, 91.
Ingolsen, Mary, 201.
Ingram, John, 272.
Inoden, David, 106.
Iron forge, 266.
Iron foundry, 265.
Ivers, Thomas, 198.

Jack maker, 266.
Jackson, Edward, 230, 231, 257, 273.
    James, 90, 225.
    John, 266.
    Mary, 225, 228-231, 254.
    Mary & William, 77.
    William, 126, 229, 230, 235.
Japanning, 23, 32, 37, 129, 237, 266, 267, 288, 298.
Jarvis & Parker, 29, 151, 164.
Jenkins, John, 106.
    Robert, 85, 156, 157, 174.
Jenkins & Son, Robert, 148.
Jennings, Jacob, 48.

Jennys, Richard, Jr., 37.
Jess, David, 48.
Jewelry, 49-53, 66-72, 123, 124, 132-149, 172, 176, 180, 235.
Johnson, ———, 48.
    Anna, 307.
    Mary, 214.
    William, 198.
Johnston, Thomas, xix, 8, 9, 28, 29-31, 298.
    William, 2.
Jones, Daniel, 31, 170, 179, 265.
    Henry, 199.
    J., 217.
    John, 213.
Jones & Griffin, 247.
Judkins, John, 199.

Kenn, Lenier, 105.
Kennedy, Dr. Hugh, 65.
Killbourn, ———, 218.
Killcup, George, 153.
George, Jr., 242, 243.
King, ———, 141.
Kipling, W., 141.
Kneeland, Edward, 73.
    Mehetabel, 34.
Kneeland & Relfast, 142.
Knives and forks, 84, 97, 225, 228.
Kover, ———, 142.

Lace, 123, 156-158, 162, 167, 168, 172, 176, 181.
Lake George, Prospect and map, 23.
Lambert, William, 102.
Lamp oil, 260.
Lamps, 97, 99, 100, 114, 124, 127.
Lamson, Joseph, xxxi.
Lane, John, 106.
    Sarah, 106.
Lang, Jeffery, 48.

Langdon, Edward, 259.
    Samuel, 32.
Lanthorns, 97, 114, 116, 127, 166, 248.
Latten ware, 234.
Law, Charles, 198.
Lawrence, R., 272.
Lead roof on Harvard College, 204.
Leather breeches, 174, 175.
Leather clothing, 183.
Leather stockings, 177.
Leason, George, 261.
Lechmere, Thomas, 123, 143.
Lee, Thomas, 24, 25, 152, 184.
Lemons, 295.
Leverett, Knight, 48.
Levi, Heyman, 152.
Lewis, Joseph, 226.
Leyland, Adam, 154.
Lime kiln, 267, 268.
Linen, Printed, 152, 154, 157, 244, 261.
Linen stamper, 268, 269.
Linen weaving, 268-270.
Linen whitener, 271.
Little, John, 305.
Liverpool ware, 83, 84, 87, 88, 90, 92, 93, 95.
Lloyd, Henry, 249.
    John, 202.
Loadstones, 271.
Locks, 230.
Locksmith, 257, 266, 271.
Looking glasses, 20, 22, 23, 25, 32, 36, 37, 80, 95, 97, 98, 106, 107, 110, 112, 114-122, 125, 127-129, 157, 177, 212.
Lord, Rupert, 106.
Lorent, Peter, 296.
Loring, Nathaniel, 87, 165, 231.
Louisbourg, Plan of, 28, 34.
Loveday, ———, 142.

Lowder, John, 196.
Luce, Capt. ———, 193.
Lutwytche, ———, 156.
Luxuries, xiv.
Lynde, Samuel, 137.
Lyman, ———, 207.
Lynes, Cornelius, 199.
Lynn, Joseph, 190.
Lyell, David, 73.

McIlvaine, Eleanor, 275.
Macintire, Robert, 200.
McIntire, Samuel, xxvi.
McLean, ———, 6.
Macsparren, James, 145.
McTaggart, Peter, 39.
Magic lantern, 114.
Mahogany, 129, 130.
Majory, Capt. Joseph, 238.
Man, Pelatiah, 201.
Manning, Richard, 175.
Maps, xv, 14-37, 300.
Marble busts, 124.
Marble chimney piece, 114.
Marble hearths, 206, 212, 214.
Marble table, 113, 115-117.
March, Clement, 22.
Marchent, William, 151.
Mark, James, 9.
Marion, Joseph, 228.
Marsh, Daniel, 164.
Mascarene, Paul, 118.
Mason, David, 267.
   George, 2.
   Isabel, 71.
   Nathaniel, Jr., 207.
Mathematical instruments, 109, 114, 119, 125, 128, 271.
Mather, Rev. Cotton, xviii, 33.
   Rev. Richard, xv, xxvii.
Mats, 112.
Mattocks, Samuel, 106.

Maxwell, James, 265.
Mayhew, Rev. Jonathan, 37.
Maylam, John, 199.
Medals, Portrait, 39.
Merritt, John, 38, 238, 263, 292, 293.
Mezzotints, xviii, xix, 3, 18, 23, 25, 28, 32, 33-37, 112, 113, 117, 151, 240, 242, 251.
Microcosm, 303.
Microscopes, 114, 119.
Middleton, Alexander, 246.
Military equipment, 271, 272, 301.
Miller, Francis, 31.
   Samuel, 264.
Millinery, 156, 158, 162, 163, 172, 273.
Minott, Samuel, 49.
Mitchelson, David, 142.
Moffet, Thomas, 185, 280.
Molineaux, William, 77, 290.
Money, 8, 9, 13, 22.
Moody, Ebenezer, 194.
Moorhead, Rev. John, 35.
   Sarah, 267.
Morland, William, 166.
Mors, Obadiah, 49.
Morse, Nathaniel, 9.
Moulton, Joseph, 49.
Mourning costume, 183.
Moving pictures, 302-304.
Muff, 178.
Mulliken, Jonathan, xvii.
   Nathaniel, 142.
Murray, Elizabeth, 162.
   William, 199.
Musgrave, ———, 59.
Music, 13-15, 17.
Musical instruments, 21, 22, 109, 114, 116, 121, 122, 170, 236, 297-301.
Mustard maker, 272.

Nail making, 273.
Needle maker, 273.
Needlework, xxx, 110, 112, 115, 159, 176, 267, 273-276.
Negroes, *see* Slaves.
Nelson, William, 282.
Netherton, William, 185.
Newell, Timothy, 79, 220.
Newman, John, 142.
    Joseph, 22.
Newspapers, List of, v.
New York, View of, 6, 15.
Nichol, James, 268.
Nichols, Capt. James, 148.
    William, 62, 158, 292.
North, Stephen, 244.

Oakes, Edward, 257, 274.
Odell, Thomas, 9.
Oil Cloths, 121, 170.
Old South Meeting House, Boston, 207.
Oliver, Andrew, Jr., 178.
    Daniel, 199.
Oliver, Clarke & Lee, 265.
Orne, Benjamin, Jr., 200.
    Timothy, xxii.
Osborne, John, 216.
Otis, James, 120.
Oursell, Nicholas, 280.

Painted canvas hangings, 119.
Painted carpets, 153.
Painter-stainer, 112, 150.
Painters, Portrait, xx-xxiii, 1-5.
Painting, House, xxi, 153, 211, 212, 215, 217, 218, 238, 239, 241, 250, 251.
Painting on glass, 12.
Paintings, 3, 5, 6.
Paints and oils, 3, 237-243, 252, 264, 293.

Palmer, Joseph, 104, 258.
Paper, 29.
Paper making, 276-278.
Paper Money, 8, 9, 13, 22, 47.
Parker, ———, 143.
    Daniel, 49-53.
    Grace, 82.
    John, 150.
Partridge, Nehemiah, 237, 302.
Pass & Stow, 256.
Paxton, Charles, 111.
Payne, William, 154.
Pearson, ———, 189.
Peaseley, Robert, 143.
Peck, John, 253.
    Moses, 143.
    Thomas Handasyd, 182.
Peirce, Moses, 244, 245.
Pelham, ———, 297.
    Henry, xvii, xxiii.
    Mrs. Mary, 13, 286.
    Peter, xviii, xxii, 9-12, 28, 33, 34, 35.
Pemberton, James, 159.
Pens, 29.
Perkins, Elizabeth, 96.
Perry, Mrs. Joanna, 26.
Persian carpets, 119, 170.
Pewter, xxix, 73-80, 117, 227, 229, 232.
Phillips, Mrs. Ann, 196.
    Gillam, 139.
    John, 84, 86, 150, 157, 164.
    Joseph, 256.
    Samuel, 26.
    Capt. Thompson, 245.
Picture framing, 17, 20, 25, 32, 37.
Picture machine, 302.
Pictures, India, 159.
Piemont, ———, 296.
Pierpont, Benjamin, 54.
Pigot, Rev. George, 190.

Pigeon, John, 36, 72.
Pim, John, 264.
Pipes, Tobacco, 126, 250.
Pistol, 272.
Pitt, Ebenezer, Jr., 54.
Pitts, Capt. James, 127.
    John, 173, 292.
Plate press, 21.
Plumber, 249, 278.
Plumber's work, 226.
Pomroy, Joseph, 45.
Portrait busts, xxxii, 39.
Portrait painting, xx-xxiii, 1-6.
Pottery, see Earthenware.
Powder maker, 278.
Powel, John, 12.
Poynton, Thomas, 202.
Prentice, Mrs. Prudence, 145.
Prentiss, Henry, 71.
Prescot, Peter, 143.
Price, William, xvi, xvii, 15-18, 20-22, 28, 107.
Price currant, 294, 307.
Prince, Capt. ———, 3.
    Rev. Thomas, 35.
Print sellers, xvii, 3.
Printing, xxvi-xxviii.
Printing press, 139.
Pritchard, William, 275.
Pue, Jonathan, 193.
Pumps, 254.
Punch bowl, 54, 60.
Puritans, Characteristics of the, xi.

Quebec, View of, 24.
Quill, John, 249.
Quillwork, 288, 289.
Quilts, 109, 112, 125, 128, 154, 159, 160, 164, 166, 168, 170-172, 176.
Quincey, Edmund, 218.
    Edmund, Jr., 31.

Rachell, John, 75.
Randal, ———, 18.
Randall, William, 86.
Randle, William, 97.
Raulisson, Paul, 190.
Ray, Caleb, 279.
Read, James, 262.
    Ruth, 143.
    Thomas, 70.
Reed, Capt. Benjamin, 200.
Remick, Christian, 2.
Revere, Paul, xvii, 13, 54, 55.
Reynolds, John, 194.
Ribright, ———, 64.
Rice, John, 298.
Richardson, ———, 300.
    Jacob, 76.
Riddell, Joseph, 185.
Rivington & Miller, 24, 222, 234, 235.
Roberts & Lee, 71.
Robinson, ———, 143.
    Sir Robert, 58.
    Thomas, 30.
Rogers, ———, 143.
    Nathaniel, 171.
Rolling stone, 99.
Rose, David, 185.
    Samuel, 203.
Roulstone, John, 144.
Rowe, John, 246.
Rowse, William, 55.
Royal, Jacob, 83, 117.
Rugar, John, 152.
Rugs, 112, 155, 167, 170, 171.
Russel, J., 126.
Russell, Benjamin, 152.
    Elizabeth, 274.
    Thomas, 226.

Salter, John, 135.
Sand for floors, 213.

# Index

Savage, Arthur, 118, 143, 206, 231, 248, 292.
    Arthur, & Co., 101.
    John, 249, 250.
    Thomas, 143, 248.
Savage & Winter, 115, 286.
Savell, Jane, 119.
Sawen, Munning, 219.
Scales and balances, 279.
School teaching, xviii, 11, 12.
Scollay, John, 248.
Scotch goods, 157, 163, 171.
Scotley, James, 186.
Scott, Joseph, 148.
Sculpture, xxxi.
Seals, 146, 147.
Sedan chair, 113, 121.
Seeds, 76, 305-308.
Selby, Thomas, xvi, 16.
Servants, 280.
Sewall, Mrs. Mary, 274.
    Samuel, xxi.
Shaw, Francis, 199.
Scheffield ware, 229.
Shelly, Abraham, 157.
Sherburne, Henry, Jr., 200.
    Thomas, 106, 122.
Shingles, 206.
Shipbuilding, xxvi.
Ship caulkers, 258.
Ship-wright, 27.
Shirley, Gov. William, 34.
Shoes, 75, 83, 123, 159, 171, 173-176, 179, 180, 183.
Shute, William, 291.
Sigourney, Andrew, 194.
Silby, Thomas, 186.
Silver and silversmiths, 41-72, 116, 117, 118, 121-124, 126, 133.
Simons, David, 81.
Simpkins, John, 172.
    William, 55.
Simpson, Hannah, 43.
Sinnett, John, 144.
Sisson, James, 194.
Skinner, John, 74.
Slate, 207, 211, 217.
Slaves, 3, 62, 109, 116, 186, 188-198, 200-203.
Smibert, John, xx, xxi, 3, 4, 28, 34.
    Nathaniel, xx, 4, 5.
Smith, James, 292.
    Oliver, 253.
    Samuel, 115, 118, 148.
    Simon, 273.
Snuff maker, 280.
Soap, 281.
Soap boiler, 259.
Southack, Capt. Cyprian, 26-28, 206.
Spectacles, 21, 64, 282.
Spice, 88, 89, 129, 157, 166, 168, 237, 252, 253, 264, 272, 292-295.
Spinning, 281, 282.
Spinning wheels, 257.
Spry, Capt. Richard, 61.
Spy glasses, 20.
Stair carpeting, 119, 121, 126, 170.
Stanbridge, ———, 238.
    Henry, 150.
Staniford, John, 209.
Stanton, Rev. Robert, 55.
Starr, Daniel, 151.
Stationery, 29, 161, 229, 277, 282.
Statuary china, 120.
    Plaster, 284.
Stay maker, 285.
Stebbins, Samuel, 286.
Stedman, ———, 18.
Stevens, Daniel, 146.
    Timothy, 197.
Stiegel glass, 101.
Stoddard, William, 173.
Stomachers, 184.

Stone, Building, 220.
Stone cutter, 217, 283-285.
Stone statues, 91.
Stone tables, 112.
Stoneware, 83, 84, 86, 87, 89, 90, 92, 93, 98-100, 102, 128.
Store, Marmaduke, 144.
Stoves, 34, 121, 125, 130, 131, 214, 225, 226, 227.
Straw carpet, 167.
Suckling, Bridget, 274.
    George, 274.
Sugar, 170, 292-296.
Sullivan, Owen, 13.
Surrage, Hugh, 198.
Surriage, Agnes, xxv.
Surveying, 254.
Surveying instruments, 271.
Sutton, Mary, 185.
Swadell, Capt. Joseph, 185.
Swan, William, 55, 56.
Sweetmeats, 109, 117, 237, 252, 258, 264, 292-296.
Sweetser, John, Jr., 260.
Swift, Ephraim, 202.
Sword, 123.
Symmes, John, 56.
    Thomas, 81.
Sympson, ———, 56.

Table decorations, 116.
Tanner, 285.
Tapestry hangings, 35, 164, 221.
Tea and coffee, 85, 88, 90, 96, 102, 155, 157-159, 169, 170, 209, 229, 245, 263, 292-295.
Telescope, 114.
Thacher, Oxenbridge, 74, 75.
    Rev. Peter, 266.
Thomas, ———, 147.
    Peter, 146.
    William, 260.

Thorn, Joseph, 173.
Thornton, Thomas, 258.
Tidmarsh, Giles Dulake, 107.
Tiles, 82, 83-85, 89, 90, 92-94, 100, 128.
Tilley, George, 215.
Tinman, 286.
Tin ware, 20.
Tobacco, 12.
Tobacco pipes, 82, 92, 100.
Tobacconist, 286.
Tomlinson, ———, 147.
Tompion, 145.
Tools, 162, 224-236, 252-291.
Toulmin, Samuel, 143.
Townley, John, 233.
Towzel, John, 56.
Toys, 17, 21, 22, 65, 94.
Trammel stick, 212, 217.
Trees, Fruit, 126.
Trott, Jonathan, 72.
Trotters, Alexander, 244.
Trowell, Thomas, 155.
Trucking, 286.
Tucker, John, 291.
Turkey carpets, 113, 114, 116, 119, 121, 124, 128.
Turner, James, 14.
    John, xvii.
Tyler, Andrew, 56.
    James, 56.
    Joseph, 182.
    Thomas, 291.
Tymms, Brown, 257.

Umbrellas, 163, 170, 265, 287.
Uniforms, 179.
Upholstery goods, 166, 172.

Van Dyke, Peter, 56.
Vardy, Luke, 5.
Vassal, Henry, 213.

# INDEX

Vernon, Fortesque, 201.
Viscount, Dorcas, 163.
   Capt. Philip, 61, 86.

Wade, Arthur, 186.
   Thomas, 130, 227.
Waghorne, ————, 297.
   John, 266.
Walker, Rebecca, 89.
   Thomas, 119.
Wall paper, 25, 84, 126, 150-153, 184, 242, 251.
Walley, Thomas, 65, 94.
Walter, Rev. Thomas, 15.
Walters, William, 156.
Wanton, Joseph, 60.
Warner, Gilbert, 55.
   Nathaniel, xix, 36.
Warton, Sarah, 280.
Warwick, Ann, 193.
Watch house, 204.
Watch makers, 6, 132-149.
Watchmaker's tools, 52, 53, 66, 67, 138, 148, 149.
Watercolors, 240, 242.
Waters & Son, Josiah, 250.
Waxwork, xxx, 122, 287-290.
Weaving, 268-270, 281, 290.
Webb, Barnabas, 57.
   Edward, 57, 58.
   Isaac, 145.
Webber, John, 81.
   Thomas, 257, 261.
Webster, Ebenezer, 201.
Welch, John, 64, 78, 117.
Welles, Samuel, 240.
Welsh, John, 72.
Welsteed, Rev. William, xviii, 36.
Wendall, Mrs. Sarah, 129.
   Jacob, Jr., 6.
Wentworth, Capt. Ebenezer, 185.

West, ————, 145.
   Benjamin, xxiii.
   Saunderson, 218.
Wetherhead, Henry, 143.
Wheeler, Samuel, 106.
   William, 213.
Wheelock, John, 216.
White, Thomas, 14.
   Timothy, 222.
Whitear, John, 256.
Whitefield, Rev.————, 289, 290.
Whitesmith, 257, 290.
Whiting, Rev. John, xviii, 36.
   Stephen, 21-25, 30-34, 37, 97, 128, 129.
   Stephen, Jr., 32, 33.
Whitman, Polly, 43.
Whitney, Samuel, 128.
   Stephen, 247.
Whittemore, Edward, 57.
Wickham & Deblois, 77.
Wig maker, 291.
Wilcox, Jeremiah, 186.
Wigglesworth, Rev. Michael, xxvii, xxxi.
Willard, Benjamin, 145.
   Rev. Samuel, 18.
Williams, John, 261.
   Jonathan, 99, 104.
   Lewis, 194.
Wilson, Ellis, 75.
   Joshua, 145.
Wine, 126, 127.
Window screens, 167.
Window weights, 218, 231, 244.
Winslow, Edward, 58.
   John, 266.
Winter, Stephen, 72.
Wise, Rev. John, 173.
Wood, Amos, 192, 225.
Wood carver, 291.
Wood engravings, xv, 37-40.

Wood turner, 267.
Wool cards, 282.
Wright, James, 255.
    Mrs. Patience, 289.

Wright, W., 58.

Yale College, View of, 21.
York, Pompey, 195.